BLACK IVORY

Slavery in the British Empire

SECOND EDITION

James Walvin

Copyright © James Walvin, 1992, 2001

The right of James Walvin to be identified as author of this work has been asserted in accordance with the Copyright, Designs and Patents Act 1988.

First published in 1992 by HarperCollins Publishers.
Second edition published in 2001 by Blackwell Publishers Ltd.

2 4 6 8 10 9 7 5 3 1

Blackwell Publishers Ltd
108 Cowley Road
Oxford OX4 1JF
UK

Blackwell Publishers Inc.
350 Main Street
Malden, Massachusetts 02148
USA

British Library Cataloguing in Publication Data

A CIP catalogue record for this book is available from the British Library.

Library of Congress Cataloging-in-Publication Data
Library of Congress data is available for this book.

ISBN 0–631–22959–0; 0–631–22960–4 (pb)

Typeset in 10.5 on 12pt Janson
by Kolam Information Services Pvt Ltd, Pondicherry, India
Printed in Great Britain by TJ International, Padstow, Cornwall
This book is printed on acid-free paper

Contents

Part IV: Resting

Part V: Fighting Back

Part VI: Consequences

Preface to the Second Edition

In the decade since this book was first published, the interest in African slavery has continued to grow. The scholarly interest in black slavery has thrived, in print and at international conferences. The history of slavery is taught at all levels of the educational system. Public interest continues to be stimulated by films and television coverage and, in Britain at least, discussion of slavery frequently takes place on the radio and in the press. Various galleries and museums have sought to interest their visitors in the material culture of the slave system.[1]

On both sides of the Atlantic, some of the finest of recent historical scholarship has emerged from this burgeoning interest in Atlantic slavery.[2] One consequence of this scholarship has been a growing appreciation of the role of African slavery in the shaping of the modern world. Where once, not long ago, Atlantic slavery seemed a marginal and rather specialized interest, today few serious historians would deny its broad importance. In part, of course, this is because we know so much more than we did a generation ago. But the *volume* of knowledge is only part of the answer. There has been a *qualitative* shift in historical sensibility and alertness; a growing recognition that the peoples of Africa played a critical role in shaping the post-Columbian development of the Americas. In the process, they also served to transform the well-being of Europe.[3]

Three continents came to be inextricably linked in the years after the European settlement of the Americas; the money, commercial expertise and migrating instincts of maritime Europe, the land and economic potential of the Americas – and the peoples of Africa. The development of the tropical and semi-tropical Americas was achieved, in large measure, through the efforts of imported African slaves. And much of the material well-being derived from those developments accrued to the commercial and maritime powers of Europe. Quite why the Africans were recruited in such number *as slaves* has become a major historical conundrum.[4] But the simple point remains; the slave system of the Atlantic – which saw some 11 million Africans loaded onto the transatlantic slave ships – was a historical episode with massive ramifications for Europe and Europeans. Put another way, though the history of the slave trade and slavery may seem, from a European vantage point, a topic of maritime or African history, it was, in addition, intimately linked to the development of Europe itself. The following book seeks to describe that process.

I initially tried to write a book with a number of different aims. First, I hoped to tell a story which was accessible to a broad readership, yet which remained faithful to the detailed scholarship on which it was based. Second, I wanted to draw together events on three continents into a single narrative account. I hoped to achieve that by conveying the sense of movement between the three distinct locations of Atlantic slavery; in Europe, West Africa and the Americas. Now, ten years on, in revising *Black Ivory* I have tried to incorporate recent scholarly findings without disturbing the narrative flow. Some of my original detail has, inevitably, been revised by subsequent findings. But the broad outlines of my basic argument remain the same.

African slavery was the key element in the European settlement and exploitation of important swathes of the Americas. In turn, all the major European maritime and colonial powers sought to enhance their commercial and political power by the creation of trading posts and colonizing settlements across the face of the Americas. But they all faced, at different times and in different forms, problems of securing the appropriate labour to tap local resources. All tried various forms of labour – free, indentured, enslaved – and mixes of all three. It was, however, the emergence of cane sugar which tipped the balance towards the use of African slaves.[5] Even then, it seems strange to modern eyes that Europeans should transport ever more Africans such vast distances, to cultivate in the Americas a produce – sugar – which had traditionally been a costly, luxury taste for European elites. Thanks to the sweat of the slaves, however, sugar and other American produce (most spectacularly tobacco) swiftly established themselves as basic essentials of everyday life, among rich and poor. What began life as a luxury was rendered a necessity. In that process the enslaved peoples of Africa were critical. To make this possible, there evolved a complex economic Atlantic system from which the European metropoles drew major material and social sustenance. But, to make a point which will act as a refrain to this book, the Africans were the lubricant of the whole system. What follows is, then, my account of that complicated history.

Scholarship published in the decade since I wrote the book has confirmed the core of my argument: that African slavery evolved as a major social and economic force in the shaping of *British* history, over a period of two centuries, from the early seventeenth to the early nineteenth centuries. What follows is, then, not simply a history of the British involvement in the Americas, or of British entanglement with African slavery in Africa and on the high seas, but an important theme in the way Britain itself was transformed. This preface also allows me to reiterate a point I made initially; that I could not have written this book without the efforts of many other historians.

J. W.
November 2000

Acknowledgements

Two men bear more responsibility than most for this book. First Avner Offer suggested I write it (having read a concise history I had written and then discarded). Without his initial prompting I would not have begun. Second, my agent Charles Walker was equally enthusiastic and was supportive throughout. Without their encouragement this book would not have been written. I am also indebted to Michael Pountney who was supportive at an early stage. More generally, I owe a great deal to Gad Heuman, my co-editor on *Slavery and Abolition*, who is always on hand to provide advice and assistance.

I first discussed the proposal at the modern social history seminar in Melbourne. There I was gently chided by John Salmond; I hope he now sees that I have tried to follow his advice. It was, however, in the wonderful atmosphere of the Research School of Social Sciences at the Australian National University that the book first took shape. My special thanks go to Oliver MacDonagh and Ken Inglis for the initial invitation to work at ANU, particularly for the friendship and facilities they afforded me in Canberra. My enthusiasm for this book was by turns encouraged and tempered by colleagues at ANU. In mentioning Eric Richards, Ngaire Naffine, John Ritchie, Iain McCalman, Anthea Hyslop and Joanna Bourke by name I am doing an injustice to others whose conversations proved so constructive. My work was also much helped by the friendship shown by a number of colleagues in Canberra: by Bill Mandle, Phil Moseley, Brian Stoddard and Chris Cuneen. Closer to home I owe a particular thanks to Edward Royle for the encouragement and practical help he always managed to offer in the midst of his own demanding career.

One man has heard all this before. Jim Axtell sat through a lecture series I gave on this topic in the sultry August–September of 1987 in Williamsburg,

Virginia. His steadfast presence and his subsequent moral support were – and remain – much appreciated. Other friends in Williamsburg helped in different ways, and I am happy to thank John Selby, Rosie and Tolly Taylor, Scott and Vivian Donaldson, Susan Axtell, Mike Meranze and Darlene Crouch.

Among the libraries I used I would like to thank especially the National Library of Jamaica, the Swem Library of the College of William and Mary, the library of the Colonial Williamsburg Foundation, the libraries of the Australian National University, the Australian National Library, and the University of York Library.

Finally, and best of all, I dedicate this book to my friend Bill Bernhardt, for twenty-five years my indefatigable guide to the curiosities of New York City.

Introduction

This book examines the history of black slavery in the British colonies of the West Indies and North America. It is not a chronological account, but seeks instead to explore those major experiences which bound together slaves from diverse African backgrounds who found themselves scattered throughout the British colonies of the Americas. It is a study of colonial life and does not concern itself with slavery in North America after the independence of the USA in 1776. Although research for the book has been conducted on both sides of the Atlantic, it is very much a view with a British perspective.

The material which forms the core of the book has been accumulated over a long period and draws upon work undertaken in Britain, Jamaica and the USA. The book is also greatly influenced by the various courses I have taught on slavery. It similarly derives from the researches of many other historians whose work, often of the most detailed kind, has so transformed our understanding of slavery over the past twenty-five years. What follows is not a book for the specialists (though I hope they too will find some interest in it); but it is a book which could not have been written without them.

There was nothing quite like black slavery, in scale, importance or consequence. No other slave system was so regulated and determined by the question of race. No other slave system forcibly removed so many people and scattered them across such vast distances – and for such wonderful returns to the slave-owning class. Black slavery in the Americas, though it differed from one place to another, was unique. Looking back, it also seems bizarre. Here was a labour system called into being by Europeans, to develop their settlements in the Americas, using labour from Africa, and all to sate the palates of Europeans. Tobacco for the pipes of Englishmen, rum to temper the squalor of life between decks on British warships, coffee for the fashionable society of

London's clubs, sugar to sweeten the miserable diet of working people – these and other tropical products spilled forth from the cornucopia that was the slave colonies of the Americas. Slaves transformed the tastes of the western world just as surely as slavery changed for ever the face of the Americas and of Africa. What follows is a description of that process.

Let us begin with a view from London.

Chronology of Main Events

1562–63. Sir John Hawkins' first English Atlantic slave voyage.

1607. English settlement of Jamestown, Virginia.

1619. First blacks sold in Jamestown, Virginia.

1632. Establishment of Maryland.

1625–55. British settle their own Caribbean islands: Barbados 1625 – Jamaica 1655.

1663. Settlement of Carolina. (Split into two in 1713.)

1672. Foundation of Royal African Company to control British slave trade.

1730–40. First Maroon war (Cudjoe), Jamaica.

1735–36. Tackey's revolt, Antigua.

1739. Stono rebellion, South Carolina.

1750–86. Thomas Thistlewood keeps detailed diary of life among Jamaican slaves.

1756–63. Seven Years War, concluded by Treaty of Paris, which granted Grenada, Dominica, St Vincent and Tobago to Britain.

1760. Tacky's revolt, Jamaica.

1771–72. Somerset case: Lord Mansfield decides that a slave cannot be removed from England against his/her will. Signals end of slavery in England.

1776–83. War of American Independence.

1780. Gordon riots in London.

1783. *Zong* case: insurance claim for the loss of 131 slaves thrown from Liverpool slave ship in 1781.

1787. Foundation of the Society for the Abolition of the Slave Trade.

1789. French Revolution: concepts of Rights of Man and equality seriously disturb slave colonies.

1789. Former slave Olaudah Equiano publishes autobiography.

1791. Slave revolt in St Domingue (Haiti).

1792–1815. Revolutionary and then Napoleonic Wars: naval warfare and disruption throughout Atlantic and Caribbean. Concluded by Treaty of Vienna, 1815.

1795–96. Second Maroon War, Jamaica.

1795–97. Fédon's rebellion, Grenada.

1800. Gabriel Prosser's revolt, Virginia.

1804. Haitian independence.

1807. Abolition of the slave trade by Britain and USA.

1816. Bussa's rebellion, Barbados.

1819. Establishment of Royal Navy anti-slave trade squadron off West Africa.

1822. Denmark Vesey's revolt, South Carolina.

1823. Slave rebellion, Demerara (Guyana).

1823. Founding of Anti-Slavery Committee, London.

1831. Nat Turner's revolt, Virginia.

1831–32. 'Baptist War'; slave revolt in Jamaica.

1834. Slavery replaced by apprenticeship in British colonies.

1838. Full freedom granted in British colonies.

1861–65. American Civil War.

1865. Thirteenth Amendment abolishes slavery in USA.

1886. Slavery abolished in Cuba.

1888. Slavery abolished in Brazil.

Maps

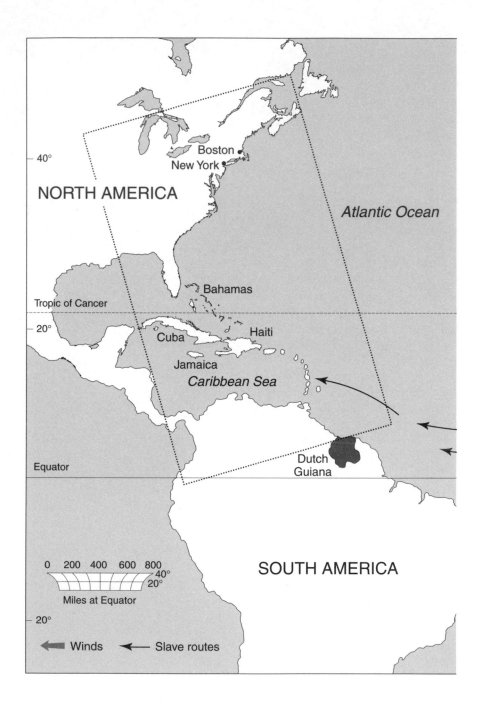

Winds ← | Slave routes ←

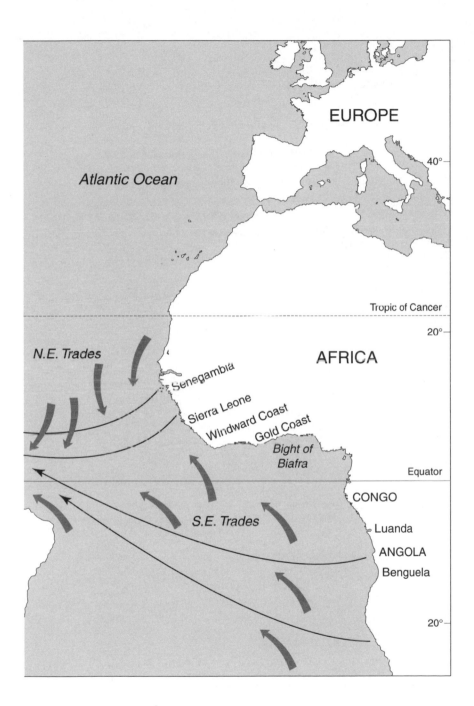

EUROPE

Atlantic Ocean

40°

Tropic of Cancer

20°

AFRICA

N.E. Trades

Senegambia

Sierra Leone

Windward Coast

Gold Coast

Bight of Biafra

Equator

CONGO

Luanda

S.E. Trades

ANGOLA

Benguela

20°

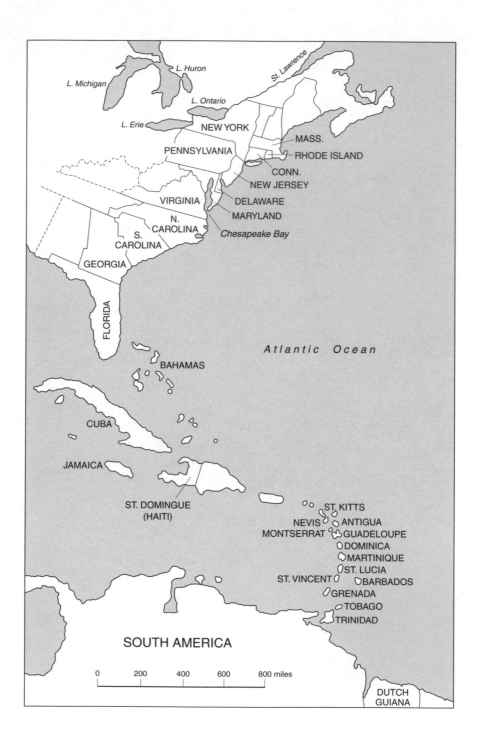

L. Michigan

L. Huron

St. Lawrence

L. Ontario

L. Erie

NEW YORK

MASS.

PENNSYLVANIA

RHODE ISLAND

CONN.

NEW JERSEY

VIRGINIA

DELAWARE

MARYLAND

N. CAROLINA

Chesapeake Bay

S. CAROLINA

GEORGIA

FLORIDA

Atlantic Ocean

BAHAMAS

CUBA

JAMAICA

ST. DOMINGUE (HAITI)

ST. KITTS

NEVIS

ANTIGUA

MONTSERRAT

GUADELOUPE

DOMINICA

MARTINIQUE

ST. LUCIA

ST. VINCENT

BARBADOS

GRENADA

TOBAGO

TRINIDAD

SOUTH AMERICA

0   200   400   600   800 miles

DUTCH GUIANA

PART I

A View from London

I

Consuming Passions

London life in the mid-eighteenth century had come to revolve round the city's coffee houses: there were some 550 of them by 1740. They were to be found in most streets, alleyways and thoroughfares of that buoyant capital city. Centres of smoky conviviality, they also served as reading rooms, places of business, a forum for political intrigue and organization, a rendezvous for artists and a warm fireside where men from the middling and lower orders could mingle on terms of friendly relaxation. Tories gravitated to the 'Cocoa Tree', Whigs to the 'St James'; Freemasons and literary men could be found at 'Anderton's' in Fleet Street; Addison, Steele, Swift and Gay favoured 'Garraway's' in the City. Gamblers drank in 'Young Man's' in Charing Cross, army officers at 'Tilt Yard' in Whitehall. Lawyers drifted to their local coffee house, 'Seale's'. Thomas Telford, the famous engineer, lived for the best part of twenty-one years at the 'Salopian Coffee House', Charing Cross. Even the famous gambling clubs of the aristocracy and of society's upper reaches – 'Boodles', 'Brooks', 'Whites' – had their own coffee rooms.

Coffee houses were more than places of refreshment, providing instead a range of functions and pleasures. They served as post offices, where friends and associates left messages for each other; as reading rooms for the expanding range of newspapers (London had four dailies and five or six tri-weekly evening papers by 1760 and there were perhaps thirty-seven provincial papers by the same time).[1] The coffee houses were the cross-roads of international trade and empire; the news, the personnel, the tittle-tattle of far-flung colonies and trading posts all passed through their doors. Virginians and Jamaicans could keep abreast of news at home by wandering down to their own coffee house where they could catch up with the colonial newsprints, merchants and travellers fresh from their homeland. Auctions often took place in coffee houses, even for black slaves bought and sold in England. And when slaves ran away, coffee houses provided a suitable place for their repossession.

In the coffee house, said one visitor: 'You have all manner of news there; you have a good Fire, which you may sit at as long as you please; you have a dish of Coffee; you meet your Friends for the transaction of Business, and all for a penny.'

The coffee houses were a mixed bunch, ranging from the fashionable to the lowlife. Most, claimed one visitor in 1726, 'are not overclean or well furnished, owing to the quantity of people who resort to these places and because of the smoke, which would quickly destroy good furniture.' They provided for a remarkable mix of people and groups.

> Workmen habitually begin the day by going to coffee-houses in order to read the latest news. I have often seen shoe-blacks and other persons of that class club together to purchase a farthing paper...Some coffee houses are a resort for learned scholars and wits; others are the resort of dandies or of politicians, or again of professional newsmongers; and many others are temples of Venus.[2]

In all the debate about the English coffee house perhaps the most curious fact of all is generally overlooked: here was an extraordinarily important institution which had come to prominence in a relatively brief period, but which depended for its very existence on produce from the tropics. It was in fact just one indication of the way European tastes had been transformed in the seventeenth and eighteenth centuries by an array of tropical goods, some previously unheard of, others too rare and costly to have a popular appeal. Tea from China, sugar and coffee from the West Indies, tobacco from Virginia, chocolate from Africa and America, rum from the Caribbean: all were consumed on an increasingly large scale. Most curious of all, the three major beverages – coffee, chocolate and tea – all had a naturally bitter taste. What made them palatable to Europeans was the addition of sugar. And the invisible ingredient which placed these exotic goods on tables throughout the western world was the toil of black slaves: Africans transported across the Atlantic, and their descendants born in the Americas. Without the slaves there would have been no sugar and without sugar there would have been no national addiction to coffee and, later, to tea.

When we think of a national British drink, it is tea not coffee which now springs to mind. It is a staple of the national diet and belongs to a much broader culture than mere food and drink. Tea-drinking is at once basic to the British way of life and a matter of curiosity to outsiders. It is surely peculiar that a product from China, later from India, and lavishly sweetened by West Indian sugar grown by slaves imported from Africa should have become a national addiction in northern Europe. It was a paradox that was appreciated from the early days of British tea-drinking: 'After all, it appears a very strange thing, that the common people of any European nation should be obliged to use, as part of their daily diet, two articles imported from the opposite sides of the earth.'

Tea was initially imported into England from China by the monopoly East India Company; prices were inevitably high. But tea began to grow in popularity, the demand partly satisfied by a thriving smuggling industry. By the early nineteenth century, the British switched tea production to India and there, eventually, on an investment of some £36 million, more than a million people found employment. It also had the effect of enhancing British political control over India.

In common with other social patterns, tea-drinking began as the fashionable preserve of the wealthy before passing down the social scale. Mass production, reduced prices and social emulation – all came together to make sweet tea a national addiction. When duties on tea were lowered in 1784, it became even more popular, dislodging in Scotland the local commitment to malt liquor. It was an odd story, when 'tea brought from the eastern extremity of the world, and sugar brought from the West Indies and both loaded with the expense of freight and insurance...compose a drink cheaper than beer.'

Those who denounced tea as a luxury had to answer the obvious question: how could a luxury become the cheapest single item in the diet of the rural and the urban poor? For the poor it was not a costly commodity: 'Spring-water, just coloured with a few leaves of the lowest-priced tea, and sweetened with the brownest of sugar, is the luxury for which you reproach them... Tea-drinking is not the cause, but the consequence of the distress of the poor.'[3] Those too poor to buy it 'begged once-used tea-leaves from neighbours, or even simulated its colour by pouring boiling water over a burnt crust.'[4]

The British used sugar in much more than their tea. More lavishly employed in the elaborate and extensive repasts of the middle and upper classes, sugar as an additive to food became equally important to working people in bread, porridge and treacle. During the eighteenth century, the British became famous for their puddings which required prodigious amounts of sugar: 'Hot puddings, cold puddings, steamed puddings, baked puddings, pies, tarts, creams, moulds, charlottes and bettys, trifles and fools, syllabubs and tansys, junkets and ices, milk puddings, suet puddings.' The British had developed the 'sweet tooth' for which they became famous; as often as not they lost their teeth altogether.[5]

The figures tell their own tale. In 1700–1709 the British per capita consumption of sugar was 4lb; by 1780–1789 it had tripled and in 1800–1809 had risen to 18lb. By 1800 the British consumption of sugar had increased 2,500 per cent in 150 years. All this was the work of the slaves.

Sugar cane cultivation was an ancient art, originating in New Guinea, moving slowly westwards and entering Europe, via the Arab conquest of the southern Mediterranean, by the eight century AD. Gradually Europeans began their own sugar cultivation in Sicily, Cyprus, southern Italy, Portugal and later Spain. These last two transplanted cane production to the Atlantic islands – Madeira, Las Palmas, the Canaries, the Azores, the Cape Verde Islands and, later, the islands of Sao Thomé and Principe José – and then to the African coast. Sugar from these islands was marketed into northern Europe through a string of major ports. Thus was created the commercial system of production and supply and, equally important, the fashionable demand for cane sugar in northern Europe.[6]

The Atlantic islands which became the centres of sugar cane cultivation, and especially the Canaries and Sao Thomé, used both forced and slave labour to work the fields. When, in 1493, Columbus made his second voyage to the Americas, he took with him sugar cane from the Canaries. By 1516 the first sugar grown in the New World, in Santo Domingo, was shipped back to Spain. It had been grown by enslaved Africans transported in the early voyages of exploration and settlement. Sugar began to flourish wherever the Europeans settled, in Brazil, the Caribbean, in Mexico and the west coast of South America. Sugar prices began to rise in Europe, warranting growing investment in African slaves. By 1568 the bigger sugar plantations in Santo Domingo had upwards of 200 slaves, some even 500. But almost as quickly as it arose, the Spanish sugar industry collapsed. Cane production and export passed to other regions and to other European nations. Initially the Portuguese were able to satisfy the European taste for sugar with the expansion of production in Brazil. But by the early seventeenth century it was the English who began to revolutionize sugar cultivation.

Early English Atlantic settlements unsuccessfully experimented with sugar production in Guiana, Virginia and Bermuda. Settlers knew there was a market for sugar if only they could find the right colony for settlement. They found the perfect place with the conquest of Barbados (1625) and the string of West Indian islands culminating in Jamaica (1655). By then, English dominance of the Caribbean had been secured. Using Dutch money and the earlier Dutch sugar experience in Brazil, British indentured (white) labour worked alongside African slaves. Barbados was slowly transformed into a luxuriant sugar island. Pioneering smallholdings were eventually amalgamated into bigger plantations; indentured labourers gave way to imported Africans. Writing in 1645, George Downing noted that Barbadians 'have brought this yeare no less than a thousand negroes, and the more they buie, the more they are able to buie, for in a yeare and a halfe they will earn with God's blessing as much as they cost.'[7] Sugar drew ever more Africans to the British islands. Barbados took most slaves up to the 1680s; thereafter more went to the Leeward Islands and, above all, to Jamaica. Between 1702 and 1808 some 830,857 Africans were shipped into Jamaica (though many were re-exported).[8]

Sugar, and other tropical produce, poured into Britain for local consumption and for re-export to other parts of Europe. By 1700 England imported

50,000 hogsheads of sugar, exporting 18,000 of them. In 1753 it imported 100,000 and exported 6,000. In return, British industries and farming disgorged volumes of produce to pay for the slaves and to feed and maintain the colonial settlements. All was controlled by an increasingly powerful state. And on the backs of the slaves there emerged a massive, lucrative and apparently unending flow of economic well-being: the maritime fleet expanded beyond imagination; ports and cities grew from simple villages to international trading centres; banking and insurance boomed as never before. With so strong and profitable an economy, the nation developed its political and military muscles – or was it the other way round? Did Britain become an ascendant global power because of the strength it acquired from its colonial possessions? Whatever the answer it was clear that much of that strength had derived from the muscles of the black slaves.

Sugar was not alone in experiencing the change from being a luxury to an item of mass consumption. Tobacco had a similar fate. Like sugar, it too was cultivated by slaves. Time and again, visitors to coffee houses in London complained of the smoke and tobacco. The tables were covered with tobacco, the atmosphere thick with tobacco smoke. By the mid-eighteenth century, the British had become addicted to the weed: they stuffed it in pipes and puffed on it, chewed it in wads, ground it to a fine dust and sniffed it. It stained their clothes, their fingers and hair, it polluted the atmosphere at any gathering – and it obviously killed them. But they loved it and could not do without it. Like sugar at precisely the same time, tobacco came from a colony, was cultivated by slaves and was part of the expansive Atlantic economy which brought such well-being to the mother-country. Early settlers in Virginia had tried – unsuccessfully – to farm sugar; their attempts with tobacco had an entirely different outcome. Once the logistical problems of survival and food had been settled, Virginians turned to the crop – tobacco – which had already developed an exclusive market in Europe. From about 1618 the colony boomed, its tobacco in massive demand (despite a pronounced hostility to it in certain fashionable British circles), its land suitably settled and the labour undertaken by a mix of free and unfree labour. From the 1620s onwards, tobacco became the region's major export, easy access to the sea provided by the complex river systems which fed into the massive Chesapeake and thence to the Atlantic. An annual average of 65,000 lb of tobacco was shipped to England in the 1620s. By the end of the 1630s, it stood at more than a million pounds each year. Forty years later, the annual export of tobacco by the Chesapeake planters was more than 20 million pounds. Throughout, the main form of labour was indentured Britons (75,000 emigrating from Britain between 1630 and 1680). But the Virginian planters could never get enough labour; immigrants were predominantly male, many simply died, others quit the land when their service was complete. Freed labour wanted land of its own; planters in Virginia and Maryland wanted a stable labour force which was tied more effectively to their land. By 1700 the supply of indentured servants from Britain had almost dried up. Thereafter, the planters turned to the kind of labour which had created the wealth of the West Indian sugar islands – black slaves.

Although Africans had been imported to Virginia in the early days of settlement, in 1660 there were only about 1,700 blacks in Maryland and Virginia (by that time Barbados had a slave population of more than 20,000), growing to 40,000 in 1670 (by which time there were 9,000 slaves in Jamaica). Planters in the Chesapeake now began to import more slaves and bought batches from the West Indies. Surely but unmistakably black slavery began to wash through the river-systems of the Chesapeake which lapped away at ever more tobacco plantations at the water's edge. White servants gave way to black slaves throughout the region.

Some 100,000 slaves were imported into the region in the eighty years between 1690 and 1770, the great majority from Africa. Planters wanted healthy males above all else but many died within a few months of landing, and many others could not be put to heavy plantation work until they had regained the strength which had drained away on the slave ships. In time, however, among locally-born slaves in the region, birth-rates began to pick up. Healthier young females, marrying early in their fertile years, had more babies than their mothers. The result was that by the early eighteenth century the black population had begun to increase. As it did so, tobacco planters had less need to buy slaves from Africa. 'The number of Negroes in the southern colonies', said an English visitor in 1759, 'is upon the whole nearly equal, if not superior, to that of the white men; and, they propagate and increase even faster.'[9]

This pattern – with a host of local variants – had a dramatic effect throughout the North American slave colonies. First, North America could manage without the costly imports of Africans. Second, having locally-born slaves rather than alien Africans (who did not even speak the language) rendered much more simple the process of socializing and acculturating the slaves to whatever norms and styles the planters desired. Finally, it ensured that there was an *internal* supply of slaves; slaves from the expanding black populations could be moved around within the colonies (later, within the states) to satisfy demand for slave labour wherever it might arise.

None of this would have happened on the scale and at the pace that it did without consumer demand for tobacco and sugar. In 1775 Virginia and Maryland exported 220 million pounds of tobacco, and the British West Indian colonies produced perhaps 100,000 tons of sugar. By the mid-eighteenth century the black population of the British Caribbean stood at 295,000; that of British North America 247,000.[10]

Mass consumption of sugar, tobacco and other tropical staples became so normal, so integrated a feature of western life that most people took it for granted. There were, it is true, isolated voices denouncing the strange economic system which had transmuted tropical exotica into temperate necessities; but such voices were generally disregarded. Who could imagine British life without sugar or tobacco? Englishmen, snug in their convivial coffee houses, might sometimes see a reminder of who did the back-breaking work in the sugar and tobacco fields with the occasional appearance of a black servant or slave. How many people made the connection? How many realized the interdependence between black slavery and the material pleasures of white life; between untold black misery and the expansion of white pleasure?

2

Murdering Men

London in the late eighteenth century, though compact by modern standards (one could walk from the centre to open fields in thirty minutes), had a large and expanding population, a substantial number of whom were outsiders. Dr Johnson, coiner of the best-remembered aphorism about London life, was himself from Lichfield, and scorned for his Staffordshire accent. Africans from the slavery coast, blacks from the West Indies, Chinese sailors, wealthy planters from Jamaica and Virginia (men who looked British but who spoke a distinctive and peculiar English), provincials from the depths of English rural life, poor people from the Celtic fringes: all these, and more, could be seen on London's streets.

Most striking, because most 'exotic', were the blacks. Sometimes attired in the height of contemporary style – as servants, footmen and coachdrivers to the wealthy – the blacks were more likely to be poor, sometimes wretched.

Of those in employment, the largest single group seems to have been in domestic service. Among their number was Elizabeth Dido Lindsay, servant to Lord Mansfield, Lord Chief Justice of England from 1756 to 1788. Like so many blacks in eighteenth-century London, Elizabeth Dido was a victim of circumstance. Labour was plentiful and there was never a shortage of young men and women keen to learn the arduous but generally secure work of domestic service. Black servants were obviously more eye-catching, more likely to reflect on their employer's wealth or status, than the ubiquitous local servants. Lord Mansfield, however, seems to have taken on the woman from a sense of family obligation. Mansfield's nephew was Sir John Lindsay, a professional sailor promoted in the last year of his life to Rear Admiral. When Lindsay died, in the summer of 1788, an obituary helps us with the life of Elizabeth Dido. Lindsay, it was recorded: 'has died, we believe, without any legitimate issue, but has left one natural daughter, a Mulatto, who has been brought up in Lord Mansfield's family almost from her infancy.'[1]

Elizabeth Dido's mother had been a slave, seized on board a captured Spanish vessel by Sir John Lindsay's ship. When she bore a child by Sir John, he passed the infant on to Lord Mansfield's family. In her adult life, Elizabeth Dido held a curious position in the Mansfield household: although employed as a domestic, she was on friendly, familiar terms with the household and visitors. Lord Mansfield was even 'reproached for showing a fondness for her'. One guest was struck by the oddness of the relationship: 'A Black came in after dinner and sat with the ladies, one of the young ladies having her arm within the other. She had a very high cap, and her wool was much frizzled in her neck, but not enough to answer...the large curls now in fashion. She is neither handsome nor genteel – pert enough.' When Lord Mansfield drafted a new will in 1782 he specified that she was to be given her freedom, and when he died in 1793 he left her £500 and an annuity of £100.[2]

This was an unusual relationship, lying somewhere between family ties and terms of employment. The blood line was clearly known to everyone; Mansfield had no qualms in describing the young woman's family origins. But she clearly did not move around the family home as an equal. Enjoying the post-dinner relaxation, Dido nevertheless remained a servant, hidden by rank, by work and by colour from the normal transactions of household and social life.

Whatever the legal questions involved, slave-holding in England clearly existed. Planters from the colonies, sailors from the slave ships, officials from the West Indies and North America, all and more returned to England in the company of their black slaves. Few people were more conscious of the law and social practice of English domestic slave-holding than Lord Mansfield, for he had patiently listened to and sifted through the conflicting social and legal evidence throughout his legal career. Not surprisingly, he took the sensible precaution of specifically emancipating Elizabeth Dido. The Lord Chief Justice was clearly not prepared to let her fall victim – like so many other blacks – to the caprice of the legal system and the unpredictable circumstances of fate.

Mansfield's dealings with slaves went far beyond owning and freeing a slave of his own. It was inevitable that blacks would find their way to England, entering the major ports on ships returning from Africa, the Caribbean and North America. In time, noticeable (though always small) black communities developed, particularly in London. What caused legal concern, and what periodically taxed English (and sometimes Scottish) courts, was the legal status of slaves in England. The British Atlantic empire had developed on the back of the slave system. Black slavery was legally sanctioned in all manner of ways; it was legal on British ships and at African trading posts, it was legal throughout the British colonies. But what happened to slaves when they set foot in Britain? For a nation which took great pride in its thriving and expanding domestic liberties, secured by the seventeenth-century revolution, it seemed odd, to put it mildly, that the British could countenance slavery surviving in Britain itself. There was a clear confusion of practice between the rise of domestic liberties and the expansion of colonial slavery. It was a confusion which would occasionally exercise the English legal mind, none more persistently so than Lord Mansfield's.

Long before Mansfield became Lord Chief Justice, slave cases had troubled English courts, but it fell to Mansfield to preside over the most significant and memorable of the slave cases. In part this was because Granville Sharp, the pioneering humanitarian, specifically set out to secure a legal confirmation that slavery could not exist in England. Sharp became a fixture in Mansfield's courtrooms, attending the various slave cases, ensuring that they were promoted in the first place, and eagerly pursuing all the related consequences of the cases through associates and men in high places. The particulars of the slave cases were often shocking, but shocking *only* because they had taken place in England. Incidents of even greater abominations were commonplace, unregarded and unexceptional on the slave ships and in the slave colonies. Even in so violent and cruel a world as mid-eighteenth-century London, the detailed sufferings of slaves in England began to disturb contemporary opinion.

Jonathan Strong was a case in point. Brought by his master from Barbados to London in 1765, he had been savagely beaten 'upon his Head with a Pistol till the Barrel and the Lock were separated from the Stock'. Scarcely able to walk, suffering from a fever and 'with so violent a disorder in his Eyes that there appeared to be the utmost danger of his becoming blind', Strong, aged seventeen, found his way to Dr William Sharp in Mincing Lane, London. It was there that the doctor's brother, Granville, encountered Strong. Thanks to the two men – and a four-month stay in St Bartholomew's hospital – the young man recovered. Two years later, Strong's former owner, John Lisle, seized him again and sold him to a Jamaican planter, James Kerr, who planned to return to the Caribbean with him. In desperation, Strong contacted Granville Sharp who secured his release. There followed a series of legal hearings and discussions about the implications of the Strong case. What remained unresolved was the simple question: could a black be removed from England, back to a slave colony, against his/her wishes? In this case Strong was freed. But the legal question remained unanswered.

Sharp's reputation as a friend of distressed and legally aggrieved blacks was now firmly established. Throughout the late 1760s he was periodically recruited to defend London blacks threatened with transportation to the colonies. A writ of Habeas Corpus normally secured their freedom. In February 1771 one such man, Thomas Lewis, already freed by Sharp's effort, petitioned Lord Mansfield's court on the central principle of a black person's right *not* to be forcibly expelled from England. Mansfield had already given two or three writs of Habeas Corpus to other slaves, but was deeply reluctant, in the Lewis case, to establish a point of principle: 'I don't know what the consequences may be, if the masters were to lose their property by accidentally bringing their slaves to England. I hope it never will be finally discussed; for I would have all masters think them free, and all Negroes think they were not, because then they would both behave better'.[3]

Mansfield did his best to avoid making a clear judgment on the issue. Even when the jury determined that the black was *not* the claimant's property (to delighted cries of 'No property, no property' from the public gallery), Mansfield refused to give appropriate compensation. Granville Sharp meanwhile continued to seek an appropriate case to bring before the English courts to secure the point that blacks were indeed free.

In 1771–72 the ideal case seemed to present itself. James Somerset, like many others before him a slave brought to England, was being forcibly removed by his owner back to the colonies. Lord Mansfield granted a writ of Habeas Corpus, referring the broader issue to a hearing in King's Bench. Mansfield knew that Granville Sharp was again active in seeking a clear decision in favour of black freedom in England.[4] There followed a series of hearings from December 1771 to June 1772. Arguments ranged back and forth on the narrow particularities of Somerset's case and on the broader issue of the legality of slavery in England. In judgment, Lord Mansfield was clear enough: 'No master ever was allowed here to take a slave by force to be sold abroad because he deserted from his service, or for any other reason whatever – therefore the man must be discharged.' James Somerset was then released and under no obligation to return against his wishes with his master to Virginia.

Almost as happy as Somerset was the sizeable black contingent which had sat through the court hearings. After Mansfield's judgment, they 'bowed with profound respect to the Judges, and shaking each other by the hand congratulated themselves upon the recovery of the rights of human nature.' At the end of June, they celebrated in style, 200 gathering 'At a public house in Westminster, to celebrate the triumph which their brother Somerset had obtained over Stewart his Master. Lord Mansfield's health was echoed round the room, and the evening was concluded with a Ball. The tickets to this Black assembly were 5s.'[5]

Had they been aware of Mansfield's real attitude, they might have hesitated in their praise. From the first he had sought ways of preventing the case coming forward (realizing its broad implications) and trying, during the hearing, to persuade Stewart to free his slave and thus avert a difficult decision. Mansfield was an expert on commercial law and was loath to make a decision which might disturb the property-basis of black slavery. So much commercial wealth flowed to Britain from its slave empire that any judgment which ran counter to that economic interest, even in so minor a fashion as slavery in England, was to be resisted. The case was followed avidly in the papers; reports described proceedings, there was a lively correspondence about the case (often at Mansfield's expense) and the case sponsored a flurry of pamphlets from planters, afraid that their long-term economic interests might be harmed. West Indian planters and merchants tried initially to secure a parliamentary Bill allowing black slavery in England. Instead, they opted for the clever ploy of persuading their slaves to sign indentures, bringing them to serve in England in return.

What Mansfield had *not* done – and he took great pains to reiterate the point at the time and later – was to free all slaves in England. As late as 1785, he claimed that the 1772 decision went 'no further than that the master cannot by force compel him to go out of the kingdom'.[6] Despite an abundance of evidence to the contrary, despite the persistence of slave sales, slave advertisements, manumission of slaves and the like long after 1772, a myth developed that Mansfield had freed all slaves in England. Yet Mansfield freed his own slave, Elizabeth Dido Lindsay, in his will drawn up in 1782. (Why go to the trouble if black freedom had been secured in 1772?) Benjamin Franklin was right when he cynically remarked that England 'piqued itself on its virtue, love of liberty, and the equity of its courts, in setting free a single negro'.[7]

Less than a year after drafting his will, Lord Mansfield presided over the most grotesquely bizarre of all slave cases heard in an English court. Strictly speaking it was not a slave case, and did not hinge on definitions of freedom or slavery. But the significance of the evidence of *Gregson v. Gilbert* (more commonly known as the *Zong* case) takes us right to the heart of the slave system, exposing the manifest contradictions between the English custom of slave-trading and the basic tenets of English law.

The *Zong* was a slave ship owned by a large Liverpool slaving company. In 1781 it was employed on the well-tried route from Liverpool to West Africa and thence with a cargo of slaves to the Caribbean. On 6 September the *Zong* sailed from West Africa with a cargo of 470 slaves bound for Jamaica. Twelve weeks later, closing on its destination, the *Zong* had already lost more than sixty Africans and seven of the seventeen-man crew. This was a high mortality level, for both black and white, but nothing like the catastrophic losses suffered by some other slave ships. But there was no end in sight to the slave deaths. Luke Collingwood, the *Zong*'s captain, called his officers together on 29 November and put forward the suggestion that sick slaves should be jettisoned – thrown overboard – both to secure the rapidly dwindling supplies of water and to allow the shipping company to claim their loss as insurance. It was, even in the age of the slave trade, a grotesque suggestion.

There were plenty of likely candidates. An abolitionist account reported that, in addition to the dead, 'a great many of the remaining slaves … were sick of some severe disorders, and likely not to live long'. Collingwood told his officers: 'if the slaves died a natural death, it would be the loss of the owners of the ship; but if they were *thrown alive into the sea, it would be the loss of the underwriters.*' As a humane, though obviously specious, justification, he suggested that 'it would not be so cruel to *throw the poor sick wretches into the sea,* as to suffer them to linger out a few days, under the disorders with which they were afflicted'.[8] No such proposal was made to put an end to the suffering of sick crewmen.

Luke Collingwood is likely to have known about contemporary maritime insurance. In that same year, a digest of insurance laws and practice was published in London. It seemed clear enough:

> The insurer takes upon him the risk of the loss, capture, and death of slaves, or any other unavoidable accident to them: but natural death is always understood to be excepted: – by natural death is meant, not only when it happens by disease or sickness, but also when the captive destroys himself through despair, which often happens: but when slaves are killed or thrown into the sea in order to quell an insurrection on their part, then the insurers must answer.[9]

Sickness alone seemed scarcely a sufficient reason for drowning the slaves. Collingwood's excuse was that the ship was running short of water, due in part to the captain's navigational error which had mistaken Hispaniola for their destination, Jamaica. Kill the sick slaves, and the healthy could be sustained on the dwindling supplies. Not to kill the slaves would be to jeopardize the safety and health of everyone on board. It was an unconvincing line of self-justification not least because water was not rationed until *after* the killing of the slaves had begun and, secondly, because no attempt was made to put ashore to replenish supplies. Moreover, before all the sick slaves had been killed, 'there fell a plentiful rain, which was admitted to have "*continued a day or two*", and which enabled them to collect *six casks of water,* which was "full allowance for 11 days, or for 23 days at half allowance."'[10] When the *Zong* landed in Jamaica on 22 December, it had 420 gallons of water on board. It had left in its wake 131 drowned slaves.

Initially, some of the crew objected to the proposal to drown the slaves but Collingwood insisted, and the killings began. The crew selected those who 'were sick, and thought not likely to live'. On 29 November, the first batch, of fifty-four, was pushed overboard. A day later forty-two more were drowned, and on the third day twenty-six were thrown into the sea. 'And this act was done, it seems, in the sight of many of the unhappy slaves who were upon deck at the time. And such an effect had the sight on them, that apprehending a similar fate, and dreading, it would seem, the being fettered, ten more of them in despair jumped overboard, and were *likewise drowned.*'[11] One of the jettisoned slaves managed to catch on to a rope and climbed back safely on board. A total of 131 slaves were coolly murdered from the deck of a Liverpool vessel,

for no good reason save the economic calculations of Captain Luke Collingwood and the physical compliance of his crewmen.

By this time Granville Sharp had spent the best part of twenty years
campaigning against the existence of slavery in England. On 19 March 1783
he was visited by Olaudah Equiano (sometimes called Gustavus Vassa), an
African and former slave who was emerging as the most prominent spokesman
for the black community living in London: 'Gustavus Vassa Negro called on
me with an account of 130 [sic] Negroes being thrown alive into the sea, from
on Board an English Slave Ship.'[12] In fact, the *Zong* affair had surfaced two
weeks earlier, when the case of *Gregson v. Gilbert* had been heard in the
Guildhall in London. Gregson, the shipowners, were claiming for the loss of
their slaves (£30 each) from their underwriters (Gilbert). The latter refused to
pay, and thus the case was a simple matter of maritime insurance.

At the initial trial, the jury sided with the shipowners, ordering the insurance company to pay compensation for the dead slaves. In a letter to the
Morning Chronicle, an eye-witness at the trial wrote: 'The narrative seemed to
make every one present shudder; and I waited with some impatience, expecting that the jury, by their foreman, would have applied to the Court for
information how to bring the perpetrators of such a horrid deed to justice.'
Perhaps one way out was the suggestion that Captain Luke Collingwood – by
now safely dead – 'was in a delirium, or a fit of lunacy when he gave the
orders'. Whatever the reason, the case retained its basic inhuman simplicity: a
claim for insurance. Yet this correspondent was absolutely correct to argue in
the newspaper that the *Zong* affair transcended the particularities of an argument about compensation:

> That there should be bad men to do bad things in all large communities, must be
> expected: but a community makes the crime general, and provokes divine wrath,
> when it suffers any member to commit flagrant acts of villainy with impun-
> ity…it is hardly possible for a state to thrive, where the perpetration of such
> complicated guilt, as the present, is not only suffered to go unpunished, but is
> allowed to glory in the infamy, and carries off the reward for it.[13]

The crime had been committed on board a British ship, and was so startling
in the crudity and extent of its violence that it clearly shook observers. But
where would the pursuit of criminality end if, let us say, the crew were
arraigned for their crimes? Although the murder of African slaves was unusual,
it was common enough in pursuit of slaves, in securing the safety of a slave
ship, in defeating ship-board resistance – to say nothing of the endemic
violence which helped keep slavery in place throughout the American slave
colonies. Slavery begat the slave trade, and the slave trade was, in origin, in
conduct and in its very being, the crudest of violations, which encompassed,
when necessary, the death of its victims. For the system to survive in its

economic viability, some slaves had to pay the ultimate sacrifice. It took no great leap of the imagination to appreciate that the logic of pursuing the murderers of the slaves on the *Zong* would be the first tug which would unravel the entire garment of the slave system. And in some respects this is precisely what happened, for it was around the small band of men of sensibility, outraged by events on the *Zong*, that there developed the first powerful body of abolitionist feeling and action. The line of dissent from the *Zong* to the successful campaign for abolition was direct and unbroken, however protracted and uneven.

Granville Sharp's initial response was to rally a body of like-minded men to pursue the prosecution of the *Zong* sailors. But when the *Zong* affair once more came to trial it did so again on a matter of insurance. The underwriters refused to pay compensation, and the matter came before Lord Justice Mansfield sitting with two other judges in May 1783. The slave-owners, claiming the insurance on the slaves, were represented by John Lee, the Solicitor-General. Lee was as conscious of the broad implications of the case as anyone. Turning towards Granville Sharp in the public gallery, he argued that there was a person in court who intended to bring on a criminal prosecution for murder against the parties concerned: *'but it would be madness: the Blacks were property.'* The line he adopted was casually dismissive:

> What is all this vast declaration of human beings thrown overboard? The question after all is, was it voluntary, or an act of necessity? *This is a case of chattels or goods.* It is really so: it is the case of throwing over goods; for to this purpose, and the purpose of the insurance, *they are goods and property: whether right or wrong, we have nothing to do with it.* This property – *the human creatures if you will* – have been thrown overboard: whether or not for the preservation of the rest, that is the real question.[14]

Stated with such boldness, this seemed an outrageous claim; in essence it was, however, true. The slave system hinged on the concept of the slave as a thing: a chattel, a piece of property. It was a concept which from the first contained an obvious contradiction: how could a human being be a thing?[15] But since law and economic practice had, from the early days of the Atlantic slave trade, accepted the chattel status of the slave, what objection could there be to the killing of chattel? Lord Mansfield himself accepted the point: 'they had no doubt (though it shocks one very much) that the case of the slaves was the same as if horses had been thrown overboard.'[16]

Mansfield conceded the importance of the case and agreed to order a new trial. But at this point the historical trail goes cold. No one has found any evidence of a further trial being held or even identified the next legal step in the *Zong* affair. But the indefatigable Granville Sharp was not prepared to let the issue slip into the anonymous recesses of legal proceedings, and the

owners of the *Zong* were not the last slave-shipowners to claim insurance for
dead slaves.

Granville Sharp tried to persuade government officers to bring murder
charges against those involved, telling Admiralty officials that he had 'been
earnestly solicited and called upon by a poor Negro for my assistance, to
avenge the blood of his murdered countrymen'. Marshalling all the supporting
evidence he could find, Sharp hoped to present an unanswerable case for a
prosecution. Again, he confronted that official silence and inactivity born of
the realization that any such action would corrode the system. Once an
English court began to discuss murder and cruelty in the conduct of the
slaving system, there was no knowing where the questions – and the consequent material damage – would end. The lessons of the *Zong* pointed down a
long road towards abolishing the slave trade and even slavery itself. But who,
in 1783 – apart from Granville Sharp, a very small band of sympathizers, and
the slaves – could even imagine such a step? The benefits of the slave system
were clear enough to British contemporaries. How many could countenance
destroying so abundant and fruitful an economic system merely from a sense
of ethical outrage? It was to take much more than the *Zong* affair – many more
lives (black and white), an incalculable fund of human suffering and misery –
before the British finally resolved to end their slave system. But in the slow
gestation of national outrage against black slavery, the events on board the
Zong in November and December 1781 played an important part. Granville
Sharp became even more determined to end the system; it became an obses-
sional, personal crusade. Within a generation, it was rewarded with success.

In the short term, it seemed that nothing had been gained from the *Zong*
affair. Ottobah Cugoano (like Equiano, a former slave living in London in the
1780s) made the melancholy remark: 'But our lives are accounted of no value,
we are hunted as the prey in the desert, and doomed to destruction as the
beasts that perish.'[17]

The *Zong* affair had alerted more than the embryonic band of abolitionists
to the problems raised by maritime insurance in the slave trade. Slave-traders
and underwriters had their own vested interest in securing legal redress for
their conflicting claims in cases of dead slaves, and it was only a matter of time
before a similar case came before an English court. Lord Mansfield once again
sat in judgment. In 1785 he listened to the disputed insurance case (*Jones v.
Schmoll*) of a Bristol slave ship whose insurance policy specified that: 'the
assurers are not to pay any loss that may happen in boats during the voyage
(mortality of Africans by natural death excepted): and not to pay for mortality
by mutiny.'

In common with so many other slave ships, this Bristol vessel had suffered a
revolt in which twelve slaves died on the African coast. A temporary calm was
followed by a more serious revolt, suppressed only by firing at the slaves.
Between the shootings, woundings, drowning and illnesses, the ship lost fifty-

five slaves. The insurance company would compensate only for those killed in the rioting itself. The jury, influenced by Lord Mansfield's guidance, confirmed the legality of this arrangement, i.e. that the insurers did *not* have to pay for slaves who merely 'died' – by suicide, illness or wasting away.

A few years later Parliament began to regulate the problem of slave insurance, although it was inevitable that disputes should continue. It is, however, worth repeating the clause of an Act of the English Parliament (of 1790), which specified that: 'no loss or damage shall be recoverable on account of the mortality of slaves by natural death or *ill treatment, or against loss by throwing overboard of slaves on any account whatsoever.*'[18] It may seem bizarre (in retrospect, though clearly not so at the time) that Parliament made specific exception to insurance cover in the case of murder. Parliament felt obliged to legislate because slaves continued to be killed on English slave ships. It had been apparent for many years that the English slave trade was built on violence. It was not simply that slaves died because of haphazard freaks of circumstance, by the accidents of fate, by illness, misfortune or at the hands of vicious (if untypical) slave-traders; it was abundantly clear that the slave trade was a system conceived, sustained and nurtured by inter-related systems of violence. At the point at which the British became most intimately and directly involved – when they took over the Africans, bought them, stored them on board and transported them to the slave colonies – violence was integral to the system. So too was death. Everyone involved in the slave trade had a keen interest in keeping slaves alive; equally, they were willing to kill and to inflict injury if necessary. To kill a slave, or a group of slaves, was an economic misfortune, but it did not constitute a human outrage which offended or worried those involved. Yet niggling doubts had been raised, from the mid-eighteenth century onwards, about the morality and the utility of so draconian a world. Such blood-letting might still be acceptable if it had a reasonable justification: for instance, it might seem acceptable to kill slaves who were in revolt (after all, those who took part in the Gordon Riots in London in 1780 were put down in a draconian and violent fashion). But what possible justification could there be for the wanton and wilful killing of slaves?

The tide had clearly begun to run against the slave-traders. At first it affected their insurance claims for slaves lost on the Atlantic crossing. What made the cases paraded through English courts between 1765 and 1796 unusual was that they allowed the courts, the public and the press to peer beyond the brutal details of a particular outrage, and to gaze, often in amazement, at the infinitely more horrible details of the Atlantic slave system itself. In 1796, a Liverpool shipper claimed insurance for the 128 slaves who had died of starvation on a crossing badly delayed by storm; only forty survived a voyage which lasted more than six months. Heard by Lord Justice Kenyon (Mansfield's successor), the case hinged upon the nature of the slaves' deaths.

Were they, because of the storm-bound crossing, caused by the perils of the sea? Lord Kenyon asked the obvious question: did the captain starve to death? Of course not. In refusing the claim, the judges determined that henceforth the deliberate killing of slaves could not be rewarded by insurance cover.

When Lord Mansfield died, in March 1793, he was laid to rest in Westminster Abbey, his memory celebrated in portraits and statues to be seen to this day in the National Portrait Gallery, Christ Church, Oxford, and Trinity Hall, Cambridge. But where are the memorials to those thousands whose lives were touched by the career of England's Lord Chief Justice?

PART II

Traumas

3

Slaves, Traders and Africa

The Atlantic slave trade drew upon a vast catchment area for slaves, and involved a far more complex economic system within Africa than we might at first imagine. In the earliest days the European presence had been more piratical than commercial. John Hawkins, the first English slave-trader in 1562, with a fleet of three ships (40, 100 and 120 tons) and a mere 100 men – though backed by money from London and with tacit royal support – was able to capture 300 Africans in Sierra Leone, 'partly by the sworde, and partly by other meanes'. He sold the slaves in Hispaniola, filling his three ships, and two more besides, with local produce: 'with hides, ginger, sugars, and some quantities of pearles'. A year after he had sailed, Hawkins returned to England, 'with prosperous successe and much gaine to himself and the afore-sayde adventurers'.[1]

Recruiting Africans 'by the sworde' had obvious drawbacks: someone would have to wield the sword or other threatening weapon. Before long, Europeans found it easier and more profitable to establish trading rather than bellicose relations on the coast. When they did raid for slaves in the old piratical fashion it was a brazen and unusual event – even counter-productive. Raids created dangers and difficulties for future trade and settlement. Where Europeans continued to snatch Africans – often people who were middlemen in the slave trade – local trade was rendered impossible. Such raids by Europeans dwindled into insignificance as the demand for slaves increased. Clear conventions and rules had developed in the conduct of the slave trade by the early eighteenth century. As with most other forms of trade, participants who flouted those conventions did so at their peril. An English captain who had seen such conflict on the coast claimed: 'our English colonies will be of no use to us for the negroes study revenge and are resolved to seize upon what they can'.[2]

The slave trade could not thrive if Africans on the coast behaved as the marauding Europeans had behaved. Both sides came to a *modus vivendi*, each providing what the other needed, though to suggest that there were only two sides, black versus white, African versus European, is to create too simple a picture from an amazing confusion of groups, places and interests which littered the African coastline and rivers. The slave trade could not have existed without a complex system of slave-trading beyond the sight and ken of the Europeans. These systems of slavery had their origins not so much in European demands for Africans but in much older, traditional systems within Africa.[3]

When Europeans made their initial maritime forays to West Africa, slavery already existed there. The overland Islamic slave trade had consumed armies of Africans, marching them north and east, long before the Atlantic trade began. Yet even before the spread of Islam into black Africa, there were forms of slavery which were endemic to Africa: certain forms of marriage, slavery for debt, concubinage, sacrifice, slavery as punishment for crime. With the coming of Islam, Africans were taken as prisoners of war; women and children were more popular than men (and were used for sexual purposes or as domestics). Arab merchants recruited Africans in abundance, shipping them across the Sahara, the Red Sea and from the East African coast. It was, however, a relatively small trade, involving perhaps no more than a few thousand each year.

By 1500 the Portuguese had effectively opened up 4,000 miles of the African coastline, their trading presence secured by a string of forts and bases in the Atlantic islands of Sao Thomé and Principe in the Gulf of Guinea. They were followed by other European nations – all keen to take Africans to the expanding economies of the Americas. This white presence on the West African coast had a dramatic impact on the nature of slavery within Africa itself. So voracious was the appetite for slaves that slavery was transformed and extended far into the African hinterland. Conflicts and even wars were created simply to provide slaves.

In the early days of the slave trade, perhaps 60 per cent had been prisoners of such wars. Over the next century, it has been calculated that upwards of 70 per cent were kidnapped. Many of these were the victims of the powerful and centralized states of Dahomey and Ashanti which had emerged in large part in response to the Atlantic slave trade. Many other Africans were captured in the plethora of small-scale and often haphazard raids and deals.

Of the very few slave narratives we posses, the most important describes an act of kidnapping. Olaudah Equiano, renamed Gustavus Vassa, wrote his memoirs in 1789. Looking back on his childhood, Equiano described how

> when the grown people in the neighbourhood were gone far in the fields to labour, the children assembled together in some of the neighbours' premises to

play; and commonly some of us used to get up a tree to look out for any assailant, or kidnapper, that might come upon us; for they sometimes took these opportunities of our parents' absence, to attack and carry off as many as they could seize.

Equiano is thought to be an Ibo from the northern Ika Ibo district, in what today is the eastern province of Benin, Nigeria. Tropical rain country, the area was criss-crossed by trade routes, one of them leading south by foot, thence by the River Ase and on to the major slave-trading region of the coast. The economy was agricultural, using both male and female labour. There was, however, tension throughout the region: 'Each little group lived with its neighbour in a state of armed neutrality which periodically gave way to open warfare.'

Violent raids and attacks had forced local people to alter their daily lives. Equiano recalled that 'when our people go out to till their land, they only go in a body, but generally take their arms with them, for the fear of a surprise'. Whenever they feared attacks, they also defended their homes, 'driving sticks into the ground, which are so sharp at one end as to pierce the foot and are generally dipt in poison'. Equiano was quite clear about the purpose of such military flurries: 'they appear to have been irruptions of one little state or district on the other, to obtain prisoners or booty'. When it did erupt, warfare took the form of 'raids, ambushes and engagements in more open country'. These engagements were conducted both with traditional African weaponry and with European arms, part of the trading system on the coast. To make good trade, Africans had to grab other Africans, and the commonest and apparently easiest way to do it was to raid and kidnap. It is instructive to listen to Equiano again: 'Perhaps they were invited to this by those traders who brought the European goods... amongst us. Such a mode of obtaining slaves in Africa is common; and I believe more are procured this way, and by kidnapping, than by any other.' Equiano's speculation on how this happened has the ring of authenticity, and is confirmed by an abundance of other evidence. 'When a trader wants slaves, he applies to a chief for them, and tempts him with his wares. It is not extraordinary, if on this occasion he yields to the temptation with as little firmness, and accepts the price of his fellow creatures' liberty with as little reluctance, as the enlightened merchant.'[4]

The slave-trading system was not quite as neat, not quite as clearly defined, as Equiano described. But we do know that on the coast Europeans had to pay levies and taxes, or offer gifts and commodities to the men who controlled the supply of slaves. In their turn, these African traders had to deal with their own suppliers of humanity from the interior. And so it continued, each link in this long and tortuous chain secured to the next negotiant by the appropriate price, commodity or barter. However deep the trade penetrated into the interior (it took Equiano 'six or seven months after I had been kidnapped' to reach the coast), and however diffused the material goods and monies made available on the coast, there came a final point where Africans were seized and enslaved.

Equiano's fate was typical of the fate of millions. He was one of seven children, his father a prosperous man who had 'many slaves' of his own. Learning the skills of local agriculture and warfare, Equiano had reached the age of eleven when disaster struck. One day he and a sister had been left alone at home when 'two men and a woman got over our walls, and in a moment seized us both'. The two children were bound and gagged and bundled away into the nearest woodland. Over-whelmed by grief and tiredness, brother and sister were propelled through the woods, day after day, eventually separated, passing through communities with alien customs and languages. In places Equiano was put to work; he tried to escape, was resold a number of times, seemed always on the move. Eventually he arrived at the coast.[5]

At certain crucial periods, warfare was the obvious and most efficient form of gathering slaves. This was especially so in the kingdom of Dahomey which came to dominate great swathes of the African trade in the eighteenth century. Europeans knew the stretch of coastline between Volta and the Lagos rivers as 'the Slave Coast'. Here was the infamous Bight of Benin (today's region of Togo and Dahomey) celebrated in contemporary doggerel for the region's dire effect on the white slave crews.

> Beware and take care
> Of the Bight of Benin;
> For one that comes out
> There are forty go in.

Here was the pestilential coast which yielded a wonderful harvest of slaves – at the cost of a high death-rate among white sailors.

Something like 2 million slaves came from this region. At first, the trade was dominated by the kingdom of Allada but by the early eighteenth century it had shifted to Whydah to the west. Over the course of that century, the interior kingdom of Dahomey dominated the supplies of slaves, Dahomey having conquered both Allada and Whydah in the 1720s. Dahomey left an indelible impression on the minds of the Europeans who traded on the coast. Whenever they wanted to paint a gory picture of the ferocious African trade, they turned to Dahomey for evidence. Images of barbaric African kings, the most savage of human sacrifices, of invincible female warriors, were paraded before the reading public. These images entered the collective British imagin-ation, and were politically useful. If the European trade in slaves could only be sustained by such levels of monstrous depravity, here was another argument against slavery itself. At a time when white people had come to think of themselves as people of refinement, the stories from Dahomey helped convince them that slavery was brutal and wrong.

Dahomey had been transformed from a small coastal state into a powerful, centralized and military kingdom controlling huge reaches of the interior slave trade. By about 1750 it had become prosperous, its fortunes based on the slave trade. As Europeans on the coast began to look elsewhere for still more slaves, the new rulers of Dahomey began to change their style of enslavement. The army was refashioned to make slave raids. Thus, by the late eighteenth century Dahomey had become a slave-raiding kingdom, its economy and army geared to the capture of other Africans. This is confirmed by someone experienced in the region writing in 1804: the Dahomean slave trade, he said, was 'carried on by a chain of merchants as it were, from the Coast indefinitely in many directions towards the interior'.[6]

Dahomey has continued to fascinate historians of slavery, in part because of its monstrous reputation but mainly because of its dominance of the supply of Africans at a crucial period of the slave trade. Earlier commentators thought that this powerful kingdom was fruitful in slaves because of its military and monarchial dominance. Now, however, it is clear that Dahomey's slaves came not solely from military raids but also from a complex trading system through which the Dahomean state acquired slaves from African middlemen. This crucial region of the African slave trade was in fact a mixture of state monopoly and private supply. For the Europeans, accommodation was the trading ideal, but the question remains: what alternatives did coastal Africans have in the matter? What power did they have to resist or turn their backs on European demands for slaves? There were cases where local African societies consciously chose not to deal in slaves, effectively cutting themselves off from European commerical inducements. Most communities did not take this route. Were they unable to resist the European presence – fuelled as it was by superior technology and firepower – or were they unable to refuse the material temptations which Europeans laid before them? The exotic goods and produce which Europeans were able to gather from their worldwide empires and trading posts quickly became the currency and exchange throughout the slave-trading region of Africa. Iron, copper and brass bars were used as currency, silks from India, refined metalware and textiles from England, the best of European drinks – all these and more besides were disgorged from the slave ships and into the maw of the African slave-trading system, quickly spreading throughout the interior.

Africans were especially keen to acquire firearms. As the slave ships approached Africa, the gunnery officer busied himself placing and testing the weapons and organizing the ammunition. Africans quickly became accustomed to staring at the guns mounted on the ships and trained on their canoes and settlements, or carried by sailors on the coast. Understandably, Africans wanted their own – with all the power they seemed to bestow. The export of arms to Africa was a massive business. By the peak years of the eighteenth century, Europeans imported between 283,000 and 394,000 guns *each year* into West Africa. In 1802 the value of weapons shipped to Africa was £145,661.[7] But the value of these weapons to Africans often transcended their monetary cost. Sought after for the power – and terror – they could create, European guns became an important lubricant of the African slave system, valuable in themselves but much more important in helping to catch more slaves. Like the rum and tobacco fed to slaves on board the slave ships, guns sold to Africans were elements of a self-sustaining international industry. Slaves produced the tobacco and rum which kept new slaves happy (or at least less miserable) in the slave ships; slave-traders sold guns to Africans to increase their own supplies of slaves.

Guns encouraged the bellicose expansion (and presumably enhanced the self-confidence) of Africans involved in the slave trade. Many of the guns were of poor quality, supplies of ammunition were uncertain and the weapons were often not as effective as carefully marshalled African troops (bowmen especially). None the less, fire-power had a decided impact on slave-trading within Africa. Guns gave strength to a state or a group (providing its neighbours did not also have them), and could tilt the balance of power in a region. It is even possible that guns persuaded some societies to become slave-traders; to protect themselves against neighbours, they needed guns. But guns could often only be acquired in return for slaves. The circle is again complete. Did Africans wage war upon their neighbours because of the aggressive and economic imperatives intruded into the region by Europeans? If, as many historians claim, most slaves were prisoners of war, were those prompted, directly or unconsciously, by the white appetite for slaves?

The enslavement of Africans and their eventual sale to Europeans was, then, made possible by a complicated trading system. On the coast the key African dealers in slaves had to be seduced into co-operative trading by the dispensing of gifts and bribes. Offering the best goods a ship carried was invariably the slave captain's first gesture on arrival. 'Treating of traders is no small article and must be done if the trade is to be carried on to its utmost,' was how Sir Dalby Thomas described it in 1709. This was merely an opening bid. Thereafter, Europeans had to provide African traders with what they required for their slaves: 'if your warehouses are not kept constantly supplied with all sorts of goods, your presents and power is to no consequence'.[8]

Double-dealing or violence, failure to satisfy African clients, duplicity or uncertainty often brought African reprisals. White sailors and traders were distrusted, but valued for the goods they brought. Disliked for their threats, whites were permanently exposed to African attacks. Understandably, Europeans often traded from fortified settlements or, safer still, from their ships riding at anchor offshore.

Forts were a characteristic of European settlements in North America, India, South-East Asia and on the African coast. Forts were both a display of strength and an unmistakable suggestion of white frailty. The Portuguese were the pioneers of African forts, with buildings at Mina (1482) and Axim (1503) constructed to defend their gold trade against other Europeans, but also to overawe Africans.[9] Local chiefs sometimes resisted the territorial encroachment needed to build the forts but they were more successful in controlling the flow of goods – and of Africans – into the European stockades. As secure as the Europeans might feel inside their walls, they remained dependent on Africans allowing goods and people to pass their way – at a price.

The British Royal African Company (founded in 1672) followed the Portuguese example, creating fortified settlements along 'their' stretch of the coast. Its main base was Cape Coast castle at Fetu, but other fortifications were built at Sekondi, Accra, Dixcove, Kommenda, Winnebah and Anomabu, with two more in Senegambia and one each in Sierra Leone and at Whydah.[10] Some were small towns – home to milling crowds of Europeans, Africans and their offspring; some were simple buildings; others were complex and substantial fortresses which survive to this day.

European trading companies, granted monopolies by their home governments over various points on the coast from the late fifteenth century onwards, maintained permanent staff in their forts, their senior men crucial in establishing fruitful and amicable relations with local Africans. Sometimes with the help of out-forts further inland, the main factor would accumulate slaves (and other African goods) to await incoming ships. Life in the forts was generally very difficult. Quite apart from discomfort and disease – and the inevitable deaths – commercial life on the coast was a permanent worry; pressured by the London company to provide certain numbers and sorts of slaves, yet subject to the uncomfortable eddies of internal African pressures, British agents resident in the forts and castles led an unenviable existence.

Life on the coast rotted the fabric of the Europeans' buildings as much as it corrupted their bodies. Supplies and tradesmen were shipped in from Britain to make good nature's wear and tear. 'Tis something strange', said the Royal African Company in 1695, 'our several forts should need so frequent and great repairs; we doubt either skill or a due care has been wanting.' Humidity, torrential rains and fierce heat – in turn or all at once – corroded the buildings. In those steamy quarters dozens of merchants, soldiers and tradesmen lived out their unpleasant and often all too brief existence in Africa.[11] At the peak of slave-trading from the forts the British had a string of seventeen establishments on the Gold Coast.[12]

Much the same was true of the Dutch, Danish and German posts. And all of them waxed and waned in importance and material strength, reflecting the ebb and flow of changing slave-trade fortunes and the freaks of accident and chance. Hundreds of white men worked on the coast – more than 300 were employed by the Royal African Company alone at its peak. There was, however, a monotonous procession of corpses to the local burial grounds. Over the years a veritable army of white men was devoured by the slave-trading machine on the coast (and on the Atlantic), but their numbers pale when compared to the numbers of Africans who died in the slave trade.

To describe the surviving slave castles as splendid may seem perverse; admiring architectural grace while overlooking the social purpose. But it would be wrong not to make some passing acknowledgement of the grace, functionalism and power of a number of the major castles – at Elmina, Cape Coast, Axim, Shama, Christianborg, Anomabu and elsewhere. They were defences against Africans and other Europeans, their big guns trained seaward against the possibility of attack from enemy ships. They were trading posts, with a host of offices, storage rooms and negotiating forums. And they provided a home – temporary or long term – for a procession of white men and for many more Africans.

At first the forts made little distinction between the kinds of goods they stored. European goods for barter, sale or consumption were stocked in rooms similar to those used for goods for export. The most valuable and most numerous exports were the African slaves. But they could not so easily be stored. Jean Barbot, writing of Cape Coast castle in 1682 noted:

> The lodgings and apartments within the castle are very large and well-built of brick, having three fonts, which, with the platform, on the south, almost make a quadrangle, answering to the inside of the walls, and form a very handsome place-of-arms well paved, under which is a spacious mansion, or place to keep the slaves in, cut out of the rocky ground, arched and divided into several rooms; so that it will conveniently contain a thousand Blacks, let down at an opening made for the purpose. The keeping of the slaves thus underground is a good security against any insurrection.[13]

'Mansion' may seem an odd description for a massive airless cellar. Plans for the English fort at Kommenda in 1756 described slave storage more simply: it was the 'Slave Hole'.

As a reminder that the slaves below were not the sole threat at Cape Coast castle, a round tower had been constructed on a nearby rock, housing six twelve-pound guns, 'which serves to keep the Blacks in the town in better awe, as well as to defend them from all other Blacks their enemies'. In time this, like other castles, changed to make allowance for the special needs of their human commodities. Fresh air was especially important, and better ventilation was incorporated into later slave quarters.[14]

In some forts, light and air filtered into the slaves' prisons from grilles set in the overhead walkways.[15] The enslaved Africans could see free people walking above them, almost precisely as they were to see the crews of the slave ships pacing the decks above them.

Above all else the slave castles and forts came to epitomize the value and apparent permanence of the slave trade. Yet it was the expansion and growing importance of the slave trade which, by the 1720s, had begun to render the castles less vital. They were buildings which spoke of the confidence of the men and the trading companies which built them. They were, however, rooted in an economic philosophy which was slowly disintegrating under the pressure for ever more slaves. As the slave colonies of the Americas thrived, as their tropical produce expanded and became basic to the diet and habits of Europeans, the Americas could not get enough Africans. From the first the monopoly companies had been scarcely able to satisfy demand for slaves. Interlopers, foreign rivals, free-trade venturers, individual skippers – these and others flitted in and out of the slaving region, always prepared to risk legal and military dangers in return for the expected profits to be had across the Atlantic.

The British Royal African Company had been hugely successful. It had built forts, dispatched 500 ships and transported 100,000 Africans, exported £1.5 million worth of goods and imported 30,000 tons of sugar.[16] But by the 1720s its time had passed. It no longer made a profit and had created a demand it could no longer supply. Henceforth, the markets of the Americas were satisfied by individual traders and companies, largely unfettered by any trace of restrictive economic philosophy and seeking only to ferry as many live Africans as they could. Not burdened by the substantial overheads of a major monopoly company (especially the maintenance of the forts), they could trade in Africans more efficiently, more nimbly – and more profitably.

From the first there had been a lively and thriving trade conducted on board ship or at the water's edge. Whereas the monopoly companies' ships might expect large numbers of Africans waiting for them in company storage quarters, individual traders had to compete, negotiate and trawl far and wide for slaves, whom they loaded in small batches. The slave ships served the same purpose as the castles on shore, offering storage space for the slowly accumulating cargo until enough were on board to head out into the Atlantic. Like the castles, the ships had to be aware of the ever-present dangers; from the slaves, from other hostile Africans and from competitors. Slave ships and castles alike had guns trained on the slaves and on the neighbourhood.

Much depended on the accidents of geography. Vast reaches of coastline were unapproachable by ocean-going vessels (thanks to sandbars, reefs, Atlantic rollers), but yielded a rich bounty of slaves. There, the slave-traders remained off-shore, sending in their yauls, or being supplied by African canoes which expertly found their way round or over the natural obstacles. The massive river systems – the Niger, Benue, Volta, Senegal, Gambia and the Congo, offered their own myriad slaving locations. In many places slave-trading was conducted on the beach; elsewhere, it took place in temporary shore-based settlements – stores, offices, living quarters and a 'baracoon' to store slaves. Africans arrived in coffles, i.e. tied 'by the neck with leather thongs, at about a yard distance from each other, thirty or forty in a string'. Even as they shuffled into bondage, the Africans were useful. In one place they arrived with 'a bundle of corn or elephants' teeth upon each of their heads'.[17]

Negotiations were often protracted. Prices and exchanges fluctuated greatly; traders, Africans, clients, local chiefs and their retinues, all had to be satisfied. Nor was it simply a matter of agreeing a price. Slave-trading on the coast developed its own conventions, rituals and etiquette, all of which had to be observed. Gifts were offered and accepted, drinks and smokes exchanged, food cooked and consumed together. Sometimes deals broke down in acrimony – not always about money or the slaves' value. Sometimes violence and bloodshed terminated proceedings. Generally, however, at the point of contact between black and white, the slave trade was a well established routine with its own protracted code of conduct which provided the essential lubricant for a potentially abrasive commerce.

Wherever we look, African negotiators were keen to assert their authority with Europeans. English agents complained in 1745 of 'the Insolence the Blacks are arrived at'. In a dispute, the Africans replied 'that the Country belongs to them'.[18] It was only at their peril that Europeans lost sight of this basic truth.

Slave-traders did not want sick or diseased Africans. Slaves were valuable only if they were healthy and strong. Not surprisingly, untold numbers of Africans were sick by the time they reached the white traders. Experience was important in spotting sick slaves. Worst of all were the contagious slaves, for their ailments could cause devastation in the squalid confines of the ships. Surgeons, captains and traders made it their business to inspect their slaves closely: 'examined by us in like manner, as our Brother Trade do Beasts in Smithfield; the Countenance, and Stature, a good set of Teeth, Pliancy in the Limbs, and Joints, and being free of Venereal Taints are the things inspected, and governs our choice in buying.'

Europeans were wise to the deceptions used by their African counterparts to disguise sickness, if only because they used the same techniques in the New World to deceive the planters. There were tricks of the trade to hide illness or physical problems and no white trader worth his salt would buy Africans without inspection. They were particularly keen to discover:

> if they are afflicted with any infirmity, or are deformed, or had bad eyes or teeth;
> if they are lame, or weak in the joints, or distorted in the back, or of slender
> make, or narrow in the chest; in short if they have been, or are afflicted in any

manner so as to render them incapable of much labour; if any of the forgoing defects are discovered in them, they are rejected.[19]

Once accepted, the slaves were normally transported to the slave ship and put into the holds. But what happened to those rejected? They had already been bought, traded and transported and clearly represented a valuable commodity to their African owners. When rejected by the Europeans the unfortunate slave often had to bear the anger of the thwarted slaver. It is another of the imponderables of the slave trade to wonder whether those rejected by white slave-traders were 'luckier' than those accepted and stowed away in the holds.

As a result of the slave trade, between 11 and 12 million Africans were loaded onto the slave ships. But huge numbers did not reach the colonies; many died, en route to the African coast and on the slave ships in mid-ocean. The 10+ million Africans landed in the Americas were the survivors of a much greater number initially enslaved in Africa.[20]

Each slave landed in the Americas with his or her own unique memory of enslavement. A mere handful left an account of their experiences, though we know a great deal from the accounts of their tormentors. The trauma of enslavement – the initial moment of capture – was but the first of an apparently endless succession of blows, some deadly but all of them painful, humiliating and unforgettable. It must have seemed barely credible to most slaves that the horrors already endured were to be followed by an even more painful and distressing experience: the voyage across the Atlantic in a slave ship.

4

Crossing the Atlantic

On Saturday 11 August 1750 the weather in Liverpool was close, with fresh gales running between the south and the west. At noon, the captain of the brig, the *Duke of Argyle* – a 'snow' of some 140 tons, 'a very old and crazy vessel…hardly fit to lye in a dock or make a Gravesend voyage' – ordered the crew to cast off from the pierhead. Only one of the ship's twelve sails was unfurled, the topsail, and the *Duke of Argyle* ran out against the flood tide.[1] Three hours later it anchored at Black Rock, joined by the *Lamb* bound for New England. Over the next few days the crew were busy preparing their ship, taking on supplies from the pilot boat, rigging out and testing the sails and equipment, and greeting the sundry collection of incoming vessels from Barbados, the Isle of Man, St Kitts, Greenland, Ireland and Denmark. Throughout the daylight hours the ship echoed to the sound of the ship's carpenter repairing the planking and plates while the crew stored the provisions and prepared the cordage. Last aboard was a sheep and a quarter of beef. When the gales moderated the *Duke of Argyle* headed down the sailing channel on 21 August, ten days after leaving the pierhead. But the weather remained poor – 'dirty' to use the captain's parlance – and the ship tacked in vain off the North Wales coast before running for shelter in Ramsay Bay in the Isle of Man. The weather was changeable and the only consolation was the night sky on Saturday 25 August: 'All night had a very wild sky, the Aurorae Borealis or Northern Lights flying about with unusual quickness.' At last they began to make good progress; on 1 September they saw Waterford, a day later Dungarvan. Thereafter the voyage gained pace. Twenty days later they closed on Tenerife and by the end of the month, as they crossed the Tropic of Cancer, new sailors paid for drinks all round rather than be subjected to the customary 'ducking'.

The *Duke of Argyle* was heading for the West African coast, and as the vessel edged closer – between the Cape Verde islands, accompanied by flying fish and a large turtle – the crew began to prepare the ship for its work on arrival. As the gunner organized the ammunition and guns, the carpenter made the necessary alterations to 'the woman's room', to the holds and to the ship's yaul (the small, six-oared boat necessary for ferrying people and goods to and from the shore). On 23 October they anchored in Frenchman's Bay, Sierra Leone, alongside the *Annapolis* of London, the *Halifax* of Bristol, a New England schooner, a sloop and three small French vessels. A day later, the ship's guns were brought up and run out. On Thursday 25 October the captain went ashore, returning with his first business transaction of the voyage: three African slaves, two men and one woman, exchanged for goods carried from Liverpool.

The *Duke of Argyle* was a slave ship, a common enough sight up and down the African coast in the mid-eighteenth century. There in Frenchman's Bay was a fairly typical, if random, collection of boats from all three major British ports – London, Bristol and Liverpool – and representatives of the North American colonies and their arch-rival, France. Theirs was a protracted business, flitting up and down the coast, following rumours and hints of good slave-trading hither and thither. Not until late May 1751 did the *Duke of Argyle*'s captain feel ready to quit the African coast and head westward to the slave colonies of the New World: 'At 3 a.m. weighed with a small brease at West bound (by God's permission) for Antigua.'

With Africa behind him, the Captain wrote to his wife:

> I have lost sight of Africa, inumerable changes and difficulties, which, without a superior protection, no man could escape or surmount, are, by the goodness of God, happily over.... It is now ten in the evening. I am going to walk the deck and think of you; and, according to my constant custom, to recommend you to the care and protection of God.

As he took exercise on deck, thinking fondly of his distant wife, his cargo – ranks of miserable Africans destined they knew not where – were firmly secured in their chains below. It is, to modern eyes, a perplexing scene: the God-fearing Englishman perfectly at ease in a godless role. There were hundreds of such men, Europeans and Americans, who praised the Lord for his blessing, giving thanks for profitable and safe business in Africa as they turned their slave ships into the trade winds and headed for the New World. To them – as to many more earlier and later – there was nothing wrong, contradictory or unchristian in their chosen trade.

The Captain of the *Duke of Argyle* was, however, an unusual man, more famous in retrospect for his piety and religiosity than for his earlier career as a slaver. (Which other slave captain wrote a hymn of abiding and widespread popularity? Captain John Newton was the author of 'Amazing Grace'.) An evangelical Christian, an associate of Wilberforce, friend and caring nurse to the poet William Cowper in his moments of madness, Newton had previously been the scourge and tyrant of hundreds of innocent Africans. Tender and affectionate to his loved ones, in his earlier career Newton had felt no qualms about violating his African slaves: 'Made a timely discovery today that the slaves were forming a plot for insurrection. Surprised two of them attempting to get off their irons...Put the boys in irons and slightly in the thumbscrews to urge them to a full confession.' When members of Newton's crew died at sea, he recorded the details: 'At 9 A.M. departed this life Gideon Measham, who came ill out of the longboat, the 28th March, of a fever which he recovered from, but has been otherwise declining ever since.' Slaves – in death as in life – were accorded a different inscription: 'Bury'd a man slave No. 84.... This morning bury'd a woman slave, No. 47.' Nameless, unmourned, unremarked, Numbers 84 and 47 were but two among armies of Africans whose bodies were consigned to the Atlantic from a passing slave ship.

It would be unrealistic to expect soft-heartedness among slave-traders; theirs was a violent, cruel, inhuman trade. Indeed, the slave trade was a notoriously unattractive occupation. Even among the low-life which found a precarious living at sea, the slave ships were avoided like the plague – literally, since sea-farers knew all too well the fearful mortality and levels of sickness among slave crews. Prospects of profit and material reward aside, why would a man join a slave ship? Why, for instance, did John Newton become a slaver?

Newton's fate was sealed by a moment of youthful infatuation. At the age of seventeen (having served at sea at the age of ten; then, aged fifteen, as an assistant to a Spanish merchant in Alicante) Newton was promised a spell of five years in Jamaica learning the plantation business. In London, awaiting his passage to the Caribbean, Newton visited friends of his mother in Chatham. There he fell hopelessly in love with the thirteen-year-old Mary Catlett. He missed his ship, and his angry father sent him on a year-long Mediterranean voyage. Newton repeated his Chatham performance a year later only to find himself press-ganged into the Royal Navy. Once again he jumped ship to see Mary Catlett. On return to HMS *Harwich* he was flogged and stripped of his rank. Clearly unsuited to the task, Newton was promptly 'exchanged' at Madeira for another sailor on a merchant vessel. This new vessel was bound for Sierra Leone to collect slaves. Thus he began to learn the peculiarities of cruising the African coast, accumulating a cargo of Africans.

John Newton was too clever for his own good. A witty man, with a talent for inventing cutting rhymes and songs, he transformed the crew into a disrespectful choir at the expense of the officers. To avoid further discipline he entered the service of a slaver resident on the African coast. It was, if anything, more hellish than life at sea, worsened by tropical sickness and neglect. After a year of ill-treatment, John Newton was released to another coastal slave-trader; this time he prospered and seems to have enjoyed his work. Early in 1748 he was 'rescued' at Kittan by the captain of the Liverpool ship the *Greyhound*. Over the next year the vessel searched the coastline a thousand miles south, collecting gold, ivory, wood and wax, but not slaves. The return leg to Liverpool was tempestuous, and Newton's fears, as the ship passed through a fierce Atlantic storm, converted him from his phase of free-thinking back to his earlier Christian zeal.

Back in Liverpool, Newton, at twenty-three, bore the qualities which were to mark the rest of his life. He remained in love with Mary Catlett, marrying her a year later; he was an experienced slave-trader and a master mariner. Above all else, he was devout and steeped in self-taught book learning which carried him in later life into ordination and a second career as an evangelical minister of the Anglican church.[2]

John Newton's home port, Liverpool, was, by mid-century, rapidly being transformed from a small town, with a steady trade to Europe, Ireland and the North American colonies, into one of the nation's major ports. The growth of the town itself and the early development of industry in its Lancastrian and Cheshire hinterland provided the necessary boosts. Liverpool had goods to trade, to the West Indies, to the Chesapeake and to and from Ireland. It was only a small step for Liverpool's merchants and shippers to copy, rival and then surpass the trade in Africans already perfected by the traders from London and Bristol. The Liverpool slave trade boomed and local merchants could not lay their hands on enough ships, especially in the years of maritime war which so disrupted the Atlantic trade throughout much of the eighteenth century.[3]

In 1746, the Liverpool merchant Joseph Manesty remarked: 'Ships are so scarce here that none is to be had at any rate.'[4] It was one of Manesty's ships which rescued John Newton from Sierra Leone and it was Manesty who offered Newton his first command as a slave-trade captain. Ships were still in short supply and thus it was that the twenty-five-year-old John Newton slipped out of Liverpool in the summer of 1750, captain of one of Manesty's ships the *Duke of Argyle*, the 'old and crazy vessel' scarcely worthy of a trip down the Thames.

From 23 May to 3 July 1751 – forty-two days – this miserable ship made its way across the Atlantic, from Shebar in Sierra Leone to the British West Indian island of Antigua. It was in many respects an unexceptional voyage; forty-two days was as fast a crossing as Newton might have expected, particularly with so old and cumbersome a ship. Slave-traders knew that the longer the voyage, the more costly the venture; the longer the slaves were at sea the more likely it was that losses would mount. Newton's log recorded the slow attrition of his slave cargo:

Thursday 23rd May...Buryed a man slave (No. 34)...
Wednesday 29th May...Buryed a boy slave (No. 86) of a flux...

Wednesday 12th June…Buryed a man slave (No. 84) of a flux, which he had
   been struggling with near 7 weeks…
Thursday 13th June…This morning buryed a woman slave (No. 47). Know not
   what to say she died of for she has not been properly alive since she first came
   on board.

This doleful litany continued across the Atlantic. A week later, they buried two
slaves, 'a man (No. 140) of a flux, and a boy (No. 170) of the gravel and
stoppage of urine'. Four days later, they were joined by a boy (No. 158), then a
girl (No. 172). Just before landfall, No. 2 succumbed to a flux which 'he has
sustained about three months'. Finally, No. 36 died of a flux the day before
they sighted land in the Caribbean. On 3 July the *Duke of Argyle* was piloted
into St John's harbour, Antigua.

Losing ten slaves and one crewman on an Atlantic crossing was not a bad
record. Many other slavers suffered much more severe losses. Yet it was a
close-run thing. Perhaps the most potent threat was slave revolt. Twice on this
voyage John Newton headed off slave resistance. On 26 May a young slave,
freed from his chains because of his ulcerous condition, managed to pass a
marlin spike through the deck gratings to the slaves below. In an hour, twenty
slaves had broken their chains and loosened the bulkheads of their hold.
Newton gave thanks that he had a full complement of sailors to put matters
right; on the African coast seven or eight of them would have been busy
off the ship. 'But I hope (by Divine Assistance) we are fully able to overaw
them now.'

Less seriously, on 16 June, Newton suspected that some of the male slaves
had tried to poison the water and was relieved to find that they had simply put
native 'fetishes' or charms into the water, 'which they had the credulity to
suppose must inevitably kill all who drank of it. But if it please God they make
no worse attempts than to charm us to death, they will not harm us.' There is a
delicious irony here. Newton had no doubt that his own deity was crucial in
securing victory over the slaves' gods.

As the *Duke of Argyle* closed on the Caribbean, Newton's crew went about
the well-tried routines of the slave trade. The slaves were paraded on deck in
batches and shaved, then washed a day later in fresh water. With the slaves
topside, their holds were cleaned out. Weather permitting, the slaves were
exercised, though always in small, manageable groups; it was far too risky to let
them gather in numbers. As the ship drew closer to its destination, Newton
anxiously looked for those tangible signs of nearby land – weeds, birds and
inshore fishes. On 29 June they saw 'several men of war, boobies and other
fowls & frequent flocks of small birds'. Swapping navigational notes with a
passing brig bound from New Providence to St Christopher, Newton realized
that the Atlantic leg of his voyage was almost finished and two days later the
Duke of Argyle passed through troublesome weather to make its first landfall.

Newton's log remains blank for the six weeks in Antigua, as he unloaded and sold his slaves, reloading with local produce for the return journey. On 13 August 1751 the ship, heavily loaded with sugar, weighed anchor 'bound (by God's permission) for Liverpool'. Running into the most terrible seas he had ever encountered, Newton feared the onset of a hurricane, but the weather cleared and a strong wind hurried the brig forward. He wrote to his wife: 'every puff pushes me nearer to you. I have shortened the distance between us about one hundred and eighty miles within the last twenty-four hours.' But how many watery miles would always remain between the slaves he had sold in Antigua and their loved ones in Africa?

One storm followed another, the old brig weathering the battering unexpectedly well. Newton wrote to his wife:

> Imagine to yourself an immense body of water behind you, higher than a house, and a chasm of equal depth just before you ... in the twinkling of an eye the ship descends into the pit which is gasping to receive her, and with equal swiftness ascends to the top on the other side before the mountain can overtake her. And this is repeated as often as you can deliberately count four.

On 5 October they sighted Ireland; two days later, they passed the landmarks of North Wales before being piloted into the Mersey. They had been away about fourteen months.

In 1754 John Newton quit the sea and was drawn increasingly to his major obsession – religion; ten years later he was ordained into the Church of England. After serving as minister in the small Buckingham-shire market town of Olney with great success – his preaching was so popular that his church had to be extended to accommodate the packed congregation – Newton moved to London in 1780. There he was drawn into the circle of those evangelicals who, later in that decade, organized the first major campaign against the slave trade. Thus did the young Liverpool slave-trade captain of the 1750s become the elderly abolitionist, directing his memories and experiences to the task of destroying the slave trade itself.

By 1789 the campaign against the slave trade had established itself as a major political force in Britain, both within Parliament and in the country at large.[5] The topic was highly emotional and both abolitionists and defenders of the trade spent a great deal of time discussing the cruelties involved. There was no shortage of witnesses willing to describe the horrors of the slave ships; no shortage of defenders anxious to deny or minimize them. From this flurry of evidence – books, pamphlets, articles, testimony to Parliament – we can begin to recapture the full horror of the slave trade.

Alexander Falconbridge had been a surgeon on African slavers and, like Newton, he lent his experience to the abolitionist side in the late 1780s with evidence to Parliament and the reading public.[6] The Africans he saw deposited before European traders on the coast had already been ill-treated and terrified. Many were delivered by river canoes, securely bound, ill-fed, exposed to the elements as they lay trussed-up in the water-logged bottom of the canoes. Once bought by the Europeans: 'The men negroes, on being brought aboard the ship, are immediately fastened together, two and two, by hand-cuffs on their wrists, and by irons rivitted on their legs. They are then sent down between the decks, and placed in an apartment partitioned off for that purpose.' Women were put into separate quarters – without irons – and small boys in another. But all were closely cramped: 'They are frequently stored so close, as to admit of no other posture than lying on their sides. Neither will the height between decks, unless directly under the grating, permit them the indulgence of an erect posture, especially where there are platforms, which is generally the case.'

These platforms were in fact deep shelves half-way between the decks which dropped down from the side of the ship towards the centre, effectively creating an extra layer of storage for slaves. Africans were packed into these platforms just as they were on to the decks, a mere two or three feet below. When a slave ship arrived from Europe, the carpenter and crew were busy putting these shelves and other bulkheads into position to receive the Africans. Similarly, once the slaves had been sold in the colonies the shelves were removed and the holds made ready to receive the bulky loads of sugar, rum or tobacco destined for Britain.

In time, vessels designed and constructed for the sole purpose of ferrying Africans across the Atlantic were developed, especially in Liverpool. Sleeker, if bigger, than the older vessels, and copper-sheathed (against rot), Liverpool's slave ships – more than a hundred were plying the trade on the eve of abolition – could be easily adapted to other, general cargoes. And it was just as well for, after abolition in 1807, they had to turn to other forms of trade. The port of Liverpool boomed in the nineteenth century and it is perfectly clear that the ending of the slave trade did not harm its commercial well-being. The reasons were complex and closely linked to the industrial development of Lancashire, but Liverpool also thrived because its slave ships (and the men who owned and sailed them) were adaptable.

The Liverpool slave ships of the late eighteenth century made some con-cession to the 'comfort' of the slaves. James Penny of Liverpool, defender of the slave trade, told Parliament:

> Great improvements have been made to Liverpool, within these Twenty Years. In the Construction of those Ships – The Space between the Decks is suffi-ciently large to contain the Number of Negroes above-mentioned [between 500 and 600], and is plained very smooth and painted: – They are also provided with Wind Sails, and most of them have Ventilators.[7]

Liverpool slave-traders were no more tender-hearted than other men in the trade; they were hard-headed businessmen, eager to learn from the experience of others. Where some might see the hand of considerate humanity in their improvements to the slave ships, we might more reasonably see the influence of enlightened self-interest. Theirs was, after all, a business. They sought the most profitable trade possible, and there was no profit in sick or dead slaves. It made economic sense to keep the Africans in as decent and reasonable a condition as money and contemporary usage would allow. Dangers and risks abounded on the slave ships – imported African diseases, contagions, the ubiquitous problem of dysentery, the threat of slave resistance – to say nothing of the unpredictable rage of the Atlantic itself. Slavers sought, as a matter of commercial common sense, to minimize and contain the dangers to the health and well-being of their human cargoes.

The slave ships from Liverpool commanded by James Penny had weighed between 200 and 300 tons, big enough, he told Parliament, to take on board 500 to 600 slaves. From the earliest days of the slave trade there had been a lively debate, economically inspired and solely with an eye to profit, about how many Africans could be packed into the holds. What was the formula which yielded the best economic returns? Should a captain squeeze in as many Africans as possible, or should he leave a little room for 'comfort' (if that word makes any sense applied to the stinking slave quarters)? Theoretically, the number of slaves was dictated by a ship's tonnage, though theory was often disregarded if the captain or owner saw fit, or (less likely) if the slave ship was faced with an unusually abundant supply of Africans waiting on the coast. Before the late 1780s British traders calculated on carrying two slaves per ton (figures which fit James Penny's account of 1789). But in 1788, as part of the abolitionist push against the slave trade, Parliament placed restrictions on the slave ships. Vessels up to 207 tons were limited to five slaves per three tons, one slave per ton above that weight. Any slave ship which was loaded to these specifications was packed to a degree that remains, to modern eyes at least, grossly overcrowded.

Even contemporaries began to feel queasy at the sight of crowded Africans on British ships. Of all the imaginative publicity coups organized by the abolitionists, few were as successful – or better remembered to this day – as the pictures of the *Brookes*, the Liverpool slave ship. It was a vessel of about 320 tons, a very large slaver indeed for the period: in 1787 only twenty-five of Liverpool's seventy-two slave ships were above 200 tons. The slaves filled the main storage decks. The neat and orderly ranks, graphically portrayed more like corpses than living beings, give little sense of space. Where the ship bulged at midship, slaves were slotted into the resulting space, filling the alleyways and gaps between the other slaves. From fore to aft, from the nose of the ship to the rudder, the Africans were arranged in tightly-packed rows which seem to owe more to the demands of geometry than of human accommodation. Where the masts obstructed the line of packing, a slave is pictured lying with one elbow casually resting on the mast.

The cross-section picture of the ship conveys a scene of even greater claustrophobia, for the packed slaves effectively halve the headroom between decks. Even the spare deck space aft of the main deck is filled with slaves. Shoulder to shoulder along the length of the ship, head to toe or head to head, this picture of ranks of slaves is the one which has endured in the popular mind. And even when we concede a degree of graphic licence, the image of the *Brookes* conveys little sense of the real pestilence and torments of the slave decks.[8]

Slaves, according to Newton, had headroom of five feet – but this was halved by the shelves. In his evangelical old age, John Newton painted a moving picture of the slaves' physical conditions, conditions which had rarely troubled him in the flesh: 'the poor creatures, thus cramped for want of room, are likewise in irons, for the most part both hands and feet, and two together, which makes it difficult for them to turn or move, to attempt either to rise or lie down, without hurting themselves, or each other.' The *Brookes* – and hence the slave ship in the mind's eye – is a still-life, devoid of that movement which was basic to a ship at sea. Again, John Newton adds to the picture:

> Nor is the motion of the ship, especially her keeling, or stoop on one side, when under sail, to be omitted; for this, as they lie athwart or across the ship, adds to the uncomfortableness of their lodgings, especially to those who lie on the leeward, or learning, side of the vessel. Dire is the tossing, deep the groans.[9]

Assume for a moment that most slave ships were *not* as crushed as the *Brookes* (although this picture allows for 454 slaves, in 1783 the ship had transported some 600), then pause to reflect that slave ships – however unlike the *Brookes* – allowed their slaves *half* the room afforded soldiers, emigrants or convicts on ships in the same period.[10] Remember too that large numbers of the slaves were sick – and most terrified. The curse of the slave trade was dysentery, 'the bloody flux'. Captains of slavers were unanimous in describing the flux as the scourge of their human cargoes. Of John Newton's twenty-four fatalities on his 1751–52 voyage to Antigua, seventeen died of dysentery. How did Africans cope with the calls of nature in crowded conditions, where slaves were chained in twos (or more) and where any movement in a rolling ship must inevitably produce collisions with other slaves?

Only those who had been on a slaver knew the appalling, stinking reality of life below the decks. It is true that the captains and their crews tried to prevent and limit the deterioration in the slaves' physical environment – it was in their economic interest to do so. But what could even the most considerate of men do in an Atlantic storm or heavy weather, when the immediate demands of the ship disrupted the routines of exercising, cleaning and feeding the slaves, to say nothing of removing and disposing of the dead or tending the sick?

The smell was overpowering. Looking back thirty years, Olaudah Equiano had not forgotten the stink:

> I was soon put down under the decks, and there I received such a salutation in my nostrils as I had never experienced in my life: so that with the loathsomeness of the stench and crying together, I became so sick and low that I was not able to eat, nor had I the least desire to taste anything.

While the slave ships languished on the coast, spending months gradually filling up with Africans, and when slaves and crew were affected by a host of local African sicknesses (the African coast was the most notoriously dangerous place for white crewmen), the air between decks was hot and fetid. Slaves rarely got the limited benefit of breezes, caught by the ship's ventilators and forced through the port-holes in between decks. Riding at anchor, the ship generally became a brew of intolerable heat and stenches.

Equiano was forced below decks:

> The stench of the holds while we were on the coast was so intolerable loathsome that it was dangerous to remain there for any time, and some of us had been permitted to stay on the deck for the fresh air; but now that the whole ship's cargo were confined together it became absolutely pestilential.

Writing at the time the *Brookes* diagram had made such an impact on British opinion, Equiano knew the political effect of rubbing his reader's nose in the mire of the slave ships. But who is to doubt or dispute the basic truth of his description? 'The air soon became unfit for respiration from a variety of loathsome smells, and brought on a sickness amongst the slaves, of which many died.' Contemporary medicine had it that disease was spread by 'miasma', travelling from one person to another through the air. There seemed plenty of reason to believe the theory in operation on the slave ships. Repugnant atmospheres seemed to be directly linked to widespread sickness and death. We might now have a more scientific appreciation of the links between the habitat of the slave ship and the sickness and deaths of the enslaved Africans. But this does not minimize the effect of the atmosphere on the slaves: 'The wretched situation was again aggravated by the galling of the chains, now become insupportable, and the filth of the necessary tubs, into which the children often fell and were almost suffocated.'[11]

Alexander Falconbridge, surgeon in the slave trade, described the slaves' lavatories, perhaps more clinically than Equiano but revealing for all that. In all the slaves' quarters were to be found 'three or four large buckets, of a conical form, being near two feet in diameter at the bottom, and only one foot at the top, and in depth about twenty-eight inches; in which, when necessary, the negroes have recourse.'

What of those slaves located at a distance from the buckets? Often, in trying to reach them, slaves 'tumble over their companions, in consequence of their being shackled. These accidents, although unavoidable, are productive of continual quarrels, in which some of them are always bruised.' Collisions, fights, curses – all in order for the slaves to relieve themselves. Many were too sick or disheartened to run the gauntlet; many simply had no strength to move. Some 'desist from the attempt; and, as the necessities of nature are not to be repelled, ease themselves as they lie'. Understandably, this too caused serious friction: 'a fresh source of broils and disturbances, and tends to render the condition of the poor captive wretches still more uncomfortable'.

With the lavatory buckets overflowing, and slaves defecating where they lay, the slaves' quarters were quickly reduced to a stable-like quagmire. Even the slave surgeons found the conditions hard to stomach. In 'wet and blowing weather' the port-holes and gratings on Alexander Falconbridge's ship were secured; he felt able to visit the slaves only 'for a very short time': 'The deck, that is the floor of their rooms, was so covered with blood and mucus which had proceeded from them in consequence of the flux that it resembled a slaughter-house. It is not in the power of human imagination, to picture to itself a situation more dreadful or disgusting.' Stripped to the waist, Falconbridge worked among the slaves for about fifteen minutes: 'I was so overcome by the heat, stench and foul air, that I nearly fainted, and it was not without assistance, that I could get upon deck.'[12] In John Newton's words: 'Epidemical fevers and fluxes...fill the ship with noisome and noxious effluvia.'

Stretched below, the Africans headed for an unknown fate, as the ship pitched and rolled its way across the Atlantic for months on end. Ideally, slaves would be regularly exercised, bathed, fed and nursed, and their quarters cleaned each day. The Atlantic took no account of the slave-traders' preferences or ideals, often lashing them with the capricious and unpredictable terrors of the deep. It was then that the slaves suffered most.

Planning an Atlantic crossing with a human cargo had become a well-practised commercial and maritime art by the mid-eighteenth century. Ample supplies of food and water were obviously essential, but even the best-stocked and provisioned ships might encounter unexpected problems. Storms, contrary winds – or no winds at all – would naturally add extra time to the crossing and deplete the ships' provisions. Water was sometimes supplemented en route by catching and storing rain water.

Feeding the slaves was an important daily routine. Merchants and captains had a clear idea of the types and quantities of food needed to maintain a given number of slaves on the voyage. Slave-traders had come to appreciate by the early eighteenth century that slaves seemed to fare better when given foods they were familiar with. Although the slave ships carried supplies of basic foods from Britain – beans, bread, cheese, beef, flour – the captains also negotiated for local African foods. Slave captains were not simply sailors but had to become commercial traders and negotiators when they reached Africa (or the Americas). They were in effect sea-borne merchants who had to supplement their maritime skills, which included maintaining a fierce discipline over a normally belligerent and difficult crew, with the hard-nosed abilities of commercial haggling and bargaining. Mistakes in provisioning, or prolonged, storm-ridden voyages, heightened and accentuated slave sufferings. Many slaves paid for such errors of management with their lives: when the *Dorothy* finally reached Barbados in June 1709, she had only 100 slaves on board, the 'great mortality' on the crossing due to 'povertie for want of provisions, as beef, oyle, malagetta etc.'; and in 1716 the *Windsor* reached Buenos Aires with only 164 slaves, not the intended 380.[13]

From the early days of the slave trade the Royal African Company took pains to provision its slave ships adequately. When the *Norman* left London in 1714 to pick up 300 slaves, it carried: '150 gallons of malt liquor; 15 bushels of salt, 11 1/2 hogsheads of vinegar; 300 pounds of tobacco; 10 gross of pipes; 4 puncheons of old beef; 3 hundredweight and 10 pounds of flour; 12 hundred weight of biscuits; and 40 quarters of beans'.[14] Whatever had been carried from London, agents of the Royal African Company were advised in 1707 to load the following in Africa: 'fifty chests of corn, forty pounds of malaguetta pepper, twenty gallons of palm oil, two bushels of salt, and twenty gallons of rum for each hundred slaves'.[15] Limes and lemons were used to counter scurvy. Some slave ships loaded extras – plantain, coconuts and even tobacco.

How many noticed the irony that tobacco and rum – products of slave labour in the West Indies and Virginia – were used to pacify and entertain new cargoes of Africans destined for the self-same slave colonies? Slavery had begun to feed upon itself; the fruits of slave labour transmuted into the lubricant of the slave trade itself.

The slaves were usually fed twice a day. Alexander Falconbridge described their meals:

> The diet of the negroes, while on board, consists chiefly of horse-beans, boiled to the consistence of a pulp; of boiled yams and rice, and sometimes a small quantity of beef or pork. The latter are frequently taken from the provisions laid in for the sailors. They sometimes make use of a sauce, comprised of palm-oil, mixed with flour, water and pepper, which the sailors called *slabber-sauce*.

Other Africans preferred different foods and as far as possible the slave-traders tried to oblige: yams for Iboes or 'Bight negroes', rice or corn for slaves from the Gold and Windward Coasts. Slaves from the Gold Coast, Falconbridge claimed, would eat anything put before them. Practically all slaves hated the beans imported from England: 'unless they were narrowly watched, when fed upon deck, they will throw them overboard, or in each others' faces when they quarrel.'

Feeding, like all aspects of running and sailing a ship full of humans, had its own routines. At eight in the morning and four in the afternoon, a small bucket of food was handed over to groups of ten slaves. Each slave was given his or her own spoon for the voyage, but these were quickly lost in the confusion of the slave deck, and the slaves 'feed themselves with their hands'. Here was an obvious source of contagion – unwashed slaves fresh from their squalid positions eating by hand from communal buckets. When the weather was good, the slaves were herded on to the deck for their food. In bad weather, slaves were fed below deck in the cramped and generally filthy quarters. Feeding – like getting to the lavatories – was a constant friction. Asking ten slaves to share a bucket of food was to invite squabbles and disputes: 'Numberless quarrels take place among them during their meal; more especially when they are put upon short allowance, which frequently happens, if the passage from the coast of Guinea to the West India island, proves of unusual length. In that case, the weak are obliged to be content with a very scanty portion.'

Many of the slaves were sick – some of them desperately ill – in need of nursing and special feeding. Yet here they were, fighting for diminishing food (if they could even manage to bring themselves to the food bucket). We do not know how much co-operation existed among the slaves. Did the strong help the weak? Or did the greedy and the desperate take advantage of their weaker shipmates to satisfy their own cravings? Slaves presumably were no different from most collections of humans thrown together in traumatic circumstances; some would have responded with noble selflessness, others with heartless greed. What seems clear enough is that the slave trade, designed for maximum efficiency in transporting crowds of humans as cheaply as possible, was unconsciously designed to create maximum human friction and suffering among legions of desperate people. Slaves were not alone in enduring overcrowding, poor food and insanitary conditions on board ships: it was the lot of indentured (free) labour travelling to America in the seventeenth century, of convict labour travelling to Australia and of naval and military personnel criss-crossing the world's oceans en route to military postings. It is not to diminish the agonies of these other groups to point out that slaves endured incomparably worse conditions.

Many slaves, from illness or depression, simply gave up the struggle and refused to eat, despite the threats and violence used to make them take their food. Slavers sometimes resorted to force-feeding to keep slaves alive.

Everyone involved in the slave trade knew what happened to the slaves on board the ships. Nor was this knowledge restricted to the slave-trading fraternity, for the slave ships docked alongside or rode at anchor close to ships of all sorts and businesses; crews of different trades and nations mingled freely, on board each other's ships, in dockside bars and taverns and in the ports and towns of Europe, West Africa and the Americas. Rumour, gossip and the evidence of seeing the slave ships come and go ensured that the grim reality of the slave trade was widely known. When the abolitionist Thomas Clarkson wanted to unearth evidence about the slave trade in the 1780s, he simply travelled to the dockside communities of Bristol and Liverpool.

Men most intimately involved in the slave trade were well aware of the dangers to the slaves' health and survival, and from an early date the slave ships carried a range of contemporary medicines likely to be needed by the human cargoes. In 1699 the Royal African Company tried to develop 'friendship with some natives that understand the best remedies for their distempers'.[16] Gradually, the slave-traders built up a reasonable knowledge of African herbal treatments, nursing customs and favourite foods and recipes. Those familiar with the coast felt sure that local treatments 'would prove more successful in the Practice of Physics than the European Preparations'.

European confidence in African medicine was often undermined by the way Africans clung to their own priests and fetish men. Like John Newton, there were many Europeans who simply dismissed as pagan superstition the beliefs and medicines of the Africans. More curious and open-minded men – Dr James Houston writing about Guinea in 1725 for instance incorporated what they regarded as successful local drugs. Houston took some local drugs 'which Herbs I infused in Brandy…and gave as a cordial to the Sick'. Another he found 'most resembling our Camomil, which I made use of for emolient fomentation and Cataplasms'. A local bay leaf was 'made use of by the Natives and our White people in the hot Bath with wonderful good success'.[17]

Slave ships often carried a medical handbook or company guide for the treatment of the slaves. Better still was to have a surgeon on board. This was a loathsome profession to which men often gravitated because of financial or personal misfortune. Many were charlatans, others were drunken incompetents; but some were industrious and capable, doing their best in appalling conditions (though encouraged by the reward – 'head money' – paid for healthy arrivals). Their work began on the African coast when, alongside experienced traders, they carefully examined the new slaves (intimately and often publicly) before deciding if the slave would make a commercial investment. At sea, the surgeons came into their own, going below each morning to inspect the slaves and to organize the transfer of the very sick to separate (though equally sparse) accommodation. There, according to Alexander Falconbridge, 'he frequently finds several dead; and among the men, sometimes a dead and living negroe fastened by their irons together. When this is the case, they are brought upon the deck, and being laid on the grating, the living negroe is disengaged, and the dead are thrown overboard'.[18]

The surgeon generally tried to supervise the regular cleansing of the overnight filth. But when an epidemic broke out or dysentery became even more rampant the surgeons were simply overwhelmed. Much the same was true in stormy weather.

Critics were quick to blame the surgeon and the captain when disaster swept through the slave holds and thus hit the pockets of the backers. Sir Dalby Thomas, agent for the Royal African Company at Cape Coast castle from 1703 to 1711, wrote: 'If the Captains, Mates, surgeons and cooks are not honest, careful and diligent and see that the slaves have always their victuals, well drest, well fed, well washt, cleanly kept and kindly used, the voyage will not be worth a farthing.' Far too often, however, the most industrious and attentive crews were overwhelmed by circumstances. Death – of slaves and crew – was an unavoidable companion on the long Atlantic crossing; the longer the voyage the higher the death-rate. Proportionately more crew members died than slaves, but of course there was a vast numerical disparity.

Not surprisingly, some of the Africans who survived to the Americas were gravely ill. Some died soon after arrival, others lingered on before finally succumbing. Nor were their troubles over if they did survive; a very large number of slaves died within the first two years of their arrival. A batch delivered to Nevis in 1714 'were very feeble and weak at their landing and many having such a contraction of nerves by their being on board and confined in irons that [they] were hardly capable to walk'.[19]

Mortality on the slave ships declined over the long history of the slave trade. By the mid-eighteenth century, British slave ships were suffering an 11 per cent mortality among slaves on the Atlantic crossing. Catastrophes might still occur, often caused by the presence of a single contagious slave brought on board on the African coast. Hence the vital role of selection and the obscene inspections by surgeons and traders before deciding which slaves to load. Losses on the Atlantic reflected problems of African diseases at work in the insanitary conditions of the slave decks. As the slave trade developed, becoming a sophisticated area of international trade, fewer Africans died on the ships. With a quick turn-around and loading on the coast and a reasonably swift crossing, deaths could be minimized. Given the contemporary state of knowledge about medicine and hygiene, there was little crews could do when disease and death struck.

The surgeon was also in charge of the daily shipboard routines of caring for the slaves. Twice a day, the slaves were exercised on the deck. In hot weather 'when they came upon Deck, there were Two Men attending with Cloths to rub them perfectly dry, and another to give them a little Cordial – the Surgeon, or his Mate, also generally attends to wash their Mouths with Vinegar or Lime juice to prevent Scurvy'[20] On deck, the slaves washed and refreshed themselves. Sailors sometimes forced the slaves to exercise themselves by dancing: 'The poor wretches are frequently compelled to sing also; but when they do so, their songs are generally as may be expected, melancholy lamentations, of their exile from their native country.'[21] Diversions were provided – beads for the women, pipes for the men: 'the utmost Attention is paid to the keeping up their Spirits and to indulge them in all their little Humours'.[22] It rarely seems to have worked. Squabbles were common, sharpened by disputes about gambling. And in any case, it would require more than the occasional musical interlude to raise the slaves' spirits.

Time and again, slaves were deeply, often catatonically, depressed by life on the slave ship. We will never know the full extent of their mental suffering, but contemporaries were in broad agreement that many slaves became unhinged by their experiences. When Olaudah Equiano was bundled on to a slave ship, others tried to talk to him to cheer him up, but to no avail, and he was left 'abandoned to despair'. As he looked round the ship, he saw 'a multitude of black people of every description chained together, every one of their countenance expressing dejection and sorrow'.[23]

Surgeons were often convinced that 'melancholy' was a cause of shipboard deaths. While it is difficult to prove the point, it seems fairly clear that depression often worsened the slaves' physical condition. Refusing to eat, to move or to help themselves in any way, the most traumatized of slaves simply faded away, succumbing more readily to the physical ailments lurking on the slave decks.

Some slaves were so depressed they killed themselves. Throughout the history of the slave trade, European and American sailors remained alert to the threat of slave suicides. Given the chance, slaves flung themselves into the ocean, diving off the main deck, slipping through port-holes, or leaping from the small boat carrying them from shore. Some slaves simply went mad and had to be restrained. Alexander Falconbridge, after describing a number of insane slaves he had dealt with, concluded: 'I think it may be clearly deduced, that the unhappy Africans are not bereft of the finer feelings, but have a strong attachment to their native country, together with a just sense of the value of liberty.'[24]

More worrying still was the slaves' tendency to revolt. They were, said Falconbridge, 'ever upon the watch to take advantage of the least negligence of their oppressors'.[25] The very organization of the slave cargoes and the slave ships' routines hinged on the need to allow slaves no opportunity to organize or resist. The slave ships needed extra hands – yet always seemed short – to keep the Africans securely in place: 'Insurrections are frequently the consequence; which are seldom suppressed without much bloodshed.'[26] Permanent viligance, the shackling of all the men in twos, the marshalling of the slaves in manageable hatches, all these were tactics common to slave ships. After all, there were hundreds of Africans and a mere handful of crew, even though slave ships tended to have bigger crews than other contemporary ships.

In a bizarre twist, it was the extremely high death-rate among the white sailors, the appalling conditions under which they worked and the brutality to which even they were subjected which proved so persuasive in the abolitionist campaign against the slave trade.[27] Yet these same men were responsible for some of the extra sufferings of the slaves.

Sailors were accustomed to a harsh and brutal life. Their conditions of work and the regime of naval discipline were appalling, on both military and mercantile ships, and sailors were themselves kept in some sort of order by the most draconian of punishments: John Newton had no hesitation in putting troublesome crew members in irons. It was hardly surprising that some of the crew on slavers found relief for their tension and sexual appetites with the slaves. Slave women were kept separately from the men. Most slave cargoes had fewer women and they were kept, with child slaves, usually unshackled, in the smaller space between decks. They were an easy target, demoralized, defenceless and exposed to the passing whims of the white sailors. Sterner captains tried to keep their crews away from the women, but the men – already at sea for months past – were not so easily deflected. The sexual licence of the slave ships was, again, a telling factor in swinging opinion behind abolition after 1787. It was easy enough to print a disgusting picture of sexual harassment, rape and general wrong-doing: 'On board some ships, the common sailor was allowed to have intercourse with such of the black women whose consent they can procure. The officers are permitted to indulge their passions among them at pleasure, and sometimes are guilty of such brutal excesses, as disgrace human nature.'[28]

John Newton would not tolerate such behaviour. Yet even with as severe a disciplinarian as Newton, a pregnant slave was vilely raped in public. How much worse was it on other, less disciplined ships? Sexual exploitation of female slaves is a familiar theme in the history of slavery and not just black slavery. Slaves in classical antiquity, and in a host of Arab societies were recruited for sexual purposes.[29] For many female slaves, the Atlantic crossing was just the beginning of the sexual harassment and violence they would experience in the Americas. Was this commonplace or unusual? The evidence, and perhaps common sense, suggests that it was common. Like death and disease in the slave ships, sexual exploitation was not *intended*; it was not a conscious and deliberate policy, but it was unavoidable. The slave trade, after all, involved the violation of millions. What we can never know about the slave trade is the extent of capricious, casual or sadistic violence involved. More outrageous incidents are well known simply because they were outrageous. Virtually unknown is the catalogue of individual and casual violence – the blows, the whippings, the ridicule – that list of personal torments which sailors could dole out with virtual impunity.

Historians of the slave trade have, in recent years, grown wary of repeating the dreadful stories of life on the slave ships. In part this has been caused by a drift away from traditional narrative history, linked to a healthy scepticism about evidence which is often partial. The drift towards a more analytical and primarily statistical approach has, however, produced problems of its own, not least the 'sanitizing' of the whole phenomenon. Cleansed of its stinks and its filth, purged of its moans of pain and its shrieks of the insane, devoid of these glimpses of corpses thrown to the accompanying sharks – thus cleansed, the slave trade looks less vile than it was. The truth of the matter remains that the slave trade – in common with many other areas of human experience – cannot be wholly distilled to a statistical outline. We now know more about the slave trade than ever before. Oddly enough, in the process the slaves have disappeared from view.

5

Landfall

To approach the West Indies by sea can be a visually stunning experience. As the ink-black water of the ocean gives way to those slashes of aquamarine inshore waters, the tropical beauties of the islands come into sharper focus. From Columbus onward visitors have been smitten by the beauty of landfall. Of the great majority of settlers arriving before the early nineteenth century, however, few could have appreciated the islands' splendours. Most of them were Africans, penned and shackled below decks in conditions of pestilential squalor for weeks past. Arrival marked the end of their seaborne horrors, but it heralded traumas of a new and totally unpredictable kind. It was the fate of all slaves, if they survived, to find one painful experience dislodged by another.

As the slave ships approached the Americas, the routines of arrival were similar to those of departure from Africa. The slaves had to be cleaned and prepared for sale, no mean task considering their wretched state. John Newton recalled:

> When the ship makes the land (usually the West India islands), and have their port in view…then, and not before, they venture to release the men slaves from their irons: and then, the sight of the land, and the freedom from long and painful confinement, usually excite in them a degree of alacrity, and a transient feeling of joy.
>
> *The prisoner leaps to lose his chains.* But this joy is short-lived indeed. The condition of the unhappy slave is a continual process from bad to worse.[1]

Newton's journal for 1753 records how, like all slave captains, he prepared his cargo for arrival. On 23 May 1753, only one month after leaving West Africa, his ship was close to the islands: 'Washed the slaves which the weather has not allowed us to do this fortnight nearly.' A day later, his crew 'shaved the slaves' foreheads'. A week later, he anchored off St Kitts. Calling in to see a local agent, Newton had to decide whether to sell in St Kitts or to sail on to Jamaica or America. 'I should be extremely loth to venture so far, for we have had the men slaves so long on board that their patience is just worn out, and I am certain they would drop fast had we another passage to make.' Newton managed to sell all but twenty at the first attempt. It took another week to sell them; a total of 167 in all.[2]

Making the slaves presentable (and saleable) was no easy task. Demoralized, run-down and often sick, the slaves needed rejuvenating before they could be paraded before potential purchasers. When the *James* reached Barbados in 1676 the Captain recorded in his log: 'I called all my slaves aft w'ch came from Wyemba and found 25 of them…gave my slaves tobacco and pipes.' As the sale day approached, he 'gave them fresh water to wash and Palme Oyle and Tobacco and Pipes'. Thus spruced and gleaming (the palm oil was used to create a healthier-looking sheen on African skin), 163 of the slaves were sold.[3]

Slave sales involved a repetition of all the indignities of the sales on the African coast. Customers, like the slave-traders themselves a few weeks earlier, were keen to buy only healthy slaves and were acutely aware that disease and illness thrived in the ships' holds. Planters or their agents were especially attentive to the slaves' physical condition and subjected them to the most intimate of examinations. In 1673 Richard Ligon described how Barbadian planters 'buy them out of the Ship, where they find them stark naked, and therefore cannot be deceived in any outward infirmity. They choose them as they do Horses in a Market; the strongest, youthfullest, and most beautiful, yield the greatest price'.[4]

One Liverpool captain with a batch of slaves suffering from dysentery 'directed the surgeon to stop the anus of each of them with oakum'. Sometimes such strategems worked. More often, slaves were so afflicted by dysentery that on landing they were 'obliged to stop almost every minute, as they passed on'.[5]

Slave-traders would go to any lengths to hide the weakness of their slaves. Anuses were plugged with wadding, grey hair dyed black, mouths thoroughly washed out, bodies cleansed and oiled. Only then were planters allowed to look.

The methods of selling slaves varied greatly. It was rare for a ship to offload its human cargo in one easy sweep. More usually, the best (i.e. the healthiest) went quickly, but days and sometimes weeks passed before the weaker slaves could be disposed of. It was no linguistic accident that slave-traders coined the phrase 'refuse slaves'; those reduced to worthlessness by sickness, age or injury: 'went on board with a Planter to sell him some o'r refuse Slaves but he did not like them'.[6] Sometimes, before the slaves were sold, 'the sick or refuse slaves, of which there are frequently many, are usually conveyed on shore, and sold at a tavern, or public auction'. Here, among the human residue of the slave trade, were to be found the most abject of scenes: the most wretched, the lame, the dying; worthless, aimless – refuse. 'It seldom happens that any, who are carried ashore in the emaciated state to which they are generally reduced by that disorder, long survive their landing.' One ship's surgeon who witnessed a parade of sixteen such wretches from ship to shore told how all soon died.[7]

Slave-traders wanted the best prices for their slaves and were prepared to leave one island for another to secure higher returns. But the slaves' condition deteriorated the longer they remained at sea. When the *James* trans-shipped slaves from Barbados to Nevis, the local governor accused the captain of importing weak slaves; and that he 'did not bring downe mine owne Gold Coast Slaves. Also said he did believe that I had on boarde all the refuse slaves of the Shippes that were off Barbados'.[8]

For the slaves, perhaps the most terrifying form of sale was the 'scramble'. Slave captains and purchasers would agree to a per capita price before the sale.

> On the day appointed, the negroes were landed and placed together in a large yard, belonging to the merchants to whom the ship was consigned … [At the appointed hour] the doors of the yard were suddenly thrown open, and in rushed a considerable number of purchasers, with all ferocity of brutes. Some instantly seized such of the negroes as they could conveniently lay hold of with their hands. Others, being prepared with several handkerchiefs tied together, encircled with these as many as they were able. While others by means of a rope, effected the same purpose.

The confusion was complete; buyers argued and disputed with each other. For their part: 'The poor astonished negroes were so much terrified by these proceedings, that several of them, through fear, climbed over the walls of the court yard, and ran wild about the town; but were soon hunted down and retaken.' When such scrambles were conducted on board ship, terrified slaves sometimes flung themselves overboard. What frightened the slaves was the sudden tumult and noise which was unleashed without any notice: 'The women in particular clung to each other in agonies scarcely to be conceived, shrieking through excess of terror, at the savage manner in which their brutal purchasers rushed upon, and seized them.'[9]

Olaudah Equiano (Gustavus Vassa) was himself sold at such a scramble when his slave vessel landed in Barbados.

> On a signal given (as the beat of a drum) the buyers rushed at once into the yard where the slaves are confined, and make choice of that parcel they like best. The noise and the clamour with which this is attended and the eagerness visible in the countenances of the buyers serve not a little to increase the apprehensive-

ness of the terrified Africans ... In this manner, without scruple, are relations and friends separated, most of them never to see each other again.[10]

Until the early eighteenth century, when the Royal African Company had controlled the British slave trade, company ships consigned their slaves to agents in the islands, who promptly resold them. Sometimes slaves were delivered to 'contractors' for a fixed price already agreed and paid in London. Company agents were on the quayside waiting to inspect the slave cargoes (and to prevent crew members selling slaves for their own advantage).[11] With the ending of this monopoly trade, however, a free trade in slaves developed. It was then that the British slave-traders came into their own and landed the largest numbers of their slaves in the Americas.

Slave captains could never predict the demand for slaves on arrival. If demand was slack, they might sail on to another colony. But wherever he made vent of his slaves, the captain normally did so through an auction, a scramble, or through a local agent. As traumatic as sale undoubtedly was, it did not mark the end of the slaves' sufferings. Nor did it mark the end of their travels.

In South Carolina and Virginia, for instance, slaves were shipped onwards, along the extensive river networks and waterways, to their immediate destinations, thence inland or to another colony. The journey to the rice fields of All Saints parish on the northern coastal stretch of South Carolina involved a twelve-hour boat trip north from the slave auctions of Charleston to Winyah Bay. From there, boats travelled further north, up the Waccamaw river, a winding waterway lined by 'swamps of cyprus, magnolia, oak and pine, reeds and rushes, and marsh', the whole region teeming with wildlife. Here were the rice plantations, large 12 to 20-acre plots hemmed in by powerful dams and lavishly watered by the fresh-water surges of the Waccamaw river. It was a luxuriant region, its natural forces gradually brought under control by slave labour and converted to rice production, and the high ground dotted by splendid great houses for the planters.[12]

By 1740 there were about 40,000 Africans in South Carolina, and the slave markets of Charleston thrived. The Waccamaw region was rapidly Africanized; the boats of its labyrinthine rivers were worked and captained by blacks famous for their singing and working chants. Further north, Maryland and above all Virginia were similarly transformed into a black society, thanks to the development of tobacco. Here, as in the Caribbean, slaves arrived in an utterly debilitated state from their protracted journey from Africa. Between 1710 and 1718 about one-twentieth of new arrivals died even before they could be sold.[13]

The sales in North America tended to differ from those in the islands. Slaves were sold on board ship, the sales spread over several days. Those sold departed with their new owners; the others returned to their chains to await the next sale. Slaves in Virginia often endured numerous sales, each with their inhuman inspection, the worries and uncertainties, and the sad departure of friends and shipmates. A slaver might take up to two and a half months to sell a complete cargo, the healthy men going first, the sick last of all. Even then, the travelling was not over. Unlike slaves on the Waccamaw rice plantations, Africans destined for the Chesapeake tobacco plantations often had to walk for miles in the wake of their new owner or agent. Once at their new home, they were put to work, usually at the most routine of field tasks, some of them not unlike crop work in their homelands.[14]

It was not enough that planters had new slaves to augment their work-force; they also needed to change them, to render them disciplined in the ways of the New World. The first step was to give them new names. Re-naming involved an attempt to change a slave's identity, a denial of his or her former self, and offered both a convenience for white owners and a confirmation of their power.

The names given were sometimes classical, sometimes African. Simple Christian names recurred time and again.[15] Yet it was likely that slaves continued to use their own names. Sometimes an African name passed down the slave family tree from one generation to another, though often in an altered form which was acceptable to both black and white.[16] The slaves' success in keeping their own names, striking in the Waccamaw region of South Carolina, was an important assertion of the most basic element of personal identity.

Above all else, the early days in the colonies were determined by a slave's physical condition. Planters often tried to break in their new slaves to routines of slave work via less demanding work, but others expected an immediate full labouring return from their new investments. When in 1730 Ayuba Suleiman Diallo (better known to Europeans as Job Ben Soloman) began work in the Maryland tobacco fields, he 'grew sick, being no way able to bear it; so that his Master was obliged to find easier work for him and therefore put him to tend the cattle'.[17] Not all planters transferred sick slaves in this way (and not all were able to); not all slaves had the chance to build up their lost strength. On the Chesapeake, one slave in four died within the first year of landing, mostly in the winter and spring. Local whites, on the other hand, tended to die in the autumn.[18]

In the British West Indies, new slaves were predominantly male ('on account of the superior strength and labour of the men')[19] but males were more at risk after arrival. One-third of imported slaves died in their first three years in the West Indies. Despite their owners' persistent conviction that it was better to buy men rather than women, males had the higher death-rate. When, in 1788, the Assembly of Jamaica scrutinized the continuing fall in the slave population, it noted 'the great Proportion of Deaths that happen among Negroes newly imported'. A local doctor, James Chisholme, reported 'that a very great number of newly imported Negroes are lost by Diseases, the predisposing Causes of which they bring in this Country along with them'.[20]

In this utterly new world, slaves even had to learn to communicate anew. Not to understand was to incur the anger of short-tempered whites who viewed incomprehension as stupidity, rewarding blank looks with blows and punishments. Slaves soon realized how important it was to understand and be understood. Among slaves from diverse tribal and linguistic groups, a lingua franca had to be created. Throughout the Americas, African languages bumped into the dominant European language – Spanish, Portuguese, Dutch, French or English. From the particular fusion of the two there emerged that plethora of pidgin and Creole languages which survive to this day. This process had already begun on the African coast and on board the slave ships, where a linguistic shorthand had evolved to cope with the major problems of communicating with hundreds of uncomprehending Africans.[21] Certain slaves acted as interpreters between traders and slaves and among themselves. Pidgin languages, enormously different one from another, quickly developed in sophistication and were passed on as a spoken language to a new generation, becoming the slaves' mother-tongues throughout the Americas.

The development of the language depended on a host of factors. Where slaves worked in small groups, close to whites, their language came closer to that of their owners. But among slaves living and working in large gangs distant from white influences – especially where there were regular influxes of new African slaves – local Creole developed quite distinctly from the local white language. On the major sugar plantations of the West Indies or on the rice plantations of South Carolina, the large labour force (predominantly African) spoke a language which their owners could scarcely comprehend. This changed, of course, when the flow of imported Africans dried up. Thereafter the African qualities in the language, as in their culture as a whole, began to fade.

The growth of Creole languages among the slaves and, later, among their freed descendants, varied greatly. In the British West Indies there were enormous differences between the islands. Often this linguistic development defies simple analysis; it was more like a mosaic than an easily discernible broad pattern. At times it produced the most remarkable mix of languages. In South Carolina, where the rice-growing slaves were predominantly African, the need both 'to learn English and to retain African speech patterns' led to the creation of a new language – Gullah.[22] Gullah-speaking slaves came from a wide area of West Africa and Gullah's accents and intonations incorporated the cadences and accents of settlers from France and Scotland, from the Caribbean islands and even embraced the regional peculiarities of Warwickshire, Lancashire and Ulster.

Understandably, whites soon began to talk like their slaves. An English visitor to South Carolina thought the local white planters had 'that peculiar accent derived from almost exclusive association with negroes'. Planters' children, allowed to mix with the slaves, 'acquired the same dialect; and today many a gentleman's son regrets that it is apparent in his speech'.[23] Similar stories emerged from the West Indies where whites seemed to speak like their slaves. Lady Nugent wrote of Jamaica in her diary in 1802:

> The Creole language is not confined to the negroes. Many of the ladies, who have not been educated in England, speak a sort of broken English, with an indolent drawling out of their words, that is very tiresome if not disgusting. I stood next to a lady one night, near a window, and, by way of saying something, remarked that the air was much cooler than usual; to which she remarked, 'Yes, ma-am, him rail-y too fraish.'[24]

Using African words or meanings, slaves could, however, invest their local Creole with words and nuances known only to them; it was a means of communicating with one another to the exclusion of the whites. Even in speech, slaves soon learned the importance of hiding beyond the reach of whites. Slaves sought to put a distance between themselves and their owners.

What went through their minds, those new slaves, as they shuffled off to their first day's work? Hectored in a language they did not understand, given tools they could not comprehend, turned loose with blacks they did not know, put to work they could not grasp; sick, weak, miserable; wretched beyond imagination, uprooted from friends and kinfolk – they were alien people in an alien land; lost in an ocean of misery. It takes a feat of imagination to recall the horrors of their last few months. For all they knew, life's torments would never end.

PART III

Working Lives

6

Plantations, Slaves and Planters

By the mid-seventeenth century the island of Barbados was rapidly being transformed. The smallholdings of the pioneer settlers had begun to give way to larger plantations on which the lucrative crop of sugar could more easily and profitably be raised. When Richard Ligon approached the island by sea, he wrote: 'For as we past along near the shoar the Plantations appear'd to us one above another: like several stories in stately buildings, which afforded us a large proportion of delight.'[1] By 1650 there were some 300 plantations on the island, most of them on the luxuriant leeward shore. Less than twenty years later there were upwards of 900; one man described counting more than 400 windmills (used for crushing the sugar cane) perched on the island's high ground. Englishmen were not only actively colonizing as many West Indian islands as they (and their military backers) could lay claim to, but in the process they were mapping and sketching the region. Each successive map of all the main inhabited West Indian islands tells much the same story: of a beautiful and bountiful wilderness slowly but surely cleared of its native peoples, its natural fecundity converted to the production of tropical staples. Travel accounts tell of intriguing islands gradually peppered with plantations – the economic and social units which converted the wilderness to profitable agriculture and which became the work-place and final resting place of armies of African slaves.[2] When Edward Slaney produced his map of Jamaica in 1678 (a mere twenty-three years after the English took the island from the Spaniards), the long sweep of Jamaica's fertile southern coast was pitted with plantations.[3] Though the island was lampooned in that period as 'the Dunghill of the Universe' (and one of its rainiest, foggiest regions described as 'the piss pot of the island'),[4] Jamaica, like Barbados before it, had begun to yield a lucrative return to its growing band of planters.[5]

By 1680 Barbados was dominated by its planters. Almost 200 planters had large-scale properties, each worked by more than sixty slaves. Another 200 or so 'middling' planters ran smaller plantations with the labour of between twenty and sixty slaves. Some of the landholdings were enormous for so small an island. The island's greatest planter owned upwards of 1,000 acres; the next, Christopher Codrington (whose land funded the library of All Souls College, Oxford), owned more than 600 acres. But land alone was not the real indicator of wealth; Barbadian planters were ranked by the numbers of their slaves.[6]

A similar story quickly unfolded in Jamaica. The invading army of 1655 ('the most prophane debauch'd persons that we ever saw') had, within a generation, become the nucleus of a prospering band of planters. The maps, again, provide evidence of what was happening. A Jamaican map of 1671 named 146 plantations; thirteen years later a new map located and named 690.[7] All sorts of tropical produce emerged from those plantations, but the single most important crop – the biggest volume of exports, the most lucrative produce and the crop which devoured the labours of ever-increasing gangs of slaves – was sugar. By the end of the seventeenth century the story of the English settlement in the West Indies had been a classic rags-to-riches tale for that small élite of planters: 'It is seldome seene that the ingenious or industrious men fail of raising their fortunes in any parts of the Indies…from little or nothing to vast estates.'[8] Naturally enough, this story of dramatic material success ignores those who fell by the wayside: the thousands of British soldiers and indentured labourers who died of disease and deprivation, who failed in a range of economic ventures, who succumbed to the natural and human savagery of life on the fringes of the islands' wilderness. And it ignores the essential labours of the imported Africans.

The transformation of the Caribbean islands into a sugar economy was dependent on slaves marshalled into a proto-industrial labour force on the plantations. In the North American colonies, however, that transformation came later. The pioneering settlers in Virginia had, as in the West Indies, been invading Britons who displaced native peoples. Africans were of little importance in the early years. Even when the whites had secured their precarious toehold on the region, along the vast river and water systems of the Chesapeake Bay, and long after tobacco had become the region's main export crop, blacks were thinly scattered. As late as 1690 blacks comprised only 15 per cent of Virginia's population (though most had arrived via an earlier sojourn in the West Indies). But from 1680 onwards Africans began to be imported direct from Africa in significant numbers. Between 1700 and 1740 54,000 blacks were imported into Virginia and Maryland, some 49,000 of whom were Africans. They entered a world of tobacco plantations which had already been shaped by white landowners and white indentured labourers with the help of the occasional black slave.[9]

Africans were introduced into small-scale operations which grew in size as the crop became more valuable and as more Africans became available for labour. But slaves were generally owned in small numbers, working side by side with local white men. As late as 1775, 63 per cent of Virginian slave-owners owned only five slaves or fewer. The sugar plantations in the British Caribbean by that time controlled an average of 240 slaves each.

Most Africans arriving in the Chesapeake were landed between June and August when the tobacco was growing rapidly. They were immediately put to work on the simpler tasks of weeding. Many slaves simply refused to accept the new routines of labour. Edward Kimber remarked in 1747: 'a new Negro must be broke... You would really be surpriz'd at their Perseverence; let an hundred Men shew him how to hoe, or drive a Wheelbarrow, he'll still take the one by the bottom, and the Other by the Wheel'.[10]

It was the first task of all slave-owners to break in their African slaves; to render them more pliable and reliable, to change them from traumatized (and often sick), reluctant immigrants into beasts of burden who might provide an economic return to their owners. The plantations became the main social instrument through which this process was achieved for the largest single group of slaves. On and around the plantations they were taught (or, in the case of the local-born, grew up with) the basic lessons for life as a slave: of work and obedience, of learning to accommodate themselves to the harsh conditions of their lives. Not all slaves were plantation slaves; substantial numbers earned their keep in the towns, on the rivers and at sea, in skilled professions or in jobbing gangs. But it was the plantation which set the mark of slavery on more slaves than any other single institution in the Americas.

In the British colonies, Barbados led the way. Like all who followed them, Barbadian slave-owners cared mainly about the labour they could extract from their Africans. Some, it is true, were worked to death, especially in the brutal pioneering days of settlement and clearing the bush, when slaves were pitted against a hostile environment in frontier conditions. With the land cleared, the island's authorities (dominated of course by the planters) created the vital infrastructure for the development of the plantations: the roads and the urban centres with their vital links to Europe and North America for capital and supplies, and to Africa for slaves. As sugar boomed, money flowed into the islands. The planters built homes in the island capitals and on their rural estates which befitted their wealth and status. Their homes grew grander (at first many bought frame-houses from New England), and interiors ever more lavish, the furnishings the best available from Europe and North America, or locally made by slave craftsmen. Gradually their plantation homes, the Great Houses, were filled with the artefacts, the bric-à-brac, which denoted wealth – silver, furniture, books and paintings which were part of an unmistakable white colonial style. It was a style which stood in stark contrast to the poverty

and general deprivation of the surrounding slaves whose labours in neighbouring fields and at their masters' tables made possible such a display.

Planters were more famous for their ostentatious and brash lifestyle than for
their cultural ambitions. Lavish parties, prodigious drinking, womanizing
(with their slaves) on an epic scale; all these from the first were the hallmark
of the West Indian planters. One commentator on mid-seventeenth-century
Barbados remarked: 'the afternoon thus passes in drinking and smoking, but
quite often one is so drunk that he cannot return home. Our gentleman found
this life extremely pleasant'.[11] The best European wines and the most potent
of West Indian rums were mingled with the best of fowl, fish and beasts.
Thomas Thistlewood, by no means a rich planter, entertained his white
Jamaican neighbours in the most lavish of fashions:

> Wednesday, 15 March 1775: John Cope, Richard Vassall, William Blake Esqr.
> dined with me, and stayed till about 9 in the evening. Mr Cope stayed all night.
> Had mutton broth, roast mutton and broccoli, carrots and asparagus, stewed
> mudfish, roast goose and paw paw, apple sauce, stewed giblets, some fine lettuce
> which Mr. Vassall brought me, crabs, cheese, mush melon, etc. Punch, porter,
> ale, cyder, madeira wine & brandy etc.

Not surprisingly, the following day he complained that he felt 'very unwell,
with drinking too much wine yesterday'.[12] Time and again Thistlewood
described similar, and even more elaborate, feasts.

Master and slaves lived cheek by jowl on the plantations; the one enjoying a
lifestyle beyond the ken and comprehension of the others. They were separated by more than colour and legal status; on every conceivable level the two
sides of the plantation system were, for all their physical proximity, as distant
and remote as could be imagined. The masters often lived in great material
comfort; slaves lived in primitive housing and wore the simplest of clothes.
The masters ate lavishly, the slaves survived on the most basic of diets. We
could of course paint a similar picture for the gulf between rich and poor in
Britain at much the same time. What made the New World contrast so
startling was its setting: the plantation. Remote, isolated and often self-con-
tained for weeks on end, the plantation was a society in miniature which
magnified and exacerbated the basic tensions and inequities of the slave
system. Yet the plantation was essential if the slaves were to be harnessed to
the prime task of tapping the wealth of the land.

Between the firm establishment of English control over the West Indian
islands through to the end of slavery, the black population of the region
increased from about 50,000 to more than one million. In those same years
more than 10 million tons of sugar cane emerged from the islands.[13] The
planters of Barbados, St Kitts, Nevis, Montserrat, Antigua and, above all,
Jamaica (between 1775 and 1824 half the region's sugar came from that island)

enriched themselves and transformed the tastes of Europe through the sugar grown by their plantation slaves.

No one doubted that slaves were the vital element in the economy of the islands. In 1718 William Wood remarked: 'The labour of negroes is the principal foundation of riches from the plantations.'[14] Plantations could not, however, function without their white élites. The ratio of black to white varied enormously. In the early days of settlements the ratio might be three to one. As the plantations became more established, blacks regularly outnumbered whites by ten to one. On some estates there were fifty slaves for every white. Black slaves were bought initially as mere beasts of burden, their sole skills thought to be their physical strength and durability. In time many became skilled in a range of occupations. As black slavery developed on the back of the sugar economy, whites were driven from the fields and into a series of occupations which became the preserve of whites alone. Slaves might become artisans and trusted craftsmen, but the literate and semi-literate office positions (clerks, book-keepers) were, like estate management and ownership, reserved for whites. No matter how essential or skilled a particular slave might be, the plantation developed its own social structure in which colour and race were more important than ability. There was a threshold beyond which no slave could step.

Plantation society was dominated, in almost every conceivable way, by men whose origins lay not, as many of them liked others to believe, in the upper reaches of European life, but in the humblest (and luckiest) of white immigrant groups. Early settlers, soldiers, fortune-seekers, even the desperate – these and more like them formed the kernel of plantation society. What distinguished them from other whites was good fortune, good health and the occasional flash of business acumen. It was no accident that this élite within an élite came to be known as the 'plantocracy' – the name an amalgam of their local rank and the status to which they aspired and whose style they so clearly aped.

Jamaica came to dominate the sugar industry in the eighteenth century, and its plantations and planters created the most popular images of West Indian wealth and dissipation. By the mid-century, half of Jamaica's landowners owned more than 500 acres. The greatest of all planters, Peter Beckford, owned eleven sugar estates and was part-owner of five more. By 1774 the medium-sized Jamaican plantation was 600 acres, worked by 200 slaves. It was the rule of thumb on sugar plantations that one slave was required for every acre of land in sugar cane.[15]

For all their wealth, the planters remained strangers in their new land. Living on the edge of untamed bush – a wilderness which would rapidly overwhelm their cultivation if they dropped their guard for a moment – surrounded by a sea of alien blacks, planters were often unhappy despite their ostentatious lifestyle. They sought refuge in drink and casual sex with their slave women. Many abandoned their plantation homes for the civilized world of London, Bath or rural Britain. The islands were rarely 'home', even three or four generations after families had settled as planters. One hundred and twenty-eight years after the Price family first settled the estate of Worthy Park in central Jamaica, Rose Price quit his inheritance to return 'home' to Cornwall in 1798.

On the smaller islands, too – St Kitts, Nevis and even Antigua – the plantocratic élite often absented itself when its fortunes had been secured. Returning 'home' to Britain, these absentee planters left their affairs in the hands of agents and overseers. This change of management has often been thought responsible for the inefficiencies which developed on the plantations. Slaves may have been more harshly treated on absentee plantations, roughly managed and handled by men who had little incentive to see to the slaves' well-being.

For those who stayed, the plantation Great House was the focal point of local life, augmented by periodic forays to the nearest urban centre or capital. Though rarely as grand as the lavish planters' homes in the American South, the West Indian Great Houses were testimony to the wealth and position of the men who built and lived in them. It was within these splendid homes that the plantocracy entertained their white guests, visitors from around the island and abroad. There were of course many planters (and even more slave-owners) of more humble means; men who could only envy the cavortings of their plantocratic superiors. But even they indulged themselves on a scale unimaginable to their contemporaries in England. All these displays of white luxury and enjoyment took place under the very noses of armies of deprived black slaves. Indeed, such extravaganzas were organized and prepared by the slaves; the cooks, servants, cleaners and domestics (all with their own helpers, friends and relatives). At its peak, plantocratic social pretensions became the stuff of caricature. Planters, their airs and graces, their styles and their vulgarities, were lampooned in cartoon and in print, in the West Indies and in Britain. Slaves too ridiculed their planters, but on the whole they knew better than to belittle them to their faces.

Plantations had little to offer but the wealth they disgorged to the favoured few. They spawned few of the social amenities which made for a civilized life. Often isolated, with poor roads leading in and out (water travel was often quicker), remote from churches, schools, social life, the printed word, political life, and distant from white neighbours and friends, the West Indian planta-tions were male-dominated laagers, breeding a coarse social life which repelled all but its *aficionados*. For the whites, there was at least the opportunity of release from the tedium of plantation life; drink, slave women, visits else-where. Such escape routes were rarely available for the slaves.

The Africans were socialized to their new lives as slaves by life on the plantations. But the first problem they faced was simply that of staying alive. In the Caribbean, one African in three did not survive the first three years in his or her new home (and this is quite apart from the deaths on the slave ships). By 1800 about 1.5 million Africans had been landed in the British islands. At first the planters bought both men and women, and seemed keen to encourage the development of slave families. But the drive towards sugar production soon changed that attitude. Work for the slaves was hard, food was often in short supply (despite the existence of small gardens, provision grounds, where slaves cultivated their own foodstuffs). Wherever we look in the eighteenth century, the plantations seem to devour their slaves. On the Codrington estates in Barbados, 5 per cent of the slaves had to be replaced each year up to the mid-eighteenth century. A similar story unfolded on the small island of Nevis. In Barbados between 1764 and 1771 more than 35,000 Africans were imported, but the overall slave population grew by a mere 5,000.

In the rush for sugar-based prosperity, planters decided that their interests were best served by young male slaves. As the proportion of female slaves dropped, the birth-rates, naturally enough, also declined. But as slave prices increased from the middle of the eighteenth century, planters once again came to appreciate the economic benefits of rearing their own slaves. Incentives were offered to encourage slaves to breed and material conditions were improved. Slowly, the slave population began to increase of its own accord.[16] But even on the eve of the abolition of the slave trade, West Indian planters still feared that they could not survive without regular importations of new Africans. There were some British colonies where slaves bred successfully, notably in the small island of Barbuda, but on the whole the slave population of the British West Indies seemed unable to grow without the supply of Africans from the slave ships.

Work in the sugar fields was extremely hard, especially in the six months of the year when the crop was being harvested. Diet was inadequate, and at times even inadequate foodstuffs were in short supply. In 1786 Thomas Thistlewood's slaves in Jamaica were all hungry. He had to give them a day off work and money 'to seek provisions, which are the scarcest ever known': 'Thursday, 20th July 1786: Abba's Mary complains of hunger much. Gave Abba a dollar to assist them. I never saw such a scarce time before, that is certain. Nothing to be had for money.'[17] Yet hunger alone cannot explain the failure of the slave population to increase. We need to look more closely at the plantation regimes.

The development of the sugar plantation spawned an agricultural literature of its own; of manuals and guides telling how to establish and manage a sugar estate. Such guides were often idealized versions of a much more varied and harsher reality. There was for instance no guaranteed way of keeping new African slaves alive. Planters knew that new arrivals were at risk and tried, where possible, to spare them the worst rigours of sugar cultivation, preferring to 'season' them in less laborious, less intensive work; weeding, guarding cattle and the like. Sometimes even that was too much.

Sugar plantation slaves were in an unusual position. They were obviously a rural labour force, but they were also disciplined and controlled like industrial workers. The rhythm of their labours was dictated as much by the routines of the sugar factory as it was by the natural pace of agricultural growth and harvesting. Sugar cane cut by the slaves was crushed in mills (hence the proliferation throughout the islands of windmills, later steam-mills), and processed in the stinking and noisy factory, curing and boiling houses. There, the manufacture of sugar and rum required more heavy labour (often employing slaves from the field gangs) as well as the highly skilled boilers and distillers. These skilled slaves determined the success or failure of the plantations' produce, and their rewards were accordingly greater. Once the crop had been processed, skilled slaves were turned over to other work around the plantation.

Approaching plantations by water or road afforded an immediate glimpse of a work-place which was part rural, part industrial. Map-makers, surveyors, painters and the words of casual visitors captured the physical appearance of these peculiar institutions. Maps of the West Indies often pictured, as well as located, plantations on the islands, with illustrations of factories and domestic buildings. Surveyors too left behind rich and detailed evidence: plans, maps and statistics of their work in plotting and drawing the lie of the land.

Today Worthy Park estate presents a magnificent sight to the visitor. As you drive across the central mountainous spine of Jamaica and turn west at the small town of Ewarton, at the foot of Mount Diablo, the road leads through an often hair-raising journey over the mountains, before dropping down on the superb panorama of Luidas Vale. From the best vantage point, the sugar fields of the estate stretch north and south, the flat lands of sugar cane neatly dissected and ordered into their various fields, fringed by the hilly surrounds of citrus crops, and the whole encircled by hills and mountains. At the centre of the estate sits the factory and that clutter of ancillary buildings and workers' homes which forms the nucleus of the modern estate. The details (and the noises of machines, tractors and factory) are modern of course. But in essence the scene remains much as it was in the days of slavery: sugar fields which swept through the fertile valley and focused on the sugar works and homes of local people. We can trace the origins of that plantation in very great detail, from the first surveyed piece of land given over to sugar production in 1670.

Today, Worthy Park dominates the valley. It even holds in its gravitational pull large numbers of other properties and small farmers scattered throughout a wide geographic area. In slave days however it was only one of a number of plantations in that valley. At the apogee of its slave fortunes, Worthy Park had almost 600 acres in cane, toiled over by a slave labour force of more than 560. The plans and maps of the late eighteenth and early nineteenth centuries provide visual confirmation of the data in the plantation's surviving slave-books.

The plantation buildings were outside the cane-growing area. The offices and the Great House were on a hill to the west of the cane fields (they are still there). To the north there was another grouping, of offices and the overseer's house. The plantation's industrial complex – the factory, water-mill, cattle-mill, curing houses and trash house – were to the south, straddling the road leading through the estate. The 'negro houses' were dotted to the west of the works.[18]

Each plantation had its own peculiarities, but all shared obvious character-istics. Black and white generally lived close to the place of work. It was obviously pointless (and counter-productive) to have master and man waste time and energy travelling long distances to work in the fields or factory. But the whites on West Indian plantations wanted to combine economic utility with social and racial segregation. They did not want to live too close to the slave labour force. On smaller slave-holdings it was, however, impossible to escape the physical proximity of slaves. Thomas Thistlewood complained in his diary on 29 December 1781: 'Pompey frequently lets such loud farts that we hear him plain and loud to my house and cookroom, between 130 & 140 yards from his hut.'[19] At such close quarters, Thistlewood complained time and again in his diary of being disturbed by his slaves whenever they drank, celebrated, made music, fought or quarrelled. Not surprisingly, planters in the Caribbean preferred to live at a quieter remove from their labour force.

Worthy Park, like other plantations of its size, kept its slaves at a distance from the whites. Surviving maps reveal the development of slave villages, clusters of huts and houses, forming a neighbouring satellite community; close to work and near enough to be scrutinized and controlled, but far enough away to be safe and quiet. Edward Long, the Jamaican writer and planter, owned Lucky Valley plantation in Clarendon, Jamaica. There the slave village formed a small huddle of buildings, housing 282 slaves, on either side of the river running through the valley, but all at a distance from the homes of the whites and the factory.[20]

Just to the west of Long's Lucky Valley plantation was Friendship estate owned by Henry Dawkins, whose family had lived in the island since the early years of English settlement. There, again, the slaves were coralled together in a village, distant (and across a river) from the centre of the estate.[21] The story was repeated across the island. On the north-east coast of Jamaica, close to the coastal town of Annotto Bay, lay Gray's Inn estate, worked in the last years of slavery by some 300 slaves. They lived in their own village, south of the main plantation complex, close to each other in 'negro houses' but, again, distant from their masters.[22]

The slaves were the most movable of all a plantation's assets. They could be shifted from one property to another, reassigned to different parts of the same colony or even sold to a different colony. They were sold off, divided from their families and friends and generally shuffled into whatever new formation their owners required. It is not surprising to find that their homes were also shifted around to suit their owners' economic interests. Various maps show land once habited by slaves, now under cultivation. On Roehampton estate immediately inland from Montego Bay in Jamaica, the slaves lived on five acres of land south of the factory in 1791. Twenty years later they had been shifted, their former land turned over to cane growing. Now they occupied a steep slope; 350 of them hemmed into terraced rows of houses on a four-acre site. The owner of Roehampton, John Baillie, tried to preserve the domestic privacy of his slaves, never entering their homes 'without asking permission'; for their part, the slaves were 'very tenacious upon that point'. He, and others, had earlier tried to provide slaves with communal barracks, constructed 'with stone, and made them a far superior description to the ordinary Negro house'. But 'the Negroes have refused to occupy them, stating that they were so much exposed to their neighbours they did not like to let them know what they were doing on all occasions'. Instead, they wanted, and got, their own houses: 'The houses upon my estate were all of stone, 16 by 24 feet in size; I had between 60 and 70. Each house and garden occupied a space of 40 feet square; they were divided according to the fancy of the Negro.' Each building was about seven feet tall, topped by a conical roof of shingles. To their owner's irritation, the slaves would not light fires in their homes, instead constructing kitchens or outbuildings in front of their houses; the owner thought it ruined the appearance of his line of slave houses.[23]

Slave homes were rarely accorded the precise surveys and measurement so common (indeed vital) in the recording of other plantation buildings. We can understand why. Slave quarters were much less permanent, more crudely and cheaply built and liable – as was the case on the Roehampton estate – to destruction or removal to another location. Occasionally the slave quarters were ignored completely by those seeking to describe or paint West Indian properties. James Hakewell painted a series of revealing views of Jamaican plantations, but he often took as his vantage point the spot where the slave houses were located; the picture looks out, towards the plantation, from the slave quarters. The result is that the modern observer could be forgiven for not realizing that slave houses were among the dominant features of the plantation landscape.[24] As the debate about black freedom reached its crisis point in Britain in the 1820s, it became obvious to West Indian planters that slave homes, like all other assets, needed careful assessment. Planters wanted to hang on to their black labour force once freedom came; they also wanted to charge rents for the homes which, in slave days, were free.

On the Jamaican plantation called Creighton Hall, astride White river in the south-east of the island, a survey in the last days of slavery provided unusual detail about the slaves' houses. It was in effect a black village, occupying fourteen acres, close to the Great House. There were eighty-one houses, fifty-one of them 'good', twenty 'indifferent' and twelve 'bad'; most homes seemed to be inhabited by three people. All seem to have had their own garden plots, close to their homes or at a distance – communal land seems to have been available to slaves who did not have their own gardens or provision grounds. Some slaves were obviously much better off than others; some had more or better land and housing. There was also a chapel in the village. As the community had grown, it had developed its own network of paths and boundaries.[25] Here was a black village emerging of its own natural accord; its main features shaped not by the fiat or orders of the white master, but by the natural demands of an emergent black community. Though rooted in slavery, where everything had been provided by white planters, such black villages had begun to transform themselves from their dependence on white control and patronage into free villages which were to characterize the West Indian islands from the end of slavery (in 1838) to the present day.[26] Sometimes slave villages were described as bucolic havens, nestling amid the undoubted beauty of a tropical landscape. Monk Lewis, describing his own slaves' houses in Westmoreland, Jamaica, wrote: 'each house is surrounded by a separate garden, and the whole village is intersected by lanes, bordered with all kinds of sweet-smelling and flowering plants'.

Most agreed that the slaves liked to live in secluded communities. And as the planters began to intervene ever more directly in the lives of their slaves, especially in their efforts to enhance the birth-rate by improving material conditions, slave villages took on a more orderly appearance. Houses were built in lines. Where new (especially coffee) plantations were established in the late eighteenth century, slave communities looked more orderly and planned. The lush tropical splendour of the surrounding vegetation, however, often disguised cramped and squalid conditions inside the wattle and daub, or timber and thatch, huts.[27] Planters traditionally regarded the provision of housing (along with clothing and basic foodstuffs) as one of their obligations. Some slaves built their own houses: 'a few planters suffer their negroes to make their own huts themselves, and in what form they please: but these will always be very incorrect, and perhaps insufficient'.[28]

Local geography often determined what could or could not be provided for the slaves on the plantation. When economic conditions changed, and marginal lands were turned over to sugar production, slaves might be uprooted from their homes and their gardens converted to the cultivation of export staples rather than food for local consumption. Looking back, it seems obvious that land should always have been set aside to allow slaves to grow their own foodstuffs. Such autonomy saved money for the planter, encouraged industrious and thrifty habits among the slaves and avoided reliance on imported foods (which might not always arrive, thanks to the vagaries of war or weather).

In the early days of West Indian slavery, planters and island assemblies sought to encourage slave cultivation by allocating land and gardens, and specifying free time for work on the slave plots. But as sugar boomed, the tendency was to convert all fertile land to export crops. Again, the plans and maps provide a clue. Sugar-cane fields called 'Old Negro Ground Piece', 'Yams Piece', 'Potato Piece', explain what happened to slaves' provision grounds. All this was a turn for the worse. Slave food was now imported from North America and Britain, and slaves were exposed to starvation and shortages. In its turn, this undermined the slaves' health and hence their ability to work effectively and to reproduce successfully. Buying corn from America, beans from England, saltfish from Newfoundland, made the slave islands' economies too dependent on external supplies and costs. It also had the long-term effect of creating national dishes (ackee and saltfish in Jamaica, for instance) from foodstuffs which were not native to the region.

In most of the islands slaves went hungry in particular years and even in certain times of the year, usually between June and September. Slaves fainted in the fields, had difficulty working (and sometimes walking) properly. Starving slaves sometimes ate dangerous plants or unripe food; some died and many more fell ill.[29] Much of the problem was caused directly by the zealous cultivation of more and more sugar.

Work for plantation slaves rarely ceased; tending crops in their own gardens, and in their owners' provision grounds, was extra work on top of the myriad tasks around the plantation. They were given time off to work their own gardens. Thomas Thistlewood recorded on 19 October 1770: 'Gave the Negroes the rest of today and tomorrow, to plant and put their grounds in order.'[30]

Planters could use the distribution of food (and other necessities) to reward favourites or more 'useful' slaves, and to punish back-sliders. There were many slaves, however, with good plots, who worked hard and who developed successful businesses, using their food supplies and the animals they reared for trade and barter. Gardens and plots, clearly vital for slave nourishment, were also important in developing an independent slave economy. Phibbah, one of Thistlewood's favourite slaves, was so astute in her business transactions that she accumulated a great deal of cash. She bought and sold animals and goods, and occasionally lent sizeable sums to her master and owner.[31] For most slaves, work in the provision grounds helped keep them alive by enhancing their diet and physical well-being.[32] But droughts and disasters – especially hurricanes – occasionally destroyed foodstuffs and sugar cane alike, leaving slaves hungry and planters deprived of their income. Even in the 'gardens of the Indies' life was always precarious and the future uncertain.

It seemed different in the North American colonies. Here, too, Africans had to endure the traumas of settlement in the New World, their numbers ravaged by death in the seasoning period and the survivors damaged and harmed by sickness and disease. Many tried to run away, to revolt or to create their own communities in the vast American wilderness. Here, too, the plantation was the crucible for shaping slave society. American plantations were, however, quite different from those in the West Indies. In Virginia, plantations were relatively small; one with more than twenty-one slaves was thought a major operation. Only one-quarter of slaves in the Chesapeake in the 1730s lived in units bigger than twenty; a half of all the slaves belonged to groups of ten or fewer.[33]

In the Caribbean the slave villages were just that; distinct social entities where black society flourished. Slaves in the Chesapeake, however, living in small numbers close to the whites, had to travel to find company, friends and lovers on other plantations. Africans, like native-born slaves, worked under the immediate supervision of their owners. They quickly learned the essential lessons for survival on the plantations. They needed to acquire basic English in order to obey instructions, to avoid punishment and to secure the necessities of life. New Africans were often herded into communal barracks – so disliked by slaves in the West Indies – but seasoned local slaves lived in their own family homes. Through to the late 1730s in the Chesapeake, this process of settling into stable routines, of work and of family, was made difficult by fresh arrivals of Africans.[34]

All this had changed by the time of the American Revolution. Fewer Africans were imported and plantation slave communities became more settled. Between 1740 and 1776 the size of the slave communities living on the plantations increased; upwards of two-thirds of slaves in the tidewater region now lived on plantations or farms in groups of twenty or more. The bigger, wealthier owners had plantations housing more than 100 slaves. And this process – of slave holdings growing in size – was equally apparent further west in the Piedmont region.[35] Plantations had grown in size and as a result more and more slaves lived away from the master's immediate control. Small villages had begun to develop, distant from the planter's home (instead of huddled at the rear of the whites' homes). Slaves' homes were, like their counterparts in the West Indies, crude and simple; providing the basics for sleeping and cooking. They also tended to be close to the slaves' provision grounds.[36] The slave family provided a focus and an encouragement for the development of independent black social life.

Like West Indian slaves, American slaves developed a degree of economic independence, their crops and animals providing goods for barter or sale. Complex and scattered ties of slave family and friendship began to spread throughout a wide area. The development of local roads and paths encouraged the movement of peoples; slaves walked great distances to seek out and visit loved ones or friends. These regular but temporary migrations of slaves criss-crossing the region were impossible to control, still less to stop. Ties of blood and marriages drew slaves from one plantation to another, from one slave quarter to the next, often even far afield.[37]

The apparent stability of slave society should not deceive us. Life remained insecure for Virginian slaves. As masters' economic or personal fortunes waxed and waned, the slaves, like other forms of chattel, were shuffled and relocated often far from family and friends. This was one of the universals of black chattel slavery; always subject to changes in their owners' fortunes, slaves could never guarantee stability in their private lives. It was all the more remarkable then that from such unpromising conditions a thriving and lively black community arose. It was, however, very different from black society in the Caribbean, thanks in large measure to the differences between the plantation systems.

Plantation slaves everywhere lived in meagre circumstances. Their homes were generally ignored by visitors or residents; when noticed they were airily dismissed. (But so too were poor domiciles in Europe.) Hovels, huts, quarters, barracks; these and other descriptions were used to describe Virginian slave homes. But, as in the West Indies, slave life had a communal vitality. Slaves huddled together, sometimes under the same roof, often sharing a cramped yard and communal facilities. We can only speculate how far this development of slave communal living was a transplantation of African village life. As slaves lived together, so they worked and celebrated together: building and repairing homes, farming and tending their provision plots; enjoying drink, music and song together.[38]

The contrast between the homes of the slaves and the homes of masters could not have been greater. This ought not to surprise us since the planters were rich, the slaves poor. Tobacco, like sugar, yielded an amazing bounty to the owners of the tobacco lands of the Americas. Through their wealth and their landownership, planters in Virginia came to dominate colonial life. Their homes reflected their wealth and status. Not all whites – even planters – were wealthy, however. Despite the development of bigger plantations, large numbers of smaller landowners survived, their lifestyles less flamboyant than those of their wealthier peers. The élite which came to dominate Virginia was, by definition, a small group; perhaps 5 per cent of the landowning white population owned 50 per cent of the wealth.

As the eighteenth century advanced, this élite secured their power and standing through a network of marriages which in effect created a series of dynasties. As their wealth grew, they built for themselves those grand homes which dominated the local high ground or which commanded the marvellous views and vantage points on riversides and creeks throughout the Chesapeake.

As the James river winds its powerful way from Richmond to the Chesapeake Bay at Norfolk, its northern shore is dotted by a string of beautiful plantation Great Houses. Shirley plantation is perhaps the most beautiful

Queen Anne house in America, the land settled in 1613, its Great House built by the Carter family in 1723. Berkeley plantation is thought to have the oldest three-storey Georgian House in Virginia (built in 1726). It was at Berkeley that the first American thanksgiving was celebrated in 1619. Westover, virtually next door, was built by William Byrd II in 1730; an elegant Georgian house, it reflects the wealth and status of its owners. But it also reveals their fears; there is an escape tunnel from the house to the riverside in case of Indian attack. Further east lies Evelynton plantation, named after William Byrd II's daughter Evelyn (she died young, allegedly of a broken heart when her father refused to allow her to marry the man of her choice).[39]

And so the list continues; wonderful houses, dotting both northern and southern banks of the river. Each house, despite modern alterations and renovations, asserts its own distinctive claim to local fame, each offering an eloquent plea for the wealth and good taste of their founding fathers. But all needed the labour of their slaves. As you wander through their grounds today, it is difficult to find physical traces of the slaves' presence. Yet they made it all possible.

These are homes which were distinctively American, but which incorporated the best of British artefacts; the furnishings and silver-ware, the books and luxuries which were the domestic and cultured hallmarks of their British counterparts. Some planters even acquired the finishing touches of British gentility by educating their sons in Britain. Unlike the West Indian planters, the Virginians did not think of Britain as home. West Indians longed for a distant 'home' (which in fact they may never have visited); their North American cousins put down local roots. Home was Virginia; Britain merely provided the market, the luxuries and the finishing school for all that made them prosperous.

This élite of the plantocracy controlled society and politics throughout the Chesapeake. They constructed provincial centres (Williamsburg and Annapolis), dominated the law and the law-making process. Like their peers in Britain, their wealth and social style effectively created an unbridgeable chasm between themselves and their less prosperous neighbours. Theirs was a world of immense material and social privilege. But it was a privilege which had been won only recently, scraped from the local soil by settler forbears and their bands of black slaves.[40] Around this small band of major planters there developed an extraordinary political and social stability. The region was peaceable and prospering, its wealth to be seen in its orderly and bountiful land, divided and neatly ordered, and worked by gangs of largely submissive slaves. Though the slave-holders of the northern colonies faced the inherent troubles of a black slave society (that range of black resistance which was endemic to slave society), they rarely, if ever, faced the major traumas of their West Indian contemporaries. At home on their Chesapeake plantations the slave-owning élite were rarely in danger from their slaves. West Indians on the other hand rarely slept easily in their beds; their dreams were of violence and slave revenge – nightmares which all too often became reality. Again, the difference seems to lie in the distinctions between the plantation systems of the two regions. Tobacco was a gentler, less malignant enterprise; the sugar plantations unleashed a host of destructive social forces.

The Chesapeake slave system was more benign than anything we can detect in the British West Indies. Slaves were, it is true, subjected to arbitrary violence, legal marginality and harsh labour. But materially the slaves in the Chesapeake were better off than slaves in the Caribbean. And proof rests in the simple but crucial differences in birth-and mortality rates between the two regions. West Indian plantations devoured their slaves; in the Chesapeake the plantations spawned new generations of black slaves. There were also major differences in the behaviour and treatment meted out by the respective planters. Slave-owners in the Chesapeake came to think of themselves as patriarchs, obliged to respect their inferiors (both black and white). Planters respected their slaves' family life, their religion (increasingly, Christianity) and their broader social lives (providing it did not loosen the essential ties and restraints of slavery itself). The end result was that slaves in the tobacco region were less rigorously controlled, less meticulously harried, than slaves on West Indian plantations. They were in effect more autonomous. Planters were secure on their tobacco lands; planters on the sugar plantations felt anything but secure, and they nervously waited for the next tremor of violence or dissent from the slaves huddled in their large villages.[41]

Nowhere in colonial North America looked more like the Caribbean than South Carolina. It was in every sense a plantation society. The climate was hostile (though not as harmful as the West Indies) and from the first days of settlement it had a strong preference for African slaves. For the first generation of settlement, it was effectively linked to the West Indies, dispatching huge amounts of local produce and foodstuffs to feed the Caribbean plantations. In return slaves, conditioned in the islands, were poured into the Carolinas. Early cultivation of tobacco and indigo succumbed, after 1690, to an expanding rice industry. Rice plantations were first established close to Charleston between 1670 and 1720, spreading rapidly through the low country until it was possible to speak and write of the 'rice coast' of South Carolina.

Like tobacco in Virginia and sugar throughout the West Indies, rice laid the basis for the wealth of South Carolina. In the process the labour force rapidly became black and enslaved. By 1720 blacks outnumbered whites by two to one. In some areas the ratio was much higher. On the rice plantations of South Carolina, societies emerged which looked remarkably similar to those which dotted the sugar lands of the Caribbean. Some historians have argued that South Carolina in these years is really best seen as the most northerly tip of the West Indies. The style and social tone were decidely West Indian, especially Barbadian.[42] And the initial rice skills were African. The crop itself was imported from Madagascar and the early rice-growing technology was introduced by the Africans; it was a crop they were familiar with in large parts of West Africa. As the industry grew there were striking similarities to the way rice was cultivated in South Carolina and West Africa; in its 'planting, hoeing, winnowing and pounding'.[43]

A neat economic formula evolved. As more rice was exported, more and more slaves were imported, the one paying for (and making necessary) the other. By 1730, 20 million pounds of rice were exported annually. It was South Carolina's most valuable export and remained so throughout the colonial years; two-thirds went to Britain. Again, like sugar and tobacco, this slave-grown staple transformed the habits and tastes of the British people. They came to love rice pudding (cooked with sugar). Rice was the fourth most valuable export from British America (behind sugar, tobacco and wheat).[44]

In the mid-1720s South Carolina was importing 600 slaves a year; a decade later 2,000 a year flowed into the colony. In 1740 there were almost 40,000 Africans in South Carolina; they were now arriving direct from Africa. Slave-owning permeated the colony. Again, a small white minority came to own vast tracts of land. Although something like two-thirds of slave-owners owned only four slaves or fewer, there was a small and powerful élite which owned slaves in large numbers. These slaves brought their masters the highest per capita income in the American colonies.

Slave labour cleared the unhealthy and dangerous swamp lands of the low-lying coastal regions; it dug the ditches, constructed the dykes and banks. Rice plantations were organized quite differently from sugar. From the early days the planters used a task, rather than a gang system.[45] Slaves were assigned particular goals or jobs each morning; once completed, the slave had finished his or her day's work. In the sugar fields of the Caribbean, the slave gangs toiled on remorselessly (though there was a drift to task work in the last years of slavery). But the negative side of task work was that a slave had to work until the job was finished; stronger, nimbler, more experienced slaves might finish quickly. Many could not. Work began at sun-up (though slaves were woken earlier than that to be on hand to start work at first light). It was unpleasant and often dangerous work – a full agricultural year's cycle of labour in swampy and snake-infested fields under a brutal sun and in sapping humidity.

Like the tobacco and sugar planters, the rice planters of South Carolina acquired great wealth from their slaves. They enjoyed remarkable levels of income (four times higher than their peers in the Chesapeake for instance). They became so rich that they accumulated cash which they would lend out at interest. Not surprisingly, their lifestyle reflected this wealth. The provincial capitals and ports, notably Charleston, developed into complex and sophisticated urban and social centres. There and on the plantations, we see planto-cratic wealth at its most ostentatious. Planters' houses were a mixture of British styles and Caribbean influences. Elegant homes on the plantations and lavish residences in Charleston; these came to characterize the region's planters. But as wealth and style gravitated to Charleston, this created a degree of absenteeism on the plantations themselves. Many even followed the West Indian pattern and quit the colony, taking their money and their ambitions back 'home' to England. On the eve of the Revolution there were as many as fifty absentee South Carolina families living in London.[46]

This was not absenteeism on the Caribbean scale. Unlike American slave-owners to the north, South Carolinians were acutely aware of their vulnerability (made worse by the threats posed by the Spanish in Florida and the French in Louisiana). Slaves were kept in check by a punitive slave code based on the Barbadian model. Slaves resisted more vigorously than anywhere in North America; runaways were common. But nowhere was there slave violence on the West Indian scale. The task system of South Carolina, unlike the gang work of the Caribbean, allowed slaves a degree of autonomy. At work, in their quarters and with their families, slaves were much freer to arrange and organize their lives than was customary for West Indian slaves. They tended to be distant from the whites; were allowed to develop their own sense of cultural identity. Local whites, whatever their fears of servile black revolt, were simply unwilling (and even unable) to supervise black life as closely and minutely as did the planters of the West Indies.[47]

Perhaps it was the nature of white supervision and regulation (allied to the associated levels of punishment) which distinguished life for the slaves on the different plantation systems of the Americas. But was that difference ultimately a result of the different crops the slaves toiled in? Once again we return to the crucial role of work. Some crops were more difficult than others. Certain tropical staples had been organized in such a way that demanded the most rigorous and minute supervision and physical control. West Indian plantation slavery was, in the words of John Reeves in 1789, based on the assumption that 'Negroes were Property, and a Species of Property that needed a rigorous and vigilant Regulation'. Throughout the islands, the laws 'had uniformly this for their Object. To secure the Rights of Owners and maintain the Subordination of Negroes'.[48] All slave societies required strict supervision and subordination of the slaves, but the West Indies became famous for the severity of their codes and the rigour of their plantocratic regulation of the slaves. The slave societies which developed throughout the English-speaking Americas differed greatly. So too did the planter classes. Plantations, which produced the tropical goods for British tastes, looked remarkably similar throughout the Americas but were in fact very different. And their major differences were shaped by their respective crops. The bitterest of slave experiences were to be found in that sweetest of all crops – sugar.

7

In the Fields

Visitors to the slave colonies were generally awed by their first glimpse of slaves *en masse*. Amazed at the slaves' appearance, confused by their alien style and manners, observers hurried to record their varied reactions. When Lady Nugent met a gang of newly-landed Ibo slaves marching to their new home in Jamaica, she ordered her driver to stop

> that I might examine their countenances as they passed, and see if they looked unhappy; but they appeared perfectly the reverse. I bowed, kissed my hand and laughed; they did the same...One man attempted to shew more pleasure than the rest, by opening his mouth as wide as possible to laugh, which was rather a horrible grin. He shewed such truly cannibal teeth, all filed as they have them, that I could not help shuddering. He was of Herculean size, and really a tremendous looking creature.[1]

Lines and gaggles of slaves, many of them half-naked, with baskets, tools, boxes, food, utensils and parcels on their heads, were a daily sight in the slave colonies. As they headed to or from the fields, or for markets at the weekends, the travelling slaves impressed outsiders with their exotic looks, their alien babble; their utter strangeness. For Britons fresh to the region, slaves in the mass presented an amazing sight. Entering any Jamaican town, Lady Nugent was struck by the industrious confusion of slaves passing back and forth. Whenever slave-owners departed or arrived, they were preceded by slaves portering their goods, with

> finery in cases, or tin boxes, on their heads. Trunks of any size are carried in the same manner. In short, everything is put upon their head, from the largest to the

smallest thing; even a smelling bottle … I have often, on our tour, seen twelve or
fourteen negroes in one line of march, each bearing some article for the toiletee
on his head.[2]

Outsiders seemed most impressed by slaves at work in the fields. Advancing
side by side through the sugar cane, working with a collective rhythm – often
to a collective song or chant – the slaves were utterly different in appearance,
sound and style from anything a European would have seen at home. A
Scottish naval officer, looking at rice slaves in South Carolina, told how they
'were working in a long string, exactly like a row of ants, with baskets of earth
on their heads'. It was sapping, debilitating work and at the end of the day the
slaves 'especially the women, looked tired enough'.[3]

Time and again, observers remarked on the regimented appearance of
slaves at work; in the fields they worked as a team, like a group of well-drilled
soldiers. Indeed, military metaphors readily sprang to mind when observers
described working slaves. They were, in the words of Thomas Roughley, 'the
field battalions', which were 'Brigaded by its chief field-officer, the head
driver.'[4]

Slaves were in the Americas to work. Whatever roles they carved out for
themselves, independently or within the slave plantations, were incidental to
their main purpose of toiling for their owners. In time, slaves came to occupy
most occupational roles throughout the Americas, from sailors to cowboys. But
the great bulk of them were employed in the fields, slaves as much to the
rhythms and cycles of the agricultural year as to the whims and fancies of their
owners. At first, however, there were no fields at all.

One of the first tasks of the slaves was to create the fields, the plots of
cultivable land, the roads and dykes, the pathways and patches of manageable
land; hacking back the frontier and wilderness and imposing an orderly and
fruitful management on the face of the environment. Across the Americas,
clearing the land to make way for cultivation was the first stage of European
settlement and it was undertaken by people of all colours living in relatively
small groups, clinging to the edge of the wild frontier but slowly and painfully
pushing forward the limits of human habitation. In the bush, work was crude;
relations between black and white were open; both undertook whatever task
needed doing. There was little sense of demarcation, little sense that certain
kinds of work were inappropriate for whites or predestined for blacks. As they
hacked at or burned the bush, black and white frequently took turns at the
same task. Often the white owner and black slave could be found holding
opposite ends of the same saw.

Just as they worked together, so they fought together. In the islands, in
Virginia and South Carolina, bands of black slaves were used as soldiers and
defenders against the ever-present threat posed by local inhabitants. But as the
tide of settlement gradually swept the native Americans back, pushed them

further and further away, or reduced them to ineffectual and dwindling bands (reduced in the main by disease and violence), the idea of arming slaves took on a different role. Black soldiers were to be found throughout the history of slavery in the Americas. But the rise of the major slave-worked staples – sugar, tobacco and rice – saw the relegation of the slaves to the fields. Armed slaves were, on the whole, too dangerous for the peace of mind of most slave-holders, though at moments of crisis – local rebellion, foreign invasion or fratricidal struggle among the whites – slaves thought to be loyal were periodically placed under arms.

As the wilderness and the Indians gradually receded before the advance of Europeans and Africans, the West Indian islands and the eastern seaboard of North America began to display a new face. The chaotic beauty of the natural wilderness gave way to fringes and pockets of organized rural development. And as the small-holdings gave way to large plantations, the easy-going pioneering relations between black and white gave way to a strict racial and occupational divide.

In the West Indies the sugar slaves were divided into gangs, a highly efficient labour system designed to squeeze from them the maximum of effort. It was also a key method for the control and discipline of crowds of slaves.

The First, Second and Third Gang each had its own distinctive but complementary function, from the most physically taxing work done by the strong slaves in the First Gang through to the gentler tasks undertaken by the very young and old in the Third Gang. The First Gang formed the plantation's shock troops, tackling the heaviest of duties. They were, said one planter, 'the flower of all the field battalions, drafted and recruited from all the other gangs, as they come of age to endure severe labour. They were drilled to become veterans in the most arduous field undertakings... They are the very essence of an estate, its support in all weathers and necessities.' It was this gang, male and female, which undertook the back-breaking and often dangerous work: building, digging, planting, manuring, cutting and burning, carrying and loading. Equipped with 'good hoes, bills and knife, and axes' they advanced like an army on the tall bank of ripe sugar cane, methodically slicing and stripping, pushing back the line of cane until they left behind them the empty land, littered with decaying trash. It was hard, punishing work, suited only to the young, healthy and fit.

Planting new cane was no less demanding. Dr Jones wrote in 1812.

It has often occurred to me that a gang of Negroes in the act of holing for canes, when hard driven appeared to be as formidable as a phalanx of infantry by the rapid movement of their hoes... while I have been astonished how such habits could enable beings to persevere, so many hours in such violent effort.[5]

Wherever there was heavy work to be done, the First Gang was drafted in; into the fields, on the roads, in the buildings and in the factories. At the busiest time, when the cane was being harvested and processed through the factory (between January and July), First Gang slaves often ended their day-long labours in the fields at sunset, before trooping off to help with the heavy jobs in the factory.

As the First Gang cut a path through the cane, they were followed by the Second Gang, 'composed of people, who are thought to be of rather weakly habits, mothers of suckling children, youths drafted from the children's gang, from 12 to 18 years of age, and elderly people that are sufficiently strong for field work'. They cleaned up the field; in the factory they cleared the factory floor of its crushed cane and trash.

Behind them lurked the Third Gang, made up of 'the rising generation', the very young or the old, who serviced the other gangs (bringing refreshments, for instance), carrying grass to the cattle and undertaking the simple field tasks. It was here that most of the children served their labouring apprenticeship, learning the skills and the routines needed for promotion to more onerous work. At Worthy Park, Jamaica, the Creole slave Kent was placed in the Third Gang when he was seven in 1814; he graduated to the Second Gang at the age of fifteen and finally into the First Gang when he was fully grown and strong.[6] In the same era, the female slave Amelia, born at Worthy Park in 1784, was put into the 'grass gang' (of children) aged six, the Third Gang three years later, moving on to the Second Gang at the age of sixteen. By 1815 she was labouring in the First Gang.

The gang system provided the planters with a perfect tool for socializing the slaves from their earliest years to a life of disciplined toil. And it was an ideal system for tapping the fruits of that most labour-intensive of crops – sugar. But what happened when the slaves' strength failed; when old age, sickness or accident reduced their usefulness? The gang system was like a game of snakes and ladders; elevation to one rank might be swiftly followed by a rapid slide to less 'useful' (and therefore less rewarded) work. When Kent, the Worthy Park slave, lost a leg in an accident in 1831 (at the age of twenty-four), he was of no further use to the First Gang. Soon he was relegated to the role of watchman (a job normally reserved for the old or infirm).[7] Duncan, another Worthy Park slave in those same years, had enjoyed a 'privileged' career, graduating from the young field gangs to domestic work in the Great House and later working for twenty-five years as a joiner. By the age of fifty-eight he was described as 'weakly', and had been reduced to the rank of watchman.

Time and again plantation papers trace the decline as well as the rise of individual slaves, as maturity took them into positions which demanded strength or skills, only for old age or infirmity to reduce them, often prematurely, to minor positions; caring for the young or the sick, tending the animals or crops. Only when they were 'useless', chronically sick, aged or disabled, did slaves cease to be assigned to tasks around the property. From their earliest years to the end of their lives, slaves were categorized and organized along the lines of economic utility. Yet it was a system – at least in the sugar islands – which by its very harshness and unremitting demands actively undermined their utility by corroding health, fertility and longevity.

It was always assumed that the best way to run a plantation was to keep the slaves at work, from their childhood to old age.

> The supernumerary invalids and superannuated persons who can do any slight work, together with such middle-aged slaves who are affflicted with asthma, boneache, or other disorders which require occasional rest, should be put under the direction of a sensible negro of their own sort, and occupied in planting and cleaning quick-fences, either round the cane or grass pieces. Though much cannot be expected from them yet it is best to keep them at some employment; and such work is easy and of utility.

Even the tiniest of children should, it was thought, be reared to the needs of the plantations. Those between the ages of three to five should be tended by a nurse 'in little playful gang': 'Each child should have a little basket, and be made somewhat useful by gathering up fallen trash and leaves, and pulling up weeds.'[8] Not until the coming of a new industrial, factory-based system in Britain in the early nineteenth century was so much thought and attention devoted to the minute management of labour.

Labouring in the sugar fields was quite different from most other forms of slave work in the Americas. What made the sugar plantations so unusual was their mixture of agriculture and industry. Cane-cutting had to be carefully meshed with the mechanical processes of the factory. Delays in the fields or mechanical breakdown in the factory could jeopardize the whole operation. The sugar industry was thought to be 'the most uncertain production upon the face of the earth',[9] a complex mix of agricultural experience (and good fortune), and the vagaries of mechanical processing. To this were added the unpredictable elements of tropical weather, the dangers of transatlantic cross-ings and the uncertainties of market prices in Europe. That so many planters stayed with sugar is an indication of the wealth it could disgorge when all went well.

The slaves, of course, did not need to worry about these various difficulties, save only when shortcomings in their own area brought retribution or hunger on their heads. On thriving estates they were pressed hard; on struggling or declining estates they were the first to suffer – short of food, clothing and care, slaves on such properties cut a pathetic figure.

Sugar slaves were busy throughout the year. Planting new cane took place between August and October (though much of the new cane sprouted from old roots, ratoons, allowed to stay in the ground and flourish again). Preparing the land and planting consumed much of the slaves' energies in the second half of the year. As the sugar cane grew it transformed the entire panorama of the plantations. Soon the bare fields became swaying walls of tall cane which made a distinctive noise when the wind whistled through the dense foliage. Experienced sugar men tested the cane and when, early in the new year, it seemed at its best, the slaves were turned loose, in gang formation, to cut it down, strip off the foliage and transport the weeping cane to the nearest factory for crushing and processing. For months before, the skilled men, black and white, had made ready the factory, trying to ensure that the mechanical process continued smoothly; breakdowns would leave cut cane rotting on the ground.

Field work in and out of crop was difficult, uncomfortable and strenuous, interrupted by sudden downpours or baked by the unrelenting sun. From dawn to dusk, the slaves bent their backs to whatever task the season demanded. And each task had its own exquisite pain. Sun-up to sunset was the normal working day for field slaves in crop time (though improvements were introduced in the last days of slavery). But, depending on the routines of the local sugar factory, slaves could be organized into shifts – partly in the fields, partly in the factories – of up to thirty hours at a stretch. In such regimes, the six-day week entailed ninety-six hours of labouring. This was the working routine for field slaves for fully six months in the agricultural year.[10]

The slave quarters were roused about 4.00 A.M. by a bell or conch shell (the conch shell was also the instrument used to rally rebellious slaves). Slaves were in the fields, depending on local custom, by 5.00 or 6.00 A.M. Jamaican slaves had breakfast in the field at nine, an hour and a half lunch break at midday, before labouring on to 6.00 P.M. All told, Jamaican field slaves worked twelve hours a day, those on the smaller islands ten hours, though the number of hours declined in the early nineteenth century.[11]

Like rural labourers everywhere, slaves used the natural unfolding of the day and the season to calculate the time and hence the pace of their work. The position of the sun provided a rough sense of time to the labouring slaves, but their hours of work, like their lives in general, were determined by their masters. There were, it is true, ways in which slaves could pace themselves; tricks and agreements that could moderate the labour demanded of them. But the field slaves' room for manoeuvre in the gang system was strictly limited. Slaves elsewhere, who worked at a task system, could hasten or retard their work as they saw fit. Gang slaves were tied much more rigidly to a rate and pace of work which they found hard to regulate.

Work in the sugar fields was team work. Slaves depended on each other for overall success and for staving off the punishments which were the inevitable consequence of back-sliding and slowness. The work was scrutinized as it proceeded by book-keepers, overseers and planters. A great deal of thought went into getting the best from the slaves: 'An animating song, struck up by one of them, should be encouraged and chorussed while at work; for they are thought good composers in their own way.' Planters came to appreciate that encouragement was more effective than brutality. 'No punishment should be inflicted, but what is absolutely necessary, and that with mercy.' Refreshments and food should be provided at regular intervals, or when needed. 'Keeping them in heart, they will work accordingly.'[12]

Like coal-mining or deep-sea fishing, work in the sugar fields was an occupation involving distinctive pains and dangers. It involved the heaviest work on the plantations and it demanded most from the slaves both in hours and physical commitment. At Worthy Park in 1789, 70 per cent of the able slaves were in the permanent field force. Of the 133 slaves involved, eighty-nine were women.[13] Whatever preference planters may have had for male slaves, they were obviously willing to use women to undertake the hard field work.

Male or female, black slaves were thought to be suited by nature for labour in the tropics. The owner of Worthy Park declared in 1832 that 'The white man cannot labour under a burning sun, without certain death, though the negro can in all climates with impunity'. A generation earlier another Jamaican planter, William Beckford, had argued that 'the climate is congenial to their natural feelings [because] the careful benevolence of Providence has thickened their skins'.[14]

Each field task was difficult and tiresome. The holes dug for the cane were deep and wide in heavy soils baked by the sun. Slaves carried manure in baskets up to 80 lb in weight on their heads. They were reported as working with baskets of dung on their heads and food in their hands. The cut cane was heavy and cumbersome; it took 20 tons of cane to produce one ton of sugar. And even the crop-over, celebrated, like harvest the world over, with music, drink and food, heralded not so much a respite as a change of pace. The slaves had to catch up on neglected tasks: making good the damage to fields, roads and buildings, to care for the plantations' animals. All this was in addition to whatever work they needed to do around their own plots and homes in the little time (and daylight) left to them at the end of the working day or on Sundays.

Work in the tobacco fields was quite different from that in the sugar plantations. Virginian planters liked to plant tobacco seed about twelve days after Christmas. Small quarter-acre beds, enriched with animal manure, were seeded and then covered with branches against possible frosts. In late April – the exact timing was a matter of the planter's judgement – the seedlings were transplanted to the main fields. The fields had been prepared and the slaves hurried the seedlings to their new location, planted by the most skilled of the field slaves.

Tobacco began to ripen throughout the summer. As it did, each leaf was given close attention; neglect, if only a matter of days, could prove disastrous. The plants needed attentive and thorough weeding. When eight to twelve leaves had appeared, the plant was 'topped' to prevent it from flowering. In September, when the planter deemed the moment right, slaves began to cut the leaves. The leaves were then hung by the slaves in large curing barns to dry. Here – as at all the earlier stages of tobacco production – there was a fine line between success and failure. Scrutinizing the drying tobacco daily, planters had to make a careful decision. When the tobacco was dry, but not brittle, the slaves began to strip it from the stalks. Tobacco was even more lucrative if it had been 'stemmed', stripped carefully from the leaf's web. Here again, slave skill was crucial. It was pernickety, time-consuming work which employed them long into the night. The tobacco was then laid, leaf upon leaf, into massive hogsheads (made by other plantation craftsmen) where it was pressed into a compact form. When the hogsheads weighed about 1,000 lb, they were rolled down to the nearest waterside and stacked into warehouses to await dispatch. In the new year the tobacco was transported to public warehouses and finally shipped to Europe in the spring – fifteen months after the initial planting. By then the new tobacco seeds were already in the ground.[15]

It was a crop cycle which allowed few periods of complete rest for the slaves, or relaxation of vigilance for the planter. Whatever free time slaves were able to find had to be squeezed from their routines of work.

It would be wrong, however, to imagine that tobacco slaves were the mere instruments of their owners and drivers. Like slaves throughout the Americas, they tried to regulate and pace their working lives. Tobacco slaves worked in small teams of between ten and twenty (though sometimes fewer), often working with or close to local whites. The smaller planter was best able to control the slaves' working lives by personal scrutiny, but the smaller the slave-holding, the more valuable were the slaves' time and effort to their owner, and the greater their influence. Bigger planters could more easily sustain losses when slaves dragged their feet, ran away or resisted in some way. In a slave team of twelve, one runaway or recalcitrant slave was a costly burden to carry.

Everywhere planters felt the need to be vigilant, if only to keep the slaves at work. George Washington himself wrote that though they were 'capable of much labour [they] require more of the master's eye'. An observer of Maryland's slaves in the 1740s commented: 'when their masters and mistresses backs are turned, they are idle and neglect their business'.[16] Slaves were driven hard from spring through the summer; replanting, weeding and harvesting (though the word 'harvest' was never used for the tobacco cycle), each stage both intensive and uncertain.

With the tobacco in the curing houses, slave-owners often had to find work for their slaves, turning them over to general labouring and repairs around their properties. But even at the busiest of times, slaves had their own ways of slowing the pace or deflecting the demands of their owners. One slave's sickness could lead to group slacking. Innovations (a new plough or cart) led to less slave effort. Sickness, feeling out of sorts, imaginary pregnancy, these and a host of human frailties were proffered as excuses for being less than industrious. In 1771 Landon Carter, the great Virginian planter, wrote in his diary: 'My Wench, McGinnis' Mary, either shams her fits, or now has fits every attack of her ague and fever. I do suppose the former, for I always have known her a violent cryer whenever anything ailed her so as to hollow to be heard all over the plantations.' His slave Sarah posed an even more peculiar problem: 'There is curiosity in this Creature. She worked none last year pretending to be with Child and this she was full 11 months before she was brought to bed.'[17]

Try as they might, tobacco planters, like their peers in the sugar islands, were never able fully to regulate and control the working lives of their slaves. Planters everywhere tried their own mix of incentive and punishment; too much of one or the other was self-defeating. Out in the fields slaves tried as best they could to impose their own pace. Yet it was in the fields where black and white were at their closest; where they met most frequently and for long periods, learning each other's foibles and weaknesses.

From the age of nine, slave children began to work part time in the tobacco fields or otherwise helped around the plantations. By their late teens they were in the fields full-time, their strength and developing expertise in their varied skills of tobacco cultivation maturing with age. Old age, sickness or disability consigned them to less demanding work, but only total incapacity brought complete relief from slave work of any kind. In 1791 fully one-half of Robert Carter's Virginian slaves were still at work between the ages of sixty-five and ninety.

The tobacco slaves of Virginia were much more fertile than slaves in the Caribbean. Planters in the Chesapeake enjoyed what West Indian planters only dreamt of: a surplus of slaves. There were too many for economic use in the tobacco fields and from about 1750 onwards the planters were able to hire out their surplus slaves for general agricultural labour on contracts of up to a year. This often had the effect of disrupting slave family life, as the (mainly male) slaves were contracted out, far and wide, to work for a new, temporary master.

Tobacco planters needed fewer slaves as the eighteenth century advanced because, unlike their West Indian counterparts, they mechanized work in the fields. In the process, lines of demarcation developed between the labourers and the semi-skilled slaves. The best field hands became foremen, well-versed and skilled in tobacco cultivation and slave management. The basic field slaves – women, young adults and a few remaining men – were left to plant, weed and harvest the tobacco.[18] What we can see on both the tobacco and sugar plantations is the emergence of a mature agricultural and labouring system which had spawned a hierarchy of labour and skills, all carefully integrated and designed both to yield the best returns while, at the same time, imposing order and discipline on the black labour force.

On the larger plantations slaves were in charge of their own patterns and routines of work. Ostensibly under the control of their owners and masters, they could, when working in larger slave groups, dictate their own pace, playing off their immediate overseer against the slave-owner. But too little work or effort, inattentive habits or slackening production would readily invite blows or lashes. It was a fine line for the field slave to tread. Too slack or indifferent, they might merely invite the pain of the whip; too industrious or energetic, they might incur the animosity of fellow-slaves.[19]

It was a truism throughout the slave colonies that slaves were lazy, indisciplined and incapable of working as their owners desired without the punishments, vigilance and constraints of slavery itself. Such accusations were, of course, part of the slave-owning ideology, part of the need to justify a system which was so clearly out of kilter with the rest of the Atlantic world. If the land-and slave-owning class were clear that industry and time were invaluable elements in the making of wealth, their views were rarely shared by their inferiors both black and white. Employers of labour on both sides of the Atlantic took pains to inculcate the lessons of industry in their labour force. The problems of encouraging a discipline of labour were especially acute among the slave-owning class, yet they had at their disposal an array of punishments denied to the employers of free labour. The systematic brutality doled out to labouring slaves was not part of the disciplinary process of free labour. It would be wrong to imagine that slaves, in the tobacco or sugar fields, were kept at work simply by fear of physical punishment. They had a range of incentives − especially when the local economy had reached a mature form − which encouraged them to work effectively and efficiently. Promotions, material rewards, free time; these and other rewards were dangled before the slaves as the crumbs which fell from the planters' tables. There is little evidence to suggest that the slaves were any more than reluctant guests in their house of bondage, but they generally tried their best to make the most of their miserable and unfortunate lot.

In sharp contrast to slaves labouring under the gang system were those who worked by task − allocated a certain job to do − and who were free to pursue their own activities when the task was completed. Task work was common among slaves working in a range of New World activities: in arrowroot, cocoa, coffee, hemp, naval stores, pimento, timber and rice. In time, more and more slave-owners came to favour the task system, even in the West Indies where the sugar gangs dominated the local economy and shaped the local white mentality. By 1838 it was remarked of the West Indies that slaves, 'weed the coffee-field, picked the coffee from the trees, billed(?) the savannah or pastures, and built the stone walls, by task'.[20] By then, the last years of British slavery, the task system had begun to intrude itself even into the sugar fields, partly at the insistence of the imperial Parliament in its efforts to curb the excesses of the planters and to limit and control the labours of the slaves.

In mainland America the task system was most common among the slaves in the rice-growing region, especially in South Carolina. Rice cultivation was horrible, filthy work. At first the rice was cultivated in inland swamps but by the mid-eighteenth century the introduction of flood-gates and irrigation schemes enabled planters to harness the tidal rivers of South Carolina. Slowly the lower reaches of the vast river systems were lined by rice plantations. There the slaves laboured in the unhealthy swamps. In late spring, the rice was sown in rows 15 inches apart; the field was flooded and the seed sprouted. Thereafter a sequence of flooding and draining allowed the rice to sprout and the slaves to weed. In August and September the rice was harvested, threshed, polished and then sold in the winter.

Most of the work was back-breaking, difficult (in mud), sometimes dangerous (the rice fields were infested with local snakes) and unhealthy (the swampy lands bred a host of diseases). And unlike work in the tobacco fields to the north, the rice was produced almost uniquely by slaves. Here – like the sugar fields in the islands – was work fit only for a slave, for a black. In the steamy heat of the summer, when the slaves were working hardest, local whites fled the plantations for the relative health and comfort of their homes in Charleston. Slaves were, in effect, left alone under the control and guidance of their black drivers (see Chapter 8). It was a labour system which evolved without the close scrutiny and personal supervision of a white slave-ownership or white managerial presence. True, the slave-drivers could be as brutal and harsh as the white overseer, but the slaves in the South Carolina rice fields could not be kept at work by the orchestrated gang system so common in other slave colonies.

Slaves were given a specific task to complete in a certain time. It was common for those tasks to be completed by mid-afternoon, a far cry from the toil throughout the daylight hours so common in the West Indies. Thereafter the local slaves were free to work on their own lands. But if a slave consistently finished the task early it was likely that the task was altered. And the tasks were calibrated according to age and physical condition.

Work began at sunrise, mainly to avoid the heat of the day. With a break at 9.00 A.M. and dinner by 3.00 P.M., the rice slave could be finished by mid-afternoon. Each job on a rice plantation was accorded specific conditions. An able-bodied slave was expected to break 1,200 square feet of land with a spade. A trench-digger had to dig three-quarters of an acre per day. A sower had to sow half an acre. In the fields, men and women worked side by side but the heavier work (ditching, banking) was left to the men.[21]

Hours of work were shorter on the rice plantations than in the tobacco fields, but the work was more strenuous. It was extremely demanding manual labour which involved a full year of effort, for much of the time in appalling physical conditions. But it was an extra-ordinarily successful labour system which secured hard labour in return for small rewards, without the savagery of the West Indian gang system. It allowed slaves a degree of flexibility in their working (and therefore their personal) lives which would have been unthinkable in the West Indies.

8

Skills

Skilled slaves were vital to the mature slave economies of the British colonies, but how many were as accomplished as the slave discussed in the *Virginia Gazette* in 1768? 'He is an indifferent shoemaker, a good butcher, ploughman and carterer; an excellent sawyer, and waterman, understands breaking oxen well, and is one of the best sythmen in *America*; in short, he is so ingenious a fellow that he can turn his hand to any thing.' He was a slave-owner's dream. Seven years later, in South Carolina, when a local man prepared to sell a group of slave painters he proclaimed: 'As to their Abilities, he thinks them evident, they having transacted the whole of his Business, without any hired Assistance; and he has taken no little Pains in initiating them in the true Principles of their Profession.'[1] Even allowing for the licence used in newspaper advertisements, these were remarkable men. Wherever we look, similarly accomplished blacks emerge from the evidence. When a Coromantee slave ran away and hid himself in Kingston, Jamaica, in 1790, readers of the *Daily Advertiser* were told: 'he is artful, speaks the English, French, Dutch, Danish and Portuguese languages'.[2]

What are we to make of such slaves, except the obvious point that they were exceptional? Even so, they give an insight into the range of skills, accomplishments and abilities which were cultivated in the slave societies of the Americas. In time, slaves and free blacks could be found in every occupational nook and cranny throughout the Americas, from sailors on the ships which served as a lifeline to Europe and beyond, to cowboys who lived on the very edge of westward American expansion.

As colonial life moved from the precarious and violent world of early settlement to the complex maturity of a highly populated and developed exporting society, more and more slaves took up new roles as skilled workers.

Slave-owners bought Africans for their muscle power; they needed healthy, young rural labourers. But the mature slave societies needed more than muscle power to thrive. The complexities of international trade, of thriving American urban life and of changing rural society throughout the slave colonies demanded and then created a host of skills. As society developed, it spawned black occupations which would have been unimaginable in the early days of slavery. The black gunsmiths, watchmakers and goldsmiths, black literate preachers, painters and builders – all these and more would have seemed unnecessary luxuries to an earlier generation of planters. Yet these slave occupations were, directly or indirectly, a consequence of the success of the plantocracy.

The plantations were built and worked by unskilled black labour. But the sugar, rum, tobacco and rice could not be extracted, processed and dispatched without skilled workers. The majority of slaves on sugar plantations were labourers, but a sizeable minority were artisans and tradesmen. When the French raided St Kitts in 1706 and 'stole' local slaves, the planters claimed compensation for their losses; their returns show that 64 per cent were field hands, 10 per cent in the factory, 14 per cent were servants and 12 per cent were tradesmen (overseers and the like).[3] On all the plantations for which we have detailed studies, local slave society took the form of an occupational pyramid; a large labouring majority at the base, above which was a smaller number of semi-skilled slaves (craftsmen, domestics) with a small élite of drivers and headmen at the top. The field gangs may have been the 'battalions' among the slaves, but they were obviously headed and complemented by a small black élite whose special skills and leadership qualities were equally vital to the economic functioning of the plantations. Nevertheless, the privileges of those élite slaves would, in time, be subsumed into the penury and miseries of old age.

Sugar plantations not only grew the sugar cane but also processed the sugar. The slave distillers and boilers knew how each stage of the manufacturing process worked – when the sugar was ready, when to add the ingredients – a vital skill, acquired by experience. Once slaves had learned this work they were generally left alone to get on with it, occasionally supervised by a book-keeper.[4] Their efforts were complemented by the work of the coopers, carpenters and smiths who made the barrels and hogsheads in which the sugar and rum left the property. Plantations needed a host of skilled men and women to keep sugar-making in full flow once crop and the factory had started up. Behind the buzz of work which consumed all and sundry on a sugar plantation in crop time there lurked other essential slaves: the smiths, masons and carpenters who kept the fabric of the estate – factories, ware-houses, hospitals, sheds, homes and workshops – in good working order.

The homes and plantation buildings were serviced by the slave craftsmen; clothing for master and man was made and repaired by slave tailors, seam-

stresses and shoemakers; household effects were made and repaired by pew-
terers and joiners. Female domestics cared for the resident whites; cleaning
and repairing their clothes and homes, preparing and cooking their meals,
nursing them in their frequent ailments (often with the help of African
medicines and cures), all the while fending off or succumbing to their sexual
advances and aggression. It shocked outsiders that whites grew lazy in the
West Indies. For people who readily complained of their slaves' incurable
laziness, the slave-owning class seemed exceptionally indolent, thanks in large
part to the ubiquity of domestic slave labour. At its worst, domestic slavery
could be more intolerable than work in the fields. Though the slave could
avoid the rigours of weather and tiring exertions, they could not escape the
attention and idiosyncrasies of resident whites.

Slave gangs worked under a driver. The head driver was described as 'the
most important personage in the slave population of an estate'. The driver
directed the slaves' labour, coaxing and threatening, generally equipped with
'the emblem of his rank and dignity, a polished staff or wand, with spongy
crooks on it to lean on, and a short-handled, tangible whip'. Ideally the driver
would be a strong, athletic man with good judgement and 'character'; clean
and tidy, accustomed to field work, respectful to white people but 'suffering no
freedom from those under him'. Thomas Roughley thought it rare 'to find this
mass of perfection in a negro'.[5] On the bigger plantations the drivers were
crucial, standing between the planters and the slaves and translating the slave-
owner's wishes and general directions into hard labouring returns. Drivers
kept the field slaves at their work, ensuring that they were both industrious
and productive, punishing shortcomings and slacking.[6] It was a position of
responsibility for which there was no formal training. Those blessed with the
right physique, experience and inclination emerged as obvious drivers. But the
driver's central position as the goader and organizer of the slaves' daily lives
could be turned to more dangerous ends. A man of physical strength and local
standing, able to lead and organize slaves, could just as easily lead the slaves
against the whites.

Africans came to the Americas with a range of their own skills and labouring
experiences; basket and pottery making, cloth-makers, certain agricultural
work (notably in rice production). But the slave artisans in the Americas
were, in general, taught their skills anew. Initially, and obviously, they learned
the new skills from white craftsmen. In Virginia the growth of slave artisans on
the tobacco plantations gradually edged out white craftsmen. For much of the
eighteenth century black and white artisans worked side by side, but in
time the slave artisans came to predominate. Thomas Jefferson 'relied almost
exclusively on his black carpenters, joiners, blacksmiths, and painters', though
all had been trained by whites.[7] Time and again, a similar pattern unfolded in
the northern colonies. A planter hired a white craftsman (or woman) to
supervise and train slave apprentices; in time they took over the skilled

work on the property. In this way, plantations came to have their own spinners and weavers, skilled iron workers, chair-makers, tailors, smiths, silversmiths and tanners. Jefferson himself remarked that numbers of slaves 'have been brought up to the handicraft arts, and from the circumstance have always been associated with the whites'.[8] In a wide range of skills, free white taught enslaved black. In their turn, the black artisans taught other slaves, often their own offspring or family. This story was repeated in the tobacco fields.

The bigger the plantation the larger the group of local craftsmen and artisans. As the planters became more wealthy, and as they effected the life-style they thought appropriate to their rank and prosperity, they began to surround themselves with domestic servants. Though not all were skilled, the training, habits and disposition of servants were obviously quite different from the labour demanded of field slaves. Domestics were expected to show greater refinement, greater familiarity with white customs and domestic manners (though this is not to deny that the domestic habits of many planters were crude in the extreme: West Indian planters were infamous for their coarse manners, their domestic drunkenness and sometimes their squalid habits). As plantations grew, there was greater scope for the skills and services of a new kind of slave class. Servants were those slaves who could satisfy their owners' domestic needs and whims, who could cook to his tastes (though those tastes were themselves clearly influenced by African ingredients and cooking), who could manage his household and maintain the physical fabric of plantocratic life: spinning, weaving and making clothes, making and repairing shoes, guns, furnishings.[9]

It was, however, in the tobacco fields that changes in slave society became more striking. In the second half of the eighteenth century the growth in plantation size and the introduction of new technology helped create a growing class of skilled slaves. Drivers (chosen from among the field hands) took over the management of slaves in the fields. Slaves with a particular skill or expertise were prized by their owners and were more valuable when sold. Three slaves, sold in 1763, were described as 'valuable young Fellows, that have been brought up to Carting and Plowing, and understand Plantation business of all Sorts'. Whenever a slave possessed a skill, it was sure to be stressed in a newspaper advertisement.[10]

In return for their skills, artisan slaves were treated better. They were better fed, rewarded and cared for by planters who appreciated their greater economic usefulness. Some of the skilled slaves became veritable jacks-of-all-trades; presumably they were allowed free rein to develop whatever natural patitudes they had. Harry, a Maryland slave, was a 'tolerable good shoemaker, clapboard carpenter, cooper, and indeed handy at anything he is put about, particularly waiting in the house, gardening, mowing, driving a carriage, and the management of horses'. Stephen Butler, a runaway in 1771, played 'on a fiddle, and is a wheelwright, Sawyer, tight Cooper, and House Carpenter by trade'.[11] Such skills provided the slaves with a much greater mobility than field slaves. They were, inevitably, sent hither and yon on tasks for their owners. They were also hired out to other employers and thus travelled more than field hands. Not surprisingly, they tended to run away more often. They were, at its simplest, exposed to a more varied and tempting social experience; they saw and experienced life well beyond the confines of their immediate plantation. Many clearly met and developed relationships with slaves on distant properties. Many found the temptations of the outside world too difficult to resist.

Skilled female labour was primarily domestic. Female slaves learned their skills in their teens. By the time they were sixteen or seventeen they were competent domestics or workers in textiles. Female domestics in Virginia, for example, rarely came to the trade late in life; it was not so much a reward for labouring work but a skill for which they were trained early on. In 1751 a sixteen-year-old was offered for sale: 'fit for Plantation Work, or very capable of making a good House Wench, having for some Months served as such in a Small Family.'[12] In the northern colonies slave domestics were generally under the close supervision of a local white woman. Whether tyrannical or tolerant, this often intimate supervision was itself a severely restrictive force in the lives of female slaves. They found it much more difficult to slack, to escape (if only for a few hours) or to seek a respite from the routines of labour by imposing their own pace.

So many of the West Indian planters and their male helpers were without resident wives that their domestics were more often under male than female control. Domestics were more numerous in the West Indies than they were in Britain at the same time. Yet it would be wrong to imagine that planters surrounded themselves with slaves whose role it was to reflect their owners' wealth and status rather than to satisfy a particular function. In any case, most sugar plantations were so isolated that there were few people on hand to impress. The truth of the matter is that the domestic servants served a series of economic purposes. As in the northern colonies, West Indian slave domestics cared for the physical fabric of the buildings and for the welfare of the whites in the house.

Work for slave domestics in the Caribbean was less demanding than for the field slaves. Escape into domestic work marked a step up; domestics were punished by relegation to the field gangs – a clear sign which job was more highly valued (by both master and slave).[13] But life in the Great House, or in the homes of the other plantation whites, was rarely easy. Female domestics were everywhere closely supervised. In the male-dominated world of the West Indian plantations they were easy prey to sexually aggressive men in and around the house. The great majority of slave domestics were female and many planters simply assumed that their favourite domestics would provide sexual favours when required, even for visiting white neighbours or friends.

In time the Caribbean planters came to favour local-born slaves for their domestics, assuming that they were more intelligent than Africans. It was claimed in 1831 that they had 'greater intelligence, greater skill and better moral feeling, because the proprietor had endeavoured to train up his people in the best manner possible adapted to the circumstance of the colony'. Just as the Africans were sought for their strength, so Creoles were thought prefer-able for the more developed social senses and skills suited to working in the Great House.[14]

Whatever the reality of these judgements, the evidence shows that planters were more likely to place local-born slaves in skilled professions and domestic service. As the plantations developed, the planters also opted for 'coloured' domestics, obviously rewarding their various paramours by giving their joint offspring the more privileged work in the house. Few planters accepted their children as legitimate offspring, but they often bestowed on them and their mothers a string of material benefits and privileges generally denied to other slaves.

The development of a large domestic slave class is also a clear sign of the way whites had come to accept living under the daily (and intrusive) control of certain blacks, allowing the most intimate corners of their lives to be ordered by their domestic slaves. In their turn, the descendants of Africans learned to provide what their owners required. Both sides began to speak the same language and to share the same vocabulary of social experience.

The use of blacks as domestics became so fashionable that it soon crossed the Atlantic. Aristocrats and then their propertied inferiors began to copy this New World habit. Blacks, often dressed in the most bizarre and colourful costumes, head-dresses and insignia, graced the homes and carriages of British landed society in the eighteenth century. They can still be seen in portraits, in contemporary cartoons and drawings, lurking in the corners, close to their masters and mistresses, providing artistic contrast to the family itself and offering a hint of their owners' wealth and status.

Peter the Great recruited black servants and slaves (from Holland) for use in his court in the late seventeenth century. Thereafter, blacks began to appear ever more prominently in and around his court, as the Russian aristocracy and wealthy vied with each other to affect the style established by their ruler.[15] In Britain and France, as we might expect, the use of black servants and slaves was more common still. But throughout Europe this employment of black slaves was a fad, a fashion which served little economic purpose save to enhance the status of the employer. There was, after all, no shortage of local white labour to use as servants.

The plantations spawned goods and styles which served an international community. Their goods graced the tables of the highest and lowest throughout the western world. The peoples and institutions of the Americas became a feature of European urban and rural life by the mid-eighteenth century. Planters and their slaves 'returned' to Europe, often in considerable style ('vulgarity' in the eyes of many curious European onlookers). Planters were famous for their wealth (often invested in stately homes) which they flaunted in capital cities and fashionable spas and retreats. But not all planters were able, or wanted, to return to Europe. Many escaped from the isolation of their plantations to the pleasures and comforts of the nearest town or city in the Americas.

Urban life had flourished on the back of the plantations and their exports. In the Caribbean, almost 10 per cent of the population lived in towns by the end of slavery. The eight largest towns in the region each had populations over 2,000; Kingston more than 12,000. Most of the major towns were also ports, serving as the vital link between the colonial interior, with their rural populations and products, and the outside world. But on the smaller islands, and even in Jamaica, the biggest British island, plantation produce went not to the major towns or cities but to the nearest point on the coast; produce was loaded on the nearest quayside, or even off the nearest beach, and imported goods were received via the same routes. None the less, as the colonies thrived, local towns grew in size and prosperity.

For the slaves, town life was quite different from that of the plantations. Planters kept the usual retinue of slaves in their town houses. So too did local merchants and traders and that emerging middle class (including a coloured middle class) whose careers were so closely bound up with the development of urban life. Many slave-owners did not provide homes or rooms for their town slaves, paying them instead to find accommodation elsewhere. This soon led to the growth of separate slave quarters, 'negro yards' in the West Indian parlance. Like towns everywhere, these new West Indian settlements tended to be dirty, unhealthy and noisy; a source of complaint for all those forced to live or stay in them against their wishes. Again, like English towns of the same period, the wealthier sited themselves in the better, more congenial and healthier areas of town. Slaves had little choice in the matter. They either lived with their owners or close by.[16]

The great majority of town slaves in the Caribbean were domestics. In all manner of ways their lives differed from those of their friends on the plantations. For a start urban slaves were outnumbered by whites. They worked for their owners as servants, undertaking all the various tasks around the house, from cleaning and washing to cooking. Towns, of course, created a much greater variety of employment for slaves and free persons. As a result there were very different groups of slave workers in the towns. Slave washerwomen (serving, for instance, the transient maritime trade), slave prostitutes, slave workers in and around local taverns and inns. In 1804 a widow in St John's, Antigua, was fined for allowing her house to be used by 'evil disposed slaves and free persons of colour [all of whom] remain drinking tippling whoring and misbehaving themselves unlawfully'.

The concentration of slaves (or free blacks) in towns made slave owners ill-at-ease. Town slaves were less easily controlled, more independent in their social lives, more vocal and boisterous than their peers on the plantations. Urban life bestowed a degree of independence which sat uneasily with the institution of slavery. A similar tale could be told in many slave towns. In Charleston, for instance, there were frequent complaints about the blatant sexual liaisons between black and white (at least on the plantations such assignations were out of sight and therefore out of mind). In the towns, it was impossible to ignore the offspring of such unions. In 1742 in Charleston they were denounced as 'the off-spring of those white Sodomites who commit fornication with their black slave women'.[17]

The offspring of such liaisons (in Charleston at least) formed a substantial proportion of those slaves who were freed in the late eighteenth century. Freed mulattos were in addition often given some property along with their freedom. There thus emerged free, non-white communities, blessed with some property, in a world where colour and property normally followed the lines of caste and social class. Towns had begun to blur the distinctions, so obvious in rural settlements, between master and man, between slave and slave-owner.

Though there was no obvious need for many of the skilled plantation trades in the towns, there was in fact a higher proportion of skilled slaves in towns than on the rural settlements. Carpenters, masons, coopers, seamstresses and tailors could all be found in abundance, plying their trade to the much broader market of urban life; working for money, fees or profits. In the towns we find slave bakers and butchers. In Georgetown, Demerara (Guyana), in 1823 it was said that 'the slave stall holders sell the best meat, and are the most punctual in the payment of the stall rents'.[18] Oddly enough, half a century earlier, in Charleston, it had been claimed that 'the Butchering Business in the Lower Market of Charles-Town has for many years past been carried on by Negroes'. The same was also true of the local fish market.[19]

Towns housed the most specialized of skills among slaves and free people: goldsmiths and watchmakers, printers and skilled carpenters. William Collins of Antigua, planning to establish a printing office, declared (in 1819) that 'I have for that purpose long since caused three young negro men named Tom, Charles and Cato belonging to me to be properly taught to read, write and spell'.[20]

Slaves living in ports shared the skills needed in the maritime industry and were employed in repairing ships and making ships' equipment – as shipwrights, ships' carpenters, sail-makers, caulkers. And this was the case in Bridgetown, Barbados, as in Charleston.[21]

The lifelines of the slave colonies were the maritime links to Africa and to Europe. The flotillas of ships which arrived and departed each year had on board not only cargoes of slaves fresh from Africa but also a number of slaves who worked as sailors. Black sailors were a common sight, not only in the Atlantic trade, but wherever Europeans traded and sailed. When in 1773 Captain Phibbs took an expedition to the Arctic, he had on board Olaudah Equiano, who, sleeping in the cramped quarters of the doctor's store-room, began to keep a journal which eventually took the form of an autobiography published in 1789. Equiano wrote of the 'one continued plain of smooth unbroken ice, bounded only by the horizon'.[22] It was far removed from his Ibo homeland and the slave colony where he had been seasoned as a slave. He was perhaps the first black to venture into the Arctic region.

Before that expedition, Equiano had made a number of major voyages along various Atlantic routes. In common with a growing number of blacks, he was caught up in the expanding world of British maritime trade and adventure. Later Equiano was used as an interpreter on board slave ships newly arrived in the Caribbean. He, and other Africans, became the important link between Africans and Europeans. Most slave sailors in the Americas, however, were involved in more prosaic but vital seafaring or river traffic. Blacks dominated the maritime and river trade centred on Charleston. It was a permanent fear that slaves would use the boats and their sailing skills to escape[23] – or help others to escape. In 1784 a Virginian law stipulated that only one-third of a local crew could be black. The planter Robert Carter had two blacks serving as masters on board his schooners *Harriet* and *Bear.*[24] When Thomas Thistlewood first arrived in Jamaica in April 1750, his boat, the *Flying Flamborough*, made landfall at Morant Bay in the east of the island: 'a Negro pilot came on board us'. Later, when he was established as a planter, close to a river and the sea, Thistlewood regularly employed slaves as fishermen, allowing them a remarkable degree of freedom, but generally scolding them if they stayed away too long or failed to catch many fish.[25] Black sailors were frequent sights on ships plying their trade throughout the Atlantic economy, and hence in all the major Atlantic ports.[26]

As towns grew in the slave colonies, they became the natural magnet for bands of slave vendors and higglers (vendors). Although only a small percentage of slaves were involved in such work, they were unavoidable, crowded as they were into the towns' markets, wharves and street corners. Produce from the plantations, and from slave plots on the plantations, imported goods and foodstuffs from other West Indian islands, manufactured articles, luxuries and essentials, meat, poultry and fish; all could be had from slave higglers in the towns and cities. Slaves wandered the streets of the towns carrying their wares on their heads (as did London's wandering hawkers), knocking on doors, selling to passers-by and sometimes irritating local propertied society by their intrusiveness.

Local authorities sought to pin down slave higglers by ordering them to trade in particular places, licensing their stalls or granting them a specific

area for trading. Wherever they settled there was instantly generated that
buzz of activity associated, now as then, with West Indian markets; noisy,
boisterous, colourful gatherings which provided customers with most articles
they needed and further enhanced the independent economic fortunes of this
small group of enterprising slaves. The market-places which evolved were
distinctive features of West Indian urban life by the early nineteenth century
and have remained among the region's more eye-catching attractions to this
day. Like the rural markets which developed close to the plantations, the
town markets attracted slaves from far and wide, some of them travelling
through the night to be there at dawn on their free days to barter and sell.
Whatever distrust the slave-owning class felt towards their local markets, they
came to depend on them for many of the goods which graced their tables in
the towns.

Much the same story was told of Charleston, where slave hawkers thronged
local wharves. A large percentage of Charleston's slave vendors were women,
who, like slave vendors throughout the colonies, were the object of suspicion
and dislike, even to the very people who used or depended on their important
services. What whites disliked most was the slaves' independence; that autonomous, self-confident and assertive black presence on the streets. It seemed
inappropriate in a slave society to have slaves operating successfully at so
important a level of economic and social activity. It was as if the higglers and
vendors had forgotten the place designated for them by the whites. Their
numbers, their noise, the stridency of their language – all these irritated and
disturbed their white owners and customers. They had become, said one
complainant in Charleston in 1774, 'so obscene in their language, so irregular
and disorderly in their conduct, and so superfluous in their Numbers'.[27]

Although slave vendors remained a minority, they became an important
force in most slave societies. Some were able to accumulate a great deal of
material prosperity: cash, foodstuffs, animals, farm produce. Thistlewood's
favourite paramour, Phibbah, sold a filly for £4.10s to another slave in 1760
and 'sold her mare Patience to the Negro man of Col. Barclay's named
Crossley for seven pounds. He paid her £5.10s down, and is to pay the
remaining 30s in three months'. Purchaser and vendor, both slaves, had cash,
and the prospect of more cash to come.[28]

Similar stories emerge whichever slave society we look at. In Barbados, a
slave offered for sale in 1829 was described as an experienced 'retailer of
goods'. There and throughout the British Caribbean, such vendors were over-
whelmingly female. On their days free from plantation labour, they marched
in single file to the nearest market or town, carrying most of their burdens on
their heads. One woman (in an account of Barbados in 1837) had a 'small black
pig doubled up under her arm'. Another 'had a brood of chickens, with the nest
coop, and all, on her head. Further along the road we were especially attracted
by a woman who was trudging with an immense turkey elevated on her head'.

Others carried 'sweet potatoes, yams, eddoes, Guinea and Indian corn, various fruits and berries, vegetables, nuts, cakes, bundles of firewood, bundles of sugar cane, etc.'[29] These are revealing scenes, not merely for their exotic and appealing details, but for the remarkable evidence they offer of the growth of an independent slave culture, linked to the world of plantation slavery but operating and thriving at an economically autonomous level. Planters often used their slaves as higglers, taking the income as their own.[30] But the growth of slave vending and higgling was more important for the slaves themselves. It was here (and on their related plots and gardens) that they established a distinct independence; creating an economic activity which survived slavery and continues to this day.

It was widely assumed that slaves, indeed blacks in general, were musical by nature; propelled towards dance, singing and music-making by inherent characteristics denied to white people. It was scarcely surprising then that slave-owners often trained chosen slaves to become professional or skilled musicians, hoping to harness the 'native' musicality of slaves (and blacks in general) and transform it by the discipline of western music. Black musicians could be found wherever music was played in the world of the British Atlantic from the late seventeenth century onwards. Indeed, the habit had started long before the flourishing of the slave colonies. Throughout medieval Europe, black musicians were employed in various royal courts, in Palermo, in Castille, in Lisbon. There was a black drummer at the Scottish Court in 1507; both Henry VII and Henry VIII employed a black trumpeter at their English Courts; the Court of Elizabeth I contained black musicians and dancers. By the mid-eighteenth century black musicians were a common sight in Britain and at fashionable gatherings in the Americas. The fanfare for the Knights Companion of the Order of the Bath in London in 1730 was blown by twelve black trumpeters. British regiments frequently used blacks as musicians, playing drums, cymbals and trumpets. The Connaught Rangers were noticed for their 'leaping Negro bandsman with his Jingling Johnnie'.[31] When fashionable balls were convened in the elegance of the major civic buildings in Spanishtown, Jamaica, music was provided by army bandsmen and black musicians.[32]

Slave musicians brought entertainment, social prestige and the veneer of sophistication to their owners' homes. In 1757 a Bristol newspaper advertised for a local runaway: 'A NEGRO LAD about 18 years of Age, near five Feet two inches high answers to the name of Starling, and blows the French Horn very well.' Equiano learnt the same instrument:

> we had a neighbour in the same court who taught the French horn. He used to blow it so well that I was charmed with it and agreed with him to teach me. Accordingly he took me in hand, and began to instruct me, and I soon learned all three parts. I took great delight in blowing this instrument.[33]

At a celebration ball in London in 1764, all the musicians were black. It was said of Soubise, friend of the Duchess of Queensbury in the 1760s, that: 'He played upon the violin with considerable taste, composed several musical pieces in the Italian style, and sang them in a comic humour that would have fitted him for a primo buffo at the Opera-house.'[34] Black musicians moved easily in fashionable British society.

Wherever Europeans travelled, explored or settled, they took blacks with them. When the British made their first tentative colonization of Australia after 1787, they deposited black criminals. Slaves from the West Indies, black criminals from late eighteenth-century London; all were dumped in the distant and therefore safe penal colony of Australia. Although the numbers were small, about 200 by the 1830s, they confirm the ubiquity of black life within the British imperial system.

John Tharpe, described as a 'doctor man', was an illiterate slave, 5 feet 7 inches tall, with tattoos of a woman on his right arm and an anchor on the left. He was a rebellious man, bearing the signs of floggings. He had been active in the Jamaican rebellion of 1832 (the 'Baptist War', see Chapter 16) but had escaped immediate arrest, and almost certain death, in the bloody aftermath of that revolt. When he was finally tried in 1834, for 'murder, rebellion, arson etc.', he was found guilty of murdering a white sailor. The death sentence was commuted to transportation. Along with seven other Jamaicans, Tharpe reached Sydney in 1836 (via trans-shipment to England and a spell in the hulks), two years before the formal ending of slavery, but none the less consigned to a lifetime's bondage. He must have been a very useful convict; in addition to his medical skills, he was a cook, servant, farrier and horse-breaker.

Those who have burrowed into the Australian archives in search of slave transportees (the Africans must surely be among the most unfortunate of travellers, having been shipped from Africa to the West Indies, from the Caribbean to Britain and then to Australia) have found a number of skilled slaves in their midst. William Steward, born in Jamaica, was a Manchester barber, transported (seven years) for stealing cutlery. Pricilla, a Jamaican domestic slave, was sent to Australia for trying to poison her master's family. Richard Holt, Jamaican, was a stableman. Thomas Butler Bonner, an African, was a servant, stockman and groom in Jamaica. Francis Smith, another Jamaican, was a cooper convicted in the 1832 rebellion. William Thomas, born in St Kitts, had worked as a messenger, clerk and letter sorter. From Antigua, Tom Tough had an unlikely name for a pastry cook; he too was sent to New South Wales for life (for robbery). A Barbadian slave, John William Adams, described as a good cooper and house servant, was transported for seven years for stealing sugar. His countryman, Toney Cat, a farm servant, joined him for stealing a goat. The list runs on, through most of the skilled and semi-skilled occupations of slave society of the early nineteenth century: groom, house

servant, cook, carpenter, driver, mason, butler, cooper, tailor, painter, fisherman, waterman, ploughman, shepherd, shoemaker, carter, laundry maid, jew-
eller (convicted of stealing silver), butcher, labourer, soldier, and even one
'engineer'.[35]

Their sentences were no more brutal than those doled out for similar
transgressions to the British themselves. But there is a bitter twist to the
story of black transportation: many were consigned to a lifetime's bondage
in Australia at a time when slavery itself was doomed and, in 1838, finally
terminated. And for those who had already endured the initial transportation
from Africa, they had to endure the fearsome voyage to Australia, as bonds-
men, at a time when the British had outlawed the maritime slave trade. They
could have been forgiven for not spotting the difference.

Australia became home to only a relatively small number of skilled black
slaves. We know a great deal about them because they were among the batches
of transportees whose personal (and criminal) details were recorded in such
detail. They offer a sample, though a peculiar one at that, of the skills and
training acquired by slaves in the mature slave colonies of the late eighteenth
and early nineteenth centuries. We are so accustomed to thinking of black
slavery in terms of its crude labouring form that we tend to overlook the ranks
of skilled men and women whose crafts, experience and abilities enhanced
the economic and social life of the slave colonies. But simply to look at the
surviving artefacts of the former slave societies – the fields, the houses, the
furnishings, the equipment – is to be confronted by the fruits of slave labours
and skills. For among the ranks of those millions of Africans imported to
labour in the fields of the slave colonies, there lurked some obviously remarkable people. Many of their descendants shook off the tighter restrictions of
field slavery and were able, by talent, effort and guile, to shape for themselves
a better material life. But for all that, despite their skills, despite their better
material fortunes, despite the talented inheritance skilled slaves were able to
bequeath to their sons and daughters, they remained slaves; bought, sold,
inherited, bequeathed and sought as other pieces of material property. Whatever his or her skill or talent, a slave was but a slave.

9

Women

Of the millions of Africans shipped across the Atlantic and deposited in the Americas, the majority were men. Women slaves were not thought as valuable as men, although in time they proved themselves to be more important than slave-owners had initially imagined. In addition, numerous African societies were loath to give up women to the slave-traders; women were too important locally, in the fields, in the communities and within the family groups, to surrender them to the slave trade. Yet as slavery developed it became clear that female slaves were doubly important: they could undertake all the heavy work undertaken by the men *and* they could produce new generations of slaves. A female slave could be a valuable worker in the fields, in white homes as a servant or in the urban settlements as a trader, as well as being a breeder; she might also be used as a provider of sexual services for the slave-owner and his coterie.

The slave trade transported twice as many men as women. This was true from one European slave-trading nation to another: Spanish, Portuguese, English, French and American – all liked to fill the holds of their slave ships with men. The percentage of males in the holds of the slave ships varied between 60 and 72 per cent.[1]

The most obvious consequence of this imbalance was on slave reproduction in the Americas. Imported women were older (had spent many of their fertile years in Africa) and were in a minority. Quite apart from the physical consequences of the Middle Passage itself (and its disastrous effect on slaves' ability to conceive and give birth), the sex ratio militated against successful or healthy breeding. Not surprisingly, the slave communities were, for a long time, kept in good demographic health only by further importations. Women were too few, too old, too sick or too debilitated to produce healthy offspring.

When they managed to conceive and give birth, their infants were far too often sickly, succumbing to that array of infant ailments which swept away so many babies in the pre-modern (and current Third) world. All slaves were exploited people, but female slaves endured extra dimensions of exploitation; worked to the limits, they were also used as breeding animals and were sexually exploited by whites throughout the Americas.

The one slave society which differed from the rest in the British Caribbean was Barbados. Here there was a 'plague' of female slaves. From about 1715 women outnumbered men. At a purely demographic level, Barbados was a woman's society. As the Africans poured into the island in the late seventeenth and early eighteenth centuries, converting the island to a sugar monoculture, local planters tried to balance the sexes on their properties: 'We buy them so as the sexes be equal; for, if they have more men than women, the men who are unmarried will come to their masters and complain, that they cannot live without wives. And he tells them, that the next ship that comes, he will buy them wives, which satisfies them for the present.'[2] Planters everywhere recognized the need to keep slaves happy by providing sexual partners. An American planter realized that slave women 'will greatly tend to keep them at home and to make them Regular'.[3] The practice of maintaining a reasonable balance was seen at its best in Barbados. There may also have been economic reasons for doing so: female slaves were cheaper than male and many planters thought them more pliant and more easily managed.[4] Whatever the reason, by the early eighteenth century, Barbadian planters had shaped a slave society in which women outnumbered men. This had major consequences for the development of local family life and slave reproduction.

Women everywhere undertook the same field work as men. Though they were never given the skilled training to become artisans, they were more than equal to the various demanding tasks of field work. Whatever the impulse – whether dictated by African forces or by the policies of the planters – Barbados came to rely for its labour on a female majority. Curiously enough this was also true of the white female population in the island. White planters in Barbados were rarely without white women partners (unlike planters in other Caribbean islands). And it seems very likely that this white female presence had a moderating effect on the behaviour of local white men. Barbadian whites were less brutal, less vile towards their slaves. It was no accident that the size of the mulatto class in Barbados was relatively small; another indication of the different relations (sexual and social) between master and slave in that island. Put simply, the presence of a more balanced population created a different set of relationships between master and slave, between black and white.[5] Men without women behaved differently.

Slave women in Barbados were found in their greatest numbers in the field gangs where the work was clearly onerous and demanding. In the other British islands, this did not become the pattern until the abolition of the slave trade in

1807 and the subsequent levelling out of the ratio between male and female slaves. In towns, too, slave women were in a majority, a reflection of the kind of work they undertook as domestics in local homes and as hawkers on the streets. But more striking still in Barbados was the fact that a growing proportion of all the slaves were born in the island and not imported from Africa. From 1760 onwards the island's slave population became less and less African. The island no longer needed the slave trade, though other British islands remained addicted to fresh supplies of Africans. Barbados was different. It showed quite clearly that slavery could take different forms. It did not have to be characterized by the brutal relations which were the hallmark of life on the Jamaican plantations for instance. The presence of women, black and white, clearly made an extraordinary difference.

Women who were imported from Africa endured the traumas of the crossing and the indignities of arrival already described in Part II. Shielded at first from the harshest aspects of slave labour, they gradually became acclimatized to field work, but in the process substantial numbers died. Of the 180,000 slaves imported into Barbados between 1700 and 1760, some 50,000 died in the first three years.[6] When strong enough, the women were slotted into the various slave gangs, their exact destination determined by their age and strength. The younger or weaker they were, the lower down the labouring chain they were employed. But experienced women field slaves could rise to levels of some command; a number of women became gang drivers, ordering and leading slaves in their charge. Whatever the rank, field work on the sugar plantations was hard: 'the great body of the slaves, the field-people on sugar plantations, are generally treated more like beasts of burden than like human creatures, since they cultivate the land, with no assistance from cattle, and suffer every hardship which can be supposed to attend oppressive toil.'[7]

Women were not shielded from the toughest field work. Nor, at first, were pregnant women, though in the last years of West Indian slavery planters began to lessen the burden on pregnant field slaves in order to encourage breeding. Newcomers were shocked to see pregnant women hard at work in the field gangs, alongside 'others whose naked infants lay exposed to the weather sprawling on a goat skin, or in a wooden tray'.[8] Working until six weeks before delivery, women were back in the fields three weeks after the birth of their baby, their new infants slung on their back.[9] This was not unique to slave societies, however.

In the fields slave women were most exposed to arbitrary punishments and blows ('stripes') from their drivers. Indeed it was the corporal punishment of female slaves, and the indignities involved, which offended a growing number of people: 'The posterior is made bare and the offender is extended prone on the ground, the hands and feet being firmly [held] by other slaves ... the driver, with his long and heavy whip, inflicts under the eye of the overseer, the number of lashes, which he may order.' Pregnancy did not deter such punishments. Two pregnant Jamaican slaves, who left the field in the rain, were put in the stocks and then flogged.[10]

Field slaves in Barbados were punished on the spot, their hands tied above their heads to a tree or pole, and their backs whipped. These physical outrages incurred the wrath of abolitionists from the 1780s onwards, and were modified in the first wave of slave amelioration. The problem facing those who disliked the flogging of female slaves was two-fold: women were flogged in English penal institutions and settlements; more important, perhaps, corporal punishment was so integral to the way West Indian slavery functioned and thrived, that to ban or qualify it was to tamper with the institution itself.

Slave women dominated the field gangs because, unlike their menfolk, they had fewer opportunities for advancement. Men and young boys were trained or directed towards a range of skilled and semi-skilled jobs on and around the estate. Those jobs remained permanently closed to female slaves. Apart from domestic work and the important tasks of seamstress, slave women were restricted to the simple tasks of labouring.[11] On Worthy Park, Jamaica, the pattern was similar to the one already described in Barbados. The great majority of that estate's skilled posts — driver, headmen and craftsmen — were reserved for male slaves. At the very time men outnumbered women on the estate as a whole, female slaves were in a great majority in the field gangs. In the 1790s about 58 per cent of the field slaves were women; forty years later it stood at more than 65 per cent.[12] We also know that in these years the field slaves were worked harder. The abolition of the slave trade in 1807 had cut off the supply of new Africans and most planters felt obliged to reorganize their gangs and make more pressing demands of them to make up the shortfall. What effect this extra effort had on the health and fertility of slave women we can only speculate.

Like slaves everywhere, female field slaves passed up the occupational ladder in their early years of health and strength, passing down the other way as they weakened or aged. Abba, an African at Worthy Park, bought about 1770, was working in the Second Gang in 1793, though already described as 'lame'. No longer able to work in the fields when she was sixty, she became a 'nurse' (1813–14). By the time she was seventy-four, in 1823, she was super-annuated, living out her last years as the estate's oldest slave, surviving on the sparse rations doled out by the plantocracy. One of her contemporaries was Whanica, born in Jamaica and bought by Worthy Park as a thirteen-year-old in 1787. She worked in the field gangs from the year of her arrival. In 1793 she was in the Second Gang, rising to the First or Great Gang in 1796; she was still there in 1825, given respites only when her five children were born. Whanica was relieved of field work only when her strength began to fade, and she became a nurse in the hospital. But in 1836 she was put back in the fields, this time as a cook for the other field slaves. She was still in the fields when, along with the rest of Britain's slaves, she was emancipated in 1838 – almost fifty years after she first toiled in Worthy Park's lush fields.[13]

Until about 1730, men remained in a majority in all the major mainland slave colonies. In Virginia in about 1700 the ratio was two to one. In frontier communities the ratio was much higher. Many Africans had little or no prospect of settling into family or sexual relations with slave women. In the absence of black women, local blacks – slaves and free – often developed relations with poor whites, normally indentured servants. There was, in those early, frontier days, a fluidity to relations between the races which was to disappear as slavery, and its plantation birthplace, gradually began to dominate the economy of the region. The exception was South Carolina. When settlers moved from Barbados to South Carolina, they brought with them slavery in its fully developed form; equipped from the first with brutal laws, punitive slave work and sharp divides between black and white. It was said that Carolinians viewed their slaves 'with half the kindness and affection with which they consider their dogs and horses'.[14]

Initially, black and white worked shoulder to shoulder at the strenuous tasks of cutting into the bush and preparing land for habitation and cultivation. Men, black and white, were often without women of their own. This changed, from 1730 onwards, when the sexual ratio between black and white levelled out. The consequences were dramatic, for it led to the establishment of stable slave families and the rapid expansion of the slave population of North America. In the century from about 1750 to the ending of slavery, the black population was extremely fertile, allowing slavery to expand to the south and west, populating and working the cotton belt of the early nineteenth century. But there is a dimension to this transformation of the American slave population which often passes unnoticed: from 1750 onwards breeding became an important economic aspect of American slavery, and thus another aspect of the continuing exploitation of slave women.[15] True to a degree in Barbados, this added exploitation was less significant a feature of life for West Indian slave women. For American slave women, however, the experience of slavery divided itself into the obvious domain of slave work and the less obvious but no less demanding tasks of bearing and rearing children. Female slaves were not famous for running away, and the reason was usually straightforward: they needed to tend their offspring.

Women's experience of slavery was, in many crucial respects, distinct and quite different from that of their male contemporaries. They were, however, far from powerless. Women slaves ruled the slave-owners' households. On the plantations and in town houses, females formed the overwhelming majority of domestic slaves.[16] Many were skilled, providing that host of services which the propertied came to expect of their servants: cleaning, cooking, child-caring and housework. Domestic work was much heavier than it is today, involving a great deal of carrying and fetching heavy implements and goods (water for instance was carried from wells and pumps; frequent and heavy loads had to be ferried round the house). Domestics could not escape the scrutiny of their owners, especially when the mistress of the house was at home. Time and again commentators in the slave colonies made a similar point: that the white mistress could be as demanding and exploitative as any field driver. She may not have used the same force or punishment with which to dominate her charges, but she could be shrewishly and inescapably intrusive.[17]

In the slave-owner's house – sometimes humble and simple, often magnificent – black and white mixed freely. For a start, slaves built those houses. Then they made them function as homes and centres of family life. The domestic slaves also lived in them, or close to them in cabins and huts huddled in the yard at the rear of the buildings. Domestics needed to be close at hand to clean and cook and to serve. Sometimes the blacks shared rooms with whites: when Mrs Priscilla Dawson, travelling in colonial Virginia, died in the night, her death was not noticed until the morning, 'notwithstanding her daughter and a Niger waiting maid was in the room all night'.[18]

Younger domestic slaves in North America wandered round the house semi-naked, to the great shock of visitors from abroad and from the north.[19] When Chateaubriand, fleeing the Revolution in France, sailed up the Chesapeake Bay in the spring of 1791 the first person to greet him was 'a Negress of thirteen or fourteen, practically naked and singularly beautiful, [she] opened the gate to us like a young Night...I gave my silk handkerchief to the little African girl: it was a slave who welcomed me to the soil of liberty'.[20]

Slave-owners' houses were often filled with black domestics. At times they resembled slave houses; the master out at work, the mistress perhaps absentee. Children in such homes were as often as not reared, taught and cared for by black domestics. Planters often complained that their families were effectively taken over by black domestics; and children of widowed fathers were brought up almost like slave children. Not surprisingly, they grew up sounding and behaving like the slaves. Slave women even breast-fed and nurtured sickly white children. Thomas Jefferson's sick daughter was revived by the milk from one of the slave servants.[21]

Visitors often disliked and disapproved of such black influence over white. Edward Kimber, a British visitor to America in 1736, wrote that there was 'one thing they are very faulty in, with regard to their Children, which is, that when young, they suffer them too much to prowl among the young Negroes, which insensibly causes them to imbibe their Manners and broken Speech'.[22] After William Byrd III left his first wife, his mother denounced the abandoned wife for allowing her child to be taken over by the slaves. While the mother lay in bed till noon, the child's 'chief time is spent with servants & negro children her play fellows, from who she has learnt a dreadfull collection of words, & is intolerably passionate'.[23] White children were spoiled by their slaves; they did little for themselves but accepted whatever their black slaves laboured to achieve. Black women were to be found wandering round the Great House nursing and cuddling white babies and children; teaching the young as they grew, allowing black and white children to play together, teaching them slave songs, stories and generally implanting in their young minds a culture which derived in substantial part from Africa. In these early years, some of the most lasting, formative and crucial impressions and lessons acquired by young whites within the Great Houses came directly from black domestics.

When the children of plantation whites were tutored or schooled on a regular basis, they headed for fun and games with the slaves when classes were over. And the reverse was often true. Plantation mistresses who reared domestic slaves from an early age often felt very attached to them; they spoke or wrote about having reared them as their own children.

All was not sweetness and light for the black domestics; they were obviously at risk of sexual exploitation. And, like slaves everywhere, domestics could expect periodic punishments and pain; the occasional cuff, a premeditated thrashing and even torture. Whenever master or mistress felt so inclined they could do whatever they wanted to their domestics. Sometimes slaves resisted but more often than not the slave had to take the pain – whatever the cause. Lucy Byrd once 'caused little Jenny to be burned with a hot iron'. On another occasion the same two women, white and black, had a serious fight; the white mistress prevailed only when the rest of her family joined in and rescued her. The slave was then 'soundly whipped'. On another occasion William Byrd had to intervene to protect the same slave woman, Jenny, from an attack by his wife.[24]

In the West Indies it was different. For a start there were fewer white women in the slave islands (hence young white widows were 'snapped up' indecently soon after their husbands' death).[25] On the plantations white women were scarce, for they generally preferred to be absent from rural properties, enjoying instead whatever pleasures and delights were available in the local towns and ports. White men on the plantations, from the planter to the book-keeper, turned to slave women for sexual companionship. Their relationships ranged from the basest of sexual intimidation and violence – against which most slave women had no defence – through to long-lasting and monogamous 'marriages'. When Lady Nugent visited Hope estate in Jamaica she found the seedy Scottish overseer ensconced with his 'chère amie...a tall black woman, well made, with a very flat nose, thick lips, and a skin of ebony, highly polished and shiny'. Described by Lady Nugent as 'the favourite Sultana of this vulgar, ugly, Scotch Sultan', this woman was but one of thousands of such slaves scattered across the slave islands; women who raised themselves a little from the crudest of slave work by their relationships with local white men.[26]

Where white women chose to remain on the plantations they soon fell under the influence of their slaves. In the West Indies, as in North America, the plantation household became the forum for the exchange of cultural influences between black and white. The black domestics greatly altered the behaviour and style of the white women they worked for. How could it be otherwise when they spent so much time together, locked into domestic routines? Cartoonists mocked the way the blacks aped their mistresses' styles; their European clothes, their airs and graces, their manners of speech. But more alarming to many was that white women allegedly picked up 'black habits' such as vulgar manners, laziness and silliness. Edward Long complained of the common sight of 'a fine young woman, awkwardly dangling her arms, with the air of a negro servant lolling almost the whole day upon beds or settees, her head muffled up with three handkerchiefs, her dress loose and without stays'.[27] It was necessary, many felt, to get young women away from the plantations at an early age; away from the sluttish influences of the black domestics, to be trained instead by a European education.

Domestics were inescapable. Houses teemed with black servants of all descriptions; cooks, cleaners, seamstresses – to say nothing of their children, husbands, boyfriends, lovers and sundry relatives and friends. Planters and visitors alike were occasionally driven to distraction by their physical presence. Home, for most planters, was not a peaceful haven away from the noise and bustle of the plantation so much as a variation on the same noisy and troublesome black presence. When Lady Nugent visited a coffee plantation in 1802 she remarked that the house was filled with a 'number of negroes, men, women, and children, running and lying about, in all parts of it. Never in my life did I smell so many'. To make matters worse, the tropical climate demanded that houses were built for coolness and comfort. But the interior walls were thin; 'one hears every word', complained Lady Nugent.[28]

For many white women, especially for newly arrived Europeans, life on the plantation was difficult and miserable. They quickly degenerated into the shrewish, temperamental caricature so frequently portrayed by cartoonists and writers. Imperious towards their servants (at least when visitors were around), they were just as likely to slide into an uneasy companionship with them, adopting their styles and language but always ready to scold and even beat them when they felt like it. If life was difficult for the white women (who were also plagued by the open and often bizarre infidelities of their menfolk with local black women), it was even more difficult for the black domestics. Expected to be different – better – than their friends and relatives in the fields (the personal and work habits of a cook or serving maid were obviously quite different from the brute strength required in the fields), black domestics found their flaws and mistakes immediately noticed and punished by their superiors in the house. If they worked for one of the 'perfect viragos' described by Lady Nugent, the slave domestic was subject to a regular and constant barrage of complaint and abuse, and sometimes (though not in front of visitors) exposed to blows and beatings. Thomas Thistlewood wrote in his diary in October

1784: 'In the morning had Damsel flogged for not keeping the cookroom clean.'[29]

Where planters lived alone – without the moderating influence of their womenfolk – hemmed in by a wilderness that constantly threatened to overwhelm their cultivation, surrounded and dominated by armies of black slaves they felt to be savage and threatening, they sometimes slid into the very barbarism they feared. One of Thomas Thistlewood's neighbours was 'Old Tom Williams' who boasted – among other foul deeds – that he once caught one of his slave domestics 'cleaning the hall when he thought it did not much want it [so] he shit in it and told her there was something for her to clean'.[30]

Training slave domestics was part of the labour problem facing West Indian planters. In the early years of settlement, white indentured women were used as servants. But as more and more Africans arrived, the more suitable women were plucked from the fields and trained in the appropriate domestic skills. In their turn they passed these skills on to their daughters and friends. An early settler in Barbados was keen to get rid of his 'sluttish' servant, but was unable to do so 'until a neger wench I have, be brought to knowledge'. In that island, by 1700 black domestics had become the norm. One man remarked in 1708 that 'the handsomest, cleanest [black] maidens are bred to menial services' in the homes of local whites.[31]

Domestic slaves often made a great show of their affection and admiration for their owners and mistresses. Whenever a planter returned to a plantation after a period away – or in some cases when visiting his properties for the first time – the domestics put on a display of effusive pleasure and friendship. When Monk Lewis visited his Jamaican estate in 1816 his slaves poured out to greet him; their pleasure 'was the loudest I ever witnessed: they all talked together, sang, danced, shouted'.[32] When Thomas Jefferson returned from Paris to his home at Monticello in December 1780 he was greeted by similar scenes: 'When the door of the carriage was opened, they received him in their arms and bore him to the house, crowding around and kissing his hands and feet – some blubbering and crying – others laughing.'[33] Such scenes were repeated from one slave society to another. Planters came to assume that their domestic slaves held them in high esteem, loved them even. One absentee Barbadian planter wrote back to his agent in 1801 that his 'old and faithful domestics will rejoice in hearing that their mistress had a very favourable time in her lying in after giving birth'.[34] When Henry Laurens of South Carolina returned to his home near Charleston, his domestics greeted him with hugs and kisses: 'affectionate Salutes and congratulations my Knees were Clasped, my hands kissed my very feet embraced...they encircled me held my hands hung upon me...Even kissed my lips'. Yet this same slave-owner also said: 'Never put your life in [Negroes'] power a moment. For a moment is sufficient to deprive you of it'.[35]

Planters and slave-owners could of course delude themselves, and could equally be deluded by the slaves, that the bonds between slaves and owners were more affectionate than they were in reality. Slaves had good reason to cultivate the sense of affection: it was a useful ploy in cementing relations with their owners and could yield material benefits. When slaves misbehaved – when they ran away, resisted or kicked over the traces in some way or other – their owners were doubly shocked. Having believed that their slaves held them in fond regard, it was doubly disappointing to discover another layer to the slaves' personality.[36]

Domestics were in a peculiar and distinctive position. They shared their owners' lives more intimately than did other slaves. They had access to the most private of plantocratic possessions: foodstuffs (which they sometimes poisoned), medicines (which they sometimes used to harm or kill the whites) and above all their children. They were privy to their owners' secrets, over-hearing family squabbles, witnessing discord between man and wife, between parents and children. They came to know their owners' weaknesses and foibles. They knew how to behave–and what not to do. Domestic slaves in certain important ways were members of the extended family which shaped life in and around the Great Houses. Never an equal member of the slave-owner's family circle, the domestic slave was none the less a distant relative, sharing the mundane features of plantocratic domestic life and finding themselves incorporated into the private world of the plantation whites.

Domestic slaves formed a sizeable group in all the mature slave colonies. Most slave-owners employed someone as a domestic. In Barbados in 1788 it was thought that upwards of 25 per cent of the overall slave population was employed as domestics. In the towns a majority of local female slaves were in domestic service. In Bridgetown almost 70 per cent of all females in the town were domestic servants.[37] Visitors often remarked on the superabundance of domestic slaves in and around the houses they visited in the slave colonies – and this from people accustomed to the benefits and the presence of domestic labour throughout the western world. There was, however, another side to the story; of large numbers of female slaves weighed down and oppressed by the punitive work of domestic labour in the pre-modern world; women struggling with cumbersome and heavy buckets of water, washerwomen spending their days by the riverside washing and drying mountains of clothes.

Domestic slaves had their own stratagems and wiles for coping with their lot. It was universally recognized that they were cunning; they stole and they lied (when caught they were soundly whipped and punished in other ways). They, like slaves in general, were thought to be impervious to any discipline short of the lash or physical punishment.

> To kindness and forbearance they return insolence and contempt. Nothing awes
> or governs them but the lash of the whip or the dread of being sent into the

fields to labour. With us, therefore, they pursue a regular course of negligence, lies, and plunder, the latter of which they carry on with a cunning and ingenuity that is surprising.[38]

The most troublesome aspect of life was the flagrant and often aggressive sexual approaches from local white men. As sons of the plantocracy grew to manhood their early familiarity with black domestics – the women who had nursed and sometimes suckled them – turned into something quite different. It was assumed that white youths, like their elders, would make free with black women. At home or visiting other planters, white men took sexual advantage of local slave women. The few who wrote diaries openly spoke of their sexual adventures from their early years. William Byrd II of Virginia made regular references to his sexual contacts with slaves. In 1720 he recorded: 'I felt the breasts of the Negro girl which she resisted little.' Similar scenes were enacted among the sons of Robert Carter, another famous Virginian planter. His oldest son Ben was accused by a younger brother of taking a young slave girl 'into your stable and there for a considerable time lock'd yourselves together'. Later Ben himself was suspected of breaking into the house in order to 'commit fornication with Sukey (a plump, sleek, likely Negro Girl about sixteen)'.

Sometimes the sexual aggression of whites led to friction with male slaves. In Virginia Thomas Sutherland, like so many other whites, made free with the slave women: 'He used to say that a likely negur wench was fit to be a Queen: and I forgot how many Queens he had among the girls on the plantations.' But he was doomed: 'He was killed by a drunken negur man, who found him over-ficious with his wife.' The slave was hung on the gibbet: 'the sun was full on him: the negur lolled out his tongue, his eyes seemed starting out from their sockets, and for three long days his only cry was Water! Water! Water!'[39] Slaves who resisted the sexual violation of their women were themselves at risk from the arbitrary power of their owners or the violence of the legal codes.

In the West Indies the abundance of domestic slaves provided planters and their sons and employees with rich sexual pickings. Observers recognized that it was all too easy for young men to 'acquire those vices of manhood' by proximity to the domestics. One lady writing about Barbados noted that 'the gentlemen are greatly addicted to their women slaves, and give the fruit of their licentiousness to their white children as slaves'.[40] Thus did family relations in the Great House become confused and complex; slave children, offspring of white masters and their slaves, became servants to their half-brothers and sisters. Throughout the Caribbean a new complex process was set in train, of the light-coloured offspring of such liaisons securing preferential treatment for themselves and their children, emerging into a full-grown 'coloured' class by the last years of slavery. They distanced themselves by colour and style from the blacks below them, but were never accepted as equals by the whites above. Slave women knew that they could improve themselves, and enhance the prospects of their children, by relations with white men.

Sometimes women deliberately chose to go this route, having long and durable 'marriages' with white men. But the casual sexual encounter, forced on slave women by white males, was more common. No one doubts the damage done to the women concerned; less easy to trace was the violation of liaisons between black men and women and the long-term repercussions of predatory white sexuality on black family life.

Few planters could have been as sexually aggressive as Thomas Thistle-wood (see Chapter 14). He took his slaves wherever he found them, in the fields, in the various plantation buildings, but most of all in his own house; in his bedroom, in the hall, kitchen, or on any piece of furniture which was nearby. In his home he ruled supreme, and any woman working there was likely to find herself pressed into sexual service for her master's pleasure. Although he had his favourites (one in particular was effectively his enslaved wife), Thistlewood seduced slaves by the dozen – each coupling recorded with an attention to detail which defies explanation. Although he lived alone, Thistlewood, like other whites in the sugar colonies, filled his house with domestics. Even at the height of the crop, with some slaves sick and the property in need of extra hands, he continued to need four domestic slaves to run his home.[41]

It seems strange that planters should need to surround themselves with domestic slaves, even when hard pressed to find enough slaves for work in the fields and around the property. They employed proportionately more domestics than were to be found among the propertied classes in Britain at much the same time. But it would be wrong to think that domestic slaves were mere luxuries; symbols of their owners' wealth and an outward sign, to the rest of the world, of their social standing. In fact the domestics worked hard for their living: cooking, washing, nursing, often in positions of great trust and confidence.

The more we know of the lives of slave domestics, the more we need to qualify the idea that they led a sheltered and more privileged life. In some respects they were spared the harsher rigours of life in the fields – of exposure to the sun and rain, the risk of the whip and the fatigue of crop time. But field slaves on the whole had their lives dictated by the natural rhythms of the seasons and the cycles of the local crop. As we have seen, there were times of the year when slave-owners had to find other work for them to do. Domestics had few such breaks. As amelioration set in, and as working conditions began to improve (shorter hours, more and guaranteed holidays), these benefits came the way of field slaves. Domestics were much more securely fastened to the unremitting daily cycle of work in and around the house. In Britain in the course of the nineteenth century, domestic servants remained the largest single occupational group; oppressed, overworked and beyond the ken of legal or social improvement. Much the same tale was true of slave domestics.

Large numbers of domestic slaves in the West Indies worked for their owners in the towns and seaports. There too they were given little respite from the demands and insistence of their employers. While other urban slaves were generally given days off, notably Sunday, domestics were expected to rise before dawn, and still be on hand long after dusk to serve, feed their owners, then prepare the house for the following day. In West Indian towns, the largest single group of slaves, up to 70 per cent, were domestics (compared to something like 10 per cent on the plantations).[42] They seem to have had more freedom of movement in the towns, but their work was no less demanding and inescapable: emptying chamber pots ('sometimes going no further than the street gutter to do so'), throwing out the domestic refuse, cleaning and cooking. They wandered round the towns buying foodstuffs, acting as messengers and often working for their masters in and around town offices and warehouses.[43]

As the towns and cities thrived, they spawned the new groups of urban slaves we have already mentioned – the hawkers, vendors and higglers. Large numbers of street slaves were women, both in the West Indies and in the northern colonies.[44] Naturally enough, some vendors were able to prosper, a facet of slave life which has generally gone unnoticed in the concentration on slavery's more abject features. There were numbers of slave women who became modestly prosperous from their economic activities or from their relationship with white men. Marketeering and vending enabled the more nimble and successful women to acquire a host of luxury goods and hard cash. Animals, clothing, furnishings, household utensils, money and various luxuries began to appear in the slave quarters, generally the reward of commercially-gifted slave women. Visitors were surprised to find luxuries in slave cabins in the last years of Caribbean slavery. Phibbah, one of Thomas Thistlewood's favourites and long-standing lover, was clearly a woman of some material standing. When in the summer of 1757 it seemed that Thistlewood and Phibbah would have to part, she gave him a keepsake: 'Thursday 23rd: Phibbah gave me a gold ring, to keep for her sake.' Later she sent him gifts: 'a fine large pumpkin, 12 cashews, and 12 crabs, & a piece of soap'. A week later she sent a turtle, dried turtles' eggs, biscuits, a pineapple and cashews. 'God bless her!'[45] Yet formally Phibbah was only a domestic, in charge of the cookhouse. She and many more like her were accustomed to possessions and sometimes to material plenty. Such women were the lucky slaves. Most could not afford gold rings for their lovers; most could find scarcely enough food for themselves and their offspring.

Slave women worked in all sorts of occupations throughout the slave colonies. They worked as prostitutes serving the low-life of New World towns and seaports, boarding visiting ships or working from local taverns. They were field hands in all the major tropical staples – rice, tobacco, and sugar – yet added to the refinement and style of the homes of the most fashion-conscious grandees in Charleston, Bridgetown or Spanishtown. As children they were turned loose on to simple tasks in the homes, in the yard, among the animals, in the fields. When old they went back to the tasks of their childhood days. Too many were old before their time – 'useless' in the unforgiving vernacular of the slave ledgers. Some were abandoned by their owners when their utility disappeared entirely. Not all slave women were doubly exploited, at work and sexually, yet it was the double jeopardy of the female slave that she was, in her younger years, at once an invaluable labourer, a source of sexual pleasure for her master or overseer and a 'breeding wench' whose offspring would secure the continuing fortunes of her owners. To a degree that historians have only recently begun to appreciate, the failings or successes of the various slave colonies need to be seen through the experiences of the female slaves.

10

Disease and Death

In December 1775 Thomas Thistlewood bought a new boy slave, Joe, at 'an incredible price indeed' from Mr James Wederburn. Within the year the young man had contracted one of the scourges of Jamaican slaves, yaws.[1] Seven years later, when Joe could scarcely have been in early adulthood, his condition was serious: 'Saturday, 16th August 1783: Joe very ill. Dawne came and bled him and laid on a blister.' A day later he was even worse and Thistlewood called for Dr Bell, who

> took a little blood from him and found it good. He is ordered to drink cornwater, with a dram of nitre dissolved in each pint, and to take every hour a tablespoon of water, in which 10 grains of emetic tartar is dissolved in each half-pint, so as to make him sickish, in hopes it may cause perspiration.

The sick slave had not been able to urinate for two days, so the doctor returned and

> put a bougi up his urethra, ordering him glysters and a warm bath, also to take a pill every hour and a half made as follows: 20 grains of James's powder and 12 of calomel, made into 6 pills, with a little bread crumb. He took of these; about 9 o'clock at night they worked him well downwards and he made water. His stools are bloody and black matter. He also parted with 4 worms.

But Joe failed to rally and the doctor recommended 'some brandy toddy, with 30 drops of laudanum in it, which was of infinite service to him and made him easier'. It was all to no avail. Within the week, on Sunday 24 August, Joe died, his master providing a wooden coffin and rum for the mourners.[2]

What was unusual about Joe was that we know the details of his sufferings. Throughout the slave societies there were millions of other slaves whose life was nasty, brutish and short; marked from first to last by pain and suffering, their demise often coming early and painfully. But they tend to remain anonymous in their sufferings; consigned at best to the statistical calculations of their owners for whom slave sickness and death was an economic blow.

All the black slave populations of the New World had developed not from natural population growth but from the economic dictates and whims of employers. Moreover, there was built into West Indian slavery a corrosive force which continued to sap the natural vitality of the slave communities. The slave trade was, paradoxically, both the sustenance and the bane of the slave communities. Without it there could be no population growth, but at the same time it infected the communities with a host of ailments; diseases from Africa and the debilities acquired on the Atlantic crossing. Sick Africans augmented slave numbers, but their ailments and deaths distorted the local figures of sickness and mortality. They died in large numbers, often infecting others around them. The slave trade was the crossroads of major diseases, mingling together the diseases of Europe, Africa and the Americas in a destructive mix which left its varied scars on all three continents.[3]

Large numbers of Africans were sick from the moment they landed in the Americas. Many lingered for a while before joining the ranks of Africans cast into the Atlantic or buried *en route* to the African coast. These early slave deaths in the Americas were victims of the slave trade; the fact that they died in America or the islands was often incidental. Africans passed through a 'seasoning' period, of up to three years, when they were apprenticed to their bondage normally via lighter, less demanding work. It was here that they were expected to regain their strength and health. But it was in that very seasoning period that many of the slaves died; perhaps upwards of 25 per cent, though percentages varied from place to place.

Planters' heaviest investments were in batches of new Africans and they began to pay them special attention. In time, the slave trade itself 'improved' (it took less time, was managed more efficiently and with less loss of life) and perhaps more Africans were healthier on arrival than in the early years of the trade. Similarly, as the estates themselves became well established, and as the harsh pioneering days receded, the work demanded of many slaves became less debilitating. Serious problems of course still remained, especially in frontier communities or on islands still in the process of slave expansion (Haiti being perhaps the best example). On Worthy Park in Jamaica, of two batches of Africans bought in 1792, more than half were dead within four years. Their owner, alarmed at the erosion of his costly purchases, shifted most of the survivors to a healthier lower location. The estate bought ninety Africans and four-fifths of them survived at Worthy Park for more than five years. Forty years later, twenty of them were still alive.

Clothed, branded, put under the supervision of established slaves, the Worthy Park Africans were given the simplest of tasks on an expansive plantation, and consigned to the crude slave barracks. They were fortunate in that the plantation employed the services of an enlightened doctor, Dr John Quier, who inoculated the slaves against smallpox; but that was not enough to secure them against the fatal ravages of yaws, leprosy and dysentery, TB, pneumonia and yellow fever.

Occasionally we catch a passing glimpse of the otherwise anonymous slaves. Clarissa was among the batch of Africans bought by Worthy Park in 1792. Described as 'Congolese', it is hard to prove her exact origins, but she was very young, perhaps only thirteen when captured and transported (though, as with most dispossessed people in the pre-modern world, ages are often guesses). Clarissa, like her shipmates, was turned loose on to various tasks on the estate and in its less demanding provision grounds. When she regained her strength, she was put into Worthy Park's Second Gang, acquiring a new name, Prattle. A mere three and three-quarter years after arriving in Jamaica, she succumbed to the flux and died at the age of seventeen. Others did not last that long. Two slaves, Fox and Boston, poisoned themselves. Others from the same batch lived to a decent old age. One of Clarissa's companions in 1792 was the unusually named Raveface, aged twenty-four on arrival. Throughout her forty years as a slave she was an active field hand. When freedom came in 1838 she was in her seventieth year; she had borne four children and had at least five grandchildren.

Even those slaves who survived tended to be dogged throughout their lives by recurring ailments and accidents. So it was with Worthy Park's slaves. Register (later renamed Charles Grant), bought by Worthy Park at the age of eleven, began to work in the Third Gang when he was twelve. After years in the fields, Register was shifted to the boiler house – infamous for its intolerable heat as the cane juice was boiled and processed – possibly in 1816. Seven years later he was described as 'diseased', at the age of forty-one. By 1830 he was lame, and six years later had become so enfeebled that he could only be employed as a watchman. When he died in August 1836 he was fifty-five.[4] For every slave in the West Indies – especially the Africans – who lived to a reasonable age, there were many more who perished in their early years.

Most spectacular, because most visible and ugly, of the slave diseases were perhaps yaws and smallpox, though neither was the main killer of slaves. Yaws was a ghastly, ugly and painful disease; contagious, with fevers, rheumatic-like pain and weeping skin eruptions which developed into stinking ulcers. Transmitted by spirochaete, it is common in the tropics and thrives in a filthy environment. It can incubate for years before bursting forth and covering the unfortunate victim with suppurating ulcers.

The havock this terrible disorder annually makes amongst Negroes in the West Indies is truly deplorable [wrote one doctor] and merits the attention of the

Statesmen, the Planters, and Physician. It may not be in our power to prevent the spreading of this disorder among the Negroes but humanity and social policy call aloud on us to alleviate the sufferings, and distresses of, this class of mankind when they are so unfortunate as to be infected with the cruel malady.

Thomas Roughley said of yaws in 1823: 'Its nauseous and loathesome appearance, its frightful ravages, its twitching pains, extending to the very marrow, brings with it a deformity of bone and flesh that strikes horror.'

Sometimes, slaves with yaws were neglected. Writing of a visit to Jamaica in 1798, Dr Williamson remarked that: 'In the progress of disease, that maintenance was not afforded them which, for curative objects, should be liberally dispensed. A disease, in itself injurious to the constitution, is aggravated from such causes; whereas, if nature were supported by fit diet, clothing, cleanliness, and comfortable housing, she would work her own cure in most cases.'[5]

Not surprisingly, most white doctors were afraid of treating slaves with yaws, from fear of contamination; 'disgrace and ruin' would inevitably follow any respectable white person contracting it. All were agreed about the 'extremely loathesome and contagious nature of this affection'.[6] In truth, the slaves' doctors had little idea how to treat yaws. Time and again, slave-owners recorded their slaves' suffering from yaws, but seemed unable to do very much about it. When the disease was bad, the slave was rested. In 1768 Thomas Thistlewood's slave Phoebe, a Coromantee, suffered another bout of yaws, so her owner felt 'obliged to make her lay up'. When, two years later, Thistlewood sent a slave gang to work on a neighbouring property, he noted: 'Dick too full of the yaws to be sent'. When he discovered that Nanny had crab yaws on her hands, Thistlewood applied a hot poultice, later holding the hands over steam. Three months later he had the infected hands treated with 'Black Dog' (black sage) and consigned her to the bilboes (the stocks).[7] Later that year, 1771, Nanny's daughter, Little Phibbah, was taken to see Dr Panton who prescribed 'equal quantities of Flour of Brimstone and Venice Treacle [?] to be given her, as much as will lie upon the small end of a teaspoon, 3 times a day in a little sugar and water.' That and a range of other treatments failed to save the child, who died in September 1771. Her mother survived, but was troubled by persistent illness. In mid-1772 she was plagued by 'ringworms on the side of her neck'. In mid-summer she gave birth to a daughter, who lived a mere three weeks.[8] Afflicted by illness, beset by personal tragedies, Nanny was unusual only in being remembered in her owner's compulsive note-taking.

Another of Thistlewood's slaves was Sally, a seventeen-or eighteen-year-old Congolese in 1770. A persistent runaway and thief, she was frequently ravished by her owner. Chains and stocks did not deter her and she continued to flee (possibly from Thistlewood's unwelcome attentions). In 1772 she was troubled by yaws, again, and one of her toes was amputated. When she recovered she ran away again, was retrieved, flogged, and was found to have VD. This did not deter Thistlewood who continued to seek her sexual favours.[9]

Yaws provided slave-owners with an all-purpose excuse for blaming the slaves for their behaviour. When in October 1775 Thistlewood discovered that 'Jimmy has got the yaws', he added, 'dare say he has infected himself purposely'.[10] So compulsive was Thistlewood's sexual appetite that even when he noticed a slave erupting with yaws he continued to press home his sexual demands.[11] When his slave Franke broke out in sores, Thistlewood none the less coupled with her ('among the lima beans'), later prescribing 'sarsparilla diet drink, etc. for the yaws'. Two months later, all but one of her ulcers had healed up. When, in the following year, Franke again complained of being unwell, Thistlewood's treatment was simple; 'pains in her back, she pretends' – he flogged her and put her in the stocks.[12]

In a more solicitous mood, Thistlewood's usual treatment for yaws was based on a formula he borrowed from a neighbour, Colonel Barclay, who said: 'put hog-plum tree bark in a pot and put to boil with water till strong; then place it over a gentle fire, and keep the feet in it as hot as can be bore for nine days and nights, and it will effectively cure the crab yaws.'[13]

White doctors and planters were often impressed by the treatment slaves used for the yaws, sometimes with striking success. Hot baths with several herbs, fermentations (but rarely medicines taken internally) seemed to work. Slaves had confidence in their own recipes but 'little Confidence in our Physicians and Surgeons'. Slaves in Jamaica, according to another observer, were 'acquainted with the use of many simples for the cure of certain disorders – as yaws, ulcers, bone-ache, etc.; and the care and management of negroes afflicted with those disorders is generally confined to an elderly negro woman who professes a knowledge of this branch of physic'.[14]

There is no doubt that slave medicine was sometimes more effective than conventional western treatment (though it is also clear that the planters' treatment of the slaves tended to be an amalgam of African and western remedies). When a planter in Grenada discovered that thirty-two of his slaves had yaws he applied the conventional western treatment: mercury pills, which made them worse. (Mercury poisoning seems to have been a major cause of sickness among men, who took the chemical for their recurring venereal infections.) The Grenadian planter then decided to use the slave remedy:

> The Negro Method is making them stand in a Cask where there is a little fire in a pot and sweating them powerfully in it twice a day, giving them decoctions of 2 woods in this Country called Bois Royale and Bois Fer and applying an Ointment of Lime Juice and Rust of Iron to their Sores.

Within two weeks, all the slaves receiving the treatment had recovered; those receiving the western treatment remained unaffected.[15]

Planters tried to isolate yaws sufferers, but this was feasible only on larger slave-holdings. The 'yaws-house' was built in a healthy spot, under the care of an experienced nurse who, naturally enough, tended to administer an African regime of care and treatment, even when supervised by a European doctor. Yet whatever the treatment, yaws remained endemic until the abolition of the slave trade cut the vital link to Africa. It killed large numbers and obscenely afflicted many more. Between 1792 and 1838 at Worthy Park (a period marked by conscious efforts to ameliorate slave conditions), death from yaws was the fourth largest killer of slaves (after 'dropsy', flux and fever).[16]

From the first, slave-owners made efforts to conserve or restore their slaves' good health, using, when it was available, the best of contemporary European medicine which was, however, in general, inadequate to the task. Doctors were available, though not always on the smaller islands. The problem was not so much the availability of medical staff, as the inadequacy of their diagnoses and treatments when confronted by that alien mix of tropical peoples and diseases. In Jamaica in 1833 there was one doctor per 1,500 slaves, though this figure breaks down into less impressive ratios in rural parts. On Barbados in 1820 the average was one doctor to 1,300 slaves – though here, and elsewhere, we need to remember that not all 'doctors' were formally qualified.

Plantations usually employed doctors on a visiting or annual basis, assisted by a local nurse, generally a slave experienced in health care. Many of the doctors had received the best of contemporary medical education, in Edinburgh or Utrecht for example. Others were woeful: ill-trained and brutish in their habits, 'They are more illiterate than you can believe, and the very negro doctors of the estates too justly vie with them in medical knowledge.'[17]

By the last days of British slavery, the islands had begun to license local physicians,[18] but it seems very likely that for most slaves the crucial health care – where it existed at all – was provided by a local slave nurse. It was the slave nurse who, in the last generation of slavery, supervised the 'hospital', often equipped with a separate ward for childbirth. In the last resort it was the planters or their agents who decided which slaves should or should not be confined to hospital or to their sick bed, or to receive medical treatment. Slaves complaining of feeling unwell had first to overcome the suspicions of the white man. Thomas Thistlewood tended to assume that slaves were feigning when first they complained, only relenting when their ill-health became obvious. A pain in the belly could be imaginary (incurring a cuffing); ulcers from yaws could not be ignored.

Sometimes the whites were successful in treating the slaves. This was especially striking in the case of smallpox, a disease introduced into the Caribbean a mere twenty-six years after Columbus's first voyage, and responsible for widespread death and disfigurement among native peoples throughout the Americas. By the late seventeenth century, smallpox epidemics periodically swept through slave quarters and slave ships with fearful results. It was spoken of as 'the most pestiferous disease that ever scourged mankind'.[19]

Africans had practised a form of immunization against the disease long before the Europeans; the Puritan Cotton Mather learned from his slave in Boston about African inoculation. Europeans were won over to inoculation by its success in Constantinople in the early eighteenth century. In the West Indies, this medical habit was, it seems, introduced by the slaves, and by the mid-eighteenth century inoculation of slaves against smallpox had become common. At the first sign of the disease, local doctors and planters began the wholesale treatment of their black charges. In 1756 Dr Thomas Fraser wrote from Antigua: 'The small-pox no sooner made its appearance here than we immediately thought of inoculation; the success of which has been remarkable among people of all ages, blacks as well as the other inhabitants, that the most obstinate were at least prevailed on to countenance this practice.' When Edward Long wrote his *History of Jamaica* in 1774 he declared that: 'The small-pox has frequently made great ravages among them [the slaves].' Now there were signs of improvement: 'The late method of inoculation, happily practised in this island, promises fair to put an end to such dreadful examples of mortality.'[20]

We can see how the system worked, again by looking at Thomas Thistlewood's slaves. In September 1768 Thistlewood decided to have his slaves treated. In the evening of Sunday the 5th he gave the adults a pill, and the children a powder. The day after, 'Gave the 17 Negroes intended to be inoculated physick this morning'. On Friday that week, 'Between 9 and 10 A.M. Dr Drummond came and inoculated 17 of my Negroes, on each arm between the elbow and the shoulder; just raised the skin with a lancet dipped in the matter and let it dry.' A week later, all but four of the slaves had developed a mild case of smallpox, and on 20 September, when Dr Drummond examined the slaves again, 'Says they are in extreme good way, and that he need not come again'. By the 27th of that month, the sores had dried and healed and Thistlewood turned the slaves out into the pastures to work.[21]

It was easy to inoculate slaves. Unlike a free population, the slaves had no say in the matter and it was simple to keep track of their reaction to the treatment. Dr John Quier, working in central Jamaica in the 1760s and 1770s, inoculated about 1,500 slaves in six years with great success. Quier's technique, his preferred regime of associated diet and related care, became an example for others. Historians continue to argue about whether or not inoculation helped to arrest smallpox in the populations of Britain and North America, but there is little reason to doubt its efficacy among the slaves, largely perhaps because they were in no position to refuse or to hide from the treatment.

After 1800 the old system of inoculation rapidly gave way to Jenner's new method of vaccination and by 1820 in Jamaica the disease had been virtually eliminated. It survived in smaller islands, where quarantine was more difficult to enforce, where local populations were more mobile (especially between the islands) and where the local sense of public health was not so well developed as in the bigger colonies.[22] In Virginia, the example of Thomas Jefferson, who vaccinated his family and his slaves, helped to popularize this attack on smallpox, winning over doubting doctors and slave-owners alike, and helping to reduce the local ravages of the disease.

On land and on the slave ships it was the 'bloody flux' which seems to have been the largest single killer of West Indian slaves – though in fact more died of 'old age'.[23] The various forms of dysentery which so afflicted the slaves were clearly related to the insanitary conditions endured by slaves on the ships and the plantations. Planters knew that the illness was also related to diet, especially to the paucity of slave diet in the late summer and early autumn. Writing in 1823 J. Stewart noted: 'the appearance of dysentery among the [Jamaican] slaves is most to be apprehended in August... This is a contagious disease and frequently fatal.'[24] The two forms of dysentery, bacillary and amoebic, are diseases of the intestine, transmitted from faeces, via fleas, hands or contaminated food and water. Dirty habits and insanitary conditions provide the ideal breeding ground and means of contagion. Bacillary dysentery in the tropics is more prevalent in the rainy season. Slave doctors tried bleeding, evacuations and emetics. One argued that at the first sign of dysentery it should be attacked by 'evacuants, such as bleeding, purging, puking, and sweating, sometimes all of them in succession'. Other doctors tried to sweat the illness out of the patient. Progress was made, however, and by the 1770s it was realized that dysentery could be effectively treated by using ipecacuanha (now recognized as a check on amoebic dysentery), and this treatment was rapidly adopted throughout the slave colonies. Among the slaves – and the population of the western world – major improvements in these and similar disorders were related to changes in personal and collective hygiene.[25]

West Indian slaves succumbed in large numbers to what contemporaries called 'dropsy', thought now to be beriberi, a deficiency disease which left the victim bloated and swollen. As the body acquired fluids, it swelled, gradually disabling the patient. Slave doctors ascribed the illness to a range of causes: to the heat and humidity, to the excessive use of spirits, to hard labour and diet. Slaves who worked in the sugar-boiling houses seemed especially prone to this ailment which, like the 'ague', was treated by purges, by 'tapping' (into the bloated body) and by the application of herbal medicines. One of these, digitalis (foxglove), proved highly effective.[26]

The disease which puzzled planters more than most others was 'dirt-eating'. It was, said Edward Long, 'a disease to which children as well as grown Negroes are subject... [and makes] incredible havok'. Sometimes known as *mal d'estomac* or *cachexia africana*, it was a slave complaint which was widely discussed in the literature and correspondence of slavery. Though planters often alleged that it made serious inroads into the slave population, studies of plantation papers do not confirm this claim. Much of this confusion – like so many other aspects of pre-modern medicine – may well be explained by difficulties of diagnosis and interpretation. Often viewed as a result of a slave's demoralization or low spirits, it is also possible that those in charge of the slaves preferred not to mention the nature of a slave's illness if it reflected poorly on themselves. What is curious about this malady is that it seems virtually to have disappeared with the ending of slavery.[27]

Dirt-eating was viewed as an especially disgusting slave habit; yet another symptom of African barbarity. It disabled slaves, often for years at a time, and sometimes culminated in serious physical complications and even death. The craving to eat dirt, especially clay, was noted throughout the slave islands and confused medical opinion as much as it disgusted and frustrated the planters. Thomas Thistlewood, locked in close proximity to his slaves in western Jamaica, viewed dirt-eating as a serious offence and punished his slaves accordingly (though Thistlewood needed little encouragement to punish his slaves in the most violent and sadistic fashion).

Dirt-eaters complained of stomach ache and loss of breath; their skin discoloured and they became bloated, nauseous and debilitated. Sometimes the afflicted slave died within a few months. But what caused this bizarre craving in the first place? One slave doctor claimed it proceeded 'from melancholy, revenge, obeah, dissatisfaction, unhealthy climate'. Even today dirt-eating – which persists in certain parts of the world – continues to perplex medical opinion. Recently it has been argued that dirt-eating stemmed from a craving stimulated by nutritional deficiencies. Often, however, what prompted the slave to eat dirt – the immediate cause rather than the long-term origins – was a changed mental state; unhappiness, for instance, itself perhaps brought about by a change of owner, location, a trauma or the threats posed by witchcraft. When pushed into dirt-eating, slaves would eat a variety of soils (some of which were, naturally enough, more dangerous or fatal than others).

Slave doctors were as confused about how to treat dirt-eating as they were about its origins. They were in broad agreement, however, that unless they acted quickly, treating a slave in the early stages of dirt-eating, they had little hope of success. A variety of purges and emetics were the popular cure, but most doctors also agreed that medicine alone would not answer the problem. In young people, said Dr Williamson in 1817, what was needed was 'early detection, and adopting a plan of treatment, with regard to medicine, diet, exercise, cleanliness, and improved clothing, which admits of no delay whatever'. The most serious obstacle to such a plan of action was that, like Thistlewood, many planters or slave-drivers viewed dirt-eating as a punishable offence. At its most bizarre this involved clamping the slave's face and head into an iron mask secured by a lock.[28]

The sufferings and early deaths of the slaves could be paralleled, though never equalled, by the sudden and unexpected pains and demise of whites in the tropics. Tropical life was hazardous for all. But if we need an irrefutable case for the particular agonies of the slaves we need only look at their patterns of reproduction. Conception, childbirth and the early days of childhood provide demographers with some of the clearest evidence about the quality of people's lives. And however we arrange the data, the evidence for West Indian slaves is appalling, and much worse than for other contemporaries.

West Indian slaves were much less fertile than their counterparts in North America. And this conundrum has puzzled historians for years. Why should slaves behave so differently from one region to another? The figures give us a stark indication of the problem. Of the 11 million slaves imported into the Americas, the smallest percentage was deposited in North America, in the region which became the USA. By 1825 that region had the largest proportion of slaves in the Americas. On the other hand, the Caribbean, which had soaked up perhaps 40 per cent of all Africans transported from Africa, had less than 20 per cent of slaves in the hemisphere. Slaves in North America developed an early and quite extraordinary natural increase. Slaves in the West Indies, on the other hand, had a dramatic rate of natural decrease. In the West Indies, the death-rate was higher and the birth-rate lower. The death-rate was higher because, in large part, the region continued for much longer to rely on imports of slaves from Africa; it was among the Africans that the slave death-rates were at their worst. But this was only part of the answer. Why, at the same time, did West Indian slaves suffer such appallingly low birth-rates?

As we have seen, West Indian slaves endured worse diet, worse housing and worse overall conditions than North American slaves. And since many more of them were Africans, their cultural habits – such as were able to survive the upheavals of the crossing and resettlement – tended to be more African and less adaptable to local, American mores. Breast-feeding was a case in point. West Indian slaves tended to breast-feed their babies for up to three years (if they survived that long). Writing in 1811 Dr Collins (familiar with the slaves in St Vincent) argued that: 'Negroes are universally fond of suckling their children for a long time. If you permit them, they will extend it to the third year.' West Indian commentators made similar remarks throughout the islands. Thomas Roughley, the Jamaican planter, said in 1823 that 'it is usually the wish of the female slaves, when they become mothers, to keep the infants suckling to an extraordinary or excessive time, sometimes for three years'. Doctors and planters in the Caribbean were fairly unanimous that their slaves suckled for far too long. Moreover, the scattered statistical evidence we have confirms that Caribbean slaves breast-fed their babies for upwards of twenty-four months – and longer in some cases. Here, it seems, was an African habit transplanted into the Americas. And whatever the flaws in the argument it seems clear that these extended periods of lactation were largely responsible for reducing fertility. If not a totally successful form of contraception, it had the effect of lengthening the periods between conceptions. Planters who were keen to have their slaves reproduce more readily (and spare them the cost of buying new Africans) – an essential move after abolition in 1807 – took pains to reduce the length of time slave mothers were allowed to breast-feed. In the last generation of slavery, planters even offered financial rewards to West Indian slaves who curtailed their breast-feeding at twelve months. Nurseries, rewards, even forcible removal of the suckling babies – all these and more testify to two related phenomena: the slaves' persistence with old, African-based social habits and the planters' determination to eradicate those habits.[29]

Slaves in North America behaved differently. They tended to breast-feed their babies for a much shorter period, usually for only twelve months. In the Chesapeake, local slaves had begun to increase naturally (rather than being augmented by African imports) as early as 1730. As the proportion of locally-born women increased, their child-bearing patterns changed. They married younger than their mothers and began to reproduce earlier (and more successfully) than slaves in the West Indies. By the 1760s the black population of the region was increasing rapidly.

Slave women in the Caribbean, on the other hand, found it hard to conceive – a combination of disease, ill-health, hard work and poor nutrition (not to mention the high incidence of venereal disease) led to an unusually low rate of conception. At any given moment a substantial proportion of slave women were suffering from a range of complaints. In 1780 on the Clarendon estates of William Beckford in Jamaica, 188 of the 604 women were sick; another thirty were 'useless'. And even among those women still toiling at the most demanding jobs in the fields, a substantial minority were less than well.

Thomas Thistlewood frequently mentioned his slaves' miscarriages, often in the most casual, dismissive fashion. In December 1761 he noted in his diary that Little Mimber was sick in the Negro House: 'It is said she miscarried last week.' Six years later, another slave aborted, under different circumstances. On 17 June 1767, 'Mountain Lucy miscarried, having I am told drank Contra-yerva lately every day on purpose.' In May 1774 Abba was ill with violent pains in her belly: 'Miscarried it seems.' Another slave, Franke, only one week after having sex with Thistlewood, miscarried: 'Her belly was pretty big.'[30] And so this dismal litany continued; slaves miscarrying as often, it seemed, as they gave birth.

It was not worth recording a slave birth until the child had survived the dangerous early weeks. Perhaps 25 per cent of all births went unrecorded because the baby died within a few days of birth. Slaves for their part seemed to display indifference to the new baby until it had survived the first nine days of life. Babies who died in that period were not accorded full burial rites, but it has to be said that much the same was true in Britain at the same time. Dead babies went unrecorded, unremarked, but it would be wrong to assume, as so many historians have, that they passed unmourned and unloved. How can we know?

All those writing about the slaves in the eighteenth century agreed that substantial numbers of slave infants died soon after birth. Of those deaths, perhaps 80 per cent took place in the first two weeks; this fell to 50 per cent in the next century. Edward Long, writing of Jamaica in 1788, argued that 'Tetanus destroys (in general) One Third of all the young children that are born here'. Dr George Farquhar, a Jamaican doctor, said in 1805 that 'one half of those born in the course of the year are not infrequently carried off'.[31] Others offered different percentages, but all were agreed that the numbers were vast. And this, we need to remind ourselves, is in a society accustomed to infant mortality. Englishmen found nothing shocking or unusual about infant deaths. What was shocking was the level, the incidence and the apparent inevitability of infant deaths in the slave quarters.[32]

Tetanus (a result perhaps of child-rearing practices, notably the swaddling of babies, and the umbilical cord, in dirty cloth), stomach complaints (directly linked to the filth and insanitary conditions of the slave quarters) and a number of infectious diseases, all made fatal inroads among the newborn.[33] This was also true among poor children in the western world at the same time. Slave babies died for much the same social and economic reasons that poor babies died (and continue to die) in many, utterly different societies.

Those babies who managed to survive the hazards of their first two weeks were then exposed to new and different dangers in their childhood. They faced those perennial killers of children, smallpox, measles, whooping cough, in addition to local dangers such as yaws; worms were especially dangerous for they 'too often baffle the prescriptions of the Doctor, and the care and attention of the Nurses'.[34] More difficult to decide is the degree to which undernourished mothers added to their infants' physical problems by not being able to provide the necessary nutrition for their newborn or growing children. The data are difficult to analyse but historians are generally agreed that children, like their elders, suffered in varying degrees from malnutrition; so many of the complaints described by planters and their medical helpers were clearly the consequences of undernourishment. Again this now seems fairly obvious. In societies where undernourishment was commonplace (though generally cyclical), children, like adults, would share in the general slave deprivation. But for growing children the consequences were more catastrophic, exposing them not only to deficiency diseases and anaemias, but to the development of physical imperfections and deformities which would last a lifetime. Slave children were, for instance, smaller than other children. On average they were 2–3 cm shorter than those children working in the factories in early industrial England; the very people regarded as enduring the worst of physical environments.

There were, as we might expect, great variations in the physical size of slaves throughout the slave colonies. The African slaves tended to be smaller than local-born slaves, and West Indian slaves were smaller than slaves in North America.[35] It seems that not only was the diet of American slaves better, but the work they undertook was less demanding, less consuming of human energy, than slave work in the Caribbean. Nevertheless, recent research has shown that slave children in the American South fared markedly worse than their white counterparts. Slave children not only inherited many of the physical problems of their parents who came from Africa, these problems were worsened by a diet that was low in calcium and high in carbohydrates and fats.[36]

Hungry slaves could often only sate their hunger by theft. Yet theft could incur the most savage of punishments. And those punishments would further sap the physical and moral well-being of people already undermined by hunger. What effect this had on their mental equilibrium, particularly among those who had endured the Atlantic crossing, we can only speculate. Slave-owners, in seeking to extract the maximum efforts from their black labour force, felt obliged to respond to slave shortcomings with a violent and often rapacious regime which often proved counter-productive, serving to debilitate still further people already living on the margins of physical and mental stability.

Death must have come as a blessing to many slaves. Some, we know, took their own lives, but it is not clear that the incidence of suicide among the slaves was any greater than among poor peoples elsewhere.

In death as in life, the slaves elude our gaze. For the millions of slaves who died in the colonies, few permanent resting places survive. Crumbling head-stones and monuments in churchyards and inside churches provide some material survival of the lost plantocracy. But what is left of the slaves? A few of them are recorded in the conventional memorials of death which provide so important and traditional a guide to lost peoples. There are few slave burial grounds that we know of, few slave gravestones. Indeed, there are precious few signs throughout the former slave colonies of the physical presence of so many slaves. The great majority have simply passed from the face of recorded history.

Death and burial form one of the most important rites of passage in most human societies. Slaves were obliged, in the main, to create their own cele-brations of death and to commemorate the deaths of friends, loved ones or neighbours as best they could. Again, this was true of poor peoples in other societies. But slaves were in an unusual position: wrenched loose from their own varied African cultures, for a long time not allowed access to the religion of their New World masters, the slaves shaped their own culture from memories and survivals of an African past which grew dimmer as time passed. This they fused with those elements of local white society which were appropriate and available. So it was, for much of the history of slavery, with burials.

Caribbean slaves, denied access to Christian churches and the graveyards, buried their dead and celebrated their passing on local land, in and around the plantation. 'The negroes...bury one another in the ground of the plantation where they die,' wrote the Governor of Barbados in 1676. As late as 1828, Anglican ministers in that island reported that slaves were buried 'in their usual burying places on the estates'. Another wrote that they were interred 'in places set apart for that purpose on each plantation'.[37] But the precise location of those burial grounds remains a mystery. Maps and local references failed to specify slave burial grounds. We know that slaves held special affection for those burial grounds and wanted them close to their homes. In 1788 it was claimed, of Barbados, that:

> Negroes are superstitiously attached to the burial places of their ancestors and friends. They are generally as near as can be to the houses in which they live. It is frequent to inter a near relation under the bedplace on which they sleep, an unwholesome and dangerous practice which they would think it the utmost tyranny to alter.[38]

Close to or within local slave villages, the graves of most slaves have simply disappeared in the years since slavery.

Few slaves were buried in local Christian cemeteries, though the numbers grew in the last generation of British slavery when missionaries made major inroads among the slaves and, naturally enough, persuaded their slave churchgoers to adopt Christian burial. For most, death and its celebration belonged to that complex culture which was mainly African, but which had been transmuted in the New World. Death was thought to herald a return to a better place, a return to the African homeland 'where riches, honour, and splendour will not be lacking, but where there will be an abundance of everything'. One man, witnessing the funeral of an African slave in Barbados in 1796, noted that the mourners 'had full faith, in Jenny's transmigration to meet her friends, at her place of nativity; and their persuasion that death was only a removal from their present to their former home – a mere change from a state of slavery to a state of freedom'.[39]

Slaves throughout the islands believed in a life after death and remained convinced that death would see them reunited with their ancestors. It was an African belief which rested comfortably with whatever influences they derived from local Christianity. In common with their Christian owners, the slaves placed great importance on the funeral.

Like people everywhere, slaves developed their own rituals of mourning and bereavement which had to be accommodated within a system of labour which consumed most of their waking hours. The digging of a grave was accompanied by a dirge. The body was prepared (for evening burial) at home, wrapped in clothing with sentimental objects placed with the deceased. The burial often involved a procession of local slaves, many of whom dressed for the occasion in whatever finery they could muster. In time the procession and the burial ceremony became even more elaborate and ritualized, incorporating many features of European funerals. When slaves were converted to Christianity this, and many other slave customs, was readily adapted to the European version of burial. Whites rarely attended slave funerals (though slaves were sometimes expected to attend an owner's burial), contenting themselves with providing the slaves with the necessary materials for a proper funeral. When Thistlewood's slave Joe died in 1783, the master provided a coffin and some rum for the funeral.[40]

Many slaves were not buried in a coffin though slaves attached great importance to having a 'handsome burial' with all the appropriate objects and ceremonies; in time the coffin became a necessary feature of a 'proper' slave burial.[41]

Interment was generally accompanied by music, singing or dirges. As early as 1657 Ligon reported from Barbados that slaves buried their dead while 'clapping and wringing their hands, and making a doleful sound with their voices'. A century later, on the same island, it was claimed that 'most young people sing and dance, and make a loud noise with rattles, as they attend the corpse to its interment'. When Parliament sought to 'civilize' slave culture in the early nineteenth century, one of its targets was the 'heathenish or idolatrous music, singing, or ceremonies' at funerals.[42] Some slaves were specialist funeral performers: John, a Barbadian runaway in 1808, was 'famous for playing the pump and singing at Negro dances and funerals'.[43]

At the graveside (according to Hans Sloane in 1707), Jamaican slaves added rum and food to the grave, 'to serve them in the other world. Sometimes they bury it in gourds, at other times spill it on the graves.' Writing about Jamaican slaves in 1687–8, John Taylor said they put into the grave 'casader bread, rosted fowls, sugar, rum, tobacco, and pipes with fier to light his pipe withall, and this they doe…in order to sustain him in his journey beyond those pleasant hills in their own country whither they say he is now going to live at rest'. In West Africa and the West Indies the dead were prepared for the journey home; goods were placed in the grave for sustenance on the journey and as gifts for long-departed ancestors.[44] Graveside ceremonies were alive with music and wailing, sometimes with jocularity; friends and mourners then adjourned to feast and drink. Those historians who have sought to link these ceremonies specifically to West Africa might also care to speculate that similar celebrations were widespread throughout Britain.

Rarely were the graves marked by permanent headstones or markings. Not until the coming of Christian graveyards did local burial sites take on the style and permanence we assume to be basic to burial grounds. It was in the same era that the more elaborate of African-based burial ceremonies, especially the graveside dancing and singing, began to wane and finally disappear. The rise of black Christianity imposed on slave burial customs that decorum and relative tranquillity which whites recognized as the sole true way of mourning. As slaves became more Christian, less African, they lost many of their old cultural habits. But for much of the history of black slavery – and certainly as long as the slave trade continued to deliver fresh batches of Africans into the slave quarters – it was inevitable that Africa would loom large in the customs of burial and mourning. It was but another aspect of the slaves' 'barbaric paganism' which, in the eyes of the whites, placed an unbridgeable gulf between black and white. A history of Barbados in 1750 remarked that: 'The negroes in general are very tenaciously addicted to the rites, ceremonies, and superstitions of their own countries, particularly in their plays, dances, music, marriages, and burials.'[45] Whites viewed these various slave ceremonies as 'superstitions'; signs of primitive peoples and their crude, unsophisticated habits. 'Superstition'; the word crops up time and again in white commentaries on black religious practices. And no 'superstitions' seemed more pronounced than those of bereavement and burial: 'There is no characteristic more strongly marked in the Negro than their superstitious veneration for the dead.'[46]

It is unclear how these habits were more 'superstitious' than those of their white Christian owners and observers. No doubt it comforted whites to place an ocean of sensibility between them and their heathen slaves. Looking back, however, the essence of the slave ceremonials of death look remarkably like those of their Christian owners. But to admit of such similarities, to concede that black and white might, in the world of black slavery, share more than the air they breathed, was to corrode that vital distinction between the two sides. To see among the slaves a mere hint of similarity was to admit of a common humanity which would undermine slavery itself. Much better to see slaves as the heathen beasts of burden whose lives were occasionally relieved by the pathetic enjoyments afforded by social habits from their African past.

When slaves died, their demise was recorded in the slave books. Like other forms of property, they were deleted from the possessions of their former owners. Born or imported into the slave colonies as chattel, valued and prized to a specific amount, the slaves left in a similar fashion. Sometimes their deaths represented a loss to their owners. A strong slave, a skilled man or woman, a recently purchased African – all these and more had a price on their head which went with them to the grave. 'Old and useless' was an economic category; the last and lowest rung on the slave ladder before consignment to the economic loss of the grave.

So many slipped away at an age when they ought to have been in their prime. And while this was and is hardly unusual among the poor, in the slave colonies it was so often a human decline and demise induced by slavery itself. The exact details will never be fully known, but it is beyond doubt that armies of black slaves slid into physical decline and an early grave *because* they were slaves. The slave system involved an international mix of peoples and diseases, kept in place by rapacious regimes of life and work unique in the modern world. The sole purpose was profit and material advancement for the minority, but at an incalculable cost to the black majority. Yet it was another irony that the system which sought to extract the best returns from its black human capital induced levels of ill-health, suffering and premature death which were obviously uneconomic. Black slavery was an economic system which appeared able to maintain itself only by a series of internal economic irregularities. But what comfort was this to the slaves?

PART IV

Resting

II

Slaves at Ease

A tutor in Virginia was alarmed, in January 1774, to discover two of his wards dancing with local slaves: 'This Evening the Negroes collected themselves into the School-Room & began to play the Fiddle & dance.'[1] They were in good company. Wherever slaves gathered in the Americas they made music. From the moment they stepped ashore, visitors to slave colonies were struck by the vigour, exuberance and inescapability of slaves enjoying themselves. They seemed especially fond of music and dance. When Thomas Thistlewood first landed in Kingston, Jamaica, he wandered 'to the westward of the Town, to see Negro Diversions – odd Music, Motions, etc. The Negroes of each Nation by themselves.'[2] As he settled into life in Jamaica, slave music often disturbed his peace. On 21 July 1766 he 'Flogged Ambo and Johnie for permitting a singing etc. at the Negro house last Saturday night'. On another occasion he was so incensed that he 'broke Job's banjar [banjo] to pieces in the mill house'.[3]

Slaves sang and made music on their improvised instruments; danced throughout the night at the ceremonies and festivals (sometimes swinging their white masters and mistresses around the floor with them). When Sir William Young visited his plantation in Barbados in 1791 he met a ninety-five-year-old slave who 'danced at the Negro-ball last Christmas; and I am to be her partner, and dance with her next Christmas'. Slaves danced when their masters returned from abroad or visited a property for the first time. Monk Lewis was amazed at their celebrations when he visited his estates in Jamaica in 1816; wherever he went he was greeted by 'strange and sudden bursts of singing and dancing'.

> Their music consisted of nothing but Gambys [Eboe drums], shaky-shekies, and kitty-katties; the latter is nothing but a flat piece of board with two sticks, the former is a bladder with a parcel of pebbles in it. But the principal part of the

music to which they dance is vocal; one girl generally singing two lines by
herself, and being answered by the chorus...The singing began about six
o'clock, and lasted without a moment's pause till two in the morning; and
such a noise never did hear till then.[4]

Local whites were so influenced by black music and dance that their own
music seemed, to outsiders at least, to be very similar to slave music. One
Virginian danced 'Congo minuets'; the 'Negro jig' became a feature of local
white dances.[5]

For people who arrived in the New World with nothing, the slaves were
quick to acquire home-made instruments. Wood, string, bones, skins, sticks,
gourds, pans and horns; all were put to good musical use. Christmas and other
formal holidays brought forth a cacophony of slave music:

the rattling of the chains and slings from the wharves, the mock-driving of hoops
by the coopers, winding the postmen's horns, beating militia and negroe drums,
the sound of the pipe and tabor, negroe flutes, gombas and jaw-bones, scraping
the violin, and singing of men, women and children, with other incidental
noises, make Kingston at this time a very disagreeable residence.[6]

It had been like this from the early days of slavery in the Americas. Richard
Ligon, describing Barbados in its transition to a slave colony in the mid-
seventeenth century, was struck by slave music. 'In the afternoons on Sundays,
they have their Musick, which is of kettle drums, and those of several
sizes; upon the smallest the best Musician plays, and the other comes in as
Chorasses.' He was captivated by the slave drumming: 'the drum all men know,
has but one tone; and therefore variety of tunes have little to do in this musick;
and yet so strangely they varie their time, as 'tis a pleasure to the most
curious ears, and it was to me one of the strangest noises that ever I heard
of one tone.'[7]

A generation later, Sir Hans Sloane, travelling through the Caribbean, was
similarly struck by slave music. Despite being 'hard wrought', the slaves 'will
at nights, or on Feast days Dance and Sing; their Songs are all bawdy, and
leading that way'. He described their lutes, made from gourds and horse hair,
or peeled climbing plants; the slaves danced with rattles tied to their ankles
and wrists and 'often tie Cow Tails to their Rumps, and add such other odd
things to their bodies in several places'.[8]

Musical instruments were, not surprisingly, similar in North America and
the Caribbean; crude drums made from wood and hide, the banjo, gourd
rattles, mandolin and other stringed instruments, and a range of percussion
instruments. They also adopted European instruments. In 1753 a Virginian
planter advertised for 'an orderly Negro or mulatto who can play well the
violin'. One slave ran away taking his fiddle with him.[9]

John Stedman described the musical instruments he found among the slaves in Surinam, listing eighteen different varieties of home-made instruments, 'to which they dance with more spirit than we do to the best bands in Europe'. In Surinam, the slaves gathered for a dance each Saturday evening, 'and generally once a quarter are indulged with a grand ball'. Neighbouring slaves were usually invited and the master often put in an appearance or donated rum. Sometimes the music lasted from Saturday night to Monday morning, when dawn heralded the return to the fields: 'thus had passed six-and-thirty hours in dancing, cheering, hallooing, and clapping of hands'. Slaves did not need a partner to join in: 'I have known a newly-imported negro, for want of a partner, figure and foot it for nearly the space of two hours, to his shadow against the wall.'[10]

Similar stories unfolded from one slave colony to another. Wherever there were slaves, music and dance dominated local social life. One correspondent from Antigua thought that the slaves' agility at dance was brought about by the 'warm climate, where elasticity is more general than in the colder latitudes'.[11] Whatever the cause, all were agreed that slaves were 'extremely fond of music and dancing; they have good ears and preserve the most perfect tune and time'. William Beckford thought that if permitted, slaves would dance 'from night to morning'.[12] Weekends were often consumed by dancing and music. And much the same was true at slave funerals (see Chapter 10) and weddings, compared by one observer to the wakes enjoyed 'by the vulgar peasantry in Ireland', where 'they dance to "tire each other down"; where they court, laugh, and sing at once; and cry, pipe and play at once; and where they gormandize and guzzle, fight and quarrel at once'.[13]

Slaves often sang when at work in the fields or factory, measuring out via songs the pattern of work, the rhythm of labour; a refrain and choral response which provided the discipline for labouring routines. John Stedman heard it among the boatmen in Surinam: 'one person constantly pronouncing a sentence extempore, which he next hums or whistles, and then all the others repeat the same in chorus.'[14]

William Beckford heard it hundreds of miles away in Jamaica at much the same period, though this time in the sugar mills:

> When the mill is at work at night, there is something affecting in the songs of the women who feed it; and it appears somewhat singular that all their tunes, if tunes they can be called, are of a plaintiff cast. Sometimes you may hear one soft, complaining voice; and now a second and a third chime in; and presently, as if inspired by the solemn impressions of night, and by the gloomy objects that are supposed to dwell around, a full chorus is heard to swell upon the ear, and then to die away again to the first original tone.[15]

Whatever the labour – however hard or tiring – slaves would set up a work song. Sometimes they were melancholy refrains about their lives and torments.

If we want to go in a Ebo
Me can't go there!
Since dem tief me from a Guinea,
Me can't go there![16]

Perhaps the most haunting and memorable was the music of black boatmen throughout the Americas. The songs of deck hands and rowers were, by turns, satirical and amorous, insulting and bawdy, entertaining passengers and observers watching the passing boats. The swish of the oars beat time with the songs from on deck.[17]

In the fields, the sounds of the field gangs – the slashing of the cane, the heaving and lifting of heavy bundles and parcels – all formed a labouring background to the songs. Field gangs worked and sang in unison; repetitive tasks were measured out by song and chorus. Musical questions drifted across the field, musical answers floated back from the work group. From Barbados in the seventeenth century through to the Deep South in the US in the mid-nineteenth century, these field songs were part and parcel of slave life and culture, not so much a response to slave work but a fundamental feature of work itself. Slave gangs continued to sing when they left the fields. Time and again, visitors were struck by the haunting music which drifted from the coffles of slaves as they plodded back to the slave quarters. Later, slaves who moved into the towns of the American South took their work songs with them. Soon the sounds of black music were to be heard in urban work-places and in the streets of nineteenth century America. Wherever slaves worked, there they sang.[18] It was a musical culture which was to live on, long after slavery had gone, throughout the Americas and which survives in so many forms to this day.

Africans among the slaves often hived off into tribal groupings for their own musical entertainment. Sharp-eyed witnesses claimed to be able to detect marked differences between the kind of music played and sung by different tribes. Bryan Edwards thought the music of the Ibos was 'soft and languishing', that of the Coromantees 'heroick and martial'. Cutting across such differences, however, was a unifying element, 'a predominant melancholy, which to a man of feeling, is sometimes very affecting'.[19] As long as the slave trade survived, it infused African cultural habits into the slave quarters; through music, different African groups expressed themselves and sought to rekindle a life they had been torn from.

Time and again, observers remarked on the 'tribal' nature of West Indian slave music. When slaves gathered for a musical evening, remarked one writer in Jamaica in 1797, 'the Negroes of each tribe or nation assemble in distinct groups with their instruments... The Coromantines far excel the others in music'.[20]

Even when outsiders could not detect tribal differences, they invariably interpreted the slaves' musicality as African. One observer said that slaves 'dance to the sound of their beloved music, and the singing of their favourite African yell. Both the music and dance are of a savage nature.' As the slaves plunged into the accelerating excitement of the dance, as the noise and confusion grew, 'a spectator would require only a slight aid from fancy to transport him to the savage wilds of Africa'.[21]

Whites were in no doubt that the musical pleasures of the slaves, however transformed by life in the Americas, were rooted in an African past. The instruments, the songs, the frenzy and carnality of the dance, the assembled crowd – part dancers, part spectators – all and more were, it was claimed, part of an African cultural background, transplanted and revived in the slave colonies of the Americas.

Not surprisingly, whites came to assume that there was something distinctively musical about blacks. They have, said John Wesley, 'the nicest ear for music'. It was a 'natural' talent on which missionaries and Christian slave-owners later sought to capitalize; hymns and psalms might lure 'pagan' slaves to Christianity. This assumption of black musicality was widely accepted in western society and pre-dated the development of black slavery in the New World (see Chapter 8). On the whole, whites regarded it as a harmless, if somewhat inexplicable, passion of a primitive people. It had its usefulness, of course. The slaves tired themselves out, burning off their energy in weekends of dancing when they might, if not at play, be up to dangerous mischief.

Slave music was not as simple as it seemed, though neither was it always as sinister as some slave-owners imagined. There were certain features of slave music which worried the whites; in particular, there seemed more to slave drumming than mere enjoyment. It was associated in the mind of the slave-owning class with African religions ('superstitions'), some of which were thought to be dangerous and subversive. Most threatening of all, it seemed the obvious way for slaves to communicate with each other. Drums, wrote Sir Hans Sloane in 1707, were used 'in their Wars at home in Africa, [and therefore] it was thought too much to inciting them to Rebellion, and so they were prohibited by the Customs of the Island'.[22] In 1789 when John Reeves tried to summarize the laws of slavery for Parliament, he wrote that throughout the islands it was unlawful for slave owners to allow 'Slaves *to assemble* together, and *beat* their Military *Drums*, empty Casks, and great Gourds, or blow their Horns or Shells.' Local laws even allowed the military 'to enter Plantations to prevent such Assembling, Drumming, and Noises. It is declared, however, that this shall not prevent Slaves assembling for their Amusement.'

The reason for such laws was simple enough: 'These restrictions proceeded from the Experience that Rebellions had often been concerted at Dances and Nightly Meetings of Slaves from different Plantations.'[23]

Slaves everywhere used their music to mock and ridicule the whites. Aping the manners, the hauteur, the idiosyncrasies of local whites, male and female, could be guaranteed to bring howls of laughter from other slaves. In South Carolina in 1772 sixty slaves gathered outside Charleston: 'The entertainment was opened by the men copying the manners of their masters and the women those of their mistresses and relating some highly curious anecdotes, to the inexpressible diversion of that company.'[24]

Slaves broke into song to ridicule the whites – to gain revenge for slights and injuries stoically endured. Derision greeted new arrivals. When a boat tied up at Port Royal Jamaica, a passenger heard slaves singing of the whites' impending fate:

> New-come buckra [whiteman]
> He get sick,
> He tak fever,
> He be die
> He be die.[25]

Throughout the West Indies, the Saturday night dance attracted slaves from a wide local area. When the music and dance was in full swing, the laws tended to be ignored (though the organizers might later be punished). The singing and dancing was often accompanied by food and (too much) drink. Outsiders were shocked by the excessive drinking, the drunkenness and the consequent sickness. Sometimes the slave arranging the dance collected money or goods for attendance; paying the musicians and covering the costs of the refreshments. Privileged slaves aped the styles of their white superiors, in dress, in the dances they performed and even down to producing crude invitations modelled on those issued for white soirées and balls. Whites rarely refused permission for such dances (often called 'plays') to take place. Beginning at eight on Saturday evening, they invariably lasted throughout the night. Some even reconvened on Sunday night.[26]

Visitors describing such scenes were usually mesmerized by the music and the dance, often referring to it as 'African': 'Outside the house, in the moonlight, a musician seated himself with his drum on the ground, and commenced singing an African air, when a circle of men and women, linked hand in hand, danced round him.'[27]

As long as the slave trade transplanted Africans into the islands, African slaves would continue to infuse their culture into the slave quarters. But as a growing proportion of slaves became Creole, a subtle process of adaptation took place. Like the slaves themselves, cultural patterns became less African, more Creole, incorporating certain qualities from the whites. Fiddles, for instance, became a popular Creole slave instrument. But however modified, music remained a permanent and ubiquitous feature of slave life in the Americas.

In the mainland colonies slave music was equally African as long as the slave trade continued. However, when American slaves began to reproduce more readily, and when the colonies had less need for importing Africans, it was inevitable that African cultural forms would become less striking. There, like the Caribbean, contemporaries frequently remarked on the black propensity for music; 'more generally gifted than the whites with accurate ears for tune and time,' was the way Thomas Jefferson described it.[28] In time, slave music was expressed most powerfully and most influentially through black religion; through those various sects which swept up so many slaves in the early nineteenth century. That process of Christianizing the slaves was itself part of the general muting and moderating of African cultures.

Like slave-owners in the West Indies, the North Americans did not always approve of slave music. For a start, it was regarded as yet another example of African barbarity; a 'heathen' survival which could not be tolerated in the more civilized world of the Americas. When Baptists began to make converts among the North American slaves, they found the blacks' musical enjoyments especially immoral. Denying themselves the public pleasures of music, gambling and other forms of worldliness, the Baptists were keen to curb those same habits among the slaves. It was immoral for anyone, black or white, 'to play the violin or banjo or sing worldly songs or to dance to dress "gaudily", to go to horse races, to bet, to drink to excess'.[29] Slaves did all of these things. More troublesome for slave-owners was the seeming link between music and slave resistance. In the Stono rebellion in South Carolina in 1739, rebels had been rallied to the cause by the sound of a drum. The Georgia slave code had such incidents in mind when it prohibited slaves from 'using and keeping drums, horns, or other loud instruments, which may call together or give sign or notice to one another of their wicked designs and intentions'.

Such prohibitions, and the vigilance of slave-owners, failed to purge slaves of their 'African' enjoyments. A commentator thought that throughout Georgia and South Carolina (in 1779), not only were slaves 'great strangers to Christianity' but their holidays were 'days of idleness, riot, wantonness and excess; in which the slaves assemble together in alarming crowds for the purpose of dancing, feasting and merriment'.[30]

In the pre-modern world, leisure for the great bulk of common people was not separated from their daily working lives; they took their pleasures as and when they could, often at work, often by absenting themselves from work; drinking, gambling, making music in and around the home and work-place. High days and holidays were exceptional and, naturally enough, were marked by mass celebrations of enjoyment in the most pleasurable fashions allowed by custom and conventions. Much the same was true for the slaves of the Americas.

Their most frequent leisure moments were provided by the weekend, from Saturday evening (sometimes Saturday lunchtime) through to dawn on

Monday morning. The northern European routine of the weekend break, imposed throughout the English slave colonies, was seized and used to the maximum. The favourite and most common recreation was, as we have seen, the weekend dance which was often drawn-out through the whole weekend.

Free time also provided that most valuable and rare of commodities for the slaves (and indeed for poor labouring people everywhere) – time to do as they pleased. It was a time to visit friends, relatives and loved ones. Slaves travelling to neighbouring properties generally needed approval from their owners or masters. Equipped with a 'ticket' or pass of authorization, they set off, often covering great distances, to spend their free time with their loved ones. Slaves were much more mobile than we might imagine. Slave-owners tended not to advertise for missing slaves as 'runaways' until some time after they had left, for the simple reason that many stayed away for a few extra days – or even a week or two – to linger with loved ones on distant properties. On the whole, slave-owners had a rough idea of their slaves' destination; when they failed to return, the resulting advertisements often specified the district or relative the slaves had headed for.

Weekends, then, were the most frequent break from slave work. But it did not leave all slaves free from labours. Now was the time to catch up with that host of domestic chores which had accumulated during the working week; mending and patching in and around the home and, most important of all, tending their own plots, gardens and provision grounds. Planters came to realize that the slaves' home-grown food was invaluable. Importing foodstuffs from Europe and North America to feed the slaves was not only costly but also risky and liable to be disrupted by warfare and bad weather. Slaves supplemented the basic diet provided by their owners by the fruit, vegetables and meat (normally pig and goat meat) which they cultivated and tended on their own lands. By the last generation of slavery in the British Caribbean, more slaves were being fed from their own provision grounds than from their masters' supplies.[31] In time, legislation in most of the islands ordered slave-owners to provide their slaves with appropriate provision grounds, though when sugar prices were high there was always the temptation to use all good land for cane cultivation.

Sometimes the provision grounds were worked under white supervision. More often, however, they were worked by the slaves in their free time, especially at the weekend. Everyone was expected to help; the whole family group, young and old, fit and disabled, each undertaking a task appropriate to their condition. The basic foodstuffs were root crops, 'yams, plantains, bananas, cassada or manioc, edoes, potatoes, ocoraes [okra], Indian corn, cale, pigeon pease, and several species of beans, and pine apples'.[32] On higher ground they grew European vegetables. Surplus produce from this weekend work was used for barter, exchange and sale among neighbours and in local markets. Goods and cash from those transactions added luxuries and refinements to their material lives. The work invested in weekend work supplemented the slaves' diet but it was perhaps more important still in laying the basis for their independent economic and social activity. The fruits of their weekend labours took the indirect form of clothing and furnishings, hard cash and refinements, animals and jewellery. Many slaves were able to acquire a host of material possessions which would have been utterly beyond their reach had they not put their free time to good use. Free time, especially at weekends, was not always as free as it seemed.

Festivals and holidays were the more obvious breaks from labour. Christian festivals (especially Christmas and Easter but also a host of locally-celebrated saints' days), New Year and harvests; these and others became major slave festivals. But so too did others which derived more from African than European roots; carnival and John Canoe for example.

Slaves took inordinate time and effort to prepare for their favourite celebrations. Christmas in the West Indies was preceded by lengthy preparations: clothes, often elaborate costumes, were specially made, food set aside and time devoted to the necessary preparations. It was a noisy, colourful and (to many Europeans) uncomfortably exuberant holiday. Slaves split into their or local groupings, paraded through the local town or property, singing and dancing and playing music. Parading slaves were often joined by the local militia in full regalia (though they were generally mustered from fear of slave exuberance spilling over into slave unrest).

Slaves might have three days holiday at Christmas. Their owners gave them extra food and drink; the senior slaves (often dressed in European styles and clothes) visited whites' homes where they played their own music and were treated in turn to food and drink. But it was the slave 'assemblies', the slave dances and 'plays' which were the highlight of the slaves' Christmas. Slaves divided themselves into groups, often marked by different coloured clothing, or processed from their property until they met converging parades of other slaves at a chosen spot, sometimes as far as twelve miles from their home. There they began their Christmas celebrations in earnest. Most danced and sang, others were 'in a constant state of intoxication' for the whole of Christmas.[33]

Whites were always bemused by the slaves' insistence on wearing finery for Christmas. Women grouped into 'sets' which took a particular colour as their theme. Led by a black fiddler, they paraded through the local streets or paths, dressed in the same colour; gold, velvet, garnet. It was, said one writer about Jamaica in 1797, 'no easy matter to account for several of them getting such finery'.[34] Lady Nugent wrote in her diary of Jamaica in 1801: 'Christmas Day! All night the music of Tom-Toms, etc. Rise early, and the whole town and house bore the appearance of a masquerade.' The passing slaves were all bedecked in their best; 'many of the blacks had really gold and silver fringe on their robes'. Nor did the day after bring a respite from the pleasurable turmoil. '26th – The same wild scenes acting over and over again.'

It was a Christmas which few Europeans would have recognized, for the slaves invested it with distinctive features derived directly from their African past. John Canoe (or Jon Kanoo) was the most striking in Jamaica. Lines and processions of singing and dancing slaves were led by John Canoe himself, a slave festooned in the most elaborate of disguises, dancing and leading the procession hither and yon. He was a sort of Puck, making fun of bystanders (especially the whites) and generally clowning his way through the day. His clothing was bizarre and colourful; baggy clothes tied by red tape, blue velvet waistcoat lavishly embroidered, his sleeves bordered by strips of metal which jingled as he walked. His long-tailed coat was similarly edged with bells and mounted by elaborate epaulettes. On his head he wore an enormous cocked hat, from which conflicting masks hung at the front and back. The whole colourful scene was rounded off by an eye-catching item pinned to his rear. Skipping along, waving a white wand in one hand, a dirty handkerchief in the other, John Canoe made mock of spectators, pretending slavishly to clean their shoes and mop their sweaty brows with his mouchoir ('murder, what a flavour of salt fish and onions it had!'). Leaping back whence he came, John Canoe pranced and wove his way through Christmas Day, calling forth music and set pieces from his following parade.

The pattern was similar from place to place, though the details varied. John Canoe incorporated flashes of white culture – images of notable statesmen and warriors, songs about Britannia, imitations of royalty and nobility. The most extraordinary of pieces flitted in and out of this amazing cultural kaleidoscope.

When Lady Nugent saw her first Christmas celebrations, the John Canoe parade included children who represented 'Tipoo Saib's children, and the man was Henry the 4th of France. – What a melange!' When Monk Lewis arrived at Black River in Jamaica on 1 January 1816 he was greeted by the local John Canoe who was 'dressed in striped doublet, and bearing upon his head a kind of pasteboard house-boat, filled with puppets, representing some sailors, others soldiers, others again slaves at work on a plantation'.[35]

Visitors found it hard to make any sense of John Canoe. On the whole they liked it, found it entertaining and good fun and thought it yet another illustration of the child-like, simple enjoyments which characterized the slaves. They knew that slaves placed great importance on it; it was clear enough that it borrowed heavily from white culture. It looked in many respects like the world of European Mardi Gras or Shrove Tuesdays; days when the world was turned upside down, when the lowest became superior and when the traditional order and conventions were suspended. It was, like Mardi Gras, a time to let off steam, to cock a snook at betters. It was, however, strictly limited. When the festival – Christmas or New Year – was over, life was expected to return, at a stroke, to its normal, harsh routines. As dawn broke on the first day back at work, yesterday's parade of John Canoe was transformed into yet another coffle of slaves shuffling off to work in the fields. Like so many aspects of popular culture, such celebrations were as useful to the masters as they were enjoyable to the slaves.

Towards the end of slavery, when the proportion of Africans began to decline, the African elements in slave celebrations began to recede or were transformed by more overtly European cultural forms. Maypoles and Jack-in-the-Green appeared at the centre of slave dances. Some visitors even thought slave celebrations similar to English Mumming players (though where English Mummers painted their faces black, the slaves painted their white).[36] In the last years of slavery in the Caribbean, some observers thought they detected a coolness among Creole slaves towards the wilder enthusiasms of the Africans. Certainly those who turned to Christianity had good reason to modify their cultural habits (though they too incorporated much of that 'enthusiasm' into their new religion).

As West Indian slaves became more Christianized, from the 1780s onwards, their energies were turned towards church and chapel and its more formal obligations and rituals. In 1826 a visitor remarked that passing through a West Indian village 'on a Christmas night, it is more common to hear psalm-singing than the sound of merriment'.[37] Others continued to find the old habits equally striking, but it is significant that local whites told their guests that now, in the 1820s and 1830s, they no longer dreaded the onset of Christmas. The slaves' celebrations had been contained; they were more acceptable because more Christian, less troublesome because more restrained, less African.

Long after slavery had ended, Christmas, New Year and Easter parades and carnivals, so obviously a fusion of African and Christian elements, remained the highlights of local black life throughout the West Indies, differing from one island to another (French islands for instance had flower carnivals).

In North America, the slaves were, from an early date, less overtly African in their public celebrations, but there was no doubting the African-based features of many of their leisure-time activities. Slaves in the Chesapeake did not develop a settled social life until after the main influx of Africans into the region. And even then they lived close to local whites whose values and lifestyles clearly influenced the evolution of slave society. Africa continued to surface, however, in transmuted form, in the cultural lives of slaves. Marriage, burial and mourning continued to bear many of the 'African' characteristics which whites so disliked and struggled to contain. There were, in the words of one man in Virginia, 'many remains ... of the savage customs of Africa': 'they cry and bawl and howl around the grave and roll in the dirt, and make many expressions of the most frantic grief ... sometimes the noise they make may be heard as far away as one or two miles.'[38]

North American slaves were most strikingly 'African' when enjoying their music and dance. At weekends they produced their banjos and gourd drums. In 1774 a British visitor wrote: 'The poetry is like the music – Rude and uncultivated. Their Dancing is most violent exercise, but so irregular and grotesque, I am not able to describe it.' Their songs, like those of their contemporaries throughout the Caribbean, were satirical and usually directed against their masters and mistresses.[39]

Slaves in South Carolina celebrated Christmas much like slaves in the West Indies. John Pierpont, a tutor working on a local plantation, described how on Christmas morning,

> the sound of serenading violins and drums saluted my ears, and for some time continued...During the whole of the second and third afternoons, the portico was crowded with these dancers...fiddlers and drumming...Some of them who were native Africans did not join the dance with the others, but, by themselves gave us a specimen of the sports & amusement with which the benighted and uncivilized children of nature divert themselves.[40]

When the slaves were converted, they invested their musical energy in carols and church singing.

Sunday was the obvious day for slave enjoyments but they often had to run the gauntlet of local priestly objection. Clerics were unhappy to see the Lord's Day made less than holy by the noisy pleasures of local slaves. It was a measure of the success of the process of Christianizing the slaves that, by the early nineteenth century, they regarded Saturday, not the Lord's Day, as the day for their festivities. Even then their music and songs remained close in style and substance to the West African communities they had sprung from. Now, however, these were directed at the particular conditions of their lives as slaves. Scipio, an African slave popular for his singing in All Saints parish, South Carolina, sang the following verse:

> Come listen, all you darkies, come listen to my song,
> It am about ole Massa, who use me bery wrong:
> In de cole, frosty mornin', it aint so bery nice,
> Wid de water to de middle to hoe among de rice.[41]

The end of the local crop provided another opportunity for slaves to indulge their musical fancies. Like agricultural workers the world over, slaves celebrated the end of the harvest with organized merriment. Masters provided drink and food and the slaves produced their musical instruments. West Indian 'crop-over', the end of the sugar harvest, saw slaves assemble near the master's or manager's house, equipped with fiddles and drums. The dancing which followed paid little regard to colour or status, for everyone on the property, black and white, joined in the festivities. Initially slaves formed into their own tribal groupings (as they did at Christmas), but as the slave population became more creolized, this tendency declined. They enjoyed European dances – Scottish reels and country-dances – orchestrated by a local fiddler.[42]

Planters everywhere, however stern and severe their daily handling of the slaves, realized the need to grant slaves a holiday at crop-over. Like Christmas, it was part of the slaves' universally accepted culture; a major break from grinding routines and a social event which surpassed mere enjoyment. Slaves viewed it as a right; masters regarded it as an obligation. Long after slavery had ended, the rural peasantry of the West Indies continued to celebrate crop-over with ceremonies that looked remarkably like the rural pleasures and formalities of European harvest festivals; workers, and the foodstuffs they produced, all bedecked in colours and ribbons, the elaborate dressing of animals and carts, speech-making and drinking; and, of course, music.

In all their breaks from work, at holidays and festivals, slaves conjured forth that fanciful web of folk stories – Anancy stories in the Caribbean, Brer Rabbit stories in North America – which both entertained and interpreted the world around them. Wherever we look at the slaves, their stories were remarkably similar. Though tales of the trickster triumphing over evil or superior forces are familiar in western literature, slave tales had clear African roots. The weak overcome the mighty; tyrants succumb to the wiles and stratagems of the meek, humility masks an invisible strength, and outward stupidity is a front for basic shrewdness and wisdom. Here, again, was a folk custom (like the John Canoe Christmas parades) which was Afro-European; elements of a varied African past transplanted and transformed by contact with European culture, itself reshaped by life in the Americas.

Folklorists have amply illustrated the direct links between slaves' folk tales and their African roots. African animals, the tortoise and the hare, the tar-baby stories – all belong to an African past. Animal tricksters were nature's weaker brethren, relatively powerless beasts, only able to survive and get their way by guile and cunning. Transplanted into the Americas they took on human form, but their role, their physical and social weakness – and of course their ultimately successful guile – remained the same. The wily rabbit outwitting the wolf, the wary rooster fooling the fox, the goat deceiving the lion; the weak, in each case, defeats the strong. In one tale, a fox takes advantage of a pig's good nature to enter his house. Seeing a pot of peas cooking, the fox sings:

> Fox and peas are very good
> But Pig and peas are better.

Pig meanwhile pretends to hear a pack of hounds, offering to hide the fox in a barrel; he then pours the scalding peas on to the fox and kills him.[43]

As slaves unravelled these tales, their audience needed no further instruction; the moral and the lesson were clear to all. Brer Rabbit invariably traps, outwits or kills the superior fox; the lion flees in terror from a goat. 'De rabbit is de slickest o' all de animals de Lawd ever made. He ain't de biggest, an' he ain't de loudest but he sho' am de slickest.'[44] Defender of the weak, conqueror of the coward and the bully, Brer Rabbit and his like spoke for and to the slaves. The most common of such tales involved food – not surprisingly among slaves who were often hungry or craving for a more varied diet. The rabbit tricks the fox out of fish, meat, animals, land, field crops; deceit outstrips gullibility; strength succumbs to guile.

The hero of the tales was the trickster. But central too was the slave story-teller. Time and again it is clear that the story-teller, the interpreter, was himself the black trickster; his tales of devious success and artful cunning won approval, applause and hoots of laughter and derision from his audience. What they heard were stories of slave life itself; of lies and deceit to outwit a master, of black chicanery to deflect oppression and shrewdness to overcome misery. Of course the tales were also good fun. They allowed slaves to laugh at their owners and at themselves; to spot and ridicule personal foibles and weaknesses, pretensions and human frailties.

West Indian slaves had their own folk tales which were different from those of North America but which contained all the same ingredients; the characters were different but the morals and conclusions were much the same. The hero was Anancy, the spider, a Brer Rabbit-like hero, common in many West African folk tales but now transplanted into the slave quarters of the Caribbean. Writing of Antigua, Mrs Lanigan said: 'After dancing, I think the next favourite pastime of the negroes, particularly among the younger ones, is to collect together upon a fine moonlight night, and talk "Nancy stories"...the far-famed "Scheherezade" of the "Arabian Nights" could scarcely invent more marvellous ones.'[45]

The story-teller was, again, held in high repute. Thomas Thistlewood was clearly intrigued by one such story-teller, the female slave Vine who visited his property from a neighbouring estate in 1768. On 17 September he recorded in his journal: 'Mr Say's Vine told many diverting Nancy stories (as Negroes call them) this evening at my house. She tells them very cleverly.' Over the following ten days she returned, telling her tales nightly.

Throughout slave societies, slaves were distinguished – as long as the slave trade persisted – by the various tribal and ethnic divides of their African homelands. Obviously they were lumped together for a host of purposes: the law, for instance, paid little regard to distinctions among the slaves. Equally, the dictates of plantation life and work often disregarded African groupings, save where they might serve the interests of economic efficiency or social control over the slaves. Planters were in fact especially alert to what they viewed as the major distinctions among the slaves. They knew (or though they knew) those groups who were particularly rebellious, those who were industrious, those who were more docile. Of course contemporary white perceptions of African tribal divisions might be crude and sometimes quite wrong. But the basic point remains: as long as Africans flowed into the Americas, their owners were forced to pay attention to the complex ramifications of having such diverse peoples living cheek by jowl on their properties.

It is equally clear that the slaves themselves observed the distinctions in their midst. Nowhere was this clearer than in their free moments; in the time free from work, Africans naturally gravitated towards other slaves of similar backgrounds who shared their language and their experiences. Time and again, commentators remarked on the way slaves automatically collected into African groupings when at leisure. They gathered, danced, sang and drank in smaller, African groups. Outsiders and local whites had no trouble in spotting the differences between the Africans and the local-born slaves. Thomas Thistlewood had been in Jamaica less than a week when, in watching the weekend dances of slaves in Kingston, he wrote in his diary of 'The negroes of each Nation by themselves.'[46] Yet this diversity of African peoples was the human and social richness which created the culture of the slave quarters, a culture which melded with and was shaped by contact with local white society.

Perhaps the most obvious (and durable) of cultural contacts between black and white was language. Slaves were forced to learn the dominant local European language, but it became transmuted into a new, Creole language (see Chapter 5). Local people – black and white – did not speak as they had once spoken in their native regions. They were obliged to adapt their language to the developing patterns of local life.

Precisely the same was true of social life. Africans enjoyed themselves as Africans, bringing their music, their songs, their stories, their dances, their broader culture, into the New World. There it collided with other cultures, more especially that of local whites. It absorbed some aspects of white culture, rejected some, and fundamentally changed others. It was, as we have seen, a mutual process; in the words of one historian, it was a world they made together. Black Christianity, in the West Indies or in the northern colonies, for instance, was quite different from the religion of their masters. And this was true of most cultural forms touched by the slaves. They celebrated Christmas – but not like the whites. They enjoyed music and song – but quite differently from the whites. There were, naturally enough, enormous differences between various slave communities. Jamaican slaves were quite different from those in Virginia, but the broader patterns of social life reveal remarkable similarities. Everywhere where black and white lived and worked together their cultures developed together. It was not a harmonious, simple development. But it was indisputably a process of cross-cultural fertilization.

Geography and the physical environment shaped the possibilities and rewards of slaves' free time. Many enjoyed smoking local tobacco in pipes fashioned from locally-grown corn. West Indian slaves drank the rum they had helped to produce; ate the fish they caught in their spare time, enjoyed the feasting and celebrations around the killing of the beasts they had tended. They played music on instruments they fashioned from whatever suitable local materials came to hand. Slaves gambled on races, on cock-fights, sometimes with spare cash, more often with whatever material possessions they had managed to accumulate.

These activities look remarkably like many of the pleasures of common people in pre-industrial Europe; their leisure moments dictated by that special mix of the rural year, prevailing religious custom and the powerful traditions of local popular culture. Yet it may seem odd, to modern readers, to think of slaves enjoying moments of leisure. It is tempting to think of slavery as so all-embracing, so demanding and enervating an institution, that it could have left slaves with little time and energy for enjoyment. Nothing could be further from the truth.

The zest of slave pleasures, the complexity and colour of their ceremonies, the energy invested in their play, may have been a reflection of the severity which characterized the rest of their lives. For people whose labouring lives were severe and often savage, it may have been all the more important to enjoy free time with a fizz and exuberance which exhausted mere bystanders. Slaves often trooped off to the fields at first light on Monday morning quite exhausted by their weekend revels. In the words of one observer: 'they undergo more fatigue, or at least more personal exertion, during their gala hours of Saturday night and Sunday, than is demanded from them, in labour, during any four days of the week.' Why should they conserve their energy for their masters? Why should they regard labour as any more than a cruel obligation, of little benefit or appeal to themselves? Work was to be endured, measured out when possible at a pace which suited the slaves. But free time, the weekend, the holiday, the high day, those belonged to the slaves. Not surprisingly, they were enjoyed greedily by people hungry for pleasures and anxious to turn their backs on the fields and the white men who owned them.

12

Religion

In the last days of 1780, Thomas Thistlewood wrote in his diary:

> Mr Wilson's Will (who is an Obiah, or Bush Man) catched in Abba's house,
> at work with his Obiah, about midnight last night, and made her believe Damsel
> is the occasion of her children being sick, and of her miscarriage, etc. A sad
> uproar. Took him home this morning, with his Obiah bag. Mr Wilson flogged
> him well.[1]

Obeah was a form of slave religion; a superstition in the eyes of the whites,
not to be compared with white religion (though precious few whites had one).
Here was a potent element of Africa transplanted into the Americas. If West
Indian planters feared anything more than the simple, brooding physical
proximity of their slaves, it was their slaves' African religions. To whites,
Africans were pagans, worshipping in ways which placed them beyond the
pale of European understanding. That they had no beliefs which whites could
recognize as religion made it all the easier to condemn them to a lifetime's
bondage (though this raised the problem of how to justify their continuing
slavery when slaves were converted to Christianity).

Slaves' religions seemed, to hostile observers, to be an unhealthy mix of
superstitious belief in spirits, of powers of curing and casting spells. It blended
folk customs (folk medicines) with mysterious rites and symbols, and its
practitioners were powerful figures in the slave community, able to inspire
and lead other slaves. Which slave-owner could feel confident that these
mysterious and personal qualities might not be used against the whites?
They might be used to harm slave-owners (to hurt, poison or kill them) or
might inspire slaves to personal or collective reprisal.

At heart the slave-owners' objections were twofold: slaves' religions were reminders, in a real and physical form, of all that was deplorable in Africa itself; equally, they represented a world beyond the masters' control. For men who felt the need to regulate and order the most minute and personal detail of their slaves' lives, slave beliefs and religious practices remained remote and worrying. They could ban them, punish the practitioners and generally fulminate against them. But as long as slavery continued, religion survived, though in time it began to be pushed aside by the emergence of Christianity among the slaves. Even then, obeah in particular – with its promises of cures and spells – was not eliminated. It survives, in altered form, down to the present day.

African religious beliefs seemed more like witchcraft to a white society which had turned its back on its own culture of witchcraft. Planters were right to worry. For a start they realized that they could not segregate religion from daily routines; slaves' beliefs permeated life itself and, to a marked degree, moulded their responses to the world at large. Yet planters resolutely refused to allow their slaves to be converted. As Christians, the slaves would inevitably be seen (or, worse still, see themselves) as believers in brotherly love. The idea that slaves might share an equality – if only of the soul – was a dangerous one. It was much easier not to have slaves as co-religionists.

Africans landed in the Americas from a range of societies with a variety of religions, but the religious beliefs of West and Central Africa had certain common characteristics. They claimed for instance to possess the ability to ward off evil. They embraced community values and expressed themselves through a series of rituals which outsiders feared and failed to understand. But African beliefs and practices inevitably had to change in the alien world of the Americas (just as all people and institutions changed when transplanted there). Slaves landed without their priests, without their religious and social organizations. They had to create life anew, drawing on what they remembered and held dear, but now transformed by the new setting of slavery in the Americas.

The religions they had left behind hinged on a belief in a supreme being but, unlike the Christian God, this being 'is the great creator but not the great lawgiver'. More important were the spirits of nature and of ancestors. West African religions believed in magic and the ability to use 'supernatural powers to achieve good or bad ends'. Specially trained priests officiated at public ceremonies and private rituals (marriage and death, for instance). The spirits in which people believed exercised a strong influence over the fortunes of everyone, and a number of religious agents, 'priests, mediums, diviners, and doctors', were used to intercede between the individual and the spirits. Everything that took place was assumed to have a significance, and these various specialists explained or cured them. Doctors could cure, but they could also curse and harm. Death was a result of bad magic or evil spirits. Eventually family and friends would be reunited in a life after death.[2]

All of these qualities featured in slave religions in the Caribbean (though in essence some of them could be seen in Christianity too). Slaves needed experts – priests – to mediate. If they were not among their imported numbers, they had to emerge from the slave ranks. Rituals of life in the slave quarters required religious sanction; slaves needed to be nursed and cured; enemies had to be plagued or punished. The newborn had to be blessed and the dead interred with suitable ceremonies. Memories and the people of Africa were thus harnessed to these various important tasks. Inevitably, what emerged was not a mere transplanting of African belief systems and practices into the Americas.

Whites in the West Indies worried most about obeah: 'An Obeah man or woman (for it is practised by both sexes) is a very wicked and dangerous person on a plantation.' Here were the slaves' priests, able to work magic, to inflict harm and pain. Large numbers were women; all were feared by the planters for the power they held over the slaves and for the role they seemed to play in a great deal of slave subversion.[3] A similar accusation was later to be hurled at Christian missionaries and in both cases it held a great deal of truth. Both for example encouraged slaves to gather, for religious ceremonies; once collected into a crowd, ideas easily circulated and charismatic leaders emerged to prompt slaves to question their lot and even to strike out against their bondage. Obeah women, wrote John Stedman, were to be seen 'dancing and whirling round in the middle of an assembly, with amazing rapidity, until they foam at the mouth, and drop down as convulsed. Whatever the prophetess orders to be done during this paroxysm is most sacredly performed by the surrounding multitude'. All of this made such meetings 'extremely dangerous, as she frequently enjoins them to murder their masters, or desert to the woods'. Not surprisingly a number of colonies expressly outlawed such gatherings, and other manifestations of slave religious practices.[4]

Obeah could be used to harm the whites but the fear of its potential harm was as great as the reality. Slaves' religions were, after all, a secret world; forms of private and collective behaviour which whites could only approach but never penetrate.

No one doubted the power of obeah in the slave quarters of the West Indies. Most of its practitioners were Africans, said Bryan Edwards, 'and they have brought the science with them from thence to Jamaica, where it is so universally practised'. Few plantations were without their local obeah men. In their turn they were revered (or feared) and consulted by the rest of the slaves for cures to illness and insults, for arbitration, punishment of wrong-doers or for prediction of future events. Charging for their charms and incantations (often administered at midnight), obeah men, understandably, hid their work from the eyes of the whites.[5] Though some slaves feared the obeah men and others held grievances against them, few were prepared to challenge them or inform on them.

Obeah curses could harm other blacks but whites were especially afraid of such threats, particularly of being poisoned by the obeah man or his disciples. Fear of poisoning, rumours and apocryphal tales abounded throughout white society. Nor were such fears totally without foundation. A Jamaican report of 1789 remarked that 'the skill of some negroes in the art of poisoning has been noticed ever since the colonists became acquainted with them'.[6] Whenever slaves or whites died in sudden or unexplained circumstances, suspicion immediately fell on local obeah men. Yet these were societies where sudden, unexpected death was all too common. In times of pain and trouble, the finger of suspicion pointed immediately at the slaves' priests.

There was evidence in abundance that obeah often preceded slave unrest and uprisings. Administering fetishes, the swearing of secret oaths sealed with a drink mixed from rum, earth and cock's blood, the killing of animals and the use of blood and feathers, all these and more formed a mysterious and threatening prelude to a number of slave revolts. Nanny, the inspirational leader of the Jamaican revolt in the 1730s, was herself a priestess. When caught, the perpetrators were savagely punished – but it was all to no avail. 'Neither the terror of this law, the strict investigation which has ever since been made after the professors of Obi, nor the many examples of those who from time to time have been hanged or transported, have hitherto produced the desired effect.' The conclusion, thought Bryan Edwards, seemed clear. Either obeah flourished under persecution, not unlike early Christianity and sects worldwide, or obeah was periodically replenished from Africa. Both seem to have been the case. Not until the rise of black Christianity was the full force of obeah diminished among the slaves.

The penalties paid by convicted obeah men were savage in the extreme, doubly so because whites hoped to extract from their victims secret information and clues about the nature of obeah. Often the dying priest was defiant to the end. 'It was not in the power of the White people to kill him', were one man's dying words. Others were subjected to experiments 'with electrical machines and magic lanterns, but with little effect, except one, who, after receiving some very severe shocks, acknowledged that "This master's obi exceeded his own"'.[7] It was more traditional to burn obeah men alive, though this habit died out in the last days of slavery and was replaced by transportation.

Like priests everywhere, obeah men had paraphernalia which had to be hidden from the whites. If discovered, punishment inevitably followed. When Cuffie was seized in Jamaica he was found to possess 'an old snuff box, several phials, some filled with liquids and some with powders, one with pounded glass; some dried herbs, teeth, beads, hair, and other trash; in short, the whole farrago of an Obeah man'.[8] In Jamaica in 1773 a slave, Sarah, was tried 'for having in her possession cats' teeth, cats' claws, cats' jaws, hair, beads, knotted cords, and other material, relative to the practice of obeah, to delude and impose on the minds of the negroes'. Three years later another Jamaican slave, Solomon, was sentenced to transportation 'for having materials in his possession for the practice of obeah'. In 1782 the slave Neptune was also transported from Jamaica 'for making use of rum, hair, chalk, stones, and other materials, relative to the practice of obeah, or witchcraft'.[9]

Tales of successful obeah healing – and successful curses – abounded among the slave-owners. All seemed able to cite examples of slaves who had recovered, or been rendered sick or even died, following the intervention of obeah men. For their part slaves were undoubtedly terrified of being cursed; the merest threat of sanctions often reduced a slave to a listless and demoralized ghost: 'A little bag, with a few trumpery and harmless ingredients, hung up over a door, was sufficient to break down the health and spirits of the stoutest-hearted African.' The fiercest of African rebels, men who faced with equanimity excruciating torture and death at the hands of their white captors, crumbled before obeah. Whites generally poured scorn on the claims of obeah – its ingredients were mere 'trumpery', its priests deluded, ignorant charlatans and even lunatics, its claims absurd – but they could not deny the power which obeah exercised over the slaves' minds and imaginations. Slaves believed in it even if their masters and mistresses did not.

There was a form of obeah – myalism – which whites disliked more than most. Myal men, claiming to be in direct contact with the spirit world, were in fact leaders of cults among the slaves that came close to forms of organized African religions. Working in groups, they generally performed their rituals close to or around trees. In March 1769 Thistlewood discovered that two slaves, Egypt Dago and Job, were both myal men and attended myal dances held 'in Phibbah's Coobah's house, at Paradise Estate'.[10] The ceremony was usually audible. In a frenzy of drumming and dance, the spirits took possession first of the myal men and then of their followers. These ceremonies may have been designed as an antidote to evil spirits ('duppies') and bore a remarkable similarity to certain ceremonies among Fanti priests in twentieth-century Africa. There is little doubt of the African roots of these ceremonies, and no doubt that they survived, in Jamaica, long after slavery had ended.

It was claimed that myal men used a 'narcotic potion made with the juice of an herb, said to be the branched Calalue, a species of Solonium, which occasions a trance, a profound sleep of certain duration [to] endeavour to convince the deluded spectators of the power to reincarnate dead bodies'.[11] The dances at the myal ceremonies were designed to show the magic of the cult leader, usually called 'Doctor'.

Among the slaves the evil spirits against whom the myal men operated were the slave-owners; the people who had taken the Africans from their homelands, inflicted on them the agonies of the Middle Passage and consigned them to a daily vision of hell on earth. That such a series of related disasters should befall the slaves could be explained only in terms of evil spirits; those spirits were the white perpetrators of black misfortune.[12] Later, with the coming of Christianity among the slaves – led by the Baptists – myalism incorporated useful aspects of the whites' religion. It absorbed the concept of the Holy Spirit and the practice of baptism by immersion. Baptism took place in rivers and the sea, which in parts of Africa were thought to be the homes of spirits. In the process protection was conferred against evil spirits.[13]

Unlike Christianity, myalism was directed towards this world and was not other-worldly. The blows of evil spirits could be deflected and the fruits of wickedness could be countered, not in the after-life but on this earth, by a process of anti-sorcery. Of course evil-doers might not be whites or slave-owners; but at heart myalism was a vehicle for actively seeking to prevent the evils of slavery. And it took its form, its direction and dynamic, from Africa.

Contemporaries tended to confuse obeah and myalism, but they were quite distinct. Whereas obeah could be directed at harming someone through charms and curses administered by a paid professional, myalism was really anti-witchcraft. Myalism tried to ward off evil; to help the triumph of good over evil; to allow slaves' social strengths to win against the evils of the slave system and its perpetrators.

The curious thing, in retrospect, is that slave-owners did not seek to root out the African religions they so disliked and feared by the simple process of conversion and baptism. Christianity came late to slaves in the West Indies – though earlier among North American slaves. Here too American slave-owners were unsure about converting their slaves. There remained the fear that baptism might confer freedom, to say nothing of narrowing the broad cultural gap between white settlers and their African slaves.[14]

Many slaves clearly had trouble recognizing Christianity as a religion at all. Both whites and slaves initially gazed at each other's religion uncomprehendingly. Africans did not divide up the world between the sacred and the secular. Whites, on the other hand (when they bothered with religion at all), tended to go to church on the Sabbath, leaving the rest of the week for secular life. Ministers for their part showed little interest in the slaves. Those who did often faced the resistance of slave-owners who, like their West Indian counterparts, were reluctant to complicate their relations with the slaves by introducing them to Christianity. There was however a lively debate, mainly among senior Anglicans, about the theological justification for converting slaves. It was commonly held that any drive towards conversion should be tailored towards the slaves' greatly inferior mental capacities. Suitably converted and fed an appropriate diet of quiescent theology, blacks could, it was claimed, become perfect slaves; compliant, accommodating and socially calm. Despite such views, Christianity generally passed the slaves by.

Before about 1750 Christianity was not a prominent force among the slaves in the northern colonies. But African survivals – unlike in the Caribbean –

were sparse. Throughout the seventeenth century 'slaves were too few and too intermixed with whites to be able to maintain more than a memory of African practices'. However some African religious practices survived – funeral rites being the most noticeable.

In the mid-eighteenth century a determined and systematic effort was made to win slaves over to Christianity. Anglican ministers had baptized slave children and married their parents but, on the whole, it was claimed, the slaves were 'living in as profound Ignorance of what Christianity really is (except as to a few outward Ordinances) as if they had remained in the midst of those barbarous Heathen Countries from whence their parents had first been imported'. From their inception, the English colonies were deemed to be Anglican. When the Virginia Company was established in 1606 it was decreed that it should provide 'the true word and service of God... according to the Rites and Doctrine of the Church of England'. Soon, however, the local church slipped away from the effective control of the Bishop of London and passed to local men who organized the church around their local vestries. They, not the Bishop, had the power of election of local ministers. And since the vestries soon fell under the sway of the planters, it was the slave-owning lobby which effectively controlled the local church. Ministers could scarcely be independent of the planters. Decent clergy refused, on the whole, to leave England to work in Virginia. Most ministers were in fact little more than deacons, subject to the control and ever attendant to the interests of their local vestries. They simply could not give offence to the plantocratic lobby. Efforts by the supervisory Bishop of London to reform the affairs of Anglican Virginia inevitably stumbled against the new orthodoxy in the slave colony. The English Church also worried about the need to convert the slaves, those fears prompted in large measure by the knowledge of the much greater and more effective measures taken by Catholic churches in other colonies.

Little progress could be made however and thus in 1701 the Society for the Propagation of the Gospel in Foreign Parts (SPG) was established, financed from England and hence separate from colonial influences. In the words of Bishop Fleetwood in 1710: 'no Man living can assign a better and more justifiable Cause, for God's with-holding Mercy from a *Christian* than that *Christian's* with-holding the mercy of *Christianity* from an Unbeliever'.[15] But this is precisely what the planters in the English colonies did.

The first major efforts to convert slaves took place in South Carolina, though the missionaries from the SPG hardly knew where to begin. Though they had secured the Church of England as the 'established' church by 1706, their potential flock was a motley crew; rough white settlers, 'savage' Indians, swarms of African slaves. 'I have here', wrote an early preacher, 'a multitude of ignorant persons to instruct.' There were, he said, 'too many profane to awaken, some few pious to build up, and many Negroes [and] Indians to begin withall'.[16]

Though the population was small, it was scattered, and ministers were few. Like others, many simply did not survive. They faced the well-worn objections of slave-owners reluctant to see their Africans baptized and converted. Some disliked the prospect of seeing slaves in the after-life: 'Is it Possible that any of my slaves could go to Heaven, & I must see them there?'[17]

Slave-owners had reason to distrust the missionaries, not least because they occasionally stood between them and their slaves, objecting to the more barbarous punishments, and heeding slave voices when no others would. The Rev. Le Jau complained in 1712 that masters 'are more Cruel Some of them of late Dayes than before. They hamstring main [maim] & unlimb those poor Creatures for small faults'.[18] But even the missionaries, like those who came a century later to the West Indies, were often dependent on slave-owners for hospitality, support and access to the slaves. They could not afford to alienate the whites too far.

The missionaries' attitude to the slaves was sometimes curious. Their most strenuous objections were directed against the slaves' 'misuse' of the Sabbath. In South Carolina, like most slave colonies, Sunday was a day free from slave labour. Slaves took the opportunity of working on their own plots and gardens; they also enjoyed themselves. In 1709, Le Jau wrote that it 'has been Customary among them to have their feasts, dances, and merry Meetings upon the Lord's day'. Preachers' dislike of the way the slaves used their Sundays was, in essence, an attack on what had emerged as the slaves' popular culture, and bore remarkable similarities to the Sabbatarian onslaught on English popular culture in the early seventeenth century and, later, in the nineteenth century. Churchmen wanted slave-owners to provide all the food and clothing needed by slaves, thus eliminating the necessity for slaves to work on the Sabbath.[19]

These early South Carolina churchmen were no less alarmed by the slaves' marital habits, though it was widely accepted that a slave worked hard to support 'his family and all that is dear to him in this world'. Ministers were especially alarmed about the slaves' habit of straying from monogamy. To curb this 'plurality of Wives' it was proposed that slaves could only marry or separate with the owners' consent.

Unconsciously, but none the less effectively, this missionary drive served to reinforce the grip of the slave masters. What countered this tendency, however, was the simple fact that the missionaries did not have great success among the slaves in South Carolina. The Anglicans insisted on preparing the slaves for baptism. Catholic missionaries on the other hand baptized and converted in a more liberal and leisurely fashion. As Anglican missionaries completed their posting and returned home, they generally bemoaned their failure to convert more than a handful of slaves: 'Tis true, indeed, that an odd slave here and there may be converted when a minister had leisure and opportunity for so doing... But alas! success must be little and inconsiderable in comparison of what might be expected.'[20]

This began to change from 1750 onwards, the period of the 'Great Awakening' which saw an evangelical nonconformist movement sweep through much of the Chesapeake and the Carolinas. The growth of revivalism was important in a number of ways. First of all it enhanced religiosity among the whites, many of whom were persuaded to allow (or encourage) their slaves to attend church. Second, it allowed conversion by the experience of God's saving grace. What mattered was that the convert understood God's work in his or her heart; it was not important if the minutiae of doctrine remained unknown and incomprehensible. Slaves could forge their own relationship with God; they did not need the intercession of a third party. Third, revivalism involved a sense of equality. Meetings took place in public; they spilled from chapels and churches into the streets and fields where excitement tipped over into ecstasy. When baptized in local rivers, amid scenes of great enthusiasm, slaves could recognize glimpses of their African past. In these years African and Christian modes of worship blended. Black and white joined together, worshipping in each other's company wherever they could find a suitable meeting place. From mid-century to the years of independence, most Baptist and Methodist churches were mixed: 'in which blacks sometimes preached to whites and in which whites and blacks witnessed together, shouted together, and shared ecstatic experiences at "dry" and wet christenings, meetings, and burials'.[21]

Nonconformist churches and chapels were simple, often crude buildings, a world removed from the elaborate, ornate and finely finished churches of local Anglicans. Like their sister chapels in Britain at precisely the same time, these new churches were for the poor; and poor whites and poor blacks worshipped together. More like barns than churches, these log cabins were home to a basic worship quite unlike anything seen before.

Slaves were not always sure why they attended: 'Many of them only seem to desire to be, they know not what; they feel themselves uneasy in their *present* condition, and therefore desire a *change*.'[22]

George Whitefield, the great Methodist preacher, travelled through the North American slave colonies, capturing (and adding to) the mood of the awakening. But he also felt pangs of conscience about the slaves. As they pressed into his meetings, touched him and worshipped with him, Whitefield urged slave-owners to think about the slaves: 'Think, your children are in any way better by nature than the poor negroes? No! In no wise! Blacks are just as much, and no more, conceived and born in sin, as white men are; and both, if born and bred up here, I am persuaded, are naturally capable of the same improvement.' Whitefield's convictions grew stronger the more intimate he became with local slaves. He wrote in his journal: 'God will highly favour them, to wipe off their reproach, and shew that He is no respecter of persons.' He began to address slaves directly, telling them that Jesus 'will wash you in his own blood'.[23]

Slaves flocked to hear Whitefield; untold numbers joined his crusade, often in scenes of ecstatic conversion. The images they rallied to were simple and stark: hell and damnation, eternal flames or eternal bliss in the heavenly home. These were sweet words to the slaves. Time and again, the 'spirit' moved them; agitated or soothed, weeping or tranquil, shrieking or peaceful, slaves turned to Whitefield's God.

Samuel Davies, a Presbyterian in Hanover Country, Virginia, converted hundreds of slaves in the 1750s. They liked the music and understood the doctrine he explained. Some converts 'lodged all night in my kitchen; and sometimes, when I have awakened about two or three a-clock in the morning, a torrent of sacred harmony poured into my chamber, and carried my mind to heaven'.[24] He declared that he expected that 'poor African *slaves* will be made the Lord's free men'. This was not what slave-owners wanted preachers to say to their slaves. It fulfilled precisely their worst fears; that the brotherhood of Christianity, if allowed to seep into the slave quarters, would serve to under-mine the very fabric of slavery itself.

Another successful preacher was the Separate Baptist, Shubal Stearns, who travelled and converted in the Carolinas and Virginia in the 1750s. His message was full of promise – for life on earth as much as in heaven – and his church organization was egalitarian where the Anglican church was élitist and exclusive. His followers were brothers and sisters, people whose equality with each other was forged by having been born again. Those who were 'saved' were assured of everlasting life. Ceremonies were marked by involvement; by holding and hugging, by total immersion, by vigorous and joyous singing. And wherever Stearns's church took root, it attracted black and white. No one challenged this mixing of the races in the fellowship of church membership. Moreover it was continued, in the 1770s and 1780s, by a new Methodist drive in Virginia. Sometimes blacks formed their own churches but, on the whole, in this generation before American Independence, the churches spawned by the revivals were mixed.[25]

In the regular conduct of these churches, local blacks secured a role for themselves which transcended their role as worshippers. They spoke and were listened to on a range of issues. The Baptist churches became courts in which disputes of any kind were aired and settled; between master and man, man and wife, between slave and slave-owner. Strict morality – especially in sexual matters – was imposed on members; 'immorality' was denounced and the virtues of marriage and monogamy insisted upon.

The 'sins' of the slaves were fairly predictable: theft, violence towards whites or sexual misbehaviour. But slave-owners could themselves be tried by their church. Churches debated the rights of whipping and burning slaves, the threat of separating families, of sexual improprieties against the slaves. In September 1775 Sherwood Walton, a member of the Meherrin Baptist Church, was accused by one of his slaves 'for being guilty of, or at least offering the Act of uncleanness to a Mulatto Girl of his own'.[26] It was only a short step from challenging particular acts of slave-owners to challenging slavery itself.

Soon, Baptist churches began to ask: 'Is it a Rituous thing for a Christian to hold or cause any of the human race to be held in slavery?' It was perhaps equally predictable that even some of the whites would be won over and come to see slavery as evil: 'I have been an advocate for Slavery, but thanks be to God, My Eyes have been Opened to see the impropriety of it.'[27]

Many slave-owners were clearly alarmed by the impact the revivals had upon their slaves (and upon some of the whites). Some made efforts to keep their slaves untainted by the message flowing from the Baptist preachers, but it proved virtually impossible to isolate slaves from church meetings or from converted slaves or whites. Some planters faced the added problem of seeing their white managers converted; the very men who were in daily charge of the slaves. Christianity, of a very distinctive kind, had seeped into the American slave quarters, and transformed the world for thousands of slaves.

The religion to which these slaves turned provided a physical forum for them to meet together away from their place of work. It gave many of them the chance to speak, and to organize, to promote their own interests and safeguard their well-being; to express themselves on a range of secular as well as spiritual issues. They spoke about slavery and slave-owners; about themselves as slaves and their treatment at the hands of their owners.

There was obviously much more to it than this. The Christianity born of the revivals before American Independence provided slaves with 'the opportunity to die and be born again'. Quite unconsciously, it fused African perceptions of death and the world of spirits 'with Christian visions of God and heaven'. Heaven was home where Jesus and the saints – and lost family members – were waiting for the slave to arrive.[28] The simplest and humblest would be raised up; the highest of tyrants cast down. It did not matter if one was a slave, for paradise was the most egalitarian of havens; a refuge for all who had been saved. The brutalities and injustices of the here-and-now would give way to everlasting peace and love. It is easy to see why this vision was enormously attractive to slaves, not least because it stood in such stark contrast to the miseries of daily life.

The consequences of the emergence of black Christianity were to reverberate throughout North America, during and after the war for independence. It was to have results which lasted into the era of the revival of American slavery, after the coming of the cotton revolution in the nineteenth century. But in the years of colonial government it had awakened slaves not only to Christianity itself but to the broader moral issues posed by slavery.

All this took place long before Christianity had made a major impact among slaves in the British Caribbean. What had happened in Virginia and the

Carolinas served as a warning to the even more resistant and unrepentant planters of the sugar islands.

There were, as we have seen, a number of obstacles to the spread of Christianity in the West Indies. Planters were, from the first, reluctant to see their slaves converted and baptized. They held fundamental objections to the prospect of black Christianity; it would come between them and their slaves, would serve to undermine their authority and perhaps persuade the slaves to get above themselves. In addition, they worried about the connection between conversion and freedom; did baptism emancipate a slave?

When Quakers sought to convert slaves in Barbados in the 1670s, the governor told the local Assembly: 'I shall leave to you to consider whether Liberty be a fit Doctrine for slaves.' But he sought to stop conversions to Christianity, 'of which they can make them understand nothing'. Yet only twenty years later, the pioneering planters of Jamaica were urged, by a local Act, to instruct their slaves in Christianity and 'cause to be baptized all such as they can make sensible of a Deity and the Christian Faith'.[29] With few exceptions, this did not happen. Unlike neighbouring Catholic islands, those under English control resolutely refused to convert their slaves. The reason was simple enough. Whereas the Catholics required little from the slaves before baptism, Protestants expected them to be prepared for baptism. They insisted on elaborate instruction before conversion and thus the English slaves remained firmly outside the Christian pale. Learning and education for the slaves was strictly restricted to plantation skills. Planters throughout the English possessions agreed with the Barbados Assembly's view (of 1681) that the slaves' 'Savage Brutishness renders them wholly uncapable' of conversion.[30]

There were exceptions to this general rule. Planters sometimes had their black mistresses and offspring baptized into the Anglican church, but the numbers were minute. Between 1670 and 1687 only thirty-four 'mulattoes and Negroes were baptized, married, or buried in St Michael's church Bridgetown'.[31] In the West Indies, as in the northern colonies, the Sabbath posed a serious problem. Either planters expected their slaves to work on Sunday, or the slaves needed the Sabbath for their own gardens and leisure. It was quite impossible for slaves to keep the Lord's Day holy. The Governor of Barbados had stated in 1695: 'I apprehend that the keeping of Christian holy days will be the greatest obstacle, most planters thinking Sunday too much to be spared from work.'[32]

With limited resources and an apparently mountainous task, the Society for the Propagation of the Gospel in Foreign Parts decided that its best efforts should be directed towards the West Indies, for it was here that more slaves languished in their native paganism than in North America. To make matters worse, the West Indian Anglican clergy were an appalling collection of men, described in 1740 as 'of character so vile, that I do not care to mention it; for except for a few, they are generally the most finished of our debauchers'.[33] They were 'better qualified to be retailers of saltfish or boatswains to privateers'.[34] They gave the planters the outer trappings of respectable Christian life – baptisms, marriages and funerals – but they gave little to the slaves. Indeed, many of the Anglican ministers were themselves involved in slave management. In the campaign against the abolitionists in the 1820s, one of the Jamaican planters' most effective scribes was an Anglican minister.[35] The Rev. William Davis of Antigua was not only the manager of a slave property but he was also indicted for the murder of Eliza, a slave woman.[36]

Some efforts had been made to bring Christianity to the slaves. When Christopher Codrington died in Barbados in 1710, supervision of his slaves was placed with the SPG who set about converting them. The first slave baptism was in 1728; five years later there were fifty-eight Christian slaves on the Codrington estates. Yet this did not involve the prospect of their emancipation.[37] There and elsewhere the conversion of the slaves was the work of missionaries. Since the local Anglicans failed to respond, it was necessary to dispatch to the islands men who would.

The first such group to arrive in Jamaica were the Moravians in 1754 but they remained a small and rather isolated group. The first significant mission was that of the Baptists – black Baptists at that – who travelled from North America to Jamaica. Led by George Leile, a former slave from Georgia, the group settled in Kingston after 1784. He soon attracted congregations of 800 slaves, and in 1793 opened a chapel. By 1802 one of his converts had established a second Kingston chapel with 500 members. Leile's associates began to spawn slave congregations in other parts of the island. Like others before and after them, they had to be cautious; they needed the planters for access to the slaves. Any resistance by the planters would simply staunch the flow of slave converts. Even then, Leile was hounded and prosecuted. Like nonconformists in Britain, Leile's most effective ploy was to preach from horseback.

Jamaica remained perhaps the major challenge to the missionaries. As a group, the missionaries were conscious of their humble social origins (most came from the world of British artisans); they were poorly paid, ill-at-ease with the planters and their roistering social style and perched uneasily on the rim of slave society. They relied on each other for support and friendship. Like their predecessors in England, the missionaries in Jamaica regarded themselves first and foremost as preachers; democratic in style, easy-going in their social relations with slaves. They were not the kind of white men and women the slaves had been accustomed to meeting. Moreover these men elevated the slaves, telling them that they were part of the brotherhood of man. In return for their hard work, the missionaries endured harsh material lives. Large numbers died young. Few survived more than ten years in Jamaica. One Wesleyan missionary wrote back to his superiors: 'I came to Jamaica by your direction and brought with me a lovely family. Within the space of two years I have lost...three children, an affectionate wife, and my own health.'[38]

Physical dangers were only the beginning of their problems. They had trouble making themselves understood among slaves whose *patois*, or African languages, they could scarcely understand. Then they had to battle against the remnants of the African religions rooted in the slave communities. Slaves had trouble accepting that they were sinful creatures. Missionaries felt they had begun to win the battle when they convinced slaves that they had a soul, the salvation of which they worked to secure. Using children's catechisms which taught by rote-learning, slowly they began to make an impression on the religious ideas and practices forged by Africa. But there was more to becoming a Christian than simply believing what the missionaries said. Converts had to behave differently. To be a good Christian involved ordering social and private life as the missionaries determined; there was a link between behaviour on this earth and the prospects of the life hereafter. To slaves accustomed to believing that they would meet their ancestors in the after-life irrespective of behaviour on earth, this was generally hard to grasp.

Sexual licence and polygamy were expected to give way to monogamous marriage. Not surprisingly, the slaves resisted many of the requirements of conversion. Missionaries did not automatically sweep all before them. Slaves clung to their traditional habits; their greater freedom with partners, the breaking of the Sabbath for necessary work or leisure, their love of drumming and dancing, their passion for drinking, especially at the weekend.

Acutely aware of the difficulties, unsure of their converts, reminded of their failing by regular backsliders, the missionaries felt their labours largely unsuccessful. Pessimism was perhaps understandable – but misplaced. Their success often lay in opening the slaves' eyes to a range of alternatives. Slaves came to realize that the world could be different and need not be like the one arranged and determined by their owners.

Missionaries tried, at all times, to stress the importance of obedience, and the Bible had an abundance of suitable quotations to support their case. The problem was, the slaves had begun to interpret the world anew and could no longer be relied on to believe what they were told. Sometimes what they heard made immediate sense. Christian visions of heaven and hell had a resonance for slaves; but hell was on earth while heaven offered the happiness denied them on earth. Planters for their part often prepared a rod for their own backs. The obstructions they placed before the missionaries, the open hostility they displayed to them personally, the violence they visited upon the chapels and homes of the preachers – all and more convinced the slaves that the missionaries were on their side. These were not normal 'buckra'; the planters' enemy was obviously the slaves' friend.

Elsewhere in the West Indies, Thomas Coke, a close associate of John Wesley, began to organize a missionary society, a move confirmed by a visit to Antigua. Thereafter it became his life's work to raise money, select suitable missionaries and visit missions in the field. At the time of his death (on his way to India in 1814) he had established missions in Sierra Leone, Newfoundland and in fifteen of the West Indian islands.[39]

These efforts in their turn inspired William Carey's Particular Baptists; in 1792 the Baptist Missionary Society was formed. This, like others before it, was able to capitalize on the extraordinary British interest in missionary work. Part of that religious revival which had transformed Britain in the late eighteenth century was the urge to convert the heathen world. Few doubted the wisdom, the justice or the practicality of converting India, for instance. And no one (excepting the plantocratic lobby) argued against the missionary drive to bring light and civilization to the West Indian slaves. Their vices were those of Africa, their failings a result of being allowed to wallow too long in the uncivilized world of slavery. At a stroke, Christianity would bring morality, family life and discipline into the barbarous slave quarters. In Britain, with the new literature of anti-slavery disgorged in thousands of tracts, pamphlets, books and sermons, the appetite for news about slaves seemed insatiable. And much of the interest was generated in poor, working-class communities, by local nonconformist sects and chapels.

What made possible the conversion of tens of thousands of British slaves was the conviction (and money) of large numbers of British people that the task was worthwhile. In retrospect it was as clear a case of cultural imperialism as we could hope to find. But it was fashioned in large part from a determination to refine the crude contours of black slavery; to civilize its victims and force slave-owners to deal with slaves as people rather than things. It was as much an attack on the slave-owners (resistant to slave Christianity at the last) as it was on the slaves' paganism. It proved successful faster and more comprehensively than its staunchest backers could have dreamed. By the time the British freed all their slaves in 1838 Christianity had become a major force in the slave quarters of the British West Indies.

The key to the missionaries' success was their preaching. In Britain and in the Caribbean nonconformists wooed tens of thousands by the persuasion of the spoken word. Their meetings, in open spaces and newly-built chapels, drew vast and growing throngs of blacks, excited by their message, intrigued by news from Britain (about the rising chorus of demands for black freedom) and keen to share the heady excitement of the noisy, public gatherings. The simple message of the brotherhood of Christ, of the equality of all believers and the fraternity of the life-hereafter sent a fizz through the slave quarters – and a cold chill through the slave-owning community.

> We will be slaves no more,
> Since Christ has made us free,

> Has nailed our tyrants to the cross,
> And bought our liberty.[40]

It was no surprise that ideas of secular freedom and equality soon swirled among the slaves. Garbled stories from Britain (that Wilberforce and Parliament had already freed the slaves) fused with images of Christian brotherhood to produce a heady political mix.

> Oh me good friend, Mr Wilberforce, make me free!
> God Almighty thank ye! God Almighty thank ye![41]

In the fifty years between the end of the American war (1783) and full black freedom in the Caribbean (1838), the impact of Christianity was seismic. The role it played in finally undermining slavery itself continues to preoccupy historians. But of the central fact there is no doubt. By the 1830s many of those slaves were Christian. Moreover, they were distinctive; enthusiastic, noisy, communal and sociable in the practice and protestation of their new faith. When they sang, chanted, danced, swooned and shrieked at their worship, they reminded outsiders of the older African slaves when worshipping. The slaves invested Christianity with a style and an energy which was African; declamatory where whites tended to be silent, ecstatic where others were tranquil, collective where others were silently individualistic. Here were some of the qualities of black Christianity which survive to this day.

A small minority of planters were themselves converted, and came to see the benefits afforded by converting their slaves. A St Vincent planter reported that after the conversion of his slaves: 'The natural result was health in promoted cleanliness, propagation in well contented families, security in property to themselves and masters in the discontinuance of former tricks and thefts, and an increasing capital in an increasing gang to the proprietor.'[42] On the whole, however, planters distrusted the missionaries. For their part the preachers trod carefully. 'I am persuaded', wrote one London Missionary Society missionary, 'that it is neither my business nor in my power to deliver from the bondage of men.' The Rev. John Smith, dispatched on his ultimately fatal mission to Demerara in 1816, was told: 'not a word must escape you in public or private which might render the slaves displeased with their masters or dissatisfied with their station. You are sent not to relieve them from their servile condition, but to afford them the consolations of religion'.[43] In time, these 'consolations' were to prove temporal as much as spiritual.

The new missionary societies, financed and encouraged by wide-spread support at home, dispatched bands of zealous agents to the West Indies (and elsewhere). By the end of slavery the slave islands provided work for sixty-three Moravian, fifty-eight Methodist, seventeen Baptist and perhaps a dozen more missionaries. The Anglicans finally responded to the challenge, through their evangelical Church Missionary Society (1799). The number of Anglican ministers was greatly increased, largely to head off the challenge of the non-conformists. The end result was that perhaps a quarter of a million slaves were converted in twenty-five years.[44]

Black churches offered an alternative society, a home-from-home where slaves from different plantations mingled for worship – but lingered for gossip and friendship. They also spawned a new breed of black leader; often from the slave élite (craftsmen and the like), but now steeped in the bible, powerful spokesmen and orators, men who interpreted the slaves' world through evocative biblical imagery. Here were men whose power of leadership and oratory the planters ought to have harnessed to their own side. Instead, they drove missionary and black preacher, slave converts and waverers, closer together in a tight-knit if uncomfortable and not always mutually-comprehending band.

The missionaries were themselves sometimes ill-at-ease with the sway their black deacons came to exercise over the slave congregations. They told of their dreams – of salvation to come – they swore oaths to pursue those dreams, they cited biblical texts which told of redemption and of fire and damnation. More important was the collision which conversion made inevitable between the ideology of the plantation and the ideals of the church. Set against the plantation which measured out worth and material rewards by colour and by the capricious whim of the whites, the churches offered salvation to anyone who truly wanted it. The one offered little more than a continuation of an earthly hell, the other, the prospects of eternal life. And which black Christian could henceforth take seriously their masters' claims to superiority? The planters had good reason to fear what was happening in the chapels, for it was little less than a social revolution among their slaves. Plantocratic night-mares periodically came true; black Christianity was at the forefront of the several major slave revolts.[45]

The slave revolt in Demerara in 1823 centred on the chapels and a number of their key worshippers. Plotters skimmed through the Bible looking for suitable quotations to assert their demands for freedom.[46] The revolt was organized through chapel connections and was launched after a communion service where the symbols of the ceremony – the oaths, the wine and bread, the story of earthly sacrifice – inspired the revolt's leaders. One group of slaves gathered with a Bible, which they kissed; they were told garbled accounts of how the King's concession of freedom was being thwarted by the planters.[47]

At the trials of the defeated rebels, the plantocracy and colonial government were determined to prove that the revolt had been fostered by the missionaries. The slave Jack Gladstone told the court: 'I solemnly avow that many of the lessons and discussions, and parts of the Scripture selected for us in Chapel, tended to make us dissatisfied with our situation as slaves; and had there been no Methodists on the East Coast, there would have been no revolt.'

True or not, the planters believed it. Yet such arguments proved their undoing, for what outraged British opinion as much as anything were the tales of plantocratic and colonial outrages against black Christians. For two centuries the British had tolerated abuses of their colonial slaves, but their attitude had begun to change now that those slaves were Christians.

Chapels, like their British counterparts, spawned other agencies which threatened the status quo. Sunday schools and Bible-reading classes taught literacy. It was claimed by 1760 that hundreds of slaves had been taught to read and write: 'The poor slaves are now commonly engaged in learning to read; some of them can read the Bible, others can only spell; and some are just learning their letters. But there is a general alteration among them for the better.'[48] The overall results of these classes were mixed, but they offered instruction to any local slave keen to improve him or herself. The literate black minority were in effect given two powerful radical forces: literacy and the Bible. Glimmers of equality were there for all to see within the chapels themselves. When a new chapel was opened on Hampden estate in Jamaica, slaves thronged the pews and refused to make space for local whites, who were forced to stand in the aisles; slaves sat and masters stood.[49] Who now could dispute the planters' fears that their world was slowly turning upside down?

13

Families and Communities

Slave-traders did not recruit Africans, nor did they import them into the Americas, as family groups. Indeed, it was widely believed that Africans did not understand the concept of family life, existing instead beyond the pale of respectability, living in conditions of barbarous crudeness, marked by promiscuity, licence and depravity. These arguments were of course self-serving; the words of men anxious to justify their trade in humanity. Such crude falsities became the commonplace of white accounts of African life and society. The Europeans thus eased their own consciences and made straight the path for the massive exploitation that was the slave trade.

There was of course an abundance of evidence to the contrary, not least in the well-recorded anguish of Africans wrenched from their loved ones and their unrequited desire to see them again, despite the vast ocean of time and water between them.

At landfall in the colonies, the Africans were alone. Olaudah Equiano wrote that when landing in Virginia in 1757, aged twelve: 'I was now exceedingly miserable and thought myself worse off than any…of my companions; for they could talk to each other, but I had no person to speak to that I could understand. In this state I was constantly grieving and pining, and wishing for death.'[1] Some slaves were lucky to arrive in the company of other Africans whose language and cultural patterns they understood. But they did not step ashore surrounded by their immediate kinsfolk.

The slaves' isolation clearly served the slavers' interests. In any case Europeans saw little reason to imagine that the slaves had left behind anything worthwhile in Africa. Though the more observant of slave-traders (especially those who subsequently repented of their ways) acknowledged the grief displayed by the slaves, few thought that they had come from societies where family ties, with their resulting emotions and affections, played any significant role.

White writers were fond of pointing to Africans' 'promiscuity' as proof that family life, as Europeans knew it, had no firm roots in Africa. African men took a number of 'wives', while African women were free with their sexual favours (as slave traders, sailors and planters were happy to discover). Such 'evidence', widely believed and frequently repeated, simply confirmed that the sexual morality which cemented family life in Europe was missing. It also helped to explain why slaves in the West Indies displayed such 'shocking licentiousness and profligacy of manners'.[2]

White men used black women as their sexual partners in Africa and the New World from the early days of slavery. Rarely, however, did they turn to them for wives, though many black–white relationships were marriages in all but name. Black women were, above all, sexual partners; they were in no position to resist the subtle seductions of personal and material advancement or the crude and brutal physical assaults of their white owners. The belief in black promiscuity, first expressed when discussing Africa but manifested most usefully (for the whites) in the Americas, provided the perfect excuse for the vicarious pleasures of white men throughout the slave colonies. Since it was thought promiscuity came naturally to the blacks, it mattered little how white men behaved towards their female slaves.

Those same white men knew however that it *did* matter; they faced the resentment, the hostility and sometimes the violence of slave men whose womenfolk had been violated or taken from them. Within the slave communities there was a deep and sullen hatred for what happened to the women. Though impossible to calculate precisely, it seems clear enough that the white sexual exploitation of slave women inspired much of the resentment and anger within the slave quarters.

Such sexual outrages undermined the fabric of the slave family. Planters were quick to dismiss their slaves for their immorality, but it is clear enough that, given the opportunity, slaves developed a family system which was precious to them individually and vital for the wider development of slave culture. Despite enormous difficulties the slave family became the cornerstone of slave life; the institution from which flowed all those lessons for life, that sense of morality and culture. It also created the most important of all personal relationships. But the emergence of the slave family was a complex business. How did Africans, taken from a myriad communities with a range of kinship ties, develop new family groups in a world which was so destructive of so much of their personal lives?

It is understandable that planters should seek to diminish the importance of their slaves' family structure. It seems more difficult to understand why historians should have followed their lead. Time and again, historians of the West Indies and North America confirmed the planters' judgement: that slaves did not develop a family structure worthy of the name. To a marked degree that was because historians – and others – have sought to measure slave life by the yardstick of conventional European morality and values. Yet slaves did not readily fit the patterns of contemporary (no less than modern) social categories and definitions. Only in recent years have historians been nudged towards a more sensitive and realistic appreciation of slave family life (often by the work of anthropologists).

Much of the discussion about the slave family has used concepts which, shaped by modern industrial society, make little sense when applied to life among the slaves and still less sense when applied to African societies. If we are looking, among the slaves, for an exact reflection of the modern western family, we will not find it. We need to remember that the family has a number of forms. The slave family – important, distinctive and crucial – was not the same as the family so idealized in early nineteenth-century Britain or North America.

The family which consists of two partners, married by local convention, living with their offspring, may be the ideal for the modern, western nuclear family. But there are many other family types, each with its own codes and moralities. Over the history of black slavery, the slave quarters provided a home for a range of family types. Moreover those families changed from the earliest days of slavery through to the coming of black freedom. What is striking is the simple *fact* of slave families.

The world of slavery was, from the start, hostile to family life. Newly-arrived Africans had been wrenched from extended kinship ties in West Africa which had shaped their personal and collective character. That web of obligation and responsibility which had flowed from African kinship ties had simply disappeared over the horizon, along with the families which made it all possible. Plucked from personal and collective networks which determined and interpreted the world at large, the African slave, dumped in the Americas, was rootless beyond compare.

In the early days of settlement – when men greatly outnumbered women – it was difficult, for many impossible, to find wives. With a small black population spread over a vast region, and with slaves living on small farms or on male-dominated plantations, many African arrivals faced a bleak personal future. In those pioneering days male slaves even faced competition from local white men, themselves settling in the Americas without womenfolk but able to command the sexual favours of slave women. Many of the early African arrivals died without finding a partner or wife. Theirs had been a miserable existence; toiling in an alien world, far removed from home and loved ones, and denied, by the quirks of demography, even the fleeting pleasures of companionship or affection. In periods of heavy African importations, there were frictions and fights among Africans for the available slave women. One Virginian slave, George, complained in 1712 that 'his country

men had poysened him for his wife'. Three months later, he died. In that same
year, another slave, Roger, wanted more than one wife, and 'hanged himself in
ye old 40 foot Tob. house not any reason he being hindered from keeping
other negroes men wifes besides his owne'. To underline the wickedness of
such desires, his owner ordered Roger's head 'cutt off and stuck on a pole to be
a terror to the others'.[3] As long as Africans poured into Virginia and Maryland
(1710–40), friction was unavoidable. At the same time, there were never
enough Africans to dominate the slave quarters (as they did a generation
later in Haiti, for example) and re-create Africa in the Americas. New male
slaves lived with other men, and though we know that many developed male
friendships (sometimes forged on the ship crossing the Atlantic), it was a far
cry from the powerful bonds of kinship they had known in Africa.

Although kinship systems were varied and differed greatly from one part of
Africa to another, cutting across any distinctions was a shared West African
belief in the importance of kinship ties. It was commonly accepted that kinship
was 'the principal way of ordering relations between individuals'.

In the Chesapeake region, if male slaves survived their early years in
slavery, they stood a good chance, eventually, of finding a wife. Invariably
she would be younger than him and she would live on a neighbouring
property. By the early eighteenth century, though many African male slaves
continued to live with other men, they had established family networks and
had begun to lay down the basis for family life. As the balance between the
sexes began to level out in Virginia and Maryland, and as fewer Africans were
imported, the lot of the new Africans improved.

By the mid-eighteenth century family life for slaves in the Chesapeake
began to stabilize and thrive. Men married younger. Their kinship networks
fanned out throughout their immediate region; they had, quite simply, many
more relatives to visit and to call upon. And as these networks developed, the
slaves' earlier reliance on white people declined proportionately. What had
emerged was not merely the slave family, but the slave community, located in
the place of work, but rooted specifically in the slave family and spreading
through extensive networks of kinfolk and friends to embrace slaves throughout a wide geographic area.

By the time of American Independence, the slave families of North America looked remarkably like the families of their white owners. Charles Carroll
of Annapolis, for example, owned almost 400 slaves in 1773; some 325 of them
lived in family units of parents and children. A similar story can be told of
other plantations; of a large majority of local slaves living in family groups of
parents and children for much of their natural life. All the evidence suggests
that the slaves chose their own partners. When they no longer liked or loved
each other, they separated or (rarely) divorced. Beneath the apparently all-
powerful regime of slave-owners lay a complex social life which defied the
owners' efforts at regulation and manipulation.[4]

Planters came to approve of slave families, but were annoyed when slaves married off their own plantations. Jefferson wrote: 'There is nothing I desire so much as that all the young people should intermarry with one another and stay at home.' His reasons were practical and financial: 'They are worth a great deal more in that case than when they have husbands and wives abroad.' Jefferson, like other Virginian planters, could not regulate slaves in this, the most personal aspect of their lives, and simply came to accept that some slaves would marry partners on neighbouring farms and plantations.

The majority of slaves in colonial America lived collectively in small communities housed in a huddle of buildings close by their place of work. In effect slaves were allowed to get on with their own domestic lives, regulating the upbringing of their children and organizing all the household chores in and around the slave quarters: food preparation, cooking, clothes-making, leisure time activities and, increasingly, religious worship. Since most slaves lived within reach of their owners and local white women, the North American slave family fell under direct white influence much more intimately and thoroughly than was the case in the West Indies. The great majority of slaves in North America were brought up by their parents, but they were also influenced by the whites, if only because their parents (but especially their slave mothers) were close to the whites. White women took a keen interest in the domestic life of female slaves on the property, their influence was to be seen most strikingly in the slaves' changing habits of child-care and child-rearing. Slave families, for all their social autonomy, drew important lessons from white people.

The development of the slave family differed greatly from one region to another. Where slaves were held in large numbers, and where slaves continued to be imported from Africa, the physical proximity of white and black, so crucial in the development of black family life in Virginia, was often missing. In South Carolina, with its large slave-holding, its absentee planters and its similarities to West Indian slavery, slave families developed in a different fashion. Again, family ties provided local slaves with their most influential and important networks. Family names were adopted – planters were generally reluctant to allow slaves to keep their African names – and family ties created that network of contacts which gave slaves a sense of identity and helped them shape a world of their own in a hostile and alien land. The newborn took family names. Later, male artisans and skilled female domestics passed their skills and privileges on to their sons and daughters, thus enhancing their children's material well-being but also providing planters with the essential skills needed on the property and in white homes. The slave family was thus as important for the slave-owner as it was for the slaves.

There were, from the first, basic threats hanging over the slave family and community. The most obvious and most serious was the threat of separation, at a moment's notice, when planters fell on bad times or when a new slave-owning generation moved westward to the challenges of the advancing American frontier. Slaves sought, where possible, to strengthen family life by bringing distant relatives closer to the main family. Often the planters complied. Jefferson bought the wife and three children of his blacksmith Moses, even though he doubted their economic value. It was always a fine balance. If planters failed to respond to the demands of slave families, they might have sullen and resentful slaves on their hands, unwilling to work and permanently disaffected. Disgruntled slaves might simply run away. One Maryland planter, faced by the problem of a persistent slave runaway (a mechanic, regularly fleeing *to* his wife), offered a qualified pardon for the latest offence in 1782: 'if he behaves well, and endeavours to make amends for his past behavior I will when I return purchase his wife if her master will sell her at a reasonable price'.

Some slaves took it as a fact of life that they would be regularly separated from their kinfolk. Servants working in white households were sometimes distant from the rest of their family. (Much the same was true of domestic servants in Britain throughout the eighteenth and nineteenth centuries.) Holidays were especially important for slaves distant from their families, for then they were able to return home.

In colonial Chesapeake at least, even when the slave family was separated (by bequest or sale), they tended to remain in the same area. Such separations were much more likely to befall those slaves living on small farms rather than larger plantations. Even then, few slaves were sold or moved great distances from their loved ones. This was to change, with terrible consequences, in the nineteenth century. Yet it needs to be stressed that, caveats aside, *most* slaves in colonial Chesapeake would experience some form of forced separation from their families at some point in their lives. Large numbers were shifted, from the mid-eighteenth century through to the end of the War of Independence, to the Piedmont region; too far away to visit relatives. But something like two-thirds of all slaves in the region lived within striking distance of their families.[5]

As colonial life moved from the bare sufficiency of early settlement to the rise of material prosperity (based on slave labour) there were direct consequences for the slaves. The process of material accumulation, of emergent prosperity or the onset of material decline among the white slave-owning class had the effect of scattering slave families in colonial America. Like fields and houses, horses and carts, the slaves were a species of property. As such they were inherited and bequeathed, bought and sold, divided up and removed. Their masters' wills and business papers document the process of the relocation of slaves.

Take for example the case of Daphne, a slave born on a plantation in 1736. By the time she was twenty-four she had had six different masters, though she still lived in her birthplace. By 1779 she had ten children, but in that year her six younger children were hived off (along with her grandchildren) when

Daphne's current master divided his slaves between his son and daughter. Though the slaves lived only a few miles away from each other, it was a sharp family divide, imposed from above to accord to the propertied interests of the slave-owning class, and paying scant attention to the needs or interests of the slaves themselves. Daphne was at the centre of a complex web of relations scattered throughout the plantations owned by her master, and having distant relatives on other neighbouring properties.[6]

Economic misfortune, relocation and resettlement, death and inheritance, marriage and maturity – all these aspects of the life cycle among the whites had direct consequences for the slaves. The wonder is that the slaves managed to maintain their families in the teeth of the periodic convulsions which shook the fabric of their lives.

The slave family lived in huts or cabins, 'negro houses', which varied enormously. On the bigger plantations, especially after 1750, planters grouped their slave families in huts huddled close to the fields they worked in. Earlier, the predominantly male slave force had sometimes been housed in barracks, catering for six men or more. But on smaller farms, slaves slept and lived where they could find room; in lofts, in the tobacco houses and in a host of outbuildings.[7] Not surprisingly, the slave families lived in simple buildings, few of which have survived, though we have sufficient evidence, especially from recent archaeological research, to reconstruct the broad outlines of slave housing. Bigger slave huts, with a variety of rooms, provided living space for more than one family, but they offered little privacy, and much of domestic life was clearly conducted communally. Families had their own rooms but used a joint fireplace, and shared outside kitchens. Given the chance, however, the slaves built separate huts; simple wooden buildings, small by modern standards – a large one might be 20 feet by 15 feet. There were, however, variations. In coastal Georgia, slave housing was built not from wood but from a mix of lime, shells, sand and water. In South Carolina slaves lived in huts with mud walls and thatched roofs, buildings which looked remarkably like African huts. In time of course the fabric of slave domestic life improved, as rising material well-being spread slowly, and unequally, through colonial society.

Slave houses were constructed cheek by jowl on the edge of a common yard. The slave house provided privacy, a physical space where mothers (and to a lesser extent fathers) passed on the cultural attributes needed by young slaves. Outside in the yard, the focal point of social life, slaves met and gossiped, gathered after work for talk, music and story-telling. Within this tight space the slave family thrived, hooked into its broader network of kinsfolk, and a constituent part of the broader slave community. Periodically it was augmented by friends, relatives and visitors from further afield. (Of course this was not the case for the knots of slaves who lived on small farms and properties.)[8]

   This picture of domestic life is, inevitably, a static caricature. From their earliest years, slaves' lives were shaped by the peculiarities of the slave system. Mothers cared for their children up to the age of ten; over the next four years children left their parents' home; some settled with other brothers and sisters, some were sold, while others moved in with other relatives. Slave women tended to marry in their late teens and then establish households of their own. The newborn was generally taken into the fields with the mother. When the child grew older, he/she was left in the company of other small children in the slave yard, possibly under the supervision of an aged slave. And like rural children the world over, as they grew a little older they were expected to care for the smaller children, allowing the mothers to work uninterrupted in the fields. By the age of seven, slave children were ready for their initiation in the local fields, learning the necessary skills and tricks of the trade from parents and white overseers. In the same way, the slave craftsmen passed on their trade to their growing progeny. It was at this point, when the young slaves had begun to work and had an economic value and potential of their own, that many of them were removed from their family home and placed in what their owners thought was more appropriate labour. We can only guess at the untold misery felt by these adolescent slaves, uprooted from their family and community, and set to work in a distant place, possibly at an alien task. Not surprisingly, many of them fled back to parents and other kinfolk.

   For young slave women, childbirth rather than marriage was the next major stage in family life. Once her child was born, she would move into her own hut and possibly receive those small privileges which slave-owners realized were so important (for them and the slave women). For the young mother, her new role was crucial, but it was less important for her spouse (who would be likely, in any case, to live elsewhere, with other men). When the father was resident in the new household, he played an important role, alongside the mother, in child-rearing, helping the children acquire skills and offering the necessary lessons for survival in slave society. The larger the plantation, the more slaves there were, many of them relatives, to help the growing slave. Lessons learned at the knee of grandparents, stories told by uncles and aunts, skills taught by cousins, family tales about various relatives – all this and more added to the accumulating store of wisdom and knowledge of the young slaves.

   At the other end of the life cycle – old age, illness or accident – the slave family once more proved crucial. Sometimes masters made provision for the decent retirement and care of their aged slaves, especially after a lifetime's faithful service; but old age generally involved a slow decline from one less demanding task to another. Unscrupulous owners sometimes sold their declining slaves, or simply freed them. But how could a former slave survive as a free person when in physical decline? It was, then, up to the family and relatives to care for the old and disabled slaves.[9]

From birth to the grave, the family provided an immediate and wider network for all stages of slave life. It was, in colonial America, and institution which emerged from the most unpromising of circumstances to become the most durable and resilient of slave institutions. To a very large degree, it made American slaves what they were. The family was the lode-star which attracted slaves from near and far. They spent much of their free time, resources and physical effort making their way back to their family group. At weekends, on holidays, on significant anniversaries (and of course when love or misery fired them), slaves left their place of labour for the bosom of the family. In time there developed a mosaic of slave family ties stretching from the family home, out through the immediate area and far beyond, even north to the growing cities which were to provide a haven from slavery in the South.[10]

Families offered a staging post for travellers and a refuge for runaways; a source of succour and comfort, strengthening the slave before silently passing him on to the next family contact. Slaves clearly viewed helping fugitive or transient relatives as a duty. And we need to remind ourselves that sudden and unexpected arrivals placed great strain not only on the host slaves' hard-pressed material resources but also on their safety. Fugitives were sometimes away from their masters for months at a time, travelling vast distances, often in hostile conditions, to see loved ones. They could not have done this without the help and support of relatives *en route*. Propelled by love, desperation, loneliness or anger, these runaway slaves, criss-crossing the face of colonial America, knew that they could depend on relatives. They could always find a home far from home.

There would, inevitably, be a variety of family systems, household arrangements and personal ties which served any slave population. There were bound to be different family systems from place to place within the same colony. What was appropriate for a major plantation was obviously impossible on small remote farms; what seemed natural in an urban setting was out of keeping with the demands of rural life. Yet despite these variations, despite the ubiquitous obstacles, the slave family became the centrepiece of slave life. True throughout the northern colonies, this was also true in the West Indies, where the greater volume of African imports – over a longer period – made the process slightly different.

When Jupiter, a fugitive slave from the Codrington estate in Barbados, returned to his master he was, despite the prospects of severe punishment, 'much rejoiced at the opportunity of getting back to his wife and children'.[11] Visitors to the islands often remarked, on the contrary, that slaves had no real attachment to families. Again, recent research has helped to clarify this confusion, though scholars continue to disagree about the nature and role of the slave family in the Caribbean.

Much of the problem is caused by the changes which took place in the development of slavery in the region. In the early days when Africans were in a

majority (and men outnumbered women), slaves continued to show strong
attachment to their tribal groups. Planters for their part were unenthusiastic
for their slaves to breed, preferring instead to buy new Africans. But this
attitude would survive only as long as new slaves remained plentiful and
cheap. By the mid-eighteenth century it had become evident that there were
financial as well as social advantages to encouraging slave breeding. That
process was aided, in Barbados initially, by the development of a local-born
slave population. In the last fifty years of slavery, from about 1780 onwards,
there was a conscious process of amelioration at work; a mix of plantocratic
encouragement for slave breeding, the first major inroads of Christianity
among the slaves and the development of nuclear families. Such families
were not, of course, universal and some of the older ties remained. But as
the Africans died out, as the local population stabilized, thrived and turned, in
growing numbers, to Christian churches with all their supporting beliefs, the
nuclear family became the norm.

The presence of such families came late in West Indian slavery, though from
the earliest days of settlement observers used the concepts 'wives', 'husbands'
and 'families' to describe slaves' private relationships. In Ligon's account of
Barbados in 1657 he claimed: 'Jealous they are of their wives, and hold it for a
great injury and scorn if another man makes the least courtship to his wife.' It
was quite common, according to Ligon, for planters to allow a slave, especially
'a brave fellow, and one that has extraordinary qualities, two or three wives'.[12]
It became widely accepted that West Indian slaves indulged in polygamy
(though polygyny is now thought the more proper term). The explanation –
for contemporaries at least – was simple: it derived directly from African
promiscuity. When whites sought to improve the slaves' lot, one point of
their attack was then to undermine the 'promiscuous polygamy' which had
been so striking a feature of West Indian slave life since the early days. Yet for
well over 150 years whites made few attempts, in that blizzard of colonial laws
regulating slavery, to encourage or enforce marriage or family life among the
slaves. Law-makers and clergy seemed uninterested in stimulating the slave
family. In part this was a legal matter: since slaves were not allowed to make
contractual arrangements, since they were mere property, they could have no
legal voice. How could chattel hold legal responsibilities?

But this reluctance had deeper reasons. It was simply assumed that Africans
were devoid of any sense of morality and had no real attachment to the
institutions through which conventional white morality functioned. For
much of the history of slavery it clearly suited white interests to give voice
to traditional beliefs in African 'promiscuity' – not least for their own sexual
gratification. The licentiousness of white males on the plantations would have
been impaired by the arrival of fully-fledged Christian marriages among the
slaves. As it was, planters and their white employees showed scant regard for
the stable slave relations they knew to exist. Whites took slave women when

and how it suited them, and it was of some general comfort to feel that their behaviour in no way offended the slaves' sense of morality. More sensitive observers realized this was not the case. Although it was recognized that slaves sometimes took more than one wife, it was a system which had its own rationale and was cemented by its own forms of affection. 'There is no such thing', said a Barbadian clergyman in 1819, 'as far as I can find, as promiscuous concubinage among them.'[13]

At the same time, planters, despite their accusations of slave promiscuity, wanted their slaves to settle down with partners on their own estate (though much depended on the number of the slaves on a property). But, as in North America, it was impossible to force slaves into such arrangements. They chose their own partners, often settling into a relationship with a spouse on a distant property, despite all the problems of travel, absenteeism and separation that this involved.

Children inherited their mother's slavery, and belonged to her master. Did this, as some have claimed, alienate the slave fathers? Were they stripped of their manhood and their sense of primacy within the family group by the superior and overriding power of the slave-owner? It is of course hard to tell and the evidence is contradictory and confusing. We know that Barbadian slave-owners tolerated conjugal visits, even though the law might disavow the necessary slave movements throughout the island. And was this greater liberalism of Barbadian planters the main factor behind the generally more peaceable nature of local slave life? What seems clear enough is that, in Barbados at least, freedom of movement was the essential lubricant of slave family life. Slaves not only had extensive family and kinship ties throughout Barbados but those family links were often known to their masters.

To imagine that absent fathers − or a father able to visit his spouse and offspring only at weekends and holidays − undermined the family unit, or sapped at the family's emotional bonds, is to ignore the degree to which such separations were common in white society. British domestic servants, men in the armed services, men with peripatetic jobs − the building trades, railway navvies, sailors, even agricultural labourers − all and more spent a great deal of time away from their wives and children. Among the slaves similar separations did not preclude or diminish the bonds of affection within the family group.

By the late eighteenth century the slave family began to reshape itself, encouraged by planters, the churches and even by slaves' self-interest. Slave women, able to secure better material conditions for themselves, began to show a clear personal preference (in Barbados) for monogamous marriages. Even slave-owners realized that stable nuclear families were more productive, not least in the number of babies they produced. With the slave trade ended in 1807 planters had very good reasons to encourage slaves to breed. There was however a marked resistance among whites in Barbados to contemplate Christian marriage among local slaves; it was felt that this would somehow undermine the sanctity of their own marriages. Although more and more slaves were baptized and buried in Christian ceremonies, formal church marriages were few and far between.

Slaves of course did not need formal marriages to sanction their family ties; they had their own ceremonies. What strengthened the slave family was the remarkable stability of local estates where ownership remained the same for more than a century. This served to minimize the re-sale and separation of slave families so common in North America and Jamaica. Distinct slave villages developed, at the heart of which were strong family groups, with links, via relations, to other slave villages across the island. The slave family, located on particular properties, rooted in their own village, developed that sense of identity we have already seen among slaves in North America. The deracination of the slave trade had been put to one side and new, local roots and identities had been forged. It was again, a remarkable phenomenon, achieved in the teeth of extraordinary difficulties.

The drive to encourage marriage and families among West Indian slaves was integral to the humanitarian campaign to improve and finally terminate slavery. In the last decades of the eighteenth century a host of British reformers saw an urgent need to make positive efforts to drive a wedge between the slaves and what survived of their African past, especially to divorce them from their polygamous habits. Edmund Burke for instance proposed, in a wide-ranging reform package for dealing with slavery, that 'all negro men and women, above eighteen years of age for the man and sixteen for the women, who have co-habited together for twelve months and upwards, shall be deemed to all intents and purposes to be married'.[14] As genuine as these humanitarian desires clearly were, they served merely to complete rather than initiate the emergence of western-type families among the slaves. The real origins of that transformation lay in the changing slave population and, ultimately, the decline of the slave trade. It was still possible of course for slave-owners to split up slave families, mainly by sale. But not until an Act of 1825 did Parliament try to enforce, by law, the embargo on owners selling mothers and children separately.

By the end of the eighteenth century, slaves in Barbados lived in unmistakable nuclear families. Parents had a household in which they lived together with their young children; older children and young adults lived in neighbouring buildings, though husbands were more likely to belong to another property.[15] Men sometimes fathered children by other women, but regarded themselves as married to a specific slave woman. The male slaves' inclination towards varied sexual relations, even when formally married, greatly troubled churchmen and reformers. Perhaps, they felt, Christian marriage with its emphasis on monogamy would purge the slaves of this 'African vice'.[16]

Thanks to some rigorous demographic research in recent years it is now possible to discuss the slave family with some confidence. Yet the topic still remains confused, not least because the institution itself was confused. There were different, and at times competing, family systems existing side by side. This was understandable enough when we remember that Africa and Europe collided in the slave colonies. Slaves clung to kinship ties which they remembered and imported from their various African homelands. No longer in Africa, circumstances forced them to accommodate themselves to the New World. The personal and family relationships which emerged were, then, a result of that fusion; that creative tension between European and African cultural values. The simple but all-important truth was that most slaves lived in family units and did so for much of the history of black slavery.[17]

Like families elsewhere, the West Indian slave family was the crucible for child-rearing and socialization. Because of the distance and absence of slave fathers, the lion's share of child-rearing fell to the womenfolk (though this, again, was hardly peculiar to slaves). It was often alleged that slaves were bad mothers; harsh, even cruel, lacking in maternal affection. But the slave discipline over children was too often mistaken for cruelty. Yet how else could slave women organize their lives, when so much was demanded of them? They were slaves to their masters and yet had to fulfil all the demanding rituals of household world and child-rearing, often without the assistance of a resident spouse. The ultimate denial of those accusations was the slaves' lifelong affection for and commitment to their mothers What served to confuse observers was that the mother child relationship, indeed family relations in general, took place within a much broader framework of ties within the slave community. Slave communities did not function like white society.

There were extended families which took on many of the roles reserved for more immediate relatives in white society. Older, established slaves, for instance, took in and effectively adopted newly-arrived African slaves. Kinsfolk rallied round in all life's trials and tribulations. Planters were sometimes amazed to discover distant relatives pleading on behalf of a slave. When the slave community cared for the old and disabled, whites assumed that it was a habit imported from Africa. It was the same with the young and the sick; neighbours and friends all helped in times of trouble. As in the slave quarters of North America, the slave family in the West Indies forged its sense of identity not only from its immediate family ties but also from its relationships with other slaves, some family, some friends or neighbours. They developed a fierce sense of attachment to that immediate community around them; to their homes – which they bequeathed to offspring – to their plots and gardens, to the sense of community which emerged from the huts and yard.[18] Again, slaves were not the only group whose attachment to local community proved vital in living under harsh circumstances.

In the most mundane of daily events – cooking, child-care, nursing, relaxing after a day's work – or during those more significant rites of passage – birth, marriage, death and bereavement – slaves, in their families and in their community, forged a sense of collective strength which steeled them against the tribulations of life under slavery. The slave family and the slave community were locked together to form the social bedrock of slave society throughout the Caribbean and colonial America. Despite everything, despite the slave trade, despite the brutalities of slave labour, despite the traumas of sales and separations and the periodic and capricious sexual approaches of white men, the slave family became the sure source of strength and resilience to slaves throughout the Americas. In essence it was to form the basis for the structure of black life and society long after the process which had brought it into being – chattel slavery – had melted away.

14

Sex in the Slave Quarters

Thomas Thistlewood was twenty-nine when he landed in Jamaica, from his native Lincolnshire, in 1750. Working first as a cattle pen keeper, later as an overseer on a sugar estate close to Savanna-la-Mar in the west of the island, Thistlewood eventually bought his own property and slaves. Throughout his adult life he kept a diary, about 10,000 pages of manuscript all told. Among the many items he recorded were details of his sex life with his slaves: the precise locations, frequency, names and pleasures of his multiple couplings, often documented in simple Latin. In English or Latin, Thistlewood's diary is a remarkable account of a man who was rarely deterred from taking sexual advantage of his slaves.

Thistlewood's first conquest seems to have been Marina, a field slave he took as his 'wife' and on whom he lavished gifts and goods: clothes, food, rum, cooking utensils, furniture. And then to bed; or in Thistlewood's Latin: '*Sup. lect. cum Marina*' [on the bed with Marina]. Having taken his pleasure of the woman, Thistlewood 'Got up first by moon rise, gave Marina a bottle of rum, water pail etc and took leave of her in my parlour.'[1]

When not fornicating with slaves, Thistlewood enjoyed the saucy tales of fellow-whites: 'Old Tom Williams says he pleases his mistress yet twice a night; first by putting his thigh over her, which pleases her by putting her in expectation – next he pleases her by taking it off, when she is weary of the weight.'[2]

Much more common were his conquests among the slaves: 'On Tuesday, 10 September 1751, about 1/2 past 10 a.m. *cum* Flora a Congo, *Super Terram* [on the ground], above the wall head, right hand of the river, toward the Negro ground. She been for water cress. Gave her 4 bits.' The very next day he turned to another slave: 'About 2 a.m. *cum* Negro girl, *super* floor, at north bed foot in the east parlour'.[3] A month later he was fornicating with a different woman: 'a.m. About eleven o'clock, *cum* Ellin, an Ebo. by the Morass side, *sup. terr.* [on the ground] toward the little plantation walk.'

It was only a matter of time before Thistlewood's promiscuity produced the inevitable results, in so diseased a society as eighteenth-century Jamaica. In October 1751 Thistlewood described his first bout of VD: 'A greater redness, with soreness, and scalding water. About 9 a.m. a running begun, of a yellowish greenish matter. Thursday, 3rd; in the night painful erections, and sharp pricking, great torment, forced to get up and walk about.' It was described by his doctor as 'A rank infection'.[4] There followed forty-four days of painful cures: bleedings, twenty-four mercury pills, salts and cooling powders, balsam, 'besides bathing the penis a long time in new milk night and morning with probes, and syringing away 2 phials of infection water'. Even as he took the treatment, he continued to take the slave women. In the middle of the treatment he took Jenny three times in one night, rewarding her with a string of gifts: 'For gifts – 2 yards of Brown Oznabrig, 4 bitts; 4 yards of striped holland, 8 bitts; and a handkerchief, 3 bitts. Gave them all to Jenny.'[5]

These are just a few, early examples of a prolific sexual appetite which feasted on slave women whenever the chance or desire arose. Thistlewood may well have been more lusty than most, but he was able to give full rein to his desires because he was surrounded by slave women who could not resist his advances and for whom his gifts and rewards were valuable commodities in a world of deprivation and hardship. He also gave them diseases and babies.

Here was the world of the plantation white, dominating his slaves in more than their working lives; able to exploit them more thoroughly than simply by work. Some of Thistlewood's lovers clearly liked him, showing signs of jealousy and anger as he strayed yet again into the arms of another slave. But it is inconceivable that all felt the same way. Most of his conquests were just that; the triumphant coupling of a dominant male who brooked no resistance to his demands. In sexual matters as at work – indeed as in life in general – the slaves were the playthings of their owners. We will need to return to Thomas Thistlewood later, hard at work in his remote home in western Jamaica, but no less industrious in his fornications with slave women of all ages and conditions. Was Thistlewood so sexually active because he lived in such a corrupt society where humanity was reduced to the level of chattel? Was there something unusual, distinctive, about sexuality in the world of the slaves?

Long before the development of the American slave empires, blacks were thought of as particularly lascivious and sexual beings. Blackness, nakedness, lust and immorality; these, in various combinations, were the stock ingredients of English accounts of Africa and Africans. More myth than reality, these concepts were embedded deep in the English imagination *before* the establishment of slavery in the British colonies. *Othello*, after all, was written some time between 1604 and 1611, years before the settlement of Barbados and Jamaica and well before the introduction of slaves into Virginia. The play is, in the words of the historian Winthrop Jordan, 'shot through with the language of blackness and sex': 'I hate the Moor', says Iago. 'And it is thought abroad that twixt my sheets He has done my office.' Later he says: 'I do suspect the lusty Moor hath leaped into my seat.' Brabantio is told that 'an old black ram is tupping your white ewe'. Shakespeare was speaking to an audience familiar with these sentiments; people alert to the powerful appeal of black sexuality and who recognized the strength of the imagery.[6]

There was plenty of printed material available to confirm these ideas about black sexuality. Accounts of the early voyages to black Africa were replete with stories of African sexuality. Hakluyt's voyages had described naked Africans, who have 'great swarms of harlots among them: where upon a man may easily conjecture their manner of living'.[7] Another early African adventurer, Walter Waterman, told how the Africans 'fall upon their women even as they came to hande without any choyse'.[8]

African nakedness made a startling impression on European explorers. Like the indigenous blackness, it was widely thought to be linked to the heat: 'throughout all Africke, under the Aequinoctinal line, and neere about the same on both sides, the regions are extreme hote, and the people very blacke'.[9] Europeans were curious for centuries about the origins of human blackness. They were no less curious about black sexuality. Was it, too, related to the heat? In 1555 William Towerson reported that men on the Guinea Coast 'are mighty big men, who all go naked except something before their private parts'. Men and women alike were naked, so that 'one cannot know a man from a woman but by their breasts, which in the most part be very foule and long, hanging down low like the udder of a goate'.[10] More striking than women's breasts were the males' penises. Over the years it came to be widely accepted that the African's 'member' was of 'extraordinary greatness'. One traveller wrote of the Africans' 'large Propagators'. Another, writing of the Mandinka in 1623, said they were 'furnisht with such members as are after a sort burthensome unto them'. By the mid-seventeenth century it had become a commonplace to write of 'their extraordinary greatness'.[11]

Quite apart from the influence of popular culture and word of mouth (those stories which sped from the dockside, from the tales of returning sailors into the community at large), there was a rich and expanding literature which apparently documented the facts of African sexuality. It was assumed that Africans − men and women − were especially lascivious; were particularly well-endowed by nature and were propelled by their hot, tropical homelands into a realm of sexuality unknown to the Europeans.

As the European trading presence on the African coast expanded, sexual relations between black and white inevitably increased. Casual sex between sailors and African women, permanent (often polygamous) relations between whites resident on the coast and their local paramours, these and a host of sexual permutations in between established the patterns of sex between black and white. African women were portrayed as lascivious, but this was a claim which was used to mask the promiscuity of the Europeans themselves. By the late seventeenth century it was widely reported that African women (all characterized by a natural 'hotness') made it their business to ensnare European men on the coast. Some claimed that Africans happily prostituted their wives and daughters to the Europeans. All the evidence suggests that, on the contrary, it was the European presence which had a corrupting effect on established local mores. Though forms of prostitution may have served the needs of transient sailors, the resident whites tended to enjoy more permanent relations. Often these families, of black and white with their locally-born offspring, proved commercially useful. Officials of the Royal African Company had local wives. One was married to a mulatto, and their four children had 'fair, flaxen hair and complexion'. More often than not, the whites took their African 'wives' and discarded them at will, using their power and influence to lure and maintain women as they saw fit. It was, said one man in 1693, 'a pleasant way of marrying, for they can turn them off and take others at pleasure, which makes them very careful to humour their husbands in washing their linen, cleaning their chambers, etc and the charge of keeping them is little or nothing'.[12]

Europeans were much more likely to comment on the baseness, the lewdness and the anarchy of African morality and sexuality. But shrewder observers appreciated the corrupting effect of the Europeans and their damaging sexual and domestic demands in a host of African societies. To condemn the immorality of the Africans was to excuse the licence and debauchery of the Europeans' themselves. It was, said one traveller, the Europeans' behaviour which 'tended to harden them in their wickedness rather than turn them from it'. Europeans were, he claimed, 'the occasion of that lewdness they seem to find fault with'.[13]

As the slave trade developed, and as thousands of Europeans settled on or travelled to the African coast, more and more observers came to accept that the whites lost their own veneer of morality when surrounded by Africans. They became as 'abandoned libertines as the Pagans'. The crew of the slave ships seemed especially vile, 'being ungovernable in their actions and appetites, pilfering from the Negroes and debauching their wives'.[14] African women were especially vulnerable on the slave ships. Many traders and captains sought to keep their crew away from the slave women, but it was an impossible task. In January 1753 one of John Newton's crew, William Cooney, 'seduced a slave down in the room and lay with her brutelike in view of the whole quarter deck, for which I put him in irons...If anything happens to the woman I shall impute it to him, for she was big with child. Her number is 83'.[15]

The brutality of sexual relations on the slave ships was only another aspect of the violence endemic throughout the slave trade. Sexually predatory sailors could effectively have their way with their helpless slave victims, deterred only by the discipline of their superiors (who often behaved no better). For many slaves, and for the broader relations between black and white, the crudity of sexuality on the slave ships established a pattern which was to recur throughout the slave colonies; of an unbridled and aggressive white sexuality towards slave women which was ubiquitous and difficult to resist. As we shall see, there may have been material advantages for some slave women in establishing a relationship with a local white man; but in most cases it was not easy to fend off the advances of their 'superiors' and their owners.

It was clear enough that the kinship and family ties which Europeans encountered on the coast were quite unlike anything they were familiar with in Europe. It was easy, if wrong, to impute to these different systems an absence of morality. Africans were widely described as immoral, wanton and lascivious; devoid of those social and sexual restraints which Europeans viewed as the distinguishing qualities of civilized people. Naked, where Europeans were clothed, black when the English believed white to be the epitome of virtue and beauty, living in societies which seemed at first sight to be devoid of family units, and sexually licensed where Europeans exhibited restraints. But it was increasingly clear that much of the 'corruption' evident in African life was a result of the contact with Europeans and was especially caused by the damages wrought by the burgeoning slave trade. By the early eighteenth century, what many observers saw as native African life was in fact the peculiar result of the unhealthy fusion of black and white habits in the disturbing world of enslavement and the slave trade.

Sexual relations between black and white in the Americas were shaped not so much by inherited attitudes as by the demography of slave societies and the power relationships which existed within those societies. As we have already seen, in many of the colonies – especially in the West Indies – slave women were outnumbered by men. Most acute in the early days of settlement, this problem was compounded by the relocation of slaves from one property to another, from one owner to another. Social, marital and sexual stability were not encouraged. Yet it was this very force – the cavalier mixing and rearranging of slaves with little regard to family or affectionate relations – that provided slave-owners with more 'proof' of slave immorality. It was widely assumed that Africans were sexually promiscuous; the process of reallocating slaves in the colonies added to the impression of a people devoid of those kinship ties and morality recognized by Europeans.

Slave women proved a temptation which owners and overseers found very difficult to resist; they were the sexual playthings of any white man who took a fancy to them. Old men looked back with nostalgia on their sexual encounters with slaves. James Masterman reflected on his time in the West Indies with 'the Black Desdimonas and Fatimas'. Now, in 1765, he was troubled by physical decay and could scarcely walk properly. He could now only make love 'between sheets or on a carpet' and he could no longer frolic sexually in the open: 'The flying fucking is over with me.'[16]

It was natural enough that men without women would turn for companionship and sex to the women they lived and worked close to. But it is impossible to speak of normal or natural relationships in so abnormal a world as that of colonial slavery. There may have been cases where white men fell in love with black women, but for every such case we have scores of examples of sexual exploitation of the basest kind. Throughout the Caribbean islands white women were in short supply, especially on the plantations, and white men simply took their pick of the available slave women, often with no regard to age, condition or the woman's existing relationships. White women clearly did not enjoy the lonely, threatening and often crude life on the plantations, preferring to live in the nearest towns, or even in Britain. One man remarked, in 1784, that the plantations were now run by 'a dissipated, careless, unfeeling young man, or a grovelling, lascivious, old bachelor (each with his half score of black or mulatto pilfering harlots)'.[17]

When Parliament and the humanitarians, notably the nonconformist churches, began to scrutinize West Indian slavery in the late eighteenth century, they were appalled by the tales of sexual laxity and licence. Slave women unable to resist the advances of their masters; slaves casually offered to visiting friends; beatings and punishments when sexual advances were spurned. All these stories, common throughout the Caribbean, were unexceptional; part of the very fabric of slave society and quite distinct from the more out rageous and sadistic acts of sexual violation. Tales spread in London of slaves sleeping with masters to avoid a beating; of reluctant women being flogged to within an inch of their lives: 'Subject to Corporal Punishment for non-compliance with the libidinous desires of the person in authority on the estate.' When whites visited friends on neighbouring estates on Sundays, it was common 'to have Women selected upon the properties for the purpose of sleeping with these visitors'.[18] White friends visiting Thomas Thistlewood expected to be provided with their favourite slave woman to complete an evening's drinking and eating. The slave quarters were the sexual hunting grounds for the predatory local whites. At first trying to persuade a slave with gifts of clothing, money, beads, food or a better post, the white man could, in the last resort, simply use physical force. Frederick Douglass, the American black leader and ex-slave, put the matter boldly, but accurately: the 'slave woman is at the mercy of the fathers, sons or brothers of her master'.[19]

The initial white surprise, horror even, at 'African' characteristics (of nakedness, different morality and apparent 'promiscuity') gave way to aggressive demands made of slave women. It was a simple progression from viewing Africans as amoral things, to feeling free to exploit them sexually and at will.

Whatever mores Africans carried with them into the Americas were rapidly abused, or at best utterly disregarded, by men who felt no compunction in demanding sexual as well as labouring services. It was all of a piece; since the slaves were there to do as the white man bid, they were to obey his sexual as much as his labouring instructions. Yet it was one of slavery's great ironies that white 'justification' for the rapacious use of slave women was the traditional or even 'natural' promiscuity of the blacks.[20]

Blessed by the freedom bestowed by a warm climate, devoid of 'normal' morality, black women were portrayed by whites in written and popular culture as naturally highly sexed. It was of course an obvious justification for everything and anything the white man chose to do to the black woman. There was however another side to this tangled web of white attitudes towards black sexuality: the common belief that black men lusted after, and were in their turn desired by, white women. Colonial society in the Caribbean and North America afforded plenty of examples of such relations, and even more illustrations of punitive efforts, in law and social practice, to prevent or punish it. Consoling to think that only women of the lowest orders would willingly couple with black men (the women most likely to meet blacks on a regular social basis), it was especially troublesome when 'superior' women took the same route to sexual or personal pleasure. Edward Long, whose writing in the 1770s remains among the most extreme of plantocratic racism, had this to say about such relations: 'The lower class of women in England, are remarkably fond of the blacks, for reasons too brutal to mention; they would connect themselves with horses and asses, if the laws permitted them.'[21] Long was directing this particular argument against black settlement in England itself, where most black settlers in the late eighteenth century were male. There were, it is true, some well-published cases. In 1794 *The Times* reported that the 'wife of a gentleman at Sheerness...had eloped with a black servant. They were pursued to the Nag's Head in the Borough on Sunday where *Blackey* fired a shot at his pursuers, for which he was taken and committed'. A day later 'the husband took her three children, and all the property he found on the coach, desired the wife to go where she pleased (after she said she'd live with no man but the Black) and *Mungo* was taken by a press gang, and put on board the tender!'[22]

Such stories were much more common, and much more subversive in their social consequences, in the slave colonies themselves. In 1681 Nell Butler, Irish maidservant to Lord Baltimore in Virginia, fell in love with her master's slave, Charles. Threatened by enslavement herself, Nell Butler replied, 'She had rather Marry the Negro under them circumstances than to marry his Lordship with his Country.'[23] Fear of male black sexuality permeated colonial life. It was frequently assumed that black violence would be accompanied by sexual licence and the ravishing of white women. Rumours abounded that rebellious slaves had targeted particular white women as sexual partners during or after a revolt. In the event most stories remained rumours – nervous fantasies of white men projecting on to the blacks their deepest sexual anxieties and their own sexual behaviour. There was violence and bloodshed in abundance in the slave revolts, especially in the West Indies, but the sexual violation of white women did not figure as a major aim of the rebels. More-over, whatever violations took place scarcely begin to compete with the ubiquitous and persistent sexual violation of slave women by white men.[24]

The degree of sexual fear of black males can best be illustrated by the use of castration in the slave colonies. At least seven of the northern colonies made legal provision for the castration of slaves, for a variety of rebellious offences such as running away or striking a white person. By the late eighteenth century changing sensibilities had effectively undermined the legal use of castration in North America. But in origin and execution it was directed against the blacks alone and had no basis in English law. Indeed English law officers, who had the duty of monitoring colonial legislation, were generally appalled by American insistence on castration. It was 'inhuman and contrary to all Christian laws' and 'such as never was allowed by or known in the Laws of this Kingdom'.[25] It was a clear indication of the degree to which slavery had debased the whites that the laws and practices needed to keep slavery in its place were thought more barbaric than anything to be found in the bloody penal code of England itself. And even when a more humane tide began to run against castration, and when slave colonies began to dispense with it, it was generally kept as a punishment for slave rape of a white woman (though not, interestingly enough, of a slave woman).

There was an obvious, deep animosity to the very idea of sexual relations between black men and white women. It would be easy to speculate on the origins of this phobia exhibited by white men on both sides of the Atlantic and in all the slave colonies. But it does not take a leap of the imagination to see that the 'problem' of sexual relations between black and white was created in the main by the behaviour of white males. It was, above all else, their unre-strained behaviour on the African coast, on the slave ships and in the slave colonies, which built up a store of resentment and hatred. Fears of black male sexuality were in part a reflection of the widespread guilt felt about white sexual behaviour towards black women. It was, inevitably, a complex phenomenon; old myths about black sexuality mingled with fears of revenge-ful blacks (inspired by a natural lust and an urge to revenge the wrongs done to their womenfolk) to poison the minds of whites throughout the slave colonies.

Planters and their white employees took slave women whenever they felt like it, or when the opportunity arose. Slave women had their own strategems for avoiding or deflecting unwelcome advances. But on the whole they remained weak in the face of such harassment. Whites constantly accused blacks of virulent promiscuity, yet of all the racial or social groups in the

Americas, few were as 'promiscuous' as those white males who lived on slave-worked rural settlements.

Thomas Thistlewood's journal records his own sexual ramblings and those of his neighbouring white friends and acquaintances. Throughout 1754 he had a passionate affair with his slave Phibbah, recording in detail the times and places they had intercourse, the nights she refused to sleep with him, the times of her menstruation; the places they used and postures they struck. But his affection for Phibbah did not keep him away from other slave women: 'Friday, 1 March: [1754] p.m. *Cum* Phibbah... and in the evening, *Cum* Susannah in the curing house, *stans*.' Thistlewood even described his response to his various couplings: 'Wednesday, 19 April 1758: About 2 p.m. *Cum mea* Abba, *Sup. Lect* (*sed non bene*) [on the bed, but not good].' When his favourites were away, he dabbled with old lovers. In January 1759 he wrote: '*Cum* Egypt Susannah, *Sup Lect* (Ter). Gave her 2 bits.' There was an extra risk in sleeping with Susannah; she was an inveterate bed-wetter: 'Last night sus[anna]h piss the bed again, makes 3 times, will bear no more.' He allowed visitors to sleep with his slaves. On 19 May 1759 John Cope stayed overnight at Thistlewood's home: 'Saturday, 19 May: at night Mr Cope come. Slept here, had Little Mimber; but suspect he has the clap.' Such a suspicion did not prevent Thistlewood from enjoying the same woman five days later: 'In the evening, *Cum* Little Mimber, a Creole, *Sup. Lect in mea domo* [parlour].'[26]

Thistlewood seems to have been untroubled by sharing his partners with slaves, visiting friends or other local white men. Sally, a woman with whom he had frequent relations in the 1760s, ran away in 1768. Put in the stocks when recaptured, Sally was clearly unwell:

> Put a collar and chain about Sally's neck, also branded her with T T on her right cheek. Note her private parts is tore in a terrible manner, which was discovered this morning by her having bled a great deal where she lay in the bilboes last night. Being threatened a good deal, she at last confessed that a sailor had laid with her while away.

When she had healed, Thistlewood returned to her: '20 October: p.m. *Cum* Sally, *mea, Sup Terr* at foot of Cotton tree by new ground side, West north West from the house.' He added '*sed non bene*'. In the light of Sally's recent experiences, it would have been amazing if it had been good.[27]

Almost as frequent as Thistlewood's varied fornications were his venereal infections. Beginning in 1753, the symptoms, cures and consequences were described in minute and painful detail. In fact the VD may simply have lain dormant throughout, flaring up periodically and sometimes, though not always, imposing a temporary halt on his sexual activities. Sometimes he took the medicines recommended by his local doctor friends. More interestingly, he occasionally adopted slave cures. Mulatto Will persuaded him to take a cure of 'Rhubarb, Cassia and Balm Capivi and some jollop scorched to make it mild over the fire'.[28] It was pointless to expect complete recovery because he could not resist the sexual temptations afforded by his slave women, even when he suspected them of being diseased. Phibbah complained in 1760 'of a violent pain at the bottom of her belly. She also has a running which stains yellowish, suppose it is Fluor Albies, but I rather suspect a venereal infection. Gave her a mercury pill at night'.[29] On 10 September 1761, troubled by VD, he none the less took Susannah, on 'Chest lid T.T. No. 2, Books and wearing apparel, *in me dom.*'

Only when he described 'emission painful' did Thistlewood abstain from sexual intercourse with his slaves.[30] He knew which of his slaves had venereal complaints, and learned that some of the friends to whom he offered slaves for the night were also badly poxed.[31] Like Thistlewood, his regular (in some cases, constant) companions were diseased year after year. His steady partner Phibbah received regular medication for VD, as did her son by Thistlewood. His friend Dr Wedderburn hazarded the disconcerting guess that 'of those who have long been in this island, he looks upon it 4/5 the die of the venereal disease, one way or other, occasioned by it'.[32]

It is relatively easy to document the venereal problems of the slaves and their white masters. More troublesome are the broader social consequences of those ailments. The casual mating so common in slave colonies, especially in the Caribbean, clearly explains the high levels of VD. Was it also responsible for the low levels of conception and successful reproduction? Planters had their own explanations for their slaves' inability (in the Caribbean, if not in North America) to breed: they were, from an early date, 'debauched' and 'promiscuous', habits imported, like many diseases, from Africa. By the end of Caribbean slavery, the detailed registration of all slaves documented their physical deformities. It was clear that substantial numbers carried with them physical imperfections, disabilities and various other physical consequences of disease. VD left many slaves with life-long scars and deformities.[33]

In the slave colonies a new class (and colour) of people was born of the relationships between black and white. The offspring of slave mothers and free white men emerged as a distinct racial and social group, creating a host of legal, social and even linguistic confusions. What was their colour? What was their status? What was their political and social standing?

In Jamaica in 1768 there were 17,000 whites to set against the 167,000 slaves; by 1809 the figures were 30,000 and 300,000. By the end of West Indian slavery there were 16,000 whites, 310,000 slaves, but also 31,000 'coloured'. The free coloured population tripled in the thirty years after 1790 and, by the 1820s, had outstripped the white population.[34]

Initially, the coloured offspring of black-white relations inherited their mothers' slave status, though they received favoured treatment from their white fathers. Some were freed or given preferential jobs on the estates. But they did *not* inherit the legal equalities of their fathers. In time, they came to form a distinct group which was accorded its own legal rights (i.e. superior to the slaves but inferior to the whites). Many acquired education and, sometimes, considerable wealth; acquisitions which troubled a plantocracy anxious to guard its monopoly of economic and political power. Individual whites may have mixed easily with their offspring, but as a rule they tried to keep a broad social distance between them. There was even a specific form of racism aimed at 'coloured' people who were often viewed as infertile mules; weak, effeminate and timid. They were thought to have inherited the worst qualities of the slaves and none of the strengths of the whites. One such man, a Jamaican, claimed that the educated 'coloured' class viewed themselves as 'barkless, branchless, and blighted trunks upon a cursed root'.[35] In their turn the coloureds, effectively denied access to the world of the whites, sought to distance themselves from the world of the slaves. They would not, it was claimed, 'cut cane, load carts, drive mules, carry trash'. A planter alleged that 'they would rather starve than engage in agricultural labour – of course I mean manual labour'.[36] Thus did the offspring of black-white sexual liaisons seek to tread a delicate and often unhappy line in a world where slavery had created the most peculiar and distinct social relations between black and white.

Attempts to forbid sexual relations were obviously doomed, though interracial marriages could more easily be outlawed. The offspring of such relations were denounced by the Virginia Assembly in 1691 as 'that abominable mixture and spurious issue'.[37] Miscegenation was in all colonies, and from an early date, a source of great local tension. Yet it would thrive as long as whites and blacks lived close together in slavery or in freedom. Whatever the law, and however strong the social taboos, white men slept with black women. How far this was true between male slaves and white women is much more difficult to decide. In 1769 a man in Maryland denied all responsibility for his wife's debts, renouncing her because she 'has, after all the love and tenderness which could possibly be shown by man to woman, polluted my bed, by taking in my stead, her own Negro slave, by whom she hath a child, which hath occasioned so much disgrace to me and my family'.[38]

Why was so much formal and social revulsion expressed about black–white sexuality? If it was so manifestly a part of the colonial world, why did Assemblies so frequently and vigorously denounce it? What was so distasteful, so repellent, about such relations that they incurred denunciation and outlawing throughout the American colonies? By 1750 all the mainland slave colonies and two of the northern colonies had specifically outlawed miscegenation, though there was some local resistance to such legislation.[39] There was a remarkable contrast between the American and the West Indian colonies. In the Caribbean it was much more common, more open and unexceptional, for whites to take black women to their beds, to have their favourites, often living with them as common-law wives, and to care for their offspring. In the words of Edward Long, anyone who denounced 'such a thing as simple fornication, would for his pains be accounted a simple blockhead: since not one in twenty can be persuaded, that there is either sin or shame in cohabiting with a slave'.[40] North Americans positively disliked and denounced miscegenation as an unnatural violation of immutable boundaries between black and white. West Indians, lost 'in a sea of blacks', took a more relaxed, more tolerant view of the matter. They might not like the collective consequences of their lust – the development of a 'coloured' social class – but they clearly did not feel that their frequent coupling with black women was in any way 'unnatural'.

Travellers in the colonial north remarked that slave-owners, or their sons, slept with their slaves in conditions of great secrecy. Local slaves were powerfully deterred from sleeping with white women by threats of castration or execution. It was a tradition which was often usurped by the local lynch mob, in slavery and in freedom. But in the Caribbean, slave-owners flaunted their liaisons with slaves. They talked, wrote and joked about them and shared their slaves out to friends and visitors for sexual services.

When the prospect of the abolition of the slave trade came closer, planters began to give serious consideration to the need to encourage breeding among their slaves. Yet it had been their own collective behaviour which had proved so disruptive of slave family life in earlier years. However 'promiscuous' the slaves, the predatory sexual demands of the whites in the islands had provided a powerful disincentive to slave stability and monogamy. Male slaves often found their wives taken from them, temporarily or permanently, for the sexual pleasures of local white men. Those who resisted, men or women, faced a range of punishments. Yet even without the corrupting presence of white males, slave women were in a peculiar position. Greatly outnumbered by men, they were, on many plantations, subjected to the natural approaches of gaggles of male slaves in search of sexual satisfaction. On estates where men had few local slave women available they made their sexual complaints known: 'the Negroe men are craving for wifes and therefore would advise girls to be bought'.[41] Some turned to prostitution as a means of enhancing their miserable material lot. But more common were the casual 'unstable' relations among young adults. Older slaves tended to have 'husbands' and 'wives', though this rarely prevented them from enjoying more casual relationships with others. It was this flexibility, the casualness, which so perplexed outside observers, including those – like the planters – who lived close to the slaves but who were greatly perplexed by relationships which differed from the European 'norm'. Edward Long, the Jamaican planter, told his readers in 1774 that the slaves 'are all married (in their way) to a husband, or wife, *pro tempore*, or have other family connections, in almost every parish throughout the island; so that one of them, perhaps, has six or more husbands or wives in several different places'.[42] Time and again, commentators returned to the theme of slaves' multiple partners. Denis Reid wrote in 1823 (of Jamaica) that 'the husband has commonly two or three wives, and the wives as many husbands which they mutually change for each other'.[43]

Sexual relations among the slaves seemed to change and flourish at particular times of the year. In Jamaica relationships flourished and adulteries began more often in November and December, and from January to April. The reason seems simple enough: local foodstuffs, and then sugar from the sugar harvest, were available. It has even been argued that the night shifts on the estates might also have provided the opportunity for illicit liaisons. Thistlewood's diary again catches the mood: 'Cobenna [a sugar boiler] catched London [a stoker] and Rosanna (Cobenna's wife) at work upon London's bed. London got a good thumping as I hear. This was after the coppers done cooling.'

With food and drink, especially rum, widely available in the harvest months, slaves may have been better nourished, keener and more able to indulge their instincts. 'Tis said eating much cane, or drinking much beverage makes a woman so loose and open, as though she has just been concerned with [a] man, and gets many a negro woman a beating from their husbands.'[44] When the harvest was over, and nutrition less easily come by, slave women seemed more willing to lend themselves to white men.

Diseased or sick, married or unattached, a good slave or indifferent, young or mature, slave women succumbed to Thistlewood's power and threats (and were generally rewarded for their services). It is a distasteful story, known only because of the man's compulsive need to record his various and varied conquests. We do not know if he was typical or unusual, though his behaviour seems all of a piece with that of his white friends and neighbours. Perhaps Thomas Thistlewood's only unusual characteristic was that he kept a diary.

PART V

Fighting Back

15

Violence

Slavery, conceived and nurtured in violence, naturally begat violence. From the beginning, the organization of the slave trade, the marshalling, loading, feeding and exercising of the slaves was determined by the paramount need for security against black violence. Guns were trained on the slaves, on other groups of Africans on shore and on the boats plying from shore to the slave ships. John Newton, lying off the African coast in 1750, aligned his ship's '4 swivel blunderbusses' along with the ship's '2 carriage guns'; together they made 'a formidable appearance upon the main deck, and will, I hope, be sufficient to intimidate the slaves from any thoughts of insurrection'.[1] A few days later, having acquired his first batch of slaves, 'began this day with chains and sentrys. Discharged, cleaned and reloaded the small arms.' If that were not enough, Newton, like most slavers of the period, kept his male slaves in chains 'till we saw the land in the West Indies'.[2]

On a later voyage, Newton noted in his diary: 'I was at first, continually alarmed with their almost desperate attempts to make insurrections upon us.' After some weeks, the mood of the slaves changed: 'they behaved more like children in one family, than slaves in chains and irons.' Such moods could never be trusted and 'we were never wanting in such methods of guarding against them as custom and prudence suggest'.[3]

Years later, when Newton had established himself as a prominent abolitionist, he discussed the threat of slave insurrection: 'It is always taken for granted, that they will attempt to gain their liberty if possible.' White men could never trust the slaves on board the slave ships: 'we receive them on board, from the first as enemies'. Slave numbers increased below decks but often the number of crew diminished:

One unguarded hour, or minute, is sufficient to give the slaves the opportunity they are always waiting for. An attempt to rise upon the ship's company, brings on instantaneous and horrid war: for, when they are once in motion, they are desperate; and when they do not conquer, they are seldom quelled without much mischief and bloodshed on both sides.

Sometimes their plans were betrayed and the ringleaders lashed or tortured mercilessly: 'continued till the poor creatures have not had power to groan under their misery'. Others were put for hours, even days, in the thumbscrews, 'a dreadful engine which, if the screw be turned by an unrelenting hand, can give intolerable anguish'. What Newton failed to mention in this new phase of his life was that he himself had administered such tortures. At least his evidence has the authenticity of experience.

Whatever the precautions, however fierce some of the deterrents, slaves took any opportunity to free themselves or harm their captors. Time and again, John Newton, an ever-vigilant slaver, managed to nip slave resistance in the bud. Good intelligence, treacherous slaves, unsleeping vigilance, and good luck, secured Newton's ships against the rumblings of slave resistance. On the whole the slave-traders were successful in overawing their human cargoes, but not all were lucky. One vessel, loading Africans not far from Newton's own ship in 1752, had an eruption among the 200 slaves; the chief mate, three or four other crew members and nineteen slaves were killed. Another, the *Adventure* of London, again trading close to Newton (this time in 1753), was overrun by rebellious slaves who ran the ship aground and destroyed it.[4]

Landfall in the Americas did not always bring an end to the threat from the slaves. In 1750 a Liverpool ship loaded with 350 slaves was taken over by them within sight of Guadaloupe. A handful of surviving crew in the ship's boat were able to raise the alarm and a sloop armed with 100 men finally overwhelmed the slaves.[5] When, in 1737, the *Prince of Orange* of Bristol finally landed in St Kitts, the captain wrote: 'I thought all our Troubles of this Voyage was over; but on the contrary I might say that Dangers rest on the Borders of Security.' Trouble simmered among the male slaves from 14 to 16 March. At five o'clock on that day 'to our great Amazement above a hundred Men Slaves jumped overboard'. The crew rescued as many as they could, but thirty-three died, men 'who would not endeavour to save themselves, but resolved to die, and sank directly down'.[6]

Vengeance for the slaves was often sweet but bloody. When the slaves on board the *King David* from Bristol overwhelmed their crew, they instantly killed the Captain and five crew and later threw nine more overboard clad in the irons designed for the slaves.[7]

The literature of the slave trade is peppered with stories about slave rebellions on the slave ships. Widely publicized in newspapers, and amply broadcast by later abolitionists, such slave violence is much harder to quantify than it is to describe. In the French slave trade in the years 1749–55 and 1763–66, ten slavers were overwhelmed by their slaves. Research from the Dutch slave trade suggests a number of cases where all slaves were lost in shipboard rebellions.[8] In the British slave trade, it has been calculated that there was a slave revolt on a slaver once every two years. In October 1786 a Dutch slave ship on the Gold Coast, almost ready to sail, was seized by the slaves. In the ensuing plunder and mayhem on board – other Africans joined in in search of booty – the ship was destroyed by a mighty explosion, 'to upwards of three or four hundred souls'.[9] It was, however, unusual for a ship to be lost completely to a slave revolt. For every overthrow of a crew there were clearly dozens of revolts on a humbler scale, acts of violence and resistance which the crews managed to suppress (generally bloodily). In 1702 on the *Tiger*, bound from Gambia, forty slaves and two crew were killed in a revolt. A year later the crew of the *Urban* killed twenty-three male slaves in suppressing a revolt. A bloody reaction by the crew usually had the desired effect. When the crew of the *Martha*, bound for Nevis in 1703, fired on rebellious slaves they 'killed 2 very lusty men and afterwards they were highly peaceable'. Crewmen were sometimes just as troubled by the women, 'on account of the noise and clamour they made'.[10]

White sailors knew that only a bloody response would settle the matter when violence erupted. No quarter was asked or expected, and the fighting was crude and ferocious. A surgeon in the Royal Navy told how, in 1721, the *Rupert* of Bristol had bought a batch of thirty slaves, one of whom, 'Captain Tomba', was a particularly powerful and fierce man. Tomba persuaded 'three or four of the stoutest of his Country-men to kill the Ship's Company'. A woman brought Tomba a hammer and 'news that there were no more than five white Men upon the Deck, and they asleep'. Tomba climbed on to the deck, where he promptly killed two of the three sleeping sailors, 'with single Strokes upon the Temples'. His accomplices were meanwhile struggling with the third sailor when Tomba turned to help them, killing the man with a hammer blow to the head. By now the noise and the fighting had alerted the watch and the Captain who 'took a hand-spike, the first thing he met with in the surprise, and redoubling his strokes home upon Tomba, laid him at length flat upon the Deck, securing them all in Irons'. Realizing that Tomba and his accomplice were valuable slaves, the Captain decided to 'whip and scarify them only'. But three others, 'Abettors but not Actors', the Captain 'sentenced to cruel deaths; making them first eat the heart and the liver of one of them killed.' The woman's fate was almost as grotesque: 'The woman he hoisted up by the thumbs, whipped and slashed her with knives, before the other slaves till she died.'[11]

Violence, the threat of violence, fearful punishments and as severe a daily regime as circumstances allowed were the factors which maintained discipline on the slave ships. Slaves were shuffled, brow-beaten, humiliated and pummelled into acceptance and obedience. However smooth and swift a voyage, however subdued or traumatized the slaves, both black and white realized that the relationship was forged by and secured in violence. This was quite apart from whatever capricious treatment the slaves might suffer at the hands of individual crew members. Sexual assaults, cuffs, blows, thorough beatings; all these were doled out in addition to the more formal and institutionalized violence of the slave system. Ultimately, the shipping of millions of Africans was made possible by the crude violence of the system itself. And the slaves responded, sometimes with aggression of their own, but often with a cowed submission born of repeated defeats and fear of the overwhelming odds.

The experience on the slave ships was like no other aspect of the slave system. It combined the very worst elements of life at sea with the worst experiences of bondage. But the slave ships were also the crucible which forged the formative relationships between slaves and between black and white. Those slaves who survived to the Americas nurtured the memories of the sufferings they endured with their shipmates. Long after they left the ships behind them, slaves in the Americas recalled their shipmates. We need to remember that black reactions to white people were shaped and sealed by these experiences. For the great majority of the millions of Africans shipped across the Atlantic, their first and only knowledge of and dealings with white men were in transit to and on board the slave ship. When Olaudah Equiano saw his first white men, 'I was now persuaded that I had got into a world of bad spirits, and that they were going to kill me. Their complexions too differing so much from ours, their long hair, and the language they spoke...united to confirm me in this belief.'[12] For the survivors the violence of the slave ships provided a basic lesson in the relationship between black and white which was to dominate their lives thereafter.

Landfall, the terror of the sales in the colonies, the separation from friends and the protracted journey to a new place of employment heralded a new regime and a new cycle of life. Many of the Africans were in a delicate state of health and needed careful nursing back to full strength and economic usefulness. Not all slave-owners could afford to allow their new Africans a period of 'seasoning' before turning them loose on the tasks required of them. But whatever new job an African was allocated – in a large field gang or in a small band of workmen, possibly working alongside white men and even the slave-owner – the threat of violence was never far away. Slaves had to be 'broken-in', taught not merely the basic skills of (mainly rural) American labour but given a new labour discipline: 'A new negro, if he must be broke, will require, more hard Discipline than a young Spaniel.'[13]

Slaves were not alone in requiring a new discipline when transplanted into an utterly alien working environment. The same was true for working people translated from rural to the first industrial occupations of early nineteenth-century Britain, and a similar story unfolded in North America among immigrants employed in new industries.[14] But harsh as life undoubtedly was for most working people, life for the black slaves entailed extra, more onerous penalties. Slaves could rarely escape the threat of violence, even if the threat did not always materialize.

White slave-owners brought together a number of theories to justify the climate of violence on which slavery depended. Africans and their descendants were savages beyond the pale of civilized life, their natural savagery kept in bounds only by the threat of punishment and reprisal. They were, in addition, lazy; indolence was not so much a personal habit as a universal racial vice: 'A planter would as soon expect to hear that sugar-canes and pineapples flourish the year round, in open-air, upon Hounslow Heath, as that Negroes when freed would be brought into the like necessity or disposition to hire themselves for plantation labour.'[15] Black indolence could be kept in check only by white discipline; and discipline without the ultimate sanction of violence was no discipline at all. Whichever slave society we look at, slave-holders said similar things about their slaves. Jamaican sugar planters mouthed the same sentiments as Virginian tobacco planters. 'I find it impossible', said a Virginian in 1772, 'to make a negro do his work well. No orders can engage it, no encouragement persuade it, nor no punishment oblige it'.[16]

The most effective discipline of all was the grinding routine of work itself. Day after day, rising at another man's call, tending the fields to a rhythm and for a duration previously unknown, bending the back to the repetitive tasks of weeding, planting, cutting and loading, all these were, ultimately, the force which shaped the slaves' discipline. But whatever the crop – sugar, rice or tobacco – the owner or his authorized agent was always close at hand to administer the encouraging blow, cuff or whipping.

Slaves were not the only people to be beaten. Whipping a child or striking an inferior were broadly accepted. For much of this period, contemporaries did not share our modern revulsion about corporal punishment. What distinguished slaves however was the persistence, the inescapability and the ubiquity of violence in their lives. Slaves who lived without a whipping in the American South were unusual. William Dunbar, a Scot living in Louisiana, wrote in 1776 that 'two or three had always behaved so well that they had never once received a stroke of the whip'.[17] 'The fear of punishment is the principle to which we must and do appeal, to keep them in awe and order.'[18]

Whipping played a central role in maintaining slavery itself; it established the nature of the relationship between master and man. Of course brute force was vital in a host of different social systems, but nowhere more crucially than in slavery. Whipping, said one historian, 'was a crucial form of social control particularly if we remember that it was very difficult for slaves to run away successfully'.[19] The violence administered by the master or his agents was the most effective way to ensure cohesion in the slave system. In the words of

Thomas Ruffin, a judge in North Carolina in 1829: 'The power of the master must be absolute, to render the submission of the slave perfect.'[20]

Whipping slaves was commonplace: to keep them at their tasks, to punish their failings, to encourage the others, ánd of course to satisfy the whims of the man wielding the whip. Whipping sometimes had a reason and it was sometimes senseless. Slaves in South Carolina were regularly whipped for not completing a set task: 'Don't done your task, driver wave that whip, put you over the barrel, beat you so blood run down.' On one plantation, eight women were given twelve lashes for 'hoeing bad corn'. Some slave-owners tried to restrain the more intemperate and violent of their slave-drivers and overseers, but it was very difficult to implement such ideas.[21] On bigger properties, the slave-owners were in the hands of men who supervised the slaves in the fields. But many slave-owners were themselves simply addicted to beating their slaves. On the Louisiana plantation of Bennet Barrow, one-half of the slaves were whipped at some point between 1840 and 1842.[22] Men who chose not to brutalize their slaves were often disappointed: 'we take away the motive that leads to labour on the neighbouring estates; that is, the dread of the lash; and we cannot substitute that which makes the English labourer industrious, namely, the fear of want'.[23] Without the threat of punishment, why should slaves work? Slave-owners created elaborate systems of rewards for their slaves – bonuses, food, clothing, rest periods and the like – but rewards alone could never prove more than a crude lubricant of the system.

In the West Indian sugar-fields, slave-drivers normally had a whip to hand. In St Kitts in the late eighteenth century, one visitor noted that the driver carried two whips, one short and one long, as he supervised the field slaves: 'They are naked, male and female, down to the girdle and you constantly observe where the application has been made.' Whippings often left life-long scars: 'I believe in some cases they remain for life, as I have seen negroes carry them very visibly to old age; the punishment is with a thong whip, which cuts deep into the flesh.' Jamaican whipping was described thus:

> The general system of flogging is to give them a certain number of stripes with a long whip, which inflicts a dreadful laceration, or a dreadful contusion; and then they follow up that by a severe flogging with ebony switches, the ebony being a very strong wirey plant, with small leaves, like a myrtle leaf, and under every leaf a very sharp tough thorn, and then after that they rub them with brine.[24]

When slaves transgressed, even in the most minor fashion, punishment was instant and often grotesque. Thomas Thistlewood wrote in 1756: 'Derby catched by Port Royal eating canes. Had him well flogged and pickled, then made Hector shit in his mouth.'[25] Thistlewood was clearly not a man who felt squeamish about violating his slaves. When some of his slaves out searching for runaways absented themselves, his reaction was ruthless; 100 to 150 lashes, the branding of the face or the loss of an ear. If he thought a slave responsible for the death of a child (all too common in the slave quarters), he had him or her flogged.

Towards the end of the eighteenth century, West Indian planters began to improve their slaves' conditions; partly under pressure from public and political opinion increasingly uneasy about the blatant violence of the slave system, partly from the self-interested realization that there might be better, more profitable ways of persuading slaves to work. But few dispensed with the whip entirely. In the words of one observer, the crack of the whip was 'a frightful sound which meets our ears every minute, in passing through estates'. Often, however, it was used to frighten slaves, to keep them up to the mark and not invariably to hurt them.[26]

Thomas Roughley, in a prescription for good management, thought that the head driver, the 'most important personage in the slave-population of an estate', should carry with him 'the emblems of his rank and dignity, a polished staff or wand, with prongy crooks on it to lean on, and a short-handled, tangible whip'. Roughley believed that, with the best of the field slaves, 'no punishment should be inflicted but what is absolutely necessary, and that with mercy'. Yet even among the very young slaves in the 'weeding gang', he thought an older woman should be in charge, 'armed with a pliant, serviceable twig, more to create dread, than inflict chastisement'.[27] For those who wanted to criticize slavery, and they increased in numbers in the early nineteenth century, corporal punishment provided a ready argument. Hostile commentators homed in on the casual and institutionalized violence of the slave fields, regaling British readers with the pain and suffering of the slaves and the random violence of their white masters and agents.[28]

Under pressure from Parliament, which was itself increasingly under the influence of abolitionist sentiment, new codes laid down regulations for slave punishments in the British West Indies from 1807. Lashes were to be limited to thirty-nine; any more than ten must be given in the presence of the overseer.[29] We know that such changes were largely window-dressing, devised by planters to persuade an increasingly hostile British public that they were not the violent barbarians many claimed them to be. And we know too that floggings continued. Missionaries among the slaves wrote back to their church organizations telling them of continuing violence against the slaves. Isaac Whitehouse, a Wesleyan missionary in St Ann's Bay, Jamaica, described one such incident:

> I saw the driver flogging a young man with a large cart whip. After he had inflicted as many strokes as he thought proper he proceeded to renew the lash on his whip. When he had done this, a female, apparently about forty years of age, was laid, her stomach upon the ground, her clothes were most indecorously

turned up and whilst two persons held her hands and one her feet…the driver inflicted stroke after stroke.[30]

This incident took place in 1828 five years *after* restrictions had been placed on the punishment of slaves. While some asserted that major changes had indeed taken place, there is an abundance of evidence to the contrary. In Barbados the local Assembly was so resistant to London's proposals for limiting slave punishment that the only restriction they accepted on flogging 'was that the indecent exposure of a woman's body should be avoided'.[31] Yet Barbadian planters were also keen to lure the slaves to work by means other than physical punishment. The latter 'should be calculated to make him feel that it is his interest to be a good member of the plantation to which he belongs, rather than to depress his spirits and produce despondence and despair.' Violence should also be administered as 'the act of cool deliberation'.[32] One problem facing all slaves was that, with capricious owners, they might be flogged even when they did work hard and dutifully.

In the long term corporal punishment did decline, at least in the last generation of slavery in the British West Indies. The cruder violation of earlier days, when settlers and their descendants felt insecurely hemmed in by a threatening frontier and a barbarous and expanding African labour force, gave way to a less savage climate. Visitors to the islands returning after a long absence sometimes recorded that daily violence against the slaves was much less frequent. Planters who completely renounced the use of the whip or banned it from their properties were few and far between. Thomas Thistlewood continued to order four or five floggings a month on his properties in the mid-1780s.

West Indian planters were effectively secure against any legal reprisal for violence to their slaves through their control over the local political and legal machinery. They remained exposed, however, as we shall see, to the reprisals of the slaves. In the main, the planters could flog with impunity, restrained only by personal inclination, a sense that excessive brutality might not serve their economic interest and from a nagging fear of slave reactions. However much they may have feared the threat of slave resistance, the planters rarely moderated their behaviour.

When legal restrictions were placed on whippings in the early nineteenth century (in Trinidad, carrying a whip was banned in 1823 and the stocks replaced floggings), they caused outrage among the planters. Not until the execution of Arthur Hodge in 1811 for having murdered several of his slaves did the belief begin to decline that planters could do anything they wished to their slaves. It is true that violence of the most extraordinarily savage kind continued to be used against slaves, but that was now reserved for slaves who had revolted, run away or been violent in their turn.

Planters tried to maintain the whip, but to use it sparingly; to impress on their slaves the inescapable presence of punishment while giving them the opportunity (through hard work and obedience) of avoiding it. And they generally recognized that the more violent of their fraternity did a disservice to the plantocracy by debasing the effectiveness of violence. In one estate in Demerara, so violent was the planter that 'the Negroes on that estate have got into a state of insensibility and desperation [so that] they quite disregard every punishment he had inflicted'.[33] Rewards came to be viewed as an equally important element in the system of social control; a carrot dangled before the slaves – but always in the knowledge that the stick was readily available.

Beating working people was not of course restricted to slaves. When industrialization began to absorb ever more people in Britain in the early nineteenth century, the most bitter complaints were often about the physical abuse of workers. In the textile industries, parents objected fiercely to the whippings and cuffings doled out to their children. It was a sign of changing mores that such incidents caused great offence to public and political opinion at large.[34] It was clear enough that the new industrial system in Europe (and later in North America) could not function properly under a regime of corporal punishment. Ironically, it was at precisely the same time (say 1800 to 1850), when industrialization began to drive out the use of corporal punishment as an important means of labour control, that corporal punishment remained vital to labour in America. With the expansion of the slave-based cotton region in the US South after 1800 (providing the new Lancastrian industry with its raw material), the crack of the whip was heard in lands which had previously been silent

In the American South, as in the West Indies before it, the planters were loath to forego the use of the whip completely. Some tried to do without but most sought to use it with moderation, alongside rewards (of all sorts) as an incentive to labour and an inducement to social stability. In the words of one slave-manager's guide:

> The object of all punishment should be 1st for correction to deter the offender from a repetition of an offence, from the fear of the like certain punishment; and 2nd, for example to all others, showing them that if they offend, they will likewise receive certain punishment. And these objects and ends of all just punishments can be better attained by the certainty than by the severity of punishment.[35]

Here was a reasonable (for the time) prescription for a management system which would combine firmness, effectiveness and benefits. Like many ideals, it tended to crumble in the hands of mortals. And few were more mortal than the men who supervised the slaves in the fields. Overseers and drivers in the Southern cotton fields were presumably no more or less inhuman, kind, sadistic or tolerant than their counterparts in the previous century throughout the Caribbean. It was the *system* which debased and corrupted. Doubtless it attracted its fair share of low life; of men, like men on the slave ships, not noted for their humanity or feelings. But even the most considerate of men generally found themselves debased by slavery. In so tainted a system, it was difficult for anyone in a position of authority not to be dragged down into slavery's corrosive mire. Whatever the management ideal (and there were plenty of whites who sought to pursue it), the reality was much coarser, much cruder, less human. Where manuals spoke of moderation, the men on the ground spoke and acted with harshness. Anger, bad judgement, drink, cruelty – all these and other human failings jostle for our attention.

Floggings were brutal; fifty to seventy-five lashes were common. Branding, tarring, burning, mutilations were perhaps less common but none the less took place. Yet how do we weigh this in the balance with the frequent examples of kindness and humanity (confirmed by the slaves) among many slave-owners? In truth, most slave-owners 'were neither pitiless fiends nor saints in their relationships with slaves'.[36] Most sought to use and treat their slaves as effectively as possible. And to do that they needed to combine firmness with consideration, punishment with incentive. Decent food, clothing, rest, medical care, housing went hand in hand with angry, punitive blows for transgressions.

Whatever reservations historians might have about the role of whipping, the slaves were clear enough. 'The whip is all in all', was the stark assertion of one slave memory. Another ex-slave (female) explained: 'I did not get many whippings because I always did what I was told, in a hurry. I hated to be whipped.' Slave voices ring loud and clear, and time and again the ex-slave and the freed slave (whose voices are captured in abundance in the USA – quite unlike the West Indies) tell of whippings administered, avoided and remembered: 'My grandfather... would tell us things! To keep the whips off your backs, you know... children, work, work, work, and work hard. You know how you hate to be whipped, so work hard.'[37]

The whip was only the most ubiquitous of an array of threats and violent punishments which kept the slave system in place. From the early days of settlement, violence was an integral part of the legal and social fabric, brought into being to contain, control and shape the slave community to economically profitable ends. All colonial settlements which came to rely on slavery devised a code of legal behaviour which sought to regulate and control the local version of black slavery. Nowhere in the English-speaking world was there a slave code like those of the French and Spanish colonies. But the legal framework in the West Indies and North America – a changing mixture of British legislation, Acts of local Assemblies and common-law traditions – was perfectly suited to the needs of slave masters. The law in each colony was instrumental in steering local slavery into the appropriate path, inevitably so since the slave lobby (led by the planters) were the key law-makers. There was a degree of copying involved; new slave colonies could look to, copy or reject the slave laws already in operation in older slave colonies.

The basic principle involved was similar. In the words of John Reeves, commenting on the slave laws in 1789: 'The leading Idea in the Negro System of jurisprudence is that, which was the first in the Minds of those most interested in its Formation; namely, that Negroes were *Property*, and a Species of Property that needed a rigorous and vigilant *Regulation*.' It was claimed that nine-tenths of the early laws of the slave colonies were concerned with regulating the slaves. These laws, beginning in Barbados, were seventeenth-century laws which reflected the violence of that earlier age fused on to a fear of black resistance. Writing about the early slave laws, John Reeves remarked:

> Death, Confinement to Hard Labour, and Whipping, are the Punishments generally inflicted by the more recent Acts; but in the older, which however are still in Force in most of the Islands, there are the Punishments of Banishments, of slitting the Nose, branding in the Forehead with a hot Iron, cutting off the Ears, and, in some Islands, even that of taking off a Limb.

Apologetically, Reeves added that such punishments 'were suggested by the necessity of a steady and watchful discipline, [rather] than by any cruel or wanton disposition to punish'. An early Act in Barbados, decreeing death for a series of offences (rape, murder, burglary, theft, killing animals), denied the slaves the right to a jury: 'being brutish Slaves, deserves not, for the Baseness of their Condition, to be tried by the legal Trial of Twelve Men of their Peers'. Less serious offences were punished by floggings. Slaves could give evidence against another slave, but never against a white person (though this was changed, along with other slave ameliorations from 1788 in a number of islands). Even with amelioration, the guiding principle was plain enough: 'the Rights of a Master be every Thing, and those of the Slave nothing'.

Wherever we look, this basic fact was central to local laws. An Act in Bermuda of 1764 prefaced its conditions with the claim that it was 'absolutely necessary that effectual provision should be made for the better ordering and governing of slaves', before proceeding to itemize a catalogue of capital crimes. Other offences could be punished, variously, by 'such corporal punishment as the Court shall think fit to inflict'; 'to have one ear nailed to a post or tree, and there to stand for the space of half an hour, and then the said ear to be cut off; and thereafter the other ear nailed in the like manner and cut off at the expiration of one other halfhour'. The mesh of the legal net designed to catch the erring slave was as fine as the slave-holder's imagination could make it. Rebellion, plots, murder, poisoning, robbery, rape or 'sodomy on the body of a white person', incendiarism, manslaughter, stealing a boat, burglary, theft of animals or money or goods (worth more than 20 shillings), food, clothes, furniture – all these were to be punished by 'death without benefit of

Clergy'.[38] Killing a slave was an economic rather than a moral problem, though this was changed by the 'amelioration' laws after 1788. For much of the history of black slavery, murdering a slave was not seriously viewed as murder; in the words of another Bermuda Act of 1730: 'here in his Majesties Colonies and plantations in America the cases and circumstances of things are wonderfully altered...' This Act determined that any slave-owner in Bermuda who might 'accidentally happen to kill any such slave or slaves...shall not be liable to any penalty or forfeiture whatsoever'.[39]

There was no such escape for slave wrong-doers. For serious crimes, the slave laws specified the most barbaric of punishments and mutilations. Transportation to another island, ears cut off, noses slit, faces branded; these were not uncommon and were quite legal. So too, until the 1780s, was amputation of a limb (usually for persistent theft or running away). The bricklayer on Drax Hall, Jamaica, who lost a leg in 1780, or the runaway whose hand was amputated in western Jamaica in 1759 – how useful could they be in so impaired a condition (assuming they survived)? Yet such cases, extreme though they may have been, were far from unusual. We remember them because they *were* so outrageous and were, accordingly, added to the abolitionists' arsenal directed against the slave system.

The legal codes governing North American slavery followed a pattern – necessary if slavery was to thrive – of relegating the slave utterly to the master's control. Like slaves in the Caribbean earlier, American slaves could not legally own property, had limited access to the courts and found their broader interests subsumed within their master's interests.[40] Time and again transgressions of the local slave code were punished by whippings ('stripes' to use the biblical imagery of some states). In Alabama, slaves wandering off the plantation without permission would receive 'twenty stripes'; possessing firearms provoked thirty-nine lashes; riots and tumults would incur 'stripes not exceeding one hundred'. The latter punishment was also reserved for slaves forging a pass. Now, however, murder and gross mistreatment of a slave were punishable by the law. For the slaves the list of capital offences was long; for conspiracy, rape, burglary, robbery with violence, murder, incendiarism. Even as late as 1852, the Alabama slave code specified branding (for breaking and entering) and for manslaughter of another slave. 'Every slave who is guilty of the crime of perjury must, on conviction, be punished with stripes not exceeding one hundred, at the discretion of the jury, and be branded in the hand with the letter P.'[41]

Executing a slave was, however, a costly affair, even when the owner was compensated by the State. Courts frequently reduced a capital sentence to imprisonment, whipping, branding and sale outside the State boundary.[42] But, from the slaves' viewpoint, the legal system in the South as in the West Indies was but another extension of slave-owners' power: 'For most slaves it was the law of the plantation, not of the state, that was relevant... Their daily lives were governed by plantation law.'[43] Slave-owners were doubly powerful; they held enormous local economic and social power and, in effect, administered the local rule of law. How could a slave distinguish the law from the slave-owner when in practice so much legal authority was vested in the same person? There were distant court-houses, jails, law officers and legal proceedings, but the law governing the slaves was most effectively implemented by the slave-owners. The planters or their employees whipped, branded, cuffed or deprived their slaves. And on those rare occasions when the local State authorities were obliged to intervene, usually because of the gravity of the offence, it was important to ram home the lesson to the local slaves. In July 1796 the slave book on Braco plantation on Jamaica's north coast recorded the following sequence of events:

July 4	Mary-Ann Died supposed to be murdered by her husband Windsor, which cut her throat...
Saturday, 23	Windsor Tried and condemned...
Sunday, 24	Windsor Being hanged at Falmouth his head cut off and brought up here and put in the cattle pen.[44]

At the hottest time in a tropical summer, someone took the trouble to carry Windsor's severed head the twenty miles or so from Falmouth along the coast road east to Braco estate. The reason was simple enough; spiked close to the cattle pen, Windsor's head was a vile reminder to the other 360-plus slaves living at Braco of the awful punishments that awaited slave wrong-doers. Human remains – severed heads, limbs, quartered corpses – had long been used on public display as an integral part of the law's fearsome and punitive ultimate response. Best remembered in the excesses of the French Revolution, displays of executed criminals – or bits of them scattered round a town at strategic points – had been commonplace in Europe. By the end of the eighteenth century, it was an aspect of the law which was slowly retreating before a changing public mood. Yet public executions *in England* did not end until 1868. In slave societies, a dead slave was an important emblem of the ultimate violence which the slave-owners were prepared to inflict on transgressing slaves.

The most violent of slave-holders' responses were, as we might expect, reserved for slaves guilty or suspected of rebellion or violence. We will return to the question of rebellion later (Chapter 16), but it is important to stress that violence was not only part of the slave-owners' daily regime but also, in its most extreme form, the ultimate exercise of plantocratic power. In the Caribbean, rebellious slaves were butchered indiscriminately, tortured for confessions and publicly executed in a style which would have been more familiar to Englishmen of the late Middle Ages: killed 'by progressive multilation, slow burnings, breaking on the wheel, or starvation in cages'.[45]

When Tacky's revolt in Jamaica failed in 1760, its leader was decapitated and the head displayed on a pole on the road leading to Spanishtown, the island's capital. One of his followers was destroyed by burning: 'his body being chained to an iron stake, the fire was applied to his feet. He uttered not a groan, and saw his legs reduced to ashes with the utmost firmness and composure'.[46] Two others were starved to death on the gibbet in Kingston's main public square; one took seven, the other nine days to die. Of slave rebels in Antigua in 1729, three were burned alive, one hanged and quartered. In the major upheaval in Barbados in 1816 (when one white and one black soldier died), fifty slaves were killed in the fighting, another seventy executed on the spot, 144 tried and executed, in public 'for the sake of example to the slaves'.[47] It was a sickening parade of plantocratic revenge. But even this was surpassed in 1831–32 in the Jamaican revolt known as the Baptist War. Some 200 slaves were killed in the fighting and another 344 executed afterwards (see Chapter 16). Even in a slave society renowned for its violence, the Jamaican blood-letting in 1832 was remarkable. Within a year, Parliament decided to abolish slavery.

The savagery of vengeful planters knew no bounds. In early days of settlement, and in America as the slave frontier pushed westwards, the slave-owners had that added violent streak of men at war with nature, with local 'savages' and with their own black slaves. Whites were debased by the frontier harshness (and neuroses) and by the very institution of slavery they conjured forth to tame the wilderness and make them prosperous. Yet Jamaica in 1832 was no longer a frontier society. It was a settled, complex and, in many respects, sophisticated society. But beneath the veneer of plantocratic sophistication (to be measured in their homes, their wealth, their glittering social world and their metropolitan connections) there lay savage and scarcely controlled violence. Scratch a planter, and a ferocious and vengeful man stepped forth to inflict death and bloodshed on the encircling blacks.

Much the same was true in the American South. Revolts, resistance or merely the hint or fear of black rebellion fanned the embers of slave-owning anger. In return for alleged violations by the slaves (usually much less outrageous than their enemies claimed), repression of the vilest kind was heaped upon them. In 1811 in Louisiana slave-owners spiked rebel slave heads along the roadside. In 1856 in Tennessee slave-owners paraded the heads of slaves suspected of plotting.[48] These displays of slave-owning deterrence were in keeping with the penal theory of the unreformed law, on both sides of the Atlantic; that justice must be seen to be done. It was a savage, remorseless justice which used the corpses of the victims to impress on everyone the power and the violence of the law. Yet white slave-owners in the Americas were not exceptionally bloodthirsty in this respect. They stood in direct line of descent from ancient slave-owning traditions which bloodily and publicly repressed slave unrest. When the Spartacus revolt was crushed, 6,000 dead slaves lined the Appian Way.

Slave violence in North America came nowhere near to threatening the stability of the slave system. The numbers involved, the destruction created and deaths left in its wake, seem minor when we compare them to the great black upheavals in the West Indies and Brazil. But the reactions of the white plantocracy cannot be gauged in direct response to the immediate threats they faced. Indeed, North American slave-owners were as prepared to do violence to their slaves at the threat or the rumour of trouble as they were in the aftermath of actual upheaval. There was a recurring numerical formula in most slave rebellions; the violent reaction of the whites took a disproportionate number of black lives, consumed immeasurably more black property than the initial upheaval. It took little to throw slave-owners into a blood-letting frenzy against their human property.

What seemed unexceptional to the slave-owners began to appear unusual to outsiders. Visitors to the colonies were frequently taken aback by the examples of judicial or casual violence they saw. When in January 1832 the Rev. Thomas Burchell (a friend of Jamaican slaves) arrived in Montego Bay in the middle of the slave revolt and its suppression, he was appalled by the violent temper of the times: 'the most ferocious and savage spirit was manifested, by some of (what are called) the most respectable white inhabitants, that ever could have occurred amongst civilized society.' Hissed at, abused, spat at, Burchell was protected by a group of local 'coloured' people: 'had I never been at Montego Bay, I must have supposed myself amongst cannibals, or in the midst of the savage hordes of Siberia, or the uncultivated and uncivilized tribes of central Africa'.[49]

The Rev. Henry Coor recalled his Jamaican host having nailed a female domestic to a tree by her ear for having broken a plate. Though the amelioration laws of the late eighteenth and early nineteenth centuries in the Caribbean tried to outlaw the worst punishments against women, in reality female slaves remained exposed to the violence of their owners both male and female. A group of slave women in St Lucia in 1828, accused of 'discontent and mutiny', were 'hung by the arms to a peg, raised so high above their heads that the toes alone touched the ground, the whole weight of the body resting on the wrists of their arms and the tips of their toes'.[50] When 'improvement' came for female slaves, they were no longer whipped; instead they were confined to the stocks, solitary confinement or snapped into a metal collar. Yet such painful humiliations carried out before the other slaves did *not* act as deterrents. Plantation records clearly show repeated offences by female slaves. From first to last, violence against slaves – legally sanctioned or merely privately administered – was a vital element in keeping slavery in place. And this was true for *all* slaves; young and old, male and female, skilled or unskilled. Simply being a slave (and black) was enough to attract the physical barbs of the white slave-owning class or their agents.

So all-encompassing was the role of violence in the slaves' lives that it is difficult to see the boundary between abnormal and normal behaviour towards them. What, today, would seem an act of unnecessary violence would pass almost unremarked in slave societies. Like cattle and other material possessions, the slaves were often branded. Slave records describe an African's tribal markings but these were commonly added to by a slave-owner's brand.[51] Thomas Thistlewood branded fresh purchases of Africans, but waited until the local slaves were five years old before branding them. It was widely recognized for what it was; a cruel, agonizing, dehumanizing act, 'a thing noted to be done only by the severest Masters or to the worst of slaves, and... very discouraging to those poor Creatures'. The Society for the Propagation of the Gospel stopped branding the title SOCIETY on the chests of its new slaves on its Barbados estate in 1732. By the 1790s a plantocratic writer thought that branding in Jamaica continued 'but is growing into disuse' and had died out in the Windward Islands. Persistently troublesome slaves continued to be branded until the end of slavery but the plantocracy had become apologetic for doing it and worried about its effect on public opinion.[52]

The public came to know about slave brandings from the frequent adverts in colonial and British newspapers for runaway slaves. The *Daily Post* of 4 August 1720 told its London readers: 'Went away 22nd July last, from the house of William Webb, in Limehouse Hole, a negro man, about 20 years old, called Dick, yellow complexion, wool hair, about five foot six inches high, having on his right breast the word "HARE" burnt.'[53] The Jamaican *Royal Gazette* in December 1780 asked for the return of a slave called Jamaica 'marked with the letter R or RS on one or both cheeks'. When the *Daily Advertiser* advertised in Kingston on 7 June 1790 for 'a NEGRO SAILOR MAN, of the Coromantee nation', it was remarked that 'he has no brand mark' – a clear suggestion that brand marks were common. When four 'NEW NEGRO MEN' ran away from the estate of Edward Woodcock in Jamaica, they were distinguished by being 'marked on the shoulder E.W.' Brand marks were often the initials of their owner or of his property.[54]

Even when such brand marks were missing, slaves often carried distinguishing physical scars. 'Country marks' (African tribal markings) on the forehead, cheeks, ears, neck; teeth filed down; the disfigurement of illness, most commonly smallpox scars; and a host of scars, holes and missing bits and pieces which testify to their violent and life-threatening experiences. 'James, of the Congo country... walks very lame' (1780); the 'negro sailor man' we have already encountered had 'his face furrowed with the smallpox marks... his back has got several lumps which in some manner resemble a bunch of grapes' (1790); a runaway 'short Creole wench named DILIGENCE alias JUNK has a large scar on her breast, occasioned by a burn, with a toe off each foot, and is troubled with the crab yaws' (1790); Pierre, a runaway in Jamaica in that same year, 'has a scar on his throat where he formerly cut it'.

Time and again adverts for slaves concentrated on their scars. Was this because runaway slaves were, by definition, more rebellious slaves, likely to manoeuvre themselves into dangerous and violent spots – hence the scars? Or were they merely a typical cross-section of a people whose daily lives were literally scarred by violence? Too common, too glaring to be simply accidental, the scarring of the slaves was not reserved for the wrong-doers or the wicked. Slaves bore physical testimony to the ubiquity and severity of the violence they endured on a daily basis.

Revolts and their repression were unusual. But violence against slaves was inescapable; a litany of stinging, smarting, unforgiven and unforgotten pain. Yet it was a violence which corrupted the whites as much as it marked the blacks. In keeping in place a system which could not function or survive without violence, whites became addicted to it. Like many other addictions, violence had its own rationale, justification and pleasures. Violence became so normal a feature of everyday life, that slave-owners ceased even to notice it. They ceased to hear the crack of the whip, the cries or whimpers of pain; they lost any sense of cruelty or reasonableness when they took their regular toll of rebellions or resistant slaves. In the process, the slave-owners were so desensitized by slavery that they failed even to notice that they had become relicts of a former age. When the English-speaking world had begun to lose its attachment to violence and violent solutions to social problems, the planters stuck out, ever more sharply, as reminders of the bad old days. Yet they were not always deliberately cruel or violent (though they could certainly be so when they put their mind to it). It was the amorality of the slave-owners which seemed their most striking characteristic by, say, 1800. Slave-owners no longer seemed to notice just how violent was the world they had created and now clung to. Others, however, had.

16

Rebellions

'The Pearl of the Antilles' is how modern-day Haiti describes itself – at least on its car number-plates. Low down in the league of Third World poverty, Haiti has for generations been exploited by its rapacious governors, its people locked into a diseased poverty which seems ineradicable. Yet two centuries ago it was the most ascendant of the Caribbean colonies, its wealth the envy of its island neighbours. From its 780 sugar estates and 2,000 coffee plantations, worked by a massive army of 465,000 slaves, boundless material prosperity flowed back to France. The French West Indies yielded £9 million-worth of exports (the British £5 million) and it was fitting that the ports of La Rochelle, Nantes and Bordeaux should emerge as elegant urban reminders of the efforts of the slaves.

St Domingue, like all slave colonies, was beset by peculiar social and economic problems; friction between colony and metropolis, between whites (30,000) and coloureds (28,000), and between black and white. Before 1788, however, such frictions were mere irritants in a successful system which disgorged such wealth to France, but within the space of a few years this imposing edifice had collapsed. Like so many of the apparently secure institutions of the *ancien régime* in France, the slave-based economy of St Domingue was swept away by revolutionary fervour.[1]

Like the English, the French enjoyed boom years in their Atlantic slave system in the eighteenth century. French slave ships carried more than one million slaves across the Atlantic, and not even the regular (and, for the French, largely unsuccessful) wars of the eighteenth century could deflect the upward curve of French slave-based wealth, from Guadeloupe, Martinique and, later, St Domingue. It was, above all, St Domingue which absorbed French slaves; about three-quarters of all Africans carried to the French colonies were deposited there. By the 1780s, more than 40,000 were being ferried across the Atlantic each year, a far higher figure than the English could manage.[2] As the century advanced, St Domingue asserted its primacy as *the* slave colony of the New World. In a mere twelve years its slave population expanded at an unprecedented rate, from 250,000 (1779) to 480,000 (1791). Perhaps as many as 10 per cent of all slaves ended up in St Domingue. With 600 ships, 15,000 sailors and the flow of unprecedented customs dues to the bankrupt royal treasury, St Domingue and the slave trade nourished the economy of France before 1788.[3]

This was a balance sheet which had an appalling deficit column. There was, for instance, the simple but alarming fact of the swift arrival of so many Africans. How could any society readily or easily absorb, accommodate and socialize so many in so brief a period? The sheer density of unassimilated Africans scattered across the island created unprecedented problems which were accentuated by the level of plantocratic absenteeism. It was inevitable, given that so large a number of slaves were new arrivals from Africa, that the rates of sickness and death would be extremely high. It was just as inevitable that in so expansive an economy – much of it on the frontiers in a harsh and debilitating physical environment – conditions for the slaves would be extremely punitive. Even by the contemporary standards of black slavery, the story unfolding in St Domingue before 1788 was miserable beyond words.

Despite the vast prosperity yielded by St Domingue it was to be predicted that, among the many complaints directed to the French government on the eve of the Revolution, the abominations of the slave trade and slavery were recurring themes. In 1789 intellectuals denounced slavery, planters defended it (nervously aware of the threats posed by the Africans) and the coloureds wanted their own share of the 'Rights of Man'. As the debates of 1789 swirled back and forth, delegates from the various colonies, and from all the groups living there (except the slaves), intruded the issue of slavery into the broader discussion about rights and representation. In the French islands, the early days of the Revolution created that *frisson* of political awakening we associate with Europe. While the *petits blancs* and the coloureds saw the exciting potential for themselves, the more circumspect in both France and the islands soon appreciated the disastrous possibilities. What would happen if the slaves began to discuss the rights of man?

Revolt in St Domingue was first raised by local coloureds, led by men fired by revolutionary egalitarianism but rebuffed in their demand for political rights by the colonial old order. Torture, execution and the public display of the dead; as in slave colonies everywhere, the first French rebels met a ghastly but predictable fate. From 1789 to 1791 conflicts in St Domingue flared and spluttered, but in August 1791 the slaves stepped in, transforming the simmering trouble into a revolt of volcanic proportions. Black rebels seized hundreds of plantations, butchering their local enemies, setting fire to properties and retreating to the hills. Perhaps 20,000 slaves set up camp in the north, and rebellion seeped slowly into the south and west. As the Revolution in France lurched to the left and then into violent confusion (and, eventually, into European war), the political fabric in St Domingue simply collapsed. French troops died in their thousands, the slaves quit their plantations, and political authority faced the added nightmare of invasion by the Spanish and the English. Early in 1793, a former slave, now military commander, Toussaint L'Ouverture, emerged, appealing to all slaves: 'Brothers and Friends. I am Toussaint L'Ouverture, my name is perhaps known to you. I have undertaken vengeance. I want liberty and equality to reign in San Domingo.' St Domingue became a battlefield, ranged over by forces from France, Spain and England. The British lost some 20,000 men (many to disease). The sugar economy collapsed and from this violent destruction there emerged the black republic of Haiti, forged from the success of black armies, created from and led by former slaves. The worst of plantocratic nightmares had come true.[4]

When independent Haiti was declared in 1804, local sugar production had fallen to one-third of the 1791 level. A decade later, Haiti simply dropped out of the sugar market. Even coffee production was halved.[5] The collapse of the Haitian economy created opportunities for other countries, many of them expanding production of sugar and coffee via slave labour. But the real consequence of Haiti in the outside world was the extra vigilance shown towards black slaves everywhere.

Whites had fled from Haiti, scattering in panic to any safe haven but mainly to Cuba and Jamaica. They were not welcome. Slave societies throughout the Americas lived in terror of the contagion of slave rebellion, and anything from Haiti – slaves, planters, even local gossip – seemed to threaten slave society. But even in wartime it was impossible to staunch the flow of peoples and ideas back and forth between slave societies. Planters and slave-owners everywhere sought to limit the potential damage caused by the news from Haiti by tightening their grip over local slaves.

Slaves also learned the lessons of Haiti. A tyrannical plantocracy and the military might of Spain, France and England had proved inadequate when faced by major slave resistance. Slaves and their owners knew that they inhabited a tinder-dry habitat which could easily be destroyed by sparks from neighbouring islands. It was a sign of the widespread alarm about potential slave rebellion that the British began to raise black regiments. By 1798 ten black West Indian regiments had been raised; 30,000 black regulars and a veritable army of irregular helpers had been rallied to support Britain's uncertain position in the West Indies. Almost one-half of the black soldiers were Africans. Only a small number survived to the end of the French wars (1815) to receive freedom and land in Trinidad, British Honduras and Sierra Leone.[6] The British needed all the military help they could muster in the 1790s, facing slave unrest in Dominica, St Lucia, St Vincent and Grenada. But their greatest and continuing concern was for the biggest, the richest and most troublesome of their slave colonies, Jamaica.

From the early days of British settlement (after 1655), Jamaica had proved a difficult island to master. The land which yielded such bounty in sugar and rum was also ideally suited for rebellious slaves. In the mountains and in the densely forested 'cockpits', where good agricultural land runs into almost impenetrable country, there was room and opportunity for escape. It was here that the famous 'Maroon' communities developed; blacks living in freedom, beyond plantocratic reach, in their own settlements, fiercely independent and resistant to any suggestions of British control. In the east of the island, local Maroons were 'acquainted with the most difficult and almost inaccessible places of the Blue Mountains where their love of Liberty induced them to settle or rather hide themselves'.[7] In the west of the island, runaway slaves formed similar communities. From the first, the British sought to flush them out and to prevent fresh runaways from joining them; descendants of those communities survive to this day in their splendid physical isolation, proud to be Maroons and proud of their past.

Throughout the eighteenth century the Leeward (western) Maroons grew in number, augmented by new runaways, able to resist British efforts to dislodge them. By the 1720s they were thought to be numbered in their thousands. Their attacks on travellers and frontier settlements provoked periodic reprisals by British and Jamaican forces who generally found the climate and topography beyond them. Time and again in guerrilla or open attacks the British failed to crush the Maroons. In 1738 Governor Trelawny wrote:

> Here the greatest difficulty is not to beat, but to see the enemy. The men are forced to march up the currents of rivers over steep mountains and precipices without a track, through such thick woods that they are obliged to cut their way almost every step...In short, nothing can be done in strict conformity to the usual military preparation and according to the regular manner, bushfighting as they call it being a thing peculiar to itself.[8]

Armed solely with rocks and stones, the Maroons could out-manoeuvre and beat a well-armed British group, unnerving them by 'blowing Horns, Conch shells and other instruments, which made a hideous and terrible noise among the mountains'. There was a succession of campaigns, some producing temporary rewards (land regained, Maroons dispersed and property destroyed), but white successes came only via the help of black auxiliaries. A peace treaty was signed with the Maroon leader, Cudjoe, in 1739; an acknowledgement of the stalemate between the British and the Maroons, concealing the Maroons' right to independence on specified land. Cudjoe and his followers subsequently helped to put down local slave revolts and in the main were free to prowl the west of the island in a state of flamboyant independence. Thomas Thistlewood bumped into Cudjoe one day in 1750:

> met Colonel Cudjoe, one of his wives, one of his sons – a Lieutenant and other attendants – he shook me by the hand and begged a dram of us, which we gave him – he had on a feathered hat, sword at his side – gun upon his shoulder and bare foot and bare legged, somewhat a majestic look – he brought to my memory the picture of Robinson Crusoe.

Six months later, Thistlewood met Cudjoe's brother, Accompong: 'about my size, in a ruffled shirt, blue broad cloth coat, scarlet cuffs to his sleeve, gold buttons... white cap and black hat, white linen breeches puffed at the knees, no stockings or shoes on. – Many of his wives, and his son there.'[9]

The British were not deceived by the extravagant displays of the Maroon leaders. These men had fought them to a standstill. However much Maroon power waned as the eighteenth century advanced, planters and colonial authorities could never rest easy, for the Maroons remained an uncontrolled threat lurking behind the plantations. In the 1790s, years of revolutionary turmoil throughout the slave islands, that threat flared up. At the very time when planters and colonial authorities were looking nervously at the disasters unfolding in Haiti, they faced disruption at home from the Maroons.

Between July 1795 and March 1796, 300 Maroons and 200 runaway slaves tied down and generally bamboozled British forces ten times their size. Jamaica seethed with rumours of French (i.e. Jacobin-inspired) plots to subvert British control and unleash black revenge. Like marginal people elsewhere, the Maroons needed no help from outside to feel a sense of grievance. Two generations after Cudjoe's treaty, the Maroons found its limitations stifling, particularly on the land where their increase in numbers had far outstripped the allocated 1,500 acres. There were other complaints, culminating in the heavy-handed and unnecessarily bellicose reactions of the island's Governor Balcarres. The British stumbled into military setbacks, losing men by the dozen with not a single Maroon 'kill' to show for it. At first the conflict promised to draw in the slaves on neighbouring plantations, and it is clear that the Maroons played up the hatred of the whites ('Buckra'), gave sustenance to local plantation slaves and hoped for support in return.

British tactics were soon adapted to the terrain and to the enemy, more successes coming from starving out the Maroon communities than in open conflict. The turning point came in December 1795 with the arrival of one hundred Cuban hunting dogs. Maroons (and slaves) were terrified by the animals, which were drawn to their prey by a strong sense for blood. The animals' fabled savagery went before them, the myth of their bloodlust more potent than the reality. Slowly over the next few months the Maroons edged forward, to parley and surrender. The more troublesome were shipped to the frozen wastes of Nova Scotia; four years later the survivors were moved on to Sierra Leone where they settled to become a local 'élite' which survives to this day. As bizarre as this may seem (shipping blacks from Jamaica to Canada, then to Africa), it was no more bizarre than the initial movement, orchestrated by the British, from Africa to the New World. The British had become adept at switching large groups of people around the globe to suit their colonial, economic or domestic problems: the Irish to Barbados, Africans to the Americas, 'criminals' to Australia, poor London blacks to Sierra Leone. The British looked to the wider world for the solution to their various problems or to enhance their domestic well-being.

Maroon communities were not unique to Jamaica. Most plantation colonies could claim to have Maroons at some stage.[10] They were to be found in St Vincent, Honduras and Dominica, but Jamaica's Maroons were the most numerous and long-lived in the British colonies. Similar communities existed throughout the Americas, especially in South America where geography conspired to offer a safe retreat. Maroons were troublesome to the British, but for all their intractability they never posed the permanent threat represented by the slaves themselves. From the origin to the termination of black slavery, slave-owners (and all who were not slaves) lived in more or less permanent fear of slave resistance and revolt.

The fear of slave revolt was ubiquitous Slave-owners often imagined revolt where there was none. White suppression of an imaginary plot could be as bloody as it was for a real uprising. In the summer of 1712, whites in New York uncovered 'a bloody conspiracy of some of the slaves of this place, to destroy as many of the inhabitants as they would'. The plot – if such it was – led to the execution of twenty-one slaves, six others killed themselves ('laid violent hands upon themselves' was how the Governor of New York described it). The litany of violence was familiar: 'twenty-one were executed, one being a woman with child, her execution by that means suspended, some were burnt others hanged, one broke on the wheele, and one hung in chains in the town'.[11]

Much more serious was the slave rising at Stono in South Carolina in 1739. On Sunday 9 September, 'the day the planters allow them to work for themselves', about twenty Angolans killed some local whites and seized arms before heading south towards Georgia and the ultimate sanctuary of the Spanish settlement of St Augustine in Florida. The slaves discriminated as they moved south, sparing a white thought to be 'a good man and kind to his slaves' but killing the less fortunate and destroying property. With drums beating, the rebels called out for liberty, recruiting more slaves to their ranks until they numbered between sixty and one hundred. Relaxing in a field, lubricated with stolen rum, the rebels 'set to dancing, singing and beating drums, to draw more Negroes to them, thinking they were now victorious over the whole Province, having marched ten miles and burnt all before them without opposition'. If so, they were sadly deluded. The militia had been raised, confronting and attacking them. The rebels were routed, some shot on the spot, others interrogated then shot: 'And this is to be said to the honour of the Carolina Planters, that notwithstanding the provocation they had received from so many murders, they did not torture one Negro, but only put them to an easy death.' Altogether, some forty slaves and twenty whites were killed.[12]

Slave-owners did not need black violence to convince them of their slaves' wicked intentions, for they had the most vivid of imaginations. The unfolding of events around Samba's 'conspiracy' in French Louisiana in 1763 provides a perfect illustration. The angry words of a slave woman, beaten by a French soldier, sowed the seeds of the suspicion that the slaves were plotting. The self-appointed investigator into the rumour 'went that very evening to the camp of the Negroes, and from hut to hut, till I saw a light'. There he discovered Samba 'plotting' with others. Eight slaves were arrested and questioned: 'The day after they were put to the torture of burning matches; which, tho' several times repeated, could not bring them to make any confession.' Knowing that Samba had been a rebel in Africa and on the slave ship, the inquisitors were not about to believe that no plot existed. Confronted by his 'record', 'Samba directly owned all the circumstances of the conspiracy; and the rest, being confronted with him, confessed also: After which, the eight Negroes were condemned to be broke on the wheel, and the woman to be hanged fore their eyes; which was accordingly done, and prevented the conspiracy from taking effect.'[13]

Who now, looking back on these bald statements, could feel much confidence in the justice of these events? Was this really a conspiracy or merely a self-fulfilling prophecy? Slaves were assumed to be potential plotters, ever alert to the prospects of freedom, settling old scores and far too willing to bad-mouth their owners. Disgruntled or resentful mutterings might readily seem to some people to be embryonic plotting. In the paranoid world of the slave-owning class, slave plots were all around; it was simply a matter of discovering them.

In the very week that American Independence was declared, July 1776, on the Louisiana frontier a local slave-owner, William Dunbar, uncovered a plot among his slaves (all recently imported from Jamaica). 'Of what avail is kindness and good usage when rewarded by such ingratitude', was the puzzled response of this Scottish settler. One slave, thoroughly (but not violently) questioned, resolutely denied all accusations of plotting. But while being transported down the river, trussed up in the bottom of a canoe, he flung himself overboard and drowned. 'This was sufficient evidence of his guilt.' Perhaps, on the other hand, he was simply terrified and keen to avoid the agonizing fate of slave plotters. This suicide sealed the fate of his acquaintances, three of whom were hanged while 'lesser punishments were inflicted on the less guilty'.[14]

There *were* slave plots – more perhaps than we shall ever discover – some of which came dangerously close to succeeding. In 1800 Gabriel Prosser's machinations among slaves in Virginia posed a serious threat. It was rumoured that thousands of slaves were to be involved in a major uprising near Richmond, Virginia. Large numbers undoubtedly knew of the plot, but the number of plotters may have been far fewer than the 1,000 alleged. In the end, about twenty were executed, and others were transported. Interestingly, many of the leaders were privileged slaves; men with a degree of freedom to move about, a freedom which allowed them to discuss, organize and plot. Slave revolts and subversion were not simply an outcome of brute physical oppression or maltreatment. This was to be a pattern repeated in the West Indies; slaves in more privileged positions were as likely to be rebellious as their more oppressed and downtrodden brothers. In Gabriel Prosser's rebellion, the evidence was clear enough and confirmed by one captured slave after another: 'My brother Gabriel was the person who influenced me to join him and others in order that (as he said) we might conquer the white people and possess ourselves of their property.' Prosser had told his associates that they would achieve this 'by falling on them [the whites] in the dead of night, at which time they would be unguarded and unsuspicious'. The aim was to seize Richmond, 'the Capital, the Magazine, the Penitentiary, the Governor's house and his person. The inhabitants were to be massacred, save those who begged for quarter and agreed to serve as soldiers with them'.[15]

Gabriel Prosser's revolt was clearly no figment of the plantocratic imagination; it was real enough, widely known among large numbers of slaves and had a core of dedicated plotters with a clear plan. Thwarted by a change in the weather (rain swept away a vital bridge) and a slave informer, it was a revolt which could have posed a serious threat to slave-holders in the Richmond area. In the event, it was suppressed before it began.

In North America this was a recurring theme. plots, real or imaginary, were discovered and resistance crushed before the slaves had time to flex their muscles. Yet how else could they organize? Too open a show invariably prompted a violent backlash; too secret or sluggish a plot might never persuade others to join. And hanging over all of them was the knowledge of what would surely happen to slaves who were caught. Africans had long and bitter memories of the violence of white people; local-born slaves were brought up on the appalling tales of their African parents and fed a diet of violent folklore and popular memory, in addition to the regular administration of blows and lashes which punctuated their lives. Plot, rebel – and fail – was a guaranteed route to the most painful of slave deaths.

The sure knowledge of what failure would bring may have deterred many slaves from joining their bolder or more desperate friends and associates. But fear and timidity were never enough to prevent slave rebellions. In 1822 Charleston, South Carolina, experienced a rebellion which was more threatening even than Prosser's. Denmark Vesey, the leader, was an impressive man; a former slave who had bought his freedom with the proceeds of lottery winnings, but who continued to speak out against the suffering of other slaves. Literate, articulate and devout, Vesey turned his talents towards goading slaves in Charleston to improve their lot. He spoke of the city of Jericho: 'And they utterly destroyed all that was in the city, both man and woman, young and old, and ox, and ass with the edge of the sword.' Aided by an Angolan slave, Gullah Jack, a man of 'grotesque physique and frightening countenance' who claimed the power of an African preacher, these two men proved a charismatic pair, the one drawing upon Africa, the other Christianity, to feed local slaves with a heady brew of discontent. Slaves of course needed no outside words to make them discontented but, at the right time and place, a clear and persuasive voice could make the difference between passive discontent and more open resistance. Slaves in South Carolina were ripe for such a voice. Thousands had been imported into the region, many from Africa and the West Indies. In the years immediately after the Haitian revolt, the ideas of black resistance and of black political successes seeped through the porous world of the American slave societies. Vesey and Gullah Jack added their own distinctive voices to these more general feelings.

Charleston was a prosperous city, effective capital of the South and a bustling entrepôt for a population that was almost evenly balanced between black and white. For the whites, it was an elegant and sophisticated city. But, like the other cities in slave societies, it was a volatile place. Obsessed by the need for black freedom, Vesey moved, in 1821, from urging local blacks to be proud, to plotting with a small handful of sympathizers to overthrow white society. Plotting, as we have seen, was a dangerous business. Of the six initial conspirators, one, Monday Gell, finally revealed the plot.

Denmark Vesey, inspired by the example of Haiti, found ample support for his arguments in the Bible:

> Behold the day of the Lord cometh, and thy spoil shall be divided in the midst of thee. For I will gather all nations against Jerusalem to battle; and the city shall be taken and the houses rifled, and women ravished.

Slowly, Vesey and his men collected arms, money and a growing band of followers. Vesey moved around the region, surreptitiously building contacts and support up to eighty miles outside Charleston.

The chosen day was 14 July 1822, a Sunday when slaves could gather in large numbers without being suspected. But before the event, word leaked out via a loyal slave. The rebels decided to bring forward their revolt by a month, but the local whites and the authorities were prepared. Blacks were arrested everywhere; 131 were paraded before a special tribunal. Eventually thirty-five were hanged including Vesey and Gullah Jack, their bodies allowed to dangle in public for several days. Forty-three others were exiled. The court's judgment on Denmark Vesey was ironically truer than it could possibly have imagined, and in a way never intended: 'Your life has become, therefore, a just and necessary sacrifice, at the shrine of indignant justice.' Vesey, steeped as he was in the language and imagery of the Old Testament, needed no lessons in biblical exegesis from the court. He got them none the less: 'Your "lamp of life" is nearly extinguished; your race is run, and you must shortly pass "from time to eternity". Let me then conjure you to devote the remnant of your existence in solemn preparation for the awful doom that awaits you.'

Gullah Jack received a similar dose of legal piety, urged to follow the example of a religion which had never been his in the first place: 'Your days are literally numbered. You will shortly be consigned to the cold and silent grave; and all the Powers of Darkness cannot rescue you from your approaching Fate!' The court offered a minister to accept Jack's full confession: 'Neglect not the opportunity, for there is no device nor art in the grave, to which you must shortly be consigned.'[16]

It was inevitable that the slaves of South Carolina would feel the sharpened hostility of the slave-owning class once the rebellion had been crushed. Black freedoms were curtailed, local black churches restricted and stern efforts taken to limit access to the printed word. It was clear in Charleston in 1822 as it was in Jamaica in 1831 that black Christianity, black literacy and a charismatic leader could become a potent social mix. And it was equally clear that black revolt, incipient or real, would be paid for by black lives.

Vesey's conspiracy might easily have engulfed Charleston. In the event it consumed only its conspirators. More threatening still was Nat Turner's revolt in Southampton County, Virginia, in 1831. Turner, born in 1800 of an African mother, had displayed precociousness; he was knowledgeable, religious and an avid reader; a loner, who revelled in the awe he inspired among other slaves. Convinced he was destined for greatness, his mature years saw him run away but then return. Gradually he turned against the institution of slavery, convincing himself that it was the Lord's will to heap destruction on the planters: 'I was ordained for some great purpose in the hands of the Almighty.' Slaves around him believed that Turner was divinely inspired. Then, in February 1831, at an eclipse of the sun, Nat Turner was convinced that he should 'arise and prepare myself and slay my enemies with their own weapons'. He immediately told his plan to a small group of followers. On 20 August 1831 they barbecued a pig in the woods. Fortified by the food – and a bottle of brandy – the group of seven slaves attacked Turner's master, Joseph Travis (a decent enough man against whom Nat Turner had no real complaint). The family of five was axed to death and the property's weapons removed. They moved on to neighbouring properties, killing whichever white folks (men, women and children) they encountered. Axes, swords, metal railings, shots – all were employed to dispatch the wretched white families. As the killing continued, more slaves joined the rebels. With a family dead, they quickly moved on to the next target. 'Having murdered Mrs Waller and her ten children, we started for Mr William Williams', then 'killed him and two little boys that were there.' Mrs Williams escaped, was caught and brought back 'and after showing her the mangled body of her lifeless husband, she was told to get down and lay by his side, where she was shot dead'.

The recitation of butchery continued, all described by Nat Turner in his condemned-cell confessions. By now, Turner's band had grown to sixty, but local white forces were rallying, as they inevitably would, to confront the rebel slaves. In the first formal clash between white hunters and black rebels, the slave band began to disintegrate. Turner tried to maintain a simple sense of military discipline, but it soon evaporated before the fire power and mobility of the rallying whites. Four days after the initial attack Nat Turner found himself alone in the woods hiding from the hunting parties. It was a wretched few weeks, living in caves and under tree trunks, scavenging for food and water, waiting for the inevitable capture. His fate was equally predictable.

Nat Turner clearly had the power to inspire people. Whether a 'fanatic' or a natural leader, his was a voice which others found hard to ignore. Though physically short, he was strong and energetic, bright and exciting. Even in his prison cell, 'clothed in rags and covered with chains', he had the power to alarm men. When he gave his confession to Dr Thomas Gray on 30 October, Turner raised 'his manacled hands to heaven; with a spirit soaring above the attributes of man, I looked on him and my blood curdled in my veins'.[17]

Nat Turner was hanged on 11 November 1831 and his body handed over to doctors who melted it down to grease. Fifty-five slaves were executed (some sixty whites had been killed) and perhaps 200 others were murdered by white mobs, panicked by the news of the rebellion. Virginia promptly followed South Carolina in curtailing black freedoms in the State. Black rebellion, white repression, then a worsening of conditions for the slaves; each followed predictably. This miserable unfolding of events was but a local, specific reprise of a very old plantocratic refrain to the tune of black rebellion. It would be heard many more times before the days of slavery were ended.

Only a month after Nat Turner was executed, slaves in Jamaica erupted in the latest of that island's apparently endless slave revolts. In scale, violence and repression it made Nat Turner's rebellion look feeble by comparison. Led by men not unlike Turner, it was a revolt which earned its reputation as a small war. By the time it had been suppressed, some 344 slaves had been executed, hundreds more summarily executed in the field. Hundreds of troops and more informal bands of armed planters, all had been stretched to the limit, first to contain black violence, then to suppress it as fiercely as they could. The damage was immense: 226 properties had been damaged; the total cost estimated at more than £1 million, 'by the slaves wilfully setting fire to buildings, by grass and canefields destroyed, robbery and plunder of every description, damage done to the present succeeding crops, the loss of the labour of Slaves, besides those killed'. Damage to slave property was also enormous for, in addition to the blood-letting, the whites laid waste to slaves' homes, crops and property. Slaves were starved back into submission.[18] Thus, both Jamaica and Virginia, two key regions in the English-speaking slave societies, experienced slave revolts at more or less the same time. Yet they were hundreds of miles apart and more socially distinct than we might expect. Their differences were never clearer than when their respective slaves rebelled: Turner's rebellion was perhaps the most serious in North America, but it would have registered only a flicker on the Richter scale of West Indian slave rebellions.

West Indian slaves seem, at first sight at least, to have been much more rebellious than North American slaves. The reason for this lies in the early days of slavery in the Caribbean. All the imported Africans were reluctant conscripts, forced to work against their will, for people they did not know, at routines and labouring systems which were utterly alien. Keeping them in their place was a major priority, as it had been on the slave ships. Nor did this problem get easier with the passage of time. British West Indian planters continued to demand fresh Africans right up to the moment the British Parliament abolished the slave trade in 1807. In many important respects slave rebellions were *African* revolts; led by Africans, planned and orchestrated by Africans and displaying tell-tale signs of African inspiration.[19] All this took place in the context of crucial geographical constraints. Although we talk readily about the West Indies, this generic term disguises a host of very different colonies. There are, for instance, 700 islands in the Bahamas chain alone. Jamaica, by far the biggest of the British islands, had a slave population equal to almost all the other islands combined. At the other extreme were St Kitts (65 square miles), Nevis (36), Montserrat (39), Anguilla (35) and Barbuda (62). Even the 'bigger' islands were compact and easily managed: Barbados (about the size of the Isle of Wight) is only 166 square miles; Antigua is 108. Some of the islands are flat; no point in the Cayman Islands, the Bahamas, Anguilla or Barbuda is higher than 200 feet.[20] Compare that to Jamaica's Blue Mountain peak, dominating the island's southern coastline at 7,400 feet. A number of the islands are in effect volcanic peaks clad in luxuriant and impenetrable jungle – Jamaica, Dominica, St Lucia, St Vincent. There are, then, enormous physical differences between the islands. In Barbados, where slave settlement was swift, the density of slave population was greater than anywhere else. But it was a small island, fully developed agriculturally from an early stage. Where could rebellious slaves escape to in such a place? In Jamaica, on the other hand, despite the vast slave population, there was free land in abundance; mountainous, rugged and wild.

The geography of each colony was especially important for the growth of Maroon societies. It is, to put it simply, difficult to see how such a society could have developed in Barbados. Slaves could rebel anywhere, however, though their chances of success were determined to a marked degree by local geography. If there was nowhere to hide, would this deter slaves in the first place? Is it mere accident that Jamaica, the biggest island with most untamed wilderness, saw the most frequent, most savage and persistent of slave revolts?

As ever more boatloads of Africans descended on the islands, the racial imbalance (thought appropriate for the growing and manufacture of sugar) created a sense of social unease. In Barbados by 1650 blacks outnumbered whites by 37,000 to 17,000. Though the slaves were divided by language and kinship, were denied access to weapons and generally kept in physical awe by the whites, many thought their numerical preponderance worrying. They were, said Richard Ligon in 1657, 'a bloody people when they think they have power or advantages'. Planters tried not to buy bellicose Africans, but they were in the hands of their suppliers and were forced to buy Africans they feared. Plots, rumours, slave rebellion, all began to unfold with predictable regularity. In the first major Barbadian slave plot in 1675, the whites moved swiftly. Martial law and swift hearings led to seventeen slaves being found guilty; six were burned alive, eleven beheaded, their bodies dragged through the streets. Later twenty-five more slaves were executed, five killed themselves in jail and seventy were severely flogged and/or deported. The planters had laid down an early marker in this gruesome colonial game of tit-for-tat.

There followed rumours of plots in 1683 and 1686 and a major concerted slave plot of 1692 which embraced privileged as well as field slaves. Its leaders were sentenced to starve to death on the gibbet, to be beheaded and their bodies quartered and burned. Plans had been carefully laid, to raise horses from the planters, weapons from the local arsenal and to rally slaves throughout the island. The plot came to nothing and Barbados, despite other rumours, was not to experience a major slave revolt until the early nineteenth century.[21]

Antigua was troubled in its early years by slave runaways, but as the island became more developed the slaves had fewer places to hide. There were the usual violent outbursts of small bands of slaves attacking local whites. Local planters (and their political arm in the Assembly) tried to remain vigilant and prepared against slave unrest. Plots were punished in the by-now traditional plantocratic fashion. But all this, as elsewhere in the West Indies, was never enough.

In 1735–36 a major plot for a slave uprising was unearthed. It was led by Tackey, an African-born slave described as 'artful, and ambitious, very proud, and of few words'. With an inner core of conspirators, the plan was to provoke an island-wide revolt by blowing up the Governor and leading planters at a major local social event in October 1736. Again, the plot was revealed. Torture and public executions (burning alive) yielded more conspirators; slaves' blood flowed freely as the courts and executioners took their predictable toll. By May 1737 eighty-six slaves had been executed; some on the gibbets, seventy-seven burned to death. Their crime had been, in some way, to be involved in a plot to kill all local whites; a plot hatched during secret obeah rites in which

cocks were slaughtered, their blood sprinkled and drunk, and elaborate ceremonies that looked remarkably 'African'. The outcome was the introduction of
severe slave laws and a tightening of plantocratic control.[22]

Both in Barbados and Antigua the nature of the slave population had begun
to change. The rise of a new, local-born (Creole) slave force working alongside
their African forbears was not enough to deflect the persistent violent threats
and rebellious plots which issued from the slave quarters. It was like the
spluttering of a dormant volcano; dormant but not inert. The slave troubles
in the smaller islands were but a prelude to the truly volcanic eruptions which
took place in the major British slave island, Jamaica.

In 1760 Jamaica was convulsed by Tacky's Revolt, coming close to plantocratic disaster. Jamaican planters had successfully thwarted local revolts in
1742 and 1745 but had, by 1760, become slack in their control. Yet Africans
continued to pour in – a large number of them Coromantees – and plantations
flourished in isolated settlements where whites were at risk from the prepon-
derant and silently threatening African masses. The revolt burst forth at Easter
1760 at Port Maria on the north coast. Between fifty and a hundred Africans
seized weapons and swung south into the island, killing whites and gathering
supporters as they progressed, and repelling counter-attacks. Led by Tacky
and perhaps inspired by the well-known freedom of the island's Maroon
communities, the rebels' aim (in the words of a contemporary enemy) was
'the entire extirpation of the white inhabitants; the enslaving of all such
Negroes as might refuse to join them; and the partition of the islands into
small principalities in the African mode; to be distributed among their leaders
and head men'.

As local planters rallied to defend themselves, the island's government, forty
miles hard-riding to the south in Spanishtown, hastily mustered militia and
regulars, force-marching them north across the island. These troops, initially,
fared badly in the fighting with the slaves. Their major success was the capture
of a rebel leader, a Coromantee obeah man, who had convinced his followers
that he could not be harmed, because 'he caught all the bullets fired at him in
his hand, and hurled them back with destruction to his foes'. This man's
execution had more than the usual trappings of a public display of lethal
deterrence: 'This old imposter was caught whilst he was tricked up with all his
feathers, teeth, and other implements of magic, and in this attire suffered
military execution by hanging.' Such a humiliating display of the slave's
mortality, bedecked in the costume of his slave office, was thought to dispirit
his followers. But the rebellion rumbled on.[23]

Slave plots, rebellions and acts of resistance began to erupt across Jamaica
from the far eastern tip, to the fertile valleys in the centre of the island, to
Westmoreland in the west. Kingston and Spanishtown were awash with
rumour and fear, but suffered no real revolt. Elsewhere, when slaves scored
a local success (usually against an inadequate militia) yet more slaves joined

their ranks. In Westmoreland the rebel band swelled to 'upwards of a thousand, including their women, who were necessary for carrying their baggage, and dressing their victual'.[24] Those who survived the tumult never forgot it. The strange behaviour of local slaves preceding the violence (the shaved heads and unexplained visits to other slaves), the swirl of rumour among neighbouring whites, were followed by a convulsion of noise and violence: slave horns (rallying rebels), the terrified arrival of half-naked men in the middle of the night raising friends and neighbours, the pitch-black, full-speed gallop to the nearest place of safety. In this jittery state, where no white man could rely on a single black, isolated slave-owners were none the less obliged to put weapons in the hands of their most trusted slaves. Pleas for help from the local militia were a mixed blessing; the militia was sometimes routed. At night the sound of burning estate houses and the smoky crackle and snapping of burning cane fields added a surreal quality to the atmosphere of terror.[25]

Gradually, however, the planters and their allies began to reassert their power. The navy directed sailors to crucial, sensitive areas and the Maroons proved effective allies of the whites. It was Maroons who cornered and killed the rebel leader, Tacky, described by Edward Long, a planter and notorious negrophobe, as 'a young man of good stature, and well made; his countenance handsome, but rather of an effeminate than manly cast'. There now began a well-tried practice of making examples of the captives. Leaders were burned or starved to death in public. Others preferred to kill themselves in the woods. When, in October 1761, the rebellion was officially suppressed, it had cost the lives of about sixty whites (and as many free coloureds and free blacks), perhaps 400 rebels killed and another 100 executed (500 more were transported).[26]

In common with other British islands and in North America later, the aftermath of Tacky's rebellion saw a sharp tightening of the Jamaican slave system. New laws restricted the movements and freedom of slaves, of free coloureds and even of whites – the latter in the hope that whites could be persuaded to be more vigilant and attentive to their slaves. New military establishments were constructed and serious thought given to the military problems of controlling slave colonies. Further violence inevitably erupted in the 1760s, but slave society in Jamaica was itself changing. As a growing proportion of the island's slaves were local-born, it seemed that the African-based threats of the past century would simply disappear. As the Africans became a minority (after 1780), planters could hope that the new, local-born slave force would find itself more at home in the system; socialized into a world which, unlike their African forbears, was their sole experience. Never having known freedom, Creole slaves would perhaps prove more manageable, less rebellious than the Africans. It was to be among the plantocracy's greatest shocks that the most savage and destructive of all slave revolts were not African revolts.

The Peace of Paris in 1763 granted Britain fresh Caribbean colonies: Grenada, Dominica, St Vincent and Tobago. Each experienced its own slave troubles. The islands seemed ideal possessions in which to repeat the lucrative sugar experiments already tried in Barbados and Jamaica. White settlers and fresh Africans were transplanted (excepting in Tobago) on to existing social systems. The end result was predictably violent.

In Grenada, slave revolt led to plantocratic repression, the import of troops and a sullen, unprofitable stalemate. More troublesome still were the Caribs, the fierce native peoples of Dominica, where jungle and mountains added to the planters' problems. Runaway slaves created new Maroon communities in virtually impenetrable enclaves. There were rebel bands all over this small island, and their attacks, especially in the 1780s, prompted stern but generally unavailing military intervention. Minor victories proved deceptive, for the rebels simply laid low, erupting again in the years between 1791 and 1813, years of major revolutionary turmoil in the entire region.

By then, the slaves were calling a different tune, one influenced by the revolutionary ideals which had washed westward from Britain and France throughout the Caribbean. Rebellious slaves in Dominica in 1791 were not inspired by ill-treatment, but by 'what they term their "rights" which in their interpretation, extend to an exemption from labour during four days out of seven'. Planters blamed British abolitionists. The situation was worsened by the arrival of French refugees and their slaves, adding an extra element to the unstable social mix. Further threats of a slave uprising in 1795 were overcome with the help of local Maroons, but trouble among the slaves continued to bubble. Even the men posted to contain them, the black Eighth West India Regiment, rebelled in 1802. Suppressed (with 100 deaths), the regiment was broken up and scattered to other islands, its leaders having been predominantly African.[27]

From 1809 to 1814 the Dominican planters were in more or less permanent pursuit of local Maroon bands. By 1812 there were an estimated 800 in nine different settlements, the problem finally resolved to white satisfaction by a new aggressive governor, Ainslie, in a year-long campaign, spearheaded by black rangers, in which the rebellious slaves were isolated and destroyed. By August 1814 the authorities claimed to have killed or captured 578 rebel slaves. But the violence caused offence in Britain. The days when planters and their allies could destroy rebels with impunity had gone. It is true that the whites could continue to kill and torture rebels, but they needed friends in high places in Britain to secure their broader economic interests. The slave trade had already been banned and plantocratic violence against resistant slaves was slowly but surely alienating more and more Britons. As they confirmed their power over the slaves, West Indian planters, by the early nineteenth century, were disqualifying themselves from British help and sympathy.

Each new possession in the Caribbean, secured by ascendant British naval power, posed problems of its own. All were inherited (except a virtually deserted Tobago) with existing indigenous, slave or white settler communities; often with a mixture of all three. On St Vincent, there were 1,300 French, 3,400 slaves and 5,000 black Caribs and some 'Yellow Caribs'. British settlements began to nibble away at the existing land settlements and the consequent resistance grew from harassment to open attacks on white settlers. If unable to secure a peace treaty, the British resolved to deport the Caribs. Open fighting in 1772 saw a repetition of the story in other islands; of successful guerrilla warfare wearing down apparently superior white forces. Within months, the British had lost seventy-two men killed and 110 dead from disease. The end result was a peace treaty of May 1773; the Caribs were granted land and freedom in return for loyalty, promising to hand over runaway slaves. It was an arrangement which was destroyed by the revolutionary turmoil of the 1790s.[28]

Caribs in St Vincent were urged, by neighbouring French revolutionaries, to act: 'Behold your chains forced and imposed by the hands of the tyrannical English! Blush, and break those ensigns of disgrace, spurn them with becoming indignation, rise in a moment.' In the following Carib rebellion, whites were slaughtered, their properties razed; the slaves (20,000 of them) wavered. Should they join the rebels or remain passive? For a year the outcome remained uncertain as butchery by both sides swept across the island, the British saved at a number of crucial junctures by the arrival of fresh forces from other islands. The fighting was fierce; at times the British were hemmed into their forts and military bases. Not until October 1796 did the British prevail. Five thousand black Caribs surrendered and were promptly shipped off to Honduras, the founders of today's 40,000 people living in the region. On their native island only a small, sad rump survives; reminder of a community which once tied down major British forces and came within a whisker of overthrowing the local plantocracy.[29]

Tobago's development came late, but as the British poured in Africans, slaves rapidly outnumbered the whites. Slave revolts became endemic. Runaways, plots, murders of planters, all took place in the years of British settlement after 1763. In the worst revolt in 1774 the captured slaves were punished in traditional plantocratic style; their arms chopped off with axes and slaves burned alive. The leader died on the gibbet.[30] A plot, at Christmas 1801, threatened a more serious rebellion but was hastily and bloodily thwarted. What puzzled the worried planters, however, was that the slave leaders were local-born. As long as the rebels were Africans, slave-owners had no trouble explaining revolt in terms of African barbarism. But who could explain the rebellious instinct in local-born slaves? Was it a nasty streak inherited from African parents, or could it be that slaves, by definition, would always seek to escape from or destroy their house of bondage?

The convulsions of the 1790s in the Caribbean were more easily explained, at least to plantocratic satisfaction. Outside influences, like 'African barbarism', seemed sufficient explanation for the series of slave upheavals which rocked the various British islands. The French repossessed a number of the British islands for a short time in their was against the British. Their presence, the threat of their arrival but, most potently, the contagion of revolutionary ideals wafting from island to island created, as we have seen, tremendous instability in the slave colonies. Though the British experienced nothing on the scale of the Haitian rebellion, they were deeply troubled by rebellious slaves throughout the West Indies. In Grenada where French influence survived strongly from its early French control, a major slave explosion took place in 1795. The British retreated to their coastal military positions, ceding the centre of the island to the rebels who, for two years (under their leader Fédon) controlled the island, attacking the British posts and creating what was in effect a state within a state.

As the British tightened their grip throughout the Caribbean, greatly helped by their naval victories, they poured troops into Grenada (and elsewhere) to restore peace. By May 1796 there were 5,000 troops in Grenada but it took another eighteen months before local officials could claim that tranquillity had returned.[31] In St Lucia, wrested from the French in the revolutionary and Napoleonic wars, the invading British were pinned down for years, despite arriving in 1796 with more than 5,000 troops. Their enemies were French planters and, above all, rebellious slaves, fired by the revolutionary attachment to freedom. The terrain, the enemy, but above all disease (especially yellow fever), sapped the morale of the British forces, and peace, of a kind, did not descend on the island till the truce of late 1797. Wherever the British took an island from the French, its economic value had to be set against the cost of local resistance. Trinidad proved no different. Taken from the Spanish in 1797, the island suffered a serious threat of revolt in 1805. But set against the bloody convulsions elsewhere, this was a minor affair.

The ending of the wars which racked Europe and the West Indies from 1793 to 1815 ought to have heralded a period of tranquillity for the slave islands. Instead it was merely the prelude to the most threatening of all West Indian slave revolts. Two factors above all others help to explain what was happening: the slave trade had been abolished in 1807. In time, the proportion of Africans in the West Indian slave population would decline. Second, the fate of the slaves had become a topic of increasing political (and humanitarian) interest in Britain itself. There was a powerful, and expanding, lobby of organized churches, humanitarians and politicians which focused its scrutiny on the slave islands. As never before, the fate of the slaves was a matter of interest in Britain itself.[32]

As we have seen, the Creole slave populations of the British islands were the target of an aggressive campaign by Christian churches, notably a group of nonconformists, to complete the process of de-Africanization by bringing the slaves within the Christian fold. Planters were right to fear black Christianity, for in the British West Indies it led the slaves to resistance and ultimately to the campaign for black freedom. Events in the West Indies strengthened the growing belief in abolitionist circles in Britain that slavery ought to be abolished. And the more the British *talked* about black freedom, the more the news of that debate filtered back to the slave quarters, sometimes utterly garbled, to encourage black aspirations. What we can see, increasingly, in the slave islands was a growing body of Christian slaves, no longer joined by 'raw' Africans, encouraged to think of freedom by news from Britain, but faced by a resistant plantocracy. Moreover, the planters had to work their slaves harder, often at tasks the slaves did not like, because the supply of Africans had dried up. As long as the slave trade continued, Africans could be thrown into the fields – the shock troops of the plantocratic system – to do the hard work. After 1808 many slaves who might (because of their 'Creole' status) expect better, more favoured work, found themselves reassigned to manual work. Disgruntlement spread rapidly.

On Easter Sunday, 14 April 1816, slaves in Barbados – a relatively quiet slave colony, not recently troubled by slave revolts – rebelled, led by Bussa, an African-born slave-driver. Martial law was declared and about 400 slaves were rounded up and executed; others were flogged and transported to Sierra Leone. The white response was, as always, violent in the extreme, borne along by a puzzled horror that such well-treated and previously quiet slaves could descend to rebellion. The rebel leaders were élite slaves who enjoyed the best of treatment and conditions among the slaves.

Trouble had been brewing for some years past and since 1800 there had been plenty of evidence that Barbadian slaves were unhappy with their lot. In the revolt, one white militia man was killed and property to the value of £175,000 destroyed. More fundamentally, it severely shook the slave-owners' self-confidence,[33] and it served to weaken still further support for slavery in Britain. Black rebellion, excessive white suppression; these seemed to be the continuing themes in the annals of British slavery. 'The Insurrection had been quelled', said the Speaker of the local Assembly in 1816, 'but the spirit is not subdued'.[34] It was to get worse, not better.

Slaves in Demerara (acquired in 1803) were among the most exploited in the region. It was a wild, frontier colony, its plantations clinging to the narrow coastal strip, its slaves worked more exploitatively and brutally than most and outnumbering whites by twenty to one. Behind them lay the vast interiors of South America and the obvious (and oft-used) escape for runaways. Long before the British took over, slave revolt and plantocratic reprisal were familiar stories, and it was these which John Gabriel Stedman captured in his narrative of 1796.[35] The new missionaries had enormous success; congregations were counted in their hundreds, converts in their thousands. At the centre of black Christianity was the Rev. John Smith of the London Missionary Society and when, in 1823, rebellion broke out, Smith was held responsible.

At its height, the revolt drew in almost all the 12,000 slaves in the colony, many convinced they had already been freed by their English king but thwarted by local planters. One British soldier reported: 'At first there was more demand for freedom and three days than anything else, but latterly when I came out again they were all for freedom, and all of them dwelt considerably on going to Church on Sunday.' So complete was the resistance that only the most draconian of punishments would suffice. Mass shootings in the field were followed by ritual public executions and the display of dismembered bodies. All told, 250 slaves died; three whites had died in the initial rebellion. The last white man to die was the Rev. John Smith, sentenced to hang for complicity but dead of consumption on 6 February 1824.[36]

Smith's death caused an outrage in Britain. Yet it is scarcely cynical to reflect that one white man's life caused infinitely more anger in Britain than the brutal slaying of 250 slaves. Perhaps it served its purpose, however. Instantly dubbed the 'Demerara Martyr', Smith's death represented the wickedness that lay at the heart of slavery. While the British fumed at the iniquity of the Rev. Smith's death (and it was indeed iniquitous), the body of one slave leader, Quamina, a black deacon, was slowly turning in the sultry tropical breeze: 'A colony of wasps had actually built a nest in the cavity of the stomach, and were flying in and out of the jaws which hung frightfully open.'[37] Such grotesqueries showed no sign of ending.

These stories, in all their putrid details, were fed back into the expanding body of British abolition sentiment by missionaries and their friends. What offended so many Britons was that the dead, whipped or humbled slaves were their co-religionists. British nonconformists found slavery offensive; even more offensive was the maltreatment of black nonconformists. After 1823 the missionaries took great care not to inflame the slaves and to discourage unrealistic expectations of early emancipation, but news from Britain was reported in the local press and growing numbers of slaves could read. White planters openly railed at the treachery afoot in Britain (their words naturally picked up by the slaves). Slaves could not be deceived about the progress of the debate about their freedom. And all this was in addition to the dramatic changes wrought by the advance of the chapels.

Nowhere had the chapels made greater progress than in Jamaica. There, at Christmas 1831, revolt broke out in the west of the island, engulfing more than 20,000 slaves but focused on areas where the Baptists had their followers and their chapels. It was here that Sam Sharpe played an important role.

Sam Sharpe could move the hearts of men. Those who heard him speak never forgot his voice of his message. A bright man, described by one who met him as 'the most intelligent and remarkable slave I have ever met with', Sharpe had a striking physical presence. He was 'of the middle size', with a sinewy frame 'handsomely moulded, and his skin as perfect jet as can be imagined'. Sharpe had a broad, high forehead, 'while his nose and lips exhibited the usual characteristics of the Negro race'. Above all else, people remembered his voice. When addressing his fellow-prisoners in a Jamaican jail in 1832, Sharpe amazed people by 'the power and freedom with which he spoke, and at the effect which was produced upon his auditory'. Then, and in countless meetings in the years before, Sharpe was the master of his audience, always able to have 'the feelings and passions of his hearers completely at his command'. It was said of Sam Sharpe that when he spoke about slavery he drove his listeners almost to a state of madness.[38]

Sam Sharpe knew as much about slavery as anyone. Technically he belonged to Croydon estate but he was remarkably mobile, regarding Montego Bay on Jamaica's north coast as his real home. He travelled far and wide throughout the interior parish of St James, his freedom of movement granted so that he could preach. Sharpe was head deacon at the Rev. Thomas Burchell's Baptist Chapel in Montego Bay and it was as a preacher that he learned how to win the hearts and minds of his congregations in Jamaica's second city and in the rugged rural hinterland. There, among the first and second generation of slaves to be won over to nonconformist Christianity, Sharpe (and other black preachers) wooed his slave congregations. Black preachers seized upon the Bible, but especially the Old Testament, as grist to their mill; the language, imagery and tales of oppression, of freedom, of promised lands, of salvation to come were ideally suited to a suggestive reinterpretation. No one made the point better than Sam Sharpe himself: 'he thought, and he learnt from his Bible, that the whites had no more right to hold black people in slavery, than black people had to make white people slaves.'[39]

The fourteen white deaths, and material damage amounting to more than £1 million, were avenged by more than 500 killings and executions. The 'Baptist War' shook Jamaican slavery just when its fate was being sealed by an assertive abolitionist campaign in Britain. Yet the revolt was not led or followed by Africans but by Creoles, many of them skilled and privileged, their leaders devout and sometimes literate. To kill such a man as Sam Sharpe was, to many in Britain, an outrage. Nine years before, the loudest British protests had been against the death of the Rev. John Smith. Opinion had swung dramatically against slavery. The planters, with their bloody apparatus of controlling the slaves, had played their part in pushing it in that direction. Perhaps the most fitting comment on the slaves' predicament had been written by John Smith in one of his last acts, scribbling on a bill (to pay for his trial): '2 Corinthians, iv, 8,9.' Translated, the quotation says: 'We are troubled on every side, yet not distressed, we are perplexed, but not in despair. Persecuted but not forsaken; cast down, but not destroyed.'[40]

Only one week after the death of Sam Sharpe, the British Parliament appointed a committee to consider ways of ending slavery. Slavery was ended, partially, on 1 August 1834; completely four years later.

From first to last, black slavery in British possessions had been marked by black resistance. From the early slave ships to the eve of full emancipation in 1838, black slaves had rebelled against their oppressors. Not all slaves rebelled; perhaps not even a majority rebelled. And why should they? All may have longed for a better world, longed for an end to the cruel violation which was the daily lot for most slaves. But slave-owners, the societies they shaped, and the colonial powers they could call upon for help had, from the first, made abundantly clear the price to be paid for unsuccessful resistance. Even by the standards of an age whose penal system was characterized by blood-letting and public execution, the fate of rebellious slaves was grotesque. Nor did the slave-owners seem to want to improve their habits as time went by. The blood-letting in Jamaica in 1831–32 spoke of a slavocracy addicted to the punitive habits of an age long gone. But so too was slavery.

17

A Leap in the Dark: Runaways

The land between the Blue Ridge Mountains and the huge stretches of Chesapeake Bay is dissected by a series of major rivers – notably the Potomac, Rappahannock, York and James – which create the four peninsulas of land which taper into the Bay. Along the shoreline, a myriad inlets, bays and spits of land give the region (and the opposite eastern shore of the Maryland peninsula) the appearance of a delicate but complex fretwork. Dense woods crowd the water's edge and the only sensible way of travel, until modern times, was by the thousands of miles of waterways, along the rivers and creeks which provided the most important routes between the major colonial settlements. It was (and in many places remains) a land of dense forests and swamps, lazily sliced by the waterways which travel from the mountains to the Chesapeake Bay.

On the eve of the American Revolution, some quarter of a million people lived in this area; perhaps 85 per cent of them white, 15 per cent black. Most of the Indians had gone, the first of the native peoples to wither, migrate or simply die out in what was to become a continuing conflict with white settlement. The whites on the other hand thrived, the early disastrous days of settlement (when death haunted their precarious toehold at the water's edge) having given way to population growth. The blacks also increased, more slowly than the whites, mixed at first by fresh imports of Africans via the Atlantic slave trade.

As the population grew, it began to spill westwards, away from the relatively crowded parishes of the early settlements where the land had been painfully wrenched from nature by burning and cutting before the rich soil was used for tobacco cultivation, moving on to the foothill regions of the Blue Ridge (Piedmont).

It was a luxuriant land, 'equal to any land in the known world' in the words of one of its early apologists (1705), yielding wealth beyond imagination to those with luck and application who managed to survive.[1] One such lucky Virginian was Colonel Landon Carter whose home was the mansion Sabine Hall, perched on the north shore of the Rappahannock in Richmond County. One of the unlucky Virginians was Simon, an ox-carter and one of Carter's slaves. On Wednesday 12 March 1766, towards the end of a cold wet spring, Simon 'complained of the belly ache and went away'. He was out and about for two weeks 'doing mischief', before returning on 24 March. Guards posted to catch Simon had shot him in the leg; later, another slave (Mangorike Will) surprised him in his hide-out, attracted there by the smoke from Simon's fire. A group of slaves tried to make Simon's return appear voluntary, but the suspicious Carter did not believe them, deciding, 'I still punish him accordingly'.

The day after Simon's return, Carter was surprised by the return of another slave, Bart: 'he has been gone ever since New Year's day'. Bart had fled to avoid a flogging, ordered because he lied to his master about some work (or at least Carter thought he lied): 'He is the most incorrigible villain I believe alive, and has deserved hanging; which I will get done if his mate in roguery can be tempted to turn evidence against him.' Both Bart and Simon broke out of their confinement that same day, 25 March. Colonel Carter's anger increased when he discovered that the men had been kept, on their last escape, by Johnny the gardener. Johnny was promptly sent to jail and his brother-in-law locked up on the estate. Slaves suspected of involvement denied all knowledge with 'great impudence', but Colonel Carter had proof to the contrary. His conclusion was that all slaves, even the favourites, 'all are liars and villains': 'I never rightly saw into the assertion that negroes are honest only from a religious principle.' After all Johnny, now in jail for harbouring the runaway, was 'the most constant churchgoer I have; but he is a drunkard, a thief and a rogue'.[2] Carter simply could not trust his slaves, even those privileged slaves who worked under his own roof. Even when they remained at home, apparently going about their business in an orderly fashion, they were harbouring and feeding a runaway.

No slave-holder, in North America or in the Caribbean, could hope to go through life without seeing slaves run away. However hard they tried, however paternal on the one hand or violent on the other, slave-owners could not staunch the regular flight of their slaves, sometimes permanently, more often for a few days.

If we turn to an utterly different slave colony, at a later period, we will see similar events. Worthy Park was (and is) a major Jamaican sugar estate. By the 1780s it had about 260 acres in sugar cane, producing 260 hogsheads (about 190 tons) of sugar and 100 puncheons of rum. All was the work of some 300 slaves; by 1820 the labour force had grown to 500 and sugar production had almost tripled. Looking at Worthy Park today it is easy to imagine the temptations facing the slaves. Despite new roads and paths, vast tracts of the surrounding hills still appear impenetrable. These beckoned those slaves, toiling below in Lluidas Vale, to run away. Between 1787 and 1835 Worthy Park recorded 1,337 slaves on the property; fifty-one of them ran away, some of them more than once. Three slaves, Jack, Bob and Mingo, were permanently absent from 1812 to 1830, but, like others, they may have died in the unforgiving bush. Worthy Park's runaways were mainly male (by three to one) and predominantly African. Creoles may simply have been more adapted to life as slaves. Africans, on the other hand, had known another life, however wretched it might have been, and many clearly found the adjustment (from Africa, to the Middle Passage, to life as a slave) difficult in the extreme. And what are we to make of the fact that four of Worthy Park's most regular absconders had deliberately degrading names: Villain, Trash, Whore and Strumpet?[3]

In December 1830, David, a nineteen-year-old Worthy Park slave, was sentenced to life in the workhouse. David, born to Big Sue (later renamed as Sukey Lowe), was one of two brothers who caused their owners no end of trouble. David and his brother Hannibal began life in the children's gang, graduating to the Second Gang in 1829. Thieving and running away led David to the workhouse; Hannibal, though an 'Incorrigible Thief and Runaway' by 1830 (still only sixteen), took his brother's fate to heart and did not err again until the end of slavery in August 1838.[4]

Two years after David was sentenced to life in the workhouse, he was joined by another Worthy Park slave, Polydore, born in 1788, one of an African woman's four children. Polydore made the usual progression through the slave gangs, finally joining the Great Gang at the age of twenty-four in 1813. He ran away often, and for as long as he could. Finally, in 1832 he was condemned, at the age of forty-three, to life in the workhouse.[5]

Among Worthy Park's female absconders was Strumpet, described as 'Field, Able, Runaway'. Absent from September to December 1787, she returned to work in the fields, now described as a 'skulker' and 'Runaway, Worthless' (1789). But her escapes came to an end with the birth of a daughter, Nina, in 1793. Her Worthy Park contemporary, Lady, had run away in 1785 and was free through much of 1786 and 1787. Caught in the summer of 1788 giving birth to a daughter, Diana, she was later returned to the Worthy Park fields, 'Able but a Runaway'. Soon after the death of her daughter, Lady took flight again in September 1791, but in the following month she was deposited in the Spanishtown workhouse. Unwilling to buy her out, Worthy Park had her sold off; 'shipped off' was the description used in the plantation ledger, as the book-keeper closed the estate's troubled dealings with yet another incorrigible runaway.[6]

So far, we have looked at only two properties, Colonel Landon Carter's Virginia estate, and Worthy Park, Jamaica. But a similar story can be found wherever we look in the slave colonies, and in England as well.

Sam was a slave attached to a Jamaican pimento plantation owned by Dr James Archer. For six days in November 1828 he was a runaway, but on return was pardoned. A few weeks later in January 1829 he escaped again, for eight days, to be pardoned, once more at the request of Mrs Archer. In the following month he ran away for five days, before being 'brought home by his mother'. In April, he was away for seven days and received thirty-nine lashes on return. Absent again from 20 May to 12 July, he was flogged again (spending twenty-two days in hospital). By August 1829 he had escaped permanently and had become a Maroon.[7]

Thomas Anson, a black, about 5 feet 6 inches tall, worked for Edmund Sill of Dent in Yorkshire. He ran away in 1758, aged twenty. 'Whoever will bring the said man back to Dent, or give information that he may be back again, shall receive a handsome reward.'[8]

In December 1780, a Jamaican slave (named Jamaica), a man of forty-five, 5 feet 3 inches tall, 'pretty stout made' with a wrinkled forehead and brand marks on both cheeks, trained as a bricklayer and a fisherman, ran away. James, another bricklayer, a Congolese slave of fifty-five 'of a very black complexion' and who 'walks very lame', ran away in the company of Sambo, 'his head quite white', who also pretended to be blind.[9]

Where could a lame man and a white-haired black, pretending to be blind, hide? Where could a runaway slave go to in the depths of rural Yorkshire? Or in the middle of London? In fact, the bolt-holes were innumerable: with friends, with relatives, within the protective and relative safety of London's black community, on the fringes of a Jamaican estate, living off the meagre crumbs falling from the table of sympathetic slaves, or even in the bush and mountains, the fastnesses of the woods and river-systems of the Chesapeake or the West Indian islands.

Wherever slavery existed, there we find slave runaways. Some formed themselves into those remarkable Maroon communities which so plagued a host of slave societies. Most runaways, however, were alone, fleeing out of desperation, or merely trying to contact friends and loved ones elsewhere. Moreover, slaves ran away long before they arrived in the Americas. On the long trek to the African coast, waiting in captivity to be sold to Europeans, on the slave ships themselves (at anchor or at sea), slaves regularly sought to escape. In the forbidding forts run by the Royal African Company and on board the slave ships, leg irons, manacles and chains were part of the fittings. In September 1820, a Royal Navy officer remarked on the disused slave baracoons of Bance Island: 'the walls of the slave-yards still prove the whole to have been so contrived as to prevent the chance of escape to the most resolute and infatuated of the miserable victims they inclosed yet with all these precautions, insurrections, as on board the slave ships, were not uncommon.'[10]

Slave-traders simply could not afford to relax their vigilance for a moment. Given the opportunity, slaves ran away from their captors or jumped into the sea. Self-destruction was as much a threat as rebellion on the slave ships. Sentinels guarded the hatches, arms primed and readily avilable on the quarterdeck, sometimes including contemporary hand-grenades. Guns were trained from the quarterdeck on to the deck. Trouble was especially likely at the twice-daily feeding time: 'all that time, what of our men are not employed in distributing their victuals…stand to their arms; and some with lighted matches at the great guns that yawn upon them, laden with partridge [shot].'[11]

When asked in 1721 why they mutinied, slaves replied to William Snelgrave on board the *Henry,* 'that I was a great rogue to buy them in order to carry them away from their own country and that they were resolved to regain their liberty if possible'.[12]

Despite the different languages the slaves spoke they soon learned that a terrible fate awaited them on the Atlantic crossing and in the New World. As slaves waited on the coast, often for months at a time, gossip and rumour from Africans long involved in the slave trade created an awareness of the horrors to come. Many captive slaves gave up hope; some even died 'by the sulks'. Slave-traders knew that they faced serious threats from their slaves and each captain had to choose his own particular way of coping with it. Should he be utterly repressive and take no risks at all, or should he try to allow the slaves a modicum of latitude so that they might not be too depressed and become a financial loss? The toughest line was obvious enough:

> I put them all in leg-irons; and if these be not enough, why then I handcuff them; if the hand-cuffs be too little, I put a collar round their neck, with a chain locked to a ring-bolt on the deck; if one chain won't do, I put two, and if two won't do, I put three; you may trust me for that…these are not cruelties; they are matters of course; there's no carrying on the trade without them.[13]

Opportunities for escape were, naturally enough, much greater once slaves had settled into the Americas (though many ran away as they were being transported or marched to their new place of enslavement).

From the earliest days of settlement, slaves and oppressed indentured servants ran away from their masters and owners. In Barbados, the local council was informed in 1655 of 'several Irish servants and Negroes' who had run away and lived 'out in rebellion in ye thicket and thereabouts'. Throughout the early years of settlement, similar complaints regularly sur-faced, despite the gradual erosion of the natural habitat as ever more of the island was cultivated. In 1655 the Barbados Council ordered that any runaway who set fire to cane fields should 'receive 40 lashes upon his naked back, and [be] branded on the forehead with the letter "R"'.[14]

In the early decades, white servants caused as much trouble as the black slaves; permission to travel, or extra time added to their servitude seemed to make little impact. It was, in one respect, easier to punish runaway slaves; they could be killed and compensated for with impunity. When George Harper recovered a female slave 'who had escaped and hid for one whole year', he received £25 compensation for her execution.[15]

After the rapid conversion of Barbados to sugar cultivation made escape and concealment difficult, what *did* remain possible, and attractive, was escape by sea. The coast was never further than ten miles away, and the many bays, jetties and beaches, often littered with boats of various descriptions, proved too tempting for many slaves. Strenuous efforts were made to prevent servants stowing away or stealing vessels; an Act of 1701 was passed 'to prevent free-men, white servants and slaves running away from the island in shallops, boats and other vessels'.[16] The maritime route to freedom was made even more attractive by Barbados' position at a major crossroads. For the slave trade and for the Royal Navy and related fleets, the island served as landfall, a victual-ling and rest stop on long Atlantic and inter-Caribbean voyages. The wars which raged against other European nations in the Americas (to 1815) made great use of Barbados. Military expeditions and convoys were especially troublesome in luring servants and slaves from their work-place to the dock-side. In wartime, threats of invasion were compounded by the fear that recalcitrant slaves might be willing to pass intelligence on to the nearest enemy. Slaves in wartime often tried to trade in their bondage for service with the enemy, or simply fled to an enemy-held island. In 1695, Josiah Jackson was rewarded for 'taking up at sea a wherry with 11 negroes which in all probability might have arrived at some of the French Islands and give intelligence of the fleet here then ready to sail'.[17] Much more likely, the slaves were taking advantage of the wartime confusion to make good their escape by sea.

Slaves fled from Barbados to St Vincent, which was effectively controlled by Caribs until 1763. A French visitor to the island wrote in 1700: 'Besides the Indians...the island is also populated by negroes, most of whom have escaped from Barbados. Barbados being to windward of St Vincent makes it an easy matter for the slaves to escape from their masters in canoes or rafts to join the savages.' Initially, the Caribs handed back slave runaways to their masters but from the 1680s generally welcomed them; the knowledge that they could find a refuge in St Vincent spurred Barbadian slaves to think of escape by sea. So numerous did the runaway slaves become that friction developed between Caribs and runaways, especially through pressure on the land and because 'the negroes continually steal their women and girls'.[18]

It was much more difficult to find an escape route in Barbados once its land had been effectively developed. There was a high ratio of white people to black (compared, for example, to Jamaica) and detection was accordingly easier. Yet despite such practical problems, slaves continued to run away. Island newspapers regularly advertised for runaway slaves as long as slavery survived. Such adverts have been mined extensively by historians, since the details provided about age, colour, skills, gender and personal characteristics are generally much fuller and more revealing than any other evidence about the slaves. When E. S. Bascom allowed his slave Chloe to go out to sell glassware in 1817, she did not return. Though an African by birth, Chloe spoke and looked like a Barbadian. Time and again, the runaways tried to pass themselves off as free people and it was easier to do this with local fluency and style rather than with African characteristics.

It was the skilled, privileged and 'coloured' slaves who were more likely to run away in the later stages of slavery in Barbados. Very few of the field slaves ran away, and many more men than women escaped. Many headed for town where they might be able to disappear in the relatively large community of free coloureds and slaves, and possibly find work. Those who headed to the country – a favourite destination for the women runaways – sought refuge or kin on other plantations. Some managed to escape from Barbados completely. Jane Frances, who ran away in 1817, 'endeavours to pass as a free woman, and in all probability will wish to quit the Island': 'All masters and owners of vessels are hereby cautioned not to take her off the Country, and other persons from harbouring or employing her.'

John Maycock, a fifteen-year-old butler, took much the same route in 1819, seemingly having 'imposed himself on the master of either the ship Constantine or Tiger, as a free man ... [and] quitted the island'.[19] The fact that captains were regularly warned against accepting runaways suggests that they provided a well-tried escape route for them.

West Indian slaves tended to run away in the summer, especially in July and August. We know that these were the months when food on the plantations was in short supply (Barbadian slaves called these months 'hungry-time' or 'hard-time'). Planters may not even have been too worried about losing slaves in the summer: the sugar crop was harvested, food was short and costly and, with luck, they would get the runaways back in time for the New Year harvest. Most runaways, at least in Barbados, did not intend to stay away from their owners, so the most likely explanation for their escape was the urge to visit loved ones or friends. Those with skills, who might be able to make their independent way in the world, were the ones who stayed away longest.

It is remarkable, in so small and compact a society as Barbados, that slaves *were* able to stay away for lengthy periods. Some cases were really astonishing. When John Beckles was discovered on Pool Plantation in 1805, he was forty-five years old; it was revealed that he 'has been living in the Pool Negro-yard for many years before the storm of 1780'. Sam, a twenty-year-old runaway, had been hidden by his father 'for nearly 16 years when by accident he was discovered to be a slave; and it was fairly proved that he was stolen by his parents when the mother was leased on Haymond's Plantation, and he was a child'. It takes a distinctive interpretation of property rights to think of a child having been 'stolen by his parents' from their joint owner.

Wherever we look, we find remarkable tales of slave runaways. Buffy, an African discovered on Lancaster Plantation, Barbados, in 1806 had mysteriously transported himself from Jamaica six years before, having come 'over as a cook on board a vessel, and…has remained on this island ever since'.[20] How *did* he manage it? How did he secure a post on a ship, sail more than 1,000 miles, and then secrete himself on a local plantation?

Slave-owners were not universally opposed to slaves running away. Provided, that is, they were someone else's slaves. A runaway harboured and employed was, at one level, a free slave for the slave-owner who took him or her in. While most slave-owners denounced runaways, realizing that it was a contagious habit which threatened slave-owners everywhere, some turned a blind eye if it was to their benefit. Advertisements for runaway slaves sometimes hinted that the slave was harboured by a white person who realized the slave was a runaway: 'some evil-disposed white person…' a reward was offered of '£10 to any person who will give information of any free subject who has employed' a runaway. Sometimes even blacks were able to harbour and employ runaway slaves. James, a one-legged fisherman, escaped in 1816, and was thought 'to be employed and harboured by some of the fishermen about Fontabelle, particularly by a man belonging to Isaac Green'.[21]

Runaways were sometimes described as dangerously disruptive, a ploy used to frighten slave-owners into a more vigilant approach. Who, for example, would want to have Appea, a fifty-year-old runaway, mixing with other slaves? In 1815 he had a

> surly countenance, has several scars about his head occasioned by fighting, and a piece of one of his ears, bit out by the same cause; he has eluded every vigilant attempt to take him. He is perhaps one of the most notorious villains the Country ever possessed; and a dangerous person to be at large amongst Plantation Negroes.

What made him attractive to the slaves, on the other hand, was his ability to draw portraits, 'by which means he gets a subsistence, going from one Estate to another'.[22]

Appea was unusual in many ways. Much more commonplace was the runaway heading for a loved one and family. Betty Beck was 'supposed to be harboured in the Plantation of Richard Cobham, Esq called Stepney, where she was born, and many of her family belong'.[23] Family provided a refuge, sometimes a job. But most important of all of course they provided that familiar and affectionate network from which many slaves had been so cruelly removed. Some slaves had family members who were free. Clarissa, a twenty-year-old slave, had a free mother 'living under the green trees in the Roebuck; and her father a black man belonging to James Halligan, Esq, called Mingo – by either of whom it is supposed she may be harboured'.

Too troublesome, too costly, too lazy, some slaves did not warrant the effort of being repossessed. Slaves caught and imprisoned were occasionally simply left there. Others were offered for sale. When Nelly ran away with £104-worth of goods, her owner advertised to 'dispose of her for £100, and her child, and give the goods into the bargain to the purchaser'.[24] Too human, too full of the frailties and strengths, the foibles and uncertainties of mere mortals ever to be pure chattel, slaves could often be more trouble than they were worth. Slave-owners sometimes simply cut their losses and got rid of them. But on a large property there was usually enough difficult and strenuous work available to find a painful niche for the most troublesome of slaves.

Running away gave some slaves the chance to bargain with their owners. The penalties and dangers were, of course, immense, but occasionally running away seems to have helped a slave to get what he wanted. In 1817 when the slave Phill ran away, his owner advertised 'should he voluntarily return, the privilege of choosing an owner will be granted to him'. Hamlet, a runaway in 1810, was promised 'if he will return of his own accord in 8 days from this date, he shall have a paper to look for another'. Here was further proof of the remarkable ability of slaves, the most marginal and oppressed of peoples, to alter the behaviour of people who had, on the surface, complete dominion over their lives.[25]

In colonial North America, slaves escaped from bondage just as in the Caribbean. It was especially noticeable in South Carolina, home to rice cultivation and a slave society which looked more African than any other in the region. In the fifty years between 1732 and 1782 there were an estimated 5,600 advertisements in South Carolina newspapers for runaway slaves (at a time when the local population was about 40,000).[26] But such figures, assiduously collected by careful scrutiny of the newspapers, tell us only part of the story, and it is perfectly clear that there were many other slaves – 'slid away', 'out considerable Time' – who were not sought through the newspapers. For a host of reasons, advertisements for runaway slaves, at least in South Carolina, were but the tip of an iceberg; the mere hint of a more substantial though generally submerged social phenomenon.

The largest group of slave runaways in South Carolina headed for other plantations and the rest headed for the towns. Some made a vain search for their distant African homelands. When five Angolans ran away in 1761 they were 'supposed to have gone on an east course as long as they could, thinking to return to their own country that way'.[27] There were enormous differences among runaways – between skilled and unskilled, English-speakers and non-English-speakers, but particularly between male and female. The overwhelming majority of women slaves ran away to visit, not to secure permanent freedom; an indication of their close attachment to kin and especially to their children.

There were many slaves who tried to live independently, away from the terrors of the slave system. Only a few miles up the Savannah river, a band of upwards of 100 slaves managed to establish their own precarious community by raiding neighbouring planters for goods. In 1786 planters launched militia raids to dislodge them but the resistance was fierce. The military returned, strafed the runaways with grape-shot, destroying or removing as much of their food as they could, burning their huts and confiscating their boats: 'The loss of their provisions it is expected will occasion them to disperse about the country, and it is hoped will be the means of most of them being soon taken up.'[28]

It was clear that most runaways had an especially strong attachment to particular districts or plantations. Some of the cases we know of testify to the remarkable determination and persistence of the slaves in seeking their 'homes' or loved ones. West Indian slaves tried to join vessels going back to their home in the Caribbean. One slave, sold from South Carolina to Jamaica, turned up in Charleston within a year. Another African, a 'Guinea' slave, made three attempts to return to the South Carolina back country where he had contacts. Time and again, slaves who were sold from one district to another tried to get 'home'; despite distance, language and the threat of punishment. Those who managed to elude arrest for any length of time obviously had friends or family to harbour and support them. Moving from place to place, from friend to friend, the runaway often managed to keep one step ahead of his or her hunter.

We tend to think of slaves as destitute people, denied all but life's basics by their oppressive owners. Many undoubtedly were, but there were clearly numbers of slaves who were able to cope with the added burdens of fugitive slaves. Slaves who worked in the kitchens, slaves who had access to markets and those who worked as fishermen could all acquire surplus goods and foodstuffs and share them with runaways. Fugitive slaves might, in some places, even find work in their new retreat. And just as runaways might find succour among kinsfolk, so too did some of them abscond in the company of kin or friends. Something like a third of South Carolina runaways absconded in groups, normally in twos.[29]

Slaves clearly had far-flung networks of relatives throughout a region (itself a result of the haphazard separation of slaves and reallocating or selling them hither and thither). Slave-owners advertising for run-aways often had to describe a slave's broad family network in the hope of alerting someone to the possible presence of a runaway. Three South Carolina runaways bought 'from Mrs Munck, in St John's Parish, in whose neighbourhood they are well known, and have a long train of acquaintance and relations, by whom they are supposed to be harboured and entertained'.[30] The great majority of runaways were young men, not yet with permanent mates and still not tied down to their locality either by family or by the prudence of experience. Sometimes the young men 'stole' women folk from a property. In their turn young women ran away to find a mate. Doll, a fifteen-year-old, was described as having 'stayed or ran away, supposed to have gone a courting'. Phillippa, similarly, ran off to go 'a sweethearting at Jacksonburgh'.[31]

This movement of slaves across the lowlands of South Carolina (the coastal belt where most of the rice was grown) was made possible by the relatively dense population of the region. And as the local population thrived, slaves developed a complexity of family and community ties from one plantation to another. In running away, slaves in the region gave ample and recurring testimony to those ties.

Further north, in North Carolina, a similar pattern was unfolding but with the added distinction created by local topography. The 'Great Dismal Swamp' stretching south from Norfolk, Virginia, into North Carolina, provided an escape route for local slaves 'for twelve, twenty or thirty years and upwards, subsisting... upon corn, hogs, and fowls.' The slaves who lived there 'could not be approached with safety because of their belligerence'.[32] Again, local runaways tended to be young males; and, as before, they were heading for families and friends. African slaves also ran away in large numbers.

On the whole slaves did not run away on the spur of the moment. However angered, insulted or hurt, slaves bided their time, letting their immediate anger subside and storing it up for the appropriate moment to make a dash for freedom. Often slaves hid their true feelings behind a deceptive façade. Slaves smiled at and flattered their owners and drivers; flattering to deceive. Joan had a 'smiling countenance', Jack 'a pleasant countenance', whereas Tom Buck had 'an uncommon flippant tongue, full of compliment'. All three of them ran away.[33]

Runaways in North Carolina tended to escape only with the clothes they wore (in the case of the Africans, this was often merely a rag or cloth). On foot, without a suspicion-arousing burden of food or extra clothing, the slaves set off with little but their optimism and the passion to escape and seek friends elsewhere. Time and again, their attempts ended in jail, flogging, torture or execution. But the example of what happened to failures simply did not deter others from striking out down the same road. Grabbing food wherever it presented itself, runaway slaves had to steal crops from the field, livestock and fowl, and cooked foodstuff close to the living quarters. Such theft often incurred the most severe of penalties, as of course it did for free people at much the same period. Early settlers in Australia included large numbers of people convicted of relatively minor thefts and other crimes against property. Blacks, according to Janet Schaw, 'a lady of quality' writing in the 1770s: 'steal whatever they can come at, and even intercept the cows and milk them. They are indeed the constant plague of their tyrants'.[34] Slaves were executed – and castrated – for a series of crimes against property in North Carolina. But the savagery of the law which, as in the West Indies, left mutilated chunks of an executed slave twisting publicly in the breeze, simply did not work. Slaves continued to run away, to thieve and to prey upon the property of the whites.

Virginia had the largest North American slave population in the colonial era. Again, from the early days, Africans fled at the first opportunity. On 7 July 1727, seven of Robert Carter's new slaves escaped by canoe on the Rappahannock river; they were brought back a week later. Such events were so common that Virginia passed laws (in 1705 and 1722) describing precisely how to deal with runaway Africans. In the early days of mass African importation into the Chesapeake, some runaway communities took root in the region. The Maryland assembly proclaimed, in 1725, that several slaves 'have of late years runaway into the Back-Woods, some of which have there perished, and others... have been entertained and encouraged to live and inhabit with the Shewan Indians'. Any slave who escaped beyond the Monocacy river, the edge of white settlement, was to lose an ear and be branded with the letter 'R' on the chin.[35] A group of fifteen runaways tried to establish a community (with stolen property) near Lexington, Virginia, in 1729, but were quickly suppressed.

Slaves were clever at hiding runaways in their midst (a sure sign of the development of a distinctive sense of slave community; see Chapter 13). Runaways clearly needed help, travelling from one property to another, skirting white folk but expecting (and in general receiving) assistance and comfort from other slaves. There was, as time passed, a veritable chain of family ties and friendships, of acquaintances and relatives which spanned the colony. Routes could be found, often with some difficulty, but clear routes none the less, which would take a runaway from point of departure to destination. Some – a small minority – were trying to escape clear out of the slave region, normally heading north to Philadelphia and New York. But most were 'visiting'; running away to spend a short time with family. When Kate, a thirty-year-old, ran away in 1756 from her master in Georgetown on the Potomac, she went thirty miles to South River, a former home. Since she was 'a great Rambler, and is well known in *Calvert* and *Anne-Arundel* Counties, besides other Parts of the country', her master thought she would 'indulge herself a little in visiting her old Acquaintance'. In fact she spent most of her time with her husband at West River.[36] For slaves to keep in touch with loved ones often involved an epic journey of endurance and ingenuity. In August 1755 one slave, Will, had to travel 100 miles, from Charles to Frederick County, to visit his wife.[37] Like tens of thousands more, the exact numbers for ever unknown, Will was a runaway.

Running away seems to have been easier in the vastness of North and South America. But how many people – slaves or free – could plunge into the wilderness and survive? How many would be prepared to exchange the pains of slavery for the terrors of the bush – the animals, the Indians, the struggle against hostile elements, the need to find food and shelter? The evidence is clear enough; slaves wanted their freedom, or at least wanted to rid themselves of the tyranny which ensnared them. Among American slaves in the South, in the early nineteenth century when cotton had revived the American attachment to black slavery, the desire for freedom was a powerful refrain in slave experience. At prayer, within the family, on reflection in later years, American slaves testified to the ubiquitous urge for freedom. Even the meanest of slaves grasped the idea of freedom; not the abstraction or the political ideal, but that freedom enjoyed by the whites in general. Solomon Northrup, a slave musician, claimed:

> They understand the privileges and exemptions that belong to it – that it would bestow upon them the enjoyment of domestic happiness. They do not fail to observe the difference between their main condition and the meanest white man's, and to realize the injustice of laws which place it within his power not only to appropriate the profits of their industry, but to subject them to unmerited and unprovoked punishment, without remedy, or the right to assist, or to remonstrate.[38]

Despite all the odds, slaves ran away time and again. Some became incorrigible runaways; footloose, resistant to the inevitable punishments and always willing to break out again and head for the hiding places in the wilderness. But slave-owners, especially in the rural communities where most slaves lived, were men who lived and worked on horseback; men who hunted, with guns and dogs, for fun and recreation. Tracking down runaways became another kind of hunt. When the runaways posed serious problems, when they threatened to merge with other rebels or with Maroons, the hunt changed from a leisurely search for a single slave into a military pursuit; men, horses and baying dogs homing in on the terrified slaves. Dogs – above all the much feared, savage blood-hounds – proved the most successful of slave catchers. To run away was, as Frederick Douglass confessed on the eve of his own escape, 'a leap in the dark'.

Trusty slaves were sometimes used to round up runaways, but even trusted slaves might run away. When Thomas Thistlewood in western Jamaica sent hunters out in search of runaways, they too stayed away. When they returned, they received 100 to 150 lashes, a brand on their face or the loss of an ear.[39] Yet Thistlewood *always* had slaves absent from his property, most away for a single day, but something like a fifth of runaways stayed absent for ten days or more. In 1815, Primus, a slave-driver on Mount Wilson plantation in Barbados, was given leave for ten days to find a runaway, Prince. Three months later, Primus himself had failed to return. Another slave, who was sent to look for Primus near his wife's home, was unsuccessful (and was murdered on the way home).[40]

Irksome as he or she was, the individual absconder was a minor and tolerable irritant. Much more threatening were the slaves who drifted into Maroon communities, living with other runaways or Indians, forming a dangerously independent and resistant core of free people on the fringes of slave society. These Maroon communities not only threatened the plantations, marauding on their lands, foods and livestock, but provided a beacon for further runaways to head for. When such Maroon communities could not be crushed, it was important to come to agreement with them for the return of future runaways. Unless that escape route could be blocked, frontier slave-owners were threatened by a permanent haemorrhage of their slaves. The Chief Justice of St Vincent, reminding all slaves that to abscond for more than six months was punishable by transportation, denounced Maroons, 'in a country like this covered with woods and abounding in fastnesses'. Slaves 'remaining so long in a fugitive state must necessarily imbibe wild and ferocious habits and consequently endanger the peace of society [and] constantly prey upon the provisions and stock of the plantation and of more domestic and orderly slaves'.[41]

Wherever the environment afforded a hiding place, slaves would run away and try to scratch an independent living for themselves. But it was as cruel and harsh a world, in its own way, as the slave plantation. How many slaves could survive in so hostile a world when most ran away without tools or foodstuffs or extra clothing? To survive in the bush required physical strength, survival skills, mental toughness and a great deal of good luck. Few slaves managed to have all these qualities, though their chances might improve in the company of other slaves. Time and again, runaways came back to their owner, to face punishment (or even a pardon); brow beaten, dishevelled and defeated by the bush in a way they had not been defeated by slavery. Nature could be as harsh a task-master as the most severe of slave-drivers. Despite the sight of defeated slaves returning to the slave plantation, freedom beckoned as long as slavery existed, however intimidating the forests, the mountains or rivers and their wild or human inhabitants.

In the late 1820s John James Audubon was exploring a Louisiana swamp, hunting and painting the local birds. As he waded across a small bayou, his dog became very excited. A voice rang out, and 'a tall firmly-built Negro' emerged from the bushy underwood, carrying a rusty and obviously unworkable gun. The two men travelled together to the runaway's hiding place, a camp where his wife and children worked and played, and where the visitor, alert to the obvious dangers, was bemused by the friendship and hospitality he received. The slaves had run away when their owner had resolved to sell them all separately. They kept in contact with old friends on nearby plantations for food and goods. It was a sentimental tale, glossed with a tarnish of romanticism and stripped of the squalor and terror of life on the run.[42] Few slaves were able to reconstitute their families in the wild. Those who did live in encampments were hunted down like (and by) animals, their homes and crops destroyed and, once captured, subject to the arbitrary violence from which they had fled in the first place.

Of all the figures we possess about slaves escaping (and none of the data is more than imprecise), there is nothing to match the convulsions brought about by the American Revolution. Both sides in that war, the British and their allies, and the American patriots, sought the support and friendship of the slaves. Wherever the two sides fought, local slaves escaped from slavery, either to join in the fighting or to flee. An estimated 5,000 slaves from the eastern shore of Virginia and Maryland and the lower reaches of the River James ran away towards the British. In South Carolina, some 13,000 slaves ran away to join the British, or to melt away into the back country, or even drift south, far away from the military confusion. Many of the slaves who fled 'died from hunger or disease or met death on the Revolution's battlefields'. Many survived. When the defeated British quit their former colonies in 1783 they took with them more than 3,000 ex-slaves, depositing them in Nova Scotia (whence many were 'repatriated' to Sierra Leone). To head off such slave escapes, planters hastily removed their slaves to safer districts whenever fighting threatened.[43]

Wherever black slavery existed, the planters and their political allies ensured that local laws made specific and severe provisions against slaves running away. Throughout the West Indies it was universally accepted that: 'No slave is to be suffered (except on Sunday) to go out of his Master's Plantation, or travel from one town to another, unless he has a ticket from his master, expressing the time of his setting out, where he is going, and the time limited for his return.' For those who broke these rules, 'The Regulations respecting the apprehending of *Runaway Slaves* are very numerous'. Running away was initially punishable by death, though laws passed in the later phase of slavery provided less severe punishments.[44] But to the end of slavery, local laws sought to tie slaves to their owners' properties. The Alabama slave code of 1852 authorized patrols to question slaves at large, and even to enter 'by force, if necessary, all negro cabins or quarters, kitchens and out houses, and to apprehend all slaves who may there be found, not belonging to the plantation or household, without a pass from their owner or overseer; or strolling from place to place without authority'. Any such unauthorized slaves could receive up to thirty-nine lashes on the spot. Slaves whose owners were unknown would be put in jail.[45]

To make slave mobility even more difficult, to render all slaves liable to scrutiny by those 'in authority' (which meant in effect any passing white man), slaves were expected to carry a pass. Once slavery had established itself as *the* major labour system in the region, the assumption grew that slaves travelling or 'wandering' did so illegally. The laws of the Caribbean islands were clear about this. But there were *hundreds* of slaves whose livelihood depended on travel; the draymen, wain and cattle drivers, the men in transport, the boat slaves of the great river systems of North and South America, the sailors working the coastal craft along the coasts and between the islands of the Caribbean. Bands of slaves were permanently distant from their home property and their owner. Carrying and transporting goods and imported items, taking produce to the nearest loading point on the riverside or the quayside or the sea; fetching and carrying, travelling hither and yon at their owners' request, such slaves had to prove their right to be travelling. Locally, travelling and transport slaves were familiar faces. But new slaves, or slaves travelling to an unfamiliar district, might not be so easily recognized. Unless they could prove their authority to travel they faced serious problems.

Mobility among the slaves was not however the major problem facing slave-owners. The most persistent problem was the flight of those supposed to be tied to the property. Viewed from the slave-owners' position, this meant that, on bigger properties, they would be permanently without some of their slaves. Runaways were costly to the owners; they had to be sought (often by other slaves), then when the absence was prolonged they were advertised for in local newspapers. When caught, the runaways had to be retrieved, often at the cost of a fee payable to the captor or local jail holding the runaway. On Barbados, the Codrington estates paid fees for runaways five or six times a year in the eighteenth century (from a slave population of some 250). Thomas Thistlewood, compulsively recording the details of his daily life among the slaves in western Jamaica, noted some twenty runaways every year; only about one-fifth were absent for more than ten days. What this meant, in practice, was that one slave in a hundred under Thistlewood's supervision would be absent.[46] On New Forest plantation in Manchester, Jamaica, at least twenty-four of the 196 slaves were absent in the years 1817–32; some were away for only four days, others for three years. Approximately 12 per cent of the slaves ran away at some time in that period (though a few ran away more than once). For slave-owners, this meant a considerable loss of slave labour (particularly troublesome when, after 1807, slaves could no longer be bought from Africa). New Forest plantation lost in effect 143 man-months of slave labour.[47]

Slave-owners were often at their wits' end with runaways. Neither punishment nor forgiveness seemed to staunch the flow. Forgiveness and pardons were common, but since they were unpredictable and personal no slave could feel safe that he or she would receive them. More likely were the blows, the lashes or, in extreme cases, transportation and the workhouse. From 1829 to 1834, 124 Jamaican slaves were transported from the island to Cuba or the prison hulks in England. From there, some of them were shipped on to Australia. It was one of the most bizarre twists to the long and sorry story of British slavery that bands of runaway slaves were transported 5,000 miles to England, then another 12,000 to Australia *after* the abolition of the slave trade.[48] Twenty-four of these slaves were Africans, who had already been shipped from Africa to the Americas. They must have been the most travelled of all their contemporaries. But how ironic that the ending of the slave trade – so disliked for its cruelties and abominations – was, for this small but rebellious group, supplemented by the longest sea voyage in the world.

In the last years of slavery in the British West Indies, recaptured runaways were punished by committal to the workhouse and the treadmill. In towns which had grown in size by the early nineteenth century there was the traditional paraphernalia of legal punishments; the jails' cages, stocks and treadmills. Although, technically, white miscreants could be consigned to the workhouse, it was generally thought inappropriate that white and black should share the same punishment. Slaves from the workhouse were used in chain-gangs on arduous public works and offered a miserable, humiliating example of the fruits of resistance.

More contentious than the workhouse were the treadmills, first introduced in Trinidad in 1823 and rapidly adopted throughout the Caribbean. Designed to instil brutal discipline, work began on them at 7 A.M. and continued until 4 P.M., in bursts of ten minutes with thirty-minute breaks; slaves were sentenced to its exhausting, repetitive routine as an alternative to corporal punishment. For some slave-owners this was not a practical alternative, living, as many did, miles from the nearest town and its punitive systems. In the three years to 1832, 255 Jamaican slaves were committed to the workhouse, a substantial number of whom were runaways, though they rubbed shoulders with slaves convicted of a list of criminal offences, from murder to theft.[49]

In that last generation of British slavery, between the ending of the slave trade (1807) and full freedom (1838), fewer slaves ran away. But, as we have already seen, the rebellious instinct among the slaves remained as sharp and unpredictable as ever. Even at its reduced level, the level of runaways remained a permanent plantocratic headache. How best to keep their slaves on the property remained a permanent difficulty facing most planters. Nothing they did could eradicate the slaves' urge to run away. In truth, the task was beyond them for no planter could eradicate the most fundamental of human passions which slaves, like other people, nurtured through the hardest and bleakest of times. From first to last, the slaves of the British colonies risked all for that leap in the dark; for a moment or two of freedom or loving compan-ionship. Not even the most barbarous of slave-owners discovered how to prevent slaves from displaying their basic humanity.

PART VI

Consequences

18

Ending it All: The Crusade against Slavery

Here is one of the major conundrums which has taxed historians in recent years: why did the British turn against their slave empire at the very point at which it seems to have been yielding such largesse to Britain? Indeed, if the slave islands were so valuable to Britain's burgeoning economy, why did the British even contemplate destroying slavery and the slave trade?

The slave trade was vital to the British West Indies. As we have seen, without regular supplies of fresh Africans the plantations' human stock would decline. Planters were thus addicted to the slave trade:

> To continue the cultivation of the West-India islands as they now stand, and to keep up their present extent of produce, will be impossible without an importation – without an importation those slaves thereon will gradually diminish, the crops decline, and the population, as the produce, will necessarily be, in the course of no inconsiderable years, extinct and at an end.[1]

When abolition of the slave trade became a possibility, West Indian planters petitioned Parliament, making similar points direct to their political masters: 'the existing proportion of female Negroes, which is inferior to that of the males, and the present manners of the Negroes, are each unfavourable to population...the only means of supplying the vacancy...depends upon new importations from Africa.'[2]

The slave-traders, too, were naturally equally keen to continue the trade. Had they wanted to leave the slave trade – with its enormous dangers, uncertainties and risks – they could simply have directed their energies and enterprise elsewhere. Though the planters felt trapped, made dependent on the slave trade by forces they were unable to control, the shippers and slave-traders could have redirected their efforts whenever they felt like it. They chose not to because it remained profitable. Throughout Britain there were substantial commercial interests, concentrated in urban centres and the ports, which were bitterly opposed to the idea of ending the slave trade. The arguments they marshalled had enormous strength and persuasion. These men were adamant – and could cite details from ledgers to prove it – that the slave trade brought profit to themselves, well-being to the immediate communities and power and prosperity to the nation.

As early as 1695, the Bristol sugar merchant, John Carey, wrote that the slave trade was 'the best Traffick the Kingdom hath ... as it doth occasionally give so vast an Imployment to our People both by Sea and Land'. The trade to Africa and the West Indies was 'the most profitable of any we drive'.[3] From the beginnings of the abolition campaign in the eighteenth century until the Abolition Act was passed in 1807, the commercial and political élite of Bristol predicted doom and depression for that city following the ending of the slave trade.

By the time abolition had gathered momentum in the late 1780s, Bristol's earlier lead in the slave trade had passed to Liverpool (better placed for shipping goods from Lancashire and Yorkshire). Here again, the commercial and political élite of the city fought the abolitionists. In 1788 a leading Liverpool slave-trader, John Tarleton, spent three and a half hours trying to persuade the Prime Minister, William Pitt, that abolition of the slave trade would bring 'total ruin'. The evidence marshalled by the Liverpool slave-traders was among the most detailed, accurate and reliable of all the evidence used in the debates about abolition inside and outside Parliament from 1787 to 1807. The city's MPs, its leading merchants and local politicians were as one, for the best part of twenty years, in believing that the slave trade was vital to the economic interests of that city and of the nation at large. Liverpool was a dangerous town for abolitionists. Sailors and the rougher side of local society were keen to threaten violence and mayhem whenever abolitionists appeared.

The nation's major port was, of course, London. There too, the West Indian merchants and the slave-traders took great exception to the idea of abolishing the slave trade. In league with their colleagues from Bristol and Liverpool they launched a vigorous defence of the trade in Africans. Although more of the slave trade sailed from Bristol and Liverpool, the London slave lobby became the main defence of the slave trade. In 1789, the London MP (and former Lord Mayor of London) Nathaniel Newnham opposed abolition because it would, if carried, fill the city with men suffering as much as the poor Africans. Another London MP, presenting a petition against abolition, thought that ending the slave trade was 'repugnant to every principle of humanity, of justice, of common sense, and of reason'.[4]

Throughout the history of the slave trade, large numbers of smaller ports also dispatched vessels to Africa and the Americas. They went from Glasgow,

Lancaster, Preston, Plymouth (from where the first English slave-trading venture had sailed under John Hawkins in 1562); from Whitehaven, Dartmouth, Cowes, Portsmouth, Poole, Southampton, Greenock and Chester. In all those towns, the shippers and the merchants who backed their ventures were unhappy at the prospects of ending the slave trade. The MP for Plymouth, Sir Charles Pole, told the Commons in 1807 that he opposed abolition because it was 'ruinous to the colonies and commerce of the country'.[5]

Here again is the conundrum. The planters of the West Indies wanted and needed the slave trade. The merchants and slave-traders of maritime Britain thought it vital. Both groups, having joined forces to defend their collective interest, assumed that the nation in general needed it. Why, then, should the British not only consider abolition but, within a relatively brief period, enact and then enforce it? Is it possible that the British could have forced through an Act of Parliament, the Abolition of the Slave Trade Act, which defied economic sense and flew in the face of self-interest? Or could it be that these various vested interests were wrong? Could it be that, despite the huffing and puffing of those involved, the British did *not* make money from the slave trade? Or is it possible that there were other considerations, non-economic factors, which came to overrule the economics of the slave empire?

Some historians continue to claim that once the British had lost the North American colonies in 1776 (whose trade to and from the West Indies was integral to the fortunes of the slave empire), the West Indies lost much of their value to the British. There is, however, a mass of evidence to the contrary; long after 1776 British trade to and from the slave islands grew in volume and value. The plantations were operating profitably as late as the 1820s.

Some historians find it hard to accept, as a matter of faith, that the British could have done anything so dramatic as ending the slave trade without furthering their own economic interests. Here is a good example, they say, of that traditional English vice: hypocrisy. Here is self-interest masquerading as morality; self-seeking passing itself off as altruism. It would be hard to ignore the degree of moral posturing by the British about abolition – especially after 1807 when they insisted that the world should follow their lead. Mathematical speculation now enters the debate: what would have been the benefits and/or disadvantages had Britain *continued* to be a slave-trading nation? That, after all, is what most of those involved wanted. A convincing case has been advanced that Britian would have been better off as a slave-trader than it was as an abolitionist power.[6] Was this a case of economic suicide – 'econocide', to use the term coined by one of the historians involved?[7]

The campaign which culminated in black freedom in the 1830s began in 1787 when a small group of Quakers launched a public campaign against the British slave trade. Few of the men who gathered in that small abolitionist circle could have imagined that the whole slave system would be brought down within a lifetime. All they wanted was an end to the trade in Africans across the Atlantic. Even that seemed a monumental task. When they heard the squeals of outrage from the slave ports and saw the opposition in Parliament, they must have doubted their chances. They were to be assisted by the social changes around them and the effectiveness of their own campaign tactics.

The campaign against slavery took place in years when more and more British people found their lives shaped by conditions in the towns. It was there that the nonconformist chapels took root and Baptist and Methodist congregations found a new social and political voice. Much of the nonconformists' attention was directed towards the slaves – the very people who were becoming their co-religionists in droves. But there was more to it than that. In a world which, after 1789, began to talk about and value the idea of liberty, slavery seemed offensive. It also seemed unnatural. At a time when British manufacturers, workers and economic theorists were promoting the virtues of free labour and the right of men to hire or rent labour without restraint, the concept of owning a worker seemed to make no sense. Slavery survived as a monument to everything that the new men of the industrial revolution, wedded to free labour and free trade, disliked. To managers and capitalists it was economic protection; to working people it was bondage of the most abject kind which even they had avoided. Slavery was one of the few, possibly the sole, issue on which master and man in the new industrial towns could unite. Of course this was also possible because it was easy to feel outraged about an institution which thrived 5,000 miles away. For all that, no one could deny the anger which began in Britain about the slave empire.

The campaign against slavery really began in the English law courts. The decision in the Somerset case of 1772 – that a slave could not be removed from England against his or her wishes – though limited, signalled the end of slavery in England. Perhaps as important, it aroused enormous interest and political controversy. Tactics had a lot to do with it. In the attack on the slave trade between 1787 and 1807, and then on slavery between 1823 and 1838, the nation was bombarded by tracts and pamphlets at a time when literacy was growing apace; petitions – most originating in churches and chapels – were signed by millions of people. There was, quite simply, no political campaign to compare to that of abolition. Abolitionists also perfected the modern tactics of lobbying Parliament and pressurizing MPs. They held public meetings and mounted brilliant press campaigns. They joined with, and gave strength to, a parliamentary abolitionist lobby led by William Wilberforce. Narrowly out-voted on a number of occasions, their campaign was made more difficult by the confusion and doubt sown by the impact of the French Revolution and the turmoil in Haiti. At the same time it became obvious that the West Indians, who for much of the eighteenth century had operated a highly effective political and economic lobby in London, were a spent political force. When success came in 1807, it was henceforth illegal for British ships to trade in slaves.[8]

Abolition of the slave trade did not end slavery in the colonies. When the last slaves had been dropped in the British West Indian islands, they joined some 600,000 slaves already there. The British waited to see whether abolition would bring about the intended improvements in the slaves' conditions. To that end, a scheme for registering the slaves was established; it would provide demographic data for assessing whether the slave population thrived or declined. In the event, people learned more about the slaves from missionaries who told them of the reality of life in the slave quarters.

It soon became clear from all accounts that the lives of slaves had not markedly improved. Nor had the ending of the slave trade seen slavery wither away. It remained as brutal and vile a system as ever. Even before formal emancipation, growing numbers of slaves were freed. Some were able, through their independent economic activities, to buy their freedom. Others, often the less useful slaves, were freed by masters keen to discard slaves whose cost outweighed any benefits they brought to their owners. Thus, from 1823 onwards a new abolitionist campaign was launched, first to improve the lot of the slaves and then finally to free them. Astute campaigning in Britain, and within Parliament, began to win over an unprecedented body of opinion in favour of black freedom. Two factors above all else aided the drift towards emancipation. First of all there was a growing demand for reform in general, black freedom was only one of a host of reforming measures on the political agenda, at the head of which was the reform of Parliament. Secondly, the slaves began to play their own role, especially through the various slave revolts, notably in Jamaica in 1831–32.

By the 1820s the British 'Establishment' – which included planters who had bought homes and land in London and rural Britain – was under attack from those on the outside. To end slavery would be to strike a below for reform; it would be a step towards a more just society. It would assuage the Christian conscience, would exonerate the sense of national virtue, please the supporters of new economic theories and confirm the justice of popular demand. An end to slavery would unite more Britons than any other issue. It was a victory for morality, for religion and good economic sense. Who but the most unreconstructed planter could argue with that?

The Parliament which resolved to end slavery between 1834 and 1838 was the reformed Parliament. The Parliamentary Reform Act of 1832 had seen the end of Old Corruption. The Act did not usher in a democratic system, nor did it incorporate the working men who had campaigned so hard for reform; but it fatally wounded the old political order, and intruded new interests into Parliament. The voice of urban and industrial Britain could now be heard inside as well as outside Parliament. The new towns and cities were, in effect, given a parliamentary voice. And for some time past much of that voice had been given over to denouncing slavery. As far as the British could see, when the slave trade ended in 1807 there was no appreciable decline in West Indian fortunes. It seemed, at first, that the West Indian lobby's rearguard defence of the slave trade, with all its horror stories of impending economic and social collapse, was mere froth. Ending the flow of slaves from Africa to the West Indies still left hundreds of thousands of slaves in place; their labours would continue (under improved conditions, the abolitionists hoped) to send the fruits of their labours to Britain.

It was at this point that the slaves took a hand. In the years when the British awaited the results of abolition, slave unrest caught the eye. Many Britons had expected the end of the slave trade to see an improvement in slave fortunes. It was hoped that slave-owners would henceforth treat their slaves better. Improved food and clothing, better working and housing conditions, attention to family life and child-care, all these would, it was claimed, flow from an end to the slave trade. Instead, the islands were buffeted by disastrous revolts and ghastly repression. It seemed to more and more people that here was a system which was beyond repair or redemption; here were men – the planters – impervious to persuasion and unaware of human decency. To cap it all, they persecuted white missionaries and harassed black Christians. It was as if the tables had been turned. Who now were the savages; who now the pagan, brutal people? In the years of emergent black Christianity, some of the most unchristian behaviour was to be found not in the slave quarters but in the Great House.

When the first reformed Parliament was elected in 1832, the government of Lord Grey was in favour of black freedom and there were sizeable (and growing) blocks in both Houses to support it. Thereafter, the battle was about what kind of emancipation would take place. In the end, and in return for compensation to the planters of £20 million, slaves were to be free on 1 August 1834. In fact it was only partial freedom. All children under six were freed. Others, however, became 'Apprentices' and had to work for their former owners for upwards of forty hours a week, for nothing, for a period of six years. Some islands (Antigua and Bermuda) decided to free their slaves immediately.

In the next few years, many doubts were expressed about the nature and usefulness of the Apprenticeship system (whose main rationale was to guarantee planters a continuing supply of labour). But on the night of 31 July 1834 the slaves showed no such doubts as they celebrated their new freedom. It was only fitting that the focus of their celebrations should be the churches. Thousands of slaves descended on the nearest churches and chapels which were decked in flowers and palm fronds and 'crowded to excess'. One was 'literally crammed, yea, almost to suffocation'. Services were held as midnight approached. Everyone rejoiced; unpleasant incidents were few and the general tone was peaceful and thankful – despite the 'gloomy expectations' of the slave-owning class. Even in Jamaica, which had been racked only two years before by the Baptist War, the celebrations passed off peacefully. When slaves raised their voices in thanksgiving, they praised their new Christian deity:

'Since dou has don dis great ting, O dat we may love dee and dy gospel more – may we be diligent in our proper calling, fervent in spirit, serving the Lord.'

Apprenticeship – closely scrutinized by missionaries and by the magistrates charged with supervising it – was soon shown to be brutal, exploitative and troublesome. When it too was finally ended, full freedom came to the slaves at midnight on 31 July 1838. Slaves once again turned to their chapels to celebrate. They held large parades, headed by appropriate banners ('Freedom come', 'Slavery is no more', 'Thy chains are broken, Africa is free!'); churches were decked in flowers and flags; bands played; speeches were made. Midnight ushered in complete freedom. At a mock funeral, the coffin of slavery was laid to rest in the grave while the congregation sang this verse:

> Now, Slavery, we lay thy vile form in the dust,
> And buried for ever there let it remain:
> And rotted, and covered with infamy's rust,
> Be every man-whip, and fetter and chain.[9]

In keeping with radical traditions, trees of liberty were planted. On special days of worship crowded churches again echoed to the names of men thought responsible for black freedom: leading abolitionists, Wilberforce, Clarkson, Buxton – now joined by the name of the eighteen-year-old Queen Victoria. One slave in the Jamaican capital of Spanishtown, Robert Peart ('but in my own country I was called Mahomed Cover'), wrote down his thanks 'to Almighty God and next the English nation, whose laws have relieved us from the bondage in which we have been held. God bless and grant long life to our Queen Victoria.'[10] It was, of course, the English nation's laws which had consigned them to slavery in the first place.

Three-quarters of a million free blacks greeted freedom with prayer and pleasure on that night in 1838. Their lives as free people were to be more arduous and uncertain than many had hoped. But for all the worries about what the future held, there is no sign that they wanted the old regime to continue. What they wanted, what they demanded and struggled for and had apparently secured, was unqualified freedom.

* * *

With British colonial slavery at an end, anti-slavery became a crusade for the rest of the century. Enforced by the power of the Royal Navy, global abolition became a major principle of British foreign policy. Between 1820 and 1870 the Royal Navy seized almost 1,600 ships and freed 150,000 slaves destined for the Atlantic crossing. The Atlantic slave trade was not effectively sealed off until 1867, by which time the British had spent something in the nature of £40 million on suppressing it.[11] Seized with the altruism of their own abolition, they set out, like zealous missionaries, to convert the world. The slave trade was evil and the British were therefore obliged to stamp out evil wherever it flourished. There were, of course, other, less noble, reasons. In 1842 Lord Palmerston remarked:

> Let no man imagine that those treaties for the suppression of the slave trade are valuable only as being calculated to promote the great interests of humanity, and as tending to rid mankind of a foul and detestable crime. Such was indeed their great object and their chief merit. But in this case as in many others, virtue carries its own reward; and if the nations of the world could extirpate this abominable traffic, and if the vast population of Africa could by that means be left free to betake themselves to peaceful and innocent trade, the greatest commercial benefit would accrue, not to England only, but to every civilized nation which engages in maritime commerce. These slave trade treaties therefore are indirectly treaties for the encouragement of commerce.[12]

It was clear that Africa offered remarkable scope for trade and commerce if only the destruction and violence of the slave trade could be uprooted. The wheel had turned full circle. When the European merchant adventurers had first sailed to Africa four centuries before they sought the fabled wealth of black Africa; its precious metals, exotic products and fashionable luxuries. Industrial Britain now looked to Africa for more of the same – and for a market for its goods. Africans were seen as producers and consumers, not as raw human material for the plantations of the Americas.

In the half-century it took to end the British slave trade and slavery the abolitionist campaign had taken on the trappings of a crusade; a good (and godly) people, brimming with pious anger, had organized themselves in a determined attack on slavery wherever it thrived. What made the extension of their campaign so difficult was the continuing success of slave systems in so many different parts of the world (some under direct British control). But their onslaught against slavery worldwide raised other moral issues: by what right did the British intervene in parts of the world which were not their own? What right did the British have to stop and search ships on the high seas? To outsiders (including many who had no truck with slavery) the British determination to eradicate slavery wherever they saw it, on land or sea, smacked of British arrogance and crude power.

The French were especially touchy and took a dim view of British abolitionists telling them how to bring about the end of French colonial slavery. In the event, French slaves were not emancipated until 1848. The Americans, having freed themselves from Britain in 1812, were similarly unhappy with British abolitionist hectoring. Slavery boomed in the American South, thanks largely to the introduction of cotton after 1800 (cotton vital to the burgeoning textile industry in Lancashire). By 1860 there were 4 million slaves at work throughout North America. Here was an obvious and natural target for British abolitionists.

Tactics formerly employed against the West Indian lobby were now turned against American slavery. Preachers, churches, pamphlets, lecture tours, drives for money, all and more fuelled British abolitionism in North America. Activists – black and white – criss-crossed the Atlantic, much as the earlier missionaries had linked British communities with the West Indian slave quarters. British abolitionists helped American campaigners against local slavery, but they often caused deep resentment by their assumption of moral superiority. The Americans had not severed their ties with Britain merely to succumb to the moral posturing of self-righteous abolitionists. None the less, there was a flourishing Anglo-American abolition movement which saw a reprise, on an international scale, of most of the political tactics directed against British slavery at an earlier date.[13]

It was to take the convulsions of the American Civil War before slavery in North America was destroyed. Indeed, before 1860 American slavery showed no sign of diminishing; its millions of victims were locked into a major economic enterprise which remained profitable and commercially attractive to the last. There is no reason to think that slavery in North America would have died a natural death.

British abolitionists had their pick of places to wax angry about. Slavery was ubiquitous. India was a case in point. Millions of slaves languished in Indian slavery (mainly as domestic slaves). The sub-continent yielded enough horror stories to slate the moral outrage of the most fanatical abolitionist. Slave concubines, many of them children, commonplace sales of children and wives, slaves as dowry and inheritance; all these transgressed the basic principles of British abolitionism. But they were ancient and indigenous. Unlike blacks in the New World, Indian slaves had not been transplanted or introduced by the British. Under pressure from British abolitionists, and as part of that drive by British missionaries to 'civilize' India by removing its native cultures, the British sought to remove slavery wherever they found it. It was, however, a long haul which could not succeed until the Indian social structure which sustained it had been changed.[14]

Through all the years of the Atlantic trade another parallel slave trade had existed, and yet had gone virtually unnoticed. Indeed, long before Europeans had begun to take Africans across the Atlantic, there had been a thriving Islamic slave trade, north across the Sahara and east to the Indian Ocean. Perhaps 4 million people had been transported to the Mediterranean and the Middle East *even before* the Atlantic trade began. In the nineteenth century another 3 million more were sold into Islamic regions.[15]

Here then was a major outrage begging for British involvement. Largely due to the explorations of David Livingstone, the full nature of the Islamic slave trade in Central and East Africa began to emerge. Livingstone felt that the slave trade could be stopped only if Europeans took over the appropriate parts of Africa; seizing Arab slave ships in the Indian Ocean would never staunch the flow of Africans. What was needed was the imposition of a different culture, British culture, on those African regions which supplied the slaves or were powerless to resist the blandishments and aggression of the slave-traders.

Efforts were made to come to an agreement with the Portuguese (the other major power with an interest in the region) to eliminate the slave trade. In the event, it was to take the 'scramble for Africa' and the direct intervention of European imperial powers in African affairs before effective measures began to bite against the slave trade throughout East Africa.[16] Even then, the demand for slaves continued.

Arabia, transformed by economic growth, wanted slaves throughout the nineteenth and well into the twentieth centuries. Africans were recruited for a variety of tasks: as workers in the Red Sea ports (after the opening of the Suez Canal in 1869), in the region's pearl fisheries, in the date gardens of Medina and the northern Hijaz, the coffee plantations of the Yemen, and to work in the sheikhdoms of Muscat and Oman. This amounted to an estimated 7,000 slaves a year in the late nineteenth century. Slaves were transported from Ethiopia, the Sudan and Somalia. Africans from Central Africa were shipped through East African ports to the Persian Gulf and south Arabia.

There was one aspect of the African slave trade which the British found especially distasteful; the trade in women, encouraged by the existence of concubinage in Islamic societies in Africa and Arabia. Although it has long been thought that slave women were required primarily for their labour and for reproductive purposes, it is clear that they were not particularly fertile. But some could provide sexual services unavailable elsewhere. Where slavery lasted longest, it was often associated with sexual slavery. Slave concubinage, in the words of a recent historian of the topic, 'was a functioning institution in the northern states of Nigeria in 1988'. The survival of sexual slavery is a reminder of the durability of slavery in its various forms.[17]

There was then, plenty of scope for British moral outrage about slavery and the slave trade long after they had abolished their own slave system in the Americas. If they gazed westwards they saw slavery survive in North America until 1863, in Cuba and Brazil until 1886 and 1888 respectively. As they turned to Central, Southern and East Africa, which they did with ever greater interest from the mid-nineteenth century, it became apparent that the slave trade was a thriving concern. Arabia showed no natural distaste for black slavery and continued to import Africans well into the twentieth century; slaves regularly sought protection and freedom in various British consulates in Arab states in the 1930s, and on the eve of the Second World War the British were negotiating with Arab leaders to outlaw the slave trade in their region. In India, the survival of local slavery was but another reminder of the many 'barbaric' customs the British needed to curb if they were ever to civilize the subcontinent.

Having purged themselves of their own collective wrong-doing, and thereby opened up new prospects of open trade, the British embarked on a crusade against the forces of darkness, rarely recognizing the role their forbears had played in unleashing those very same forces. The problems they faced can be gauged from the simple fact that the Anti-Slavery Society survives to this day.

Historians continue to argue fiercely about the economic consequences of the slave system for Britain. What role did slavery play in the transformation of Britain into an industrial power?

The most beguiling connection between slavery and the rise of industrial capitalism is the simple coincidence of timing. The British abolished the slave trade (1807) and then slavery (1834–38) at the very moment when modern industry began to emerge. It was no accident that when early factory reformers began to campaign for social reform at home they spoke of 'factory slaves'. What was the precise link between these two changes – the end of British slavery and the rise of British industry?[18]

It would be hard to dispute the simple point that slavery was economic in origin and development. The British – and other Europeans – did not recruit millions of Africans simply for racial reasons (though in time they came to offer racial justifications for black slavery). The Africans filled a labouring void, especially after the switch to labour-intensive sugar production. There was not enough indigenous or European migrant labour to work the sugar plantations, and Africans could be obtained relatively cheaply and in abundance.

From the early days, the system of recruiting and shipping Africans into the Americas had been a capitalist undertaking. Capital from European bankers and merchant houses was the crucial ingredient which enabled plantations to be developed and Africans to be bought and transported. Trade from Britain was inexorably lured to the Americas as slavery and tropical produce transformed the region. British goods, and European goods re-exported through Britain, poured into the Caribbean. As the Atlantic trade in all its forms became the central feature of British maritime trade in the eighteenth century, the whole edifice hinged on the labour of the slaves. Even the non-slave colonies of North America were sucked into the process, for their foodstuffs and raw materials (especially their wood) went to the Caribbean. The links between the various parts of Britain's Atlantic maritime empire were often remote, but they were held together by the slave labour of the islands and the northern colonies.

This valuable trading nexus naturally lured a vast amount of investment[19] (£37 million in 1773), and spat out profits and growth. Money made from the slave crops provided a major stimulus to British industry, which grew faster than would have been possible from satisfying a purely domestic demand. Up to the 1790s there is little room to doubt the remarkable influence which the slave system had upon the development of the British economy.[20]

The British had become major consumers by the late eighteenth century, their taste transformed by luxury goods which would have been beyond their means and desires a generation earlier: foodstuffs, clothing, exotic drinks, tobacco, coffee, sugar, books, toys and a range of leisure activities. There was, quite simply, an amazing rise in consumer demand in Britain itself, and a great deal of that demand was for tropical produce, much of which was the fruit of slave labour. As the British consumed ever more sugar and tobacco, those products created further opportunities for export of British goods to the Americas and Africa.[21]

By the third quarter of the eighteenth century demand for slaves increased markedly in the slave colonies. Slave prices rose, but planters were able to pay the costs because they earned so much from sugar sales. At the heart of this formula lay a massive growth in the British consumption of sugar. Here, then, we return to the point made at the beginning of this book: the British were consuming gallons of tea and coffee laced with pounds of sugar.[22] Sugar consumption was especially pronounced in new industrial regions which enjoyed a rise in material prosperity in the years 1775 to 1800.

In these same decades British overseas trade began to change. West Riding woollen goods, copper, brass and wrought iron were exported to Africa and the Americas; by the end of the eighteenth century some 40 per cent of all British exports went to those two regions, both linked to slavery and the slave trade. At the heart of this growth of the British export trade lay the purchasing power of the Caribbean, made possible by the remarkable increase in sales of sugar. The more the planters sold, the more they bought from Britain, from Africa, from North America and from Ireland. By the 1770s the average annual value of goods exported from Britain to the Caribbean was in excess of £1.33 million.[23] But it would be wrong to think of this as a simple 'triangular' trading system, for its ramifications were vast. The increase in West Indian purchasing power stimulated other areas of British overseas trade. For example, the trade to Africa (for slaves destined for the Caribbean) did not consist solely of goods from Britain itself. About one-quarter of all the goods shipped from Britain to Africa were in fact of East Indian origin; the rise of the export trade to West Africa served to increase British trade to and from India. West Indian planters also bought growing volumes of food and building materials from the North American colonies and from Ireland. This enabled those regions to conduct an enhanced trade with Britain.

From this welter of evidence (which is a simplification of much greater and complex findings of economic historians) we can glean some basic points. Something like a third of the growth in British exports in the generation before American Independence, and perhaps a half of all the increase in British goods produced for export, went to satisfy demand in the West Indies. This means that from the mid-eighteenth century onwards demand from the Caribbean stimulated an enormous growth in British industrial output (perhaps to the value of £1.26 million in the years 1750–75). This is not to claim that the slave colonies laid the basis for the industrial revolution, but it is perfectly clear that major industrial sectors would not have developed when and as they did without the prompting and the money from the West Indies. Slavery's important contribution was not so much profits as the stimulus to British economic growth (although it is also true that many people *did* make profits from slavery which they invested in Britain).[24]

The West Indian slave system drew together regions which were geographically and economically distinct. The industrial regions of Lancashire and Yorkshire (textiles), of the Midlands (metal) and west-central Scotland (foodstuffs) were drawn into satisfying the needs and the tastes of the slave islands. This was made possible by the burgeoning British demand for slave-grown sugar. What this complex process did was not so much create the industrial revolution as to lay the foundations for economic and social conditions which prevailed in Britain in the next century.

The economic importance of slavery can be gauged in any number of ways. It made the colonies attractive places for British investment. It has been calculated that, again on the eve of American Independence, some £37 million was invested in the West Indies and perhaps £5 million in the American slave colonies. Profits and income flowed back from those investments, to be spent as the investor wished. There is no real evidence that such money went to finance industrial developments in Britain. But that is really beside the point for, in whatever way the money was spent – splendid houses in Bristol or Liverpool, fashionable country retreats, or the pursuit of pleasure – here was further proof (if more is needed) of the value of the West Indian slave colonies.

Yet by the 1840s those same colonies, and the once-vital maritime trade which sustained them, had collapsed. British slavery had been brought down by a sustained political campaign which seemed to pay scant attention to Britain's economic interests. Those armies of ex-slaves, a dwindling band of ageing Africans and their local-born descendants, were now cast adrift as free people. It was to be yet another of the great ironies of British imperial history that the people for whom the British had waxed so indignant – the blacks of the West Indies – were soon relegated to the ranks of the unimportant and the unnoticed. Not until the descendants of those same people began to arrive in Britain a full century later, after the Second World War, did the British once more begin to pay serious attention to the West Indian societies they had conjured forth for their own economic interests.

19

The Plight of Africa

Much of this book has recounted a litany of horrors visited upon innocent people by a rapacious system. The victims of this story were Africans and their New World descendants. It is the story of lives shaped by the Atlantic crossing and in the plantations of the Americas. But what did all this mean for Africa? Was Africa left a desolate vale of tears, permanently mourning the loss of millions of its sons and daughters; made to pay for generations to come for the sinful greed of the slave-traders? Or was the outcome less cataclysmic than we might instinctively imagine?

In the last twenty years, much of the debate about the Atlantic slave trade has been about statistics. A highly sophisticated and complex army of statistically-minded scholars has marched back and forth through the available data, reassessing the evidence and refining the received wisdom of earlier generations. Sometimes it has been difficult to catch a glimpse of the slaves buried beneath the statistics paraded by historians, but without these efforts we would have nothing but impressions and inspired guesses when discussing the slave trade and its impact on Africa.

Until the 1960s, the figures quoted for the numbers of Africans forced into the Atlantic slave trade varied enormously – not surprisingly since most of them were guesses. Some thought 15 million, others cited 50 million. The effort since then to produce a more 'scientific' estimate has been criticized and dismissed as an attempt at 'measuring the immeasurable'. A recently published CD-ROM, containing all the known data from the Atlantic slave trade, has, however, confirmed the irrefutable importance of attention to the statistics. The numbers involved clearly *do* matter.[1]

The problems are clear enough, and begin and end with the sources. Evidence for the Atlantic trade exists in a range of materials: in African, shipping, New World and European sources. We know a great deal about the slave trade in particular places at certain times. We have good shipping records for particular countries and companies; there are excellent details of slave imports into certain regions of the Americas and there are some revealing details available in plantation papers. It is a patchy, uneven set of sources; a rich mosaic with some vivid sections showing in full detail but with lots of important pieces missing.

The broad outlines of the Atlantic slave trade are now clear enough. Almost 12 million Africans were loaded onto the Atlantic slave ships, but a substantial minority died en route. Something like 10+ million were landed in the Americas. Of the major slave-trading nations, the British became the pre-eminent power. In the years 1662–1810, British, and British American, ships carried almost 3 million slaves from Africa. By the end of the eighteenth century something like 80,000 Africans were being transported every year.[2] By any standards, these figures are enormous (the population of Britain in 1800 was only 10 million) even though they were spread over a long period. The first slaves transported by the English crossed in the reign of Elizabeth I; the English were still trying to intercept slave ships in the mid-years of Queen Victoria's reign. The sheer durability of the slave trade is as stunning as the numbers involved.

The bald statistics hide as much as they reveal. Closer scrutiny illustrates the more detailed, hidden consequences – none more dramatic than for Africa itself. At its peak, the slave trade drew upon an African coastline stretching from Senegambia, east and south to the Angolan coast and even round the Cape to East Africa. As the slave trade evolved, Europeans switched their attention to new parts of the coast, and to new river systems, gradually moving further south. By 1700 the British were trading not only in Senegambia, Sierra Leone, the Windward and Gold Coasts, but had moved into the Bight of Biafra. Slaves from the Niger Delta were being fed into the British slave trade even before 1700. Forty years later both the British and French were operating even further south and were buying slaves in the area immediately north of the Zaire river.[3]

In the eighteenth century the British drew 20 per cent of their slave cargoes from the Loango coast – rivalling the volume of slaves recruited from the Bight of Benin. Though most of the formative impressions about the slave trade (especially those conveyed in the abolitionist debates) derived from older slave-trading regions to the north, it seems clear enough that perhaps 40 per cent of all slaves shipped across the Atlantic came from Angola and the Zaire river interior. French slave-traders took their slave cargoes from the following regions, in descending order of priority: the Bight of Benin, west-central Africa and (much less important) the Bight of Biafra. North Americans on the other hand, with the trade centred on Rhode Island, trawled for slaves in Sierra Leone, Senegambia and the Gold Coast.

It is important to know precisely where slaves came from. How else can we understand the nature of slavery in the Americas or make some assessment of the consequences of the slave trade on Africa itself? About 40 per cent – possibly even 50 per cent – of all slaves came from Bantu-speaking people. We now know that slaves were drawn not solely from coastal regions but also came from the African interior. Historians have studied the ethnic origins of slaves on the New World plantations (planters and slave-traders kept records of their slaves' home region). Slaves on the plantations of St Domingue for instance came from the far interior of west-central Africa; something like a fifth of slaves described as coming from the Slave Coast were in fact drawn from a distant interior.[4]

The Africans taken as slaves were not a natural cross-section of the societies they came from. Planters and slave-traders wanted young, healthy males. Of course they did not always get what they sought, but they did get more men than women. From the late seventeenth to the nineteenth centuries some 60+ per cent of all Africans transported were male. Ideally, slave-traders would have preferred to ship two males for every female slave. As the slave trade moved further south along the African coast, the ratio of men to women shipped out came closer to the ideal. In fact it was only when the traders were slaving on the Loango coast by the 1740s that they were able to get male slaves in the ratios they desired; this fact alone may have lured ever more slave-traders to that region. In the nineteenth century the Atlantic trade registered a persistently high ratio of male slaves; upwards of 70 per cent of all slaves taken to Cuba for instance.[5] The simple point from this welter of evidence is that Africa lost a consistently higher number of men than women. What effect did this have upon the birth-rates of the home communities? What economic results followed from removing so many young men? Is it possible that, far from being the human and economic disaster we might expect, this human loss might have been sustained – for instance by a population explosion?

Throughout the era of the slave trade, children made up about 34 per cent of the African population. But before 1800 fewer than 20 per cent of slaves carried across the Atlantic were children. There were, as we might expect, striking variations in the proportion of children shipped from different slave-trading regions (perhaps 35 per cent of slaves from Sierra Leone were children, for instance). But as the trade developed the overall percentage of children found on the slave ships rose quite markedly. By the nineteenth century, when the centre of the trade was west-central Africa, there was a dramatic increase in the number of boys being shipped. This was largely a way round recent Portuguese regulations governing slave transportation. It was easier to pack more young slaves tightly into the holds.[6] It might also be the case that healthier, younger slaves were better able to withstand the long trek from their interior homelands to the slave ports on the Angolan coast. However we arrange the figures for the nineteenth century slave trade, we find ourselves staring at children. Between 1811 and 1867 more than 41 per cent of all slaves shipped across the Atlantic were children. Of the slaves sailing from north of the Zaire river, 52 per cent were children. Children made up 59 per cent of Angolan slaves; from south-eastern Africa the ratio was even higher, a remarkable 61 per cent. Understandably, it has been claimed that, by the nineteenth century, 'The Atlantic trade had become a trade in children'.[7]

Perhaps the most curious aspect of this lowering of the age of slaves was its link with the distance from the African coast. At a time when a large proportion of slaves originated from the interior, an increasing proportion of those slaves were boys. It seems likely that boys aged about ten and over were able to withstand long marches from the interior and were now viewed as the most valuable of potential slaves. But what did all this mean for Africa?

The evidence about the slave trade becomes more voluminous and reliable in its more modern epochs. Whereas the earlier history of the trade is uncertain and patchy, we know a great deal about the slave trade in the nineteenth century – the very century when the British turned against it and sought to stamp it out. Yet here is a crucial point. Slavery survived – in some places thrived – in a period characterized by powerful opposition. In the century when many Europeans came to view it as the great evil, more Africans crossed the Atlantic than ever before. Those who wanted to buy Africans established so powerful an institution that the development of slavery and enslavement within Africa took on local form – seemed even indigenous in places – and proved fiercely resistant to demands that it should stop. For every outside call for an end to slavery in the nineteenth century, there were men on hand, Arabs, Europeans, Africans, Brazilians, Cubans and others, prepared to buy still more slaves. Slavery had become so ubiquitous in Africa, so integral to the way a host of different African societies conducted their economies, that it was no easy matter to uproot it and direct local commerce to other less oppressive channels. There were many thousands of Africans involved in the trade who saw no good reason for heeding European moral suggestions. And in any case, in vast tracts of Africa, slavery had become an unquestioned way of life and death.

We know that for every African landed in the Americas, there were many others who were trapped in the expanding slave systems of Africa itself. Millions remained slaves within Africa; ensnared by systems which thrived as a by-product of the external demands for African slaves. Of those who were fed into African slavery, the majority were women. When Europeans began to push into regions of Africa as yet untouched by whites they were often appalled to discover the extent and violence of slavery within the continent. It seemed to them yet another example of African barbarism visited upon other Africans. When accounts of grotesque African brutalities were paraded before the British reading public, few recognized their own creation.

Europeans found it easy to assert that African slavery was indigenous – the result of savage and uncivilized local habits which owed little to the influence or consequences of white interests.

The most important, but invisible, end result of all these upheavals was the impact on the African population. By 1850 the population of Africa was something like 25 million. Historians calculate that *without* the slave trade it would have been twice that figure; somewhere in the region of 46–53 million people. The difficulties and arguments raised by such calculations (which involve complex mathematical models and speculations) can easily be ima- gined. But can we doubt that the loss of the young and the healthy would have had a deeply harmful impact on those regions of black Africa sucked into the overseas slave trades? We can only speculate on what sort of economic impact this loss of manpower had upon Africa. Was it one of the basic causes which underpinned Africa's persistent underdevelopment? Was it the beginning of a process which has continued into the twentieth century of European and American economic forces draining Africa of its raw materials and perman- ently exploiting its cheap and pliant labour, offering little in return but enhanced privation?[8]

In addition to the Africans exported overseas and the Africans enslaved in Africa were those who simply died. The enslavement of Africans generated by the Atlantic trade was, in the words of the most prominent historians of Angola, the 'way of death'; a brutal machine of mass destruction which destroyed as many Africans as it exported. Something like 40 per cent of all slaves went to the Americas from west-central Africa; 50,000–60,000 each year by the late eighteenth century. But a similar number of Africans died each year in the same region, as a direct result of the process of enslavement. African legend had it that the routes taken by Africans trekking westwards from their homeland led to death. It was a legend born of reality and suffering on an epic scale. The diseases, indignities and death suffered by armies of Africans would not have happened had it not been for the Atlantic slave trade.[9]

The Atlantic slave trade not only made possible the emergence of slavery in the Americas, but it also breathed life into African slavery. By about 1800 there were perhaps '3 million slaves in those parts of Africa that serviced the Atlantic trade' – more or less the same number as in the Americas.[10] Slavery blighted Africa in more ways than simply the obvious exporting of its native peoples.

As important as the Atlantic trade undoubtedly was, there was a great deal of African slavery which owed its origins and growth to other factors. Wars and enslavement took place in regions remote from, and quite unconnected to, the movement of peoples and goods to the Atlantic coast. That said, the Atlantic and Islamic slave trades had driven enslavement and slavery so deep into African societies that slavery had been transformed throughout Africa.[11] Long after slavery had been ended in the Americas, it continued to survive and grow in Africa. Statistics provide the basic data which underpin the case. By 1800 there were almost 3 million slaves in the Americas;[12] sixty years later there were upward of 6 million slaves in the USA, Brazil and Cuba. Research on Africa at a later date provides some startling comparisons. In 1900 there were about 2.5 million slaves in the Sokoto Caliphate (a quarter of the entire population). A few years later perhaps 1,192,000 slaves lived in French Western Sudan (from an overall population of 5,134,000). There were quite simply 'twice as many slaves in Islamic West Africa as there had been in Brazil and Cuba in 1870'[13] But what is the relevance of this for the story of British colonial slavery?

Historians of the Americas have long been aware that Africa and its peoples shaped the course of slavery in the Americas. It is now equally clear that the drain of slaves westwards across the Atlantic set in train enormous changes within Africa itself. Moreover those changes continued to reverberate long after the Atlantic slave trade had died, and they penetrated deep into regions apparently untouched by the Atlantic slave trade. We know that black slavery in the Americas involved vast numbers, had massive economic consequences and was unfathomable in its scale of human suffering. We now know that slavery in Africa was comparable in scale to slavery in the Americas. Why should we doubt that the ramifications of African slavery were no less important in economic, social and personal terms?

There is however a school of historians – in fact some of the most imaginative and pioneering historians in the field – who have sought to minimize the effect of slavery on Africa. The *prima facie* evidence might seem to make such an undertaking difficult, though closer inspection suggests a plausibility for their case. Slavery was not the sole source of human destruction in Africa. There were other sources of human loss which far outstripped the numbers of people enslaved. Far more Africans were lost to high rates of infant mortality than were lost to the slave trade. The death of babies was ten times higher than the number of captures for enslavement.[14] The traditional devastations caused by disease and natural disasters swept away many more Africans than did the slave trade. Drought uprooted whole communities, killed untold numbers, permanently debilitated many others and exposed all to the ravages of diseases they would otherwise have resisted.

The bitter twist to this scenario is that many Africans dispersed by such natural disasters fell into the open arms of the slave-traders. At least one major epidemic each century ravaged the slave-trading regions of Africa, removing perhaps one-third of the population in a process comparable to the devastation of the Black Death in Europe in the fourteenth century. In regions untouched by slave-trading, vast numbers of people were scattered by major wars. Fleeing from conflict and dislocation caused human suffering, loss and destruction on a scale every bit as great as in the slave trade. Rootless, enfeebled and often with no means of support, thousands of Africans were

easy prey for slave-traders. Some were simply enslaved by force, others –
especially children – were handed over to slavers by hungry and weakened
parents.[15] Often, though, the sufferings of the enslaved had been so profound
that large numbers died en route or arrived sick and weak.[16]

What took place within Africa was nothing less than a major transformation.
Slavery grew where it did not exist before, and old forms of bondage were
transformed and revitalized by the external demands for slaves. At the heart of
this complex transformation lay a violent upheaval in a series of African
societies. The slave trade, and trade for a range of European goods (especially
firearms), transformed Africa, pushing back the slave-trading frontier from its
coastal and river bases deep into the interior. New patterns of human settlement and trade developed, the reaction to disease and illness changed; so too
did patterns of population growth. It was, as one historian of Angolan slavery
has written, 'a moving frontier zone of slaving violence'. Atlantic slavery cast
the malignant spores of enslavement throughout great regions of black Africa,
corroding and damaging life and transforming society beyond recall. In the
process millions were dispatched to an early grave. In a phrase which could
stand as the leitmotif for the whole Atlantic system, a Portuguese governor
described Angolan slaves as 'a commodity that died with such ease'.[17] Theirs
was a way of death which surpassed even the wildest fantasies of African
folklore.

20

The Problems of Freedom

In the British West Indies, almost three-quarters of a million slaves were given their full freedom in 1838. All of them had their roots in Africa. The free descendants of those West Indian slaves soon found that freedom brought poverty and in the course of the nineteenth century many left the depressed rural circumstances of their impoverished homelands to seek material salvation wherever it was available – and wherever they were allowed to travel and settle. They migrated to neighbouring Cuba to work on the sugar and tobacco plantations. Thousands migrated to Panama to labour on the railway and later the Panama Canal, where thousands of them died in the epidemics which blighted that massive development. West Indians migrated to Central America, to toil on the new banana plantations. Others took to the sea, joining the growing numbers of black sailors, West Indian and West African, who provided cheap labour for the new steamship lines plying the world's trade routes.

The West Indian islands, for so long the economic jewel in the British imperial crown, slipped into neglect and disregard. In the years after slavery, the crop which had underpinned Caribbean fortunes and British prosperity – sugar – could be produced more abundantly (and cheaply) elsewhere. New areas turned to sugar cultivation (often without the use of slave labour); European sugar beet added to the worldwide glut of sugar production. The figures speak for themselves. In 1800 world sugar production stood at 250,000 tons; eighty years later it was 3.8 million tons and in 1914, 16 million tons.[1]

The West Indies did not share in this boom. They had thrived because of the economic protection afforded by the old slave system, their sugar prices guaranteed by British subsidies. In an age of free trade, however, such subsidies no longer found economic or political favour. As Britain moved into a different phase, favouring more open trade, and scorning its old protected habits and ideas, the West Indies slipped out of focus. Once the area which commanded British political and strategic attention, the area where the Royal Navy enforced British might, ensuring the primacy of British economic interests, the Caribbean now became a scenic sideshow; a troublesome reminder of past greatness.

Many of the former slaves no longer wanted to be associated with the plantations and they left them in droves. But their new-found freedom had its costs. Whatever else the plantations had done, they had provided a modicum of paternalistic material protection. They had, after a fashion, housed, clothed and fed their black labour force. Those who stayed on the plantations found that what had once been free now had to be paid for – housing, gardens and plots, clothing and food – from the pittance paid by planters (themselves nostalgic about the world they had lost).

Ex-slaves who simply quit the plantations became, in general, impoverished peasants, eking out a meagre living on land which was often marginal and often legally disputed. The West Indian peasantry grew, and developed a remarkable economy based on their rural plots linked with a network of villages and markets (which had emerged from the markets of slave society). But they remained a poor, depressed and marginal people, enjoying their new-found freedom but denied the material well-being which many, including their British supporters, had expected to follow full freedom.

A new diaspora began. The modern West Indies had been forged by the enforced diaspora of Africans and the creation of slave societies throughout the islands. Now, free descendants of those slaves migrated to seek work elsewhere, sending remittances home to provide for their families.

In another curious twist to the story of those islands, in the years when West Indians began to leave for work abroad, other peoples were encouraged to migrate *to* the former slave islands. For all the contraction and gloom of the nineteenth-century sugar industry, the planters continued to complain about the availability of labour. Slaves, for all the 'problems' they caused, were, at the very least, at their owner's beck and call, available to be roused and driven into the fields at a moment's notice. Their free descendants were quite different. In some islands (and in some places in the bigger islands) black workers had few alternatives to working for the local sugar-planter. But the development of free black lands and the diversification of local economies offered alternatives for large numbers of West Indian rural workers. Planters found that they could no longer get the labour they wanted, as and when they wanted it. No longer as powerful in London as their eighteenth-century predecessors, the sugar lobby still had influence with the British Colonial Office. From their demands for fresh supplies of labour to take the place of the departing ex-slaves there evolved that peculiar, new migration of imperial peoples – the indentured labour scheme from India.

Planters had heard that Indian 'coolies' had proved successful in Mauritius. By 1841, 7,000 had been imported into the West Indies. Despite objections from the powerful abolitionist body in Britain (its strength revitalized by the success of 1838), the scheme won official approval. With agents in India to recruit and regulate the trade, an organized migration of poor Indians developed, continuing until the First World War, by which time more than a quarter of a million Indians had been imported into Guiana, some 134,000 into Trinidad, 33,000 into Jamaica, with scatterings in the smaller islands. By the time it ended, the indentured immigration scheme had brought more than half a million Indians into the British Caribbean.[2] To many it was a scheme which had unhappy reflections of the older scheme which had shipped Africans into the islands.

Few of the Indians took up the opportunity of repatriation at the end of their five-year indenture. Most merged into the local labour force, many of them joining the ex-slaves in rural impoverishment, others emerging from their labouring roots to become a new generation of shop-keepers. To this remarkable racial mix was added, from the mid-century, the Chinese. They too rose from labouring ranks to become grocers and laundry workers. Later in the century, they were joined by Lebanese and Syrians. The result was the emergence of extraordinary polyglot societies. In some of the colonies, Guiana and Trinidad especially, the Indian populations were, in time, to equal and then surpass the local black population. But in all cases the newer immigrants brought with them their own cultures which became part of the broader culture of the Caribbean peoples. There also developed new divides between local peoples which fragmented social and political life in the years to come.[3]

The purpose of those nineteenth-century migrations had been to enhance local economic fortunes. In fact, conditions for the great bulk of West Indians did not improve. Throughout that century, the West Indian peasantry, African or Indian in origin, remained abject and, in places, seemed to deteriorate. Visitors from Europe and North America told a uniformly depressing tale of widespread rural poverty and hopelessness, of general urban decay and overall economic despair. When the novelist Anthony Trollope travelled through the Caribbean in 1858–60 he painted a gloomy picture, though the sugar-planters, for all their complaints, were still able to entertain their guest in lavish style with the extravagance (and excessive drink) so beloved of their slave-owning forefathers. Like the planters, Trollope was not impressed by local blacks: 'The negro's idea of emancipation was, and is, emancipation not from slavery but from work.' Trollope took up some old themes, expressed in a style which must have warmed the cockles of plantocratic hearts. The negro, he thought:

is capable of the hardest bodily work, and that probably with less bodily pain than men of any other race; but he is idle, unambitious as to worldly position, sensual, and content with little...I think that he seldom understands the

purpose of industry, the objects of truth, or the results of honesty. [The blacks]
are a servile race, fitted by nature for the hardest physical work, and apparently
at present fitted for little else.[4]

Slavery had been a 'sin' which Trollope was happy to see ended. But
emancipation had left the ex-slaves to flounder. Happy to survive by minimal
effort in a land which yielded a plentiful bounty, the black population of the
West Indies, he believed, were content to see their former masters, and the
economy as a whole, slide into decay.

Coming so soon after black freedom, these views were an unhappy reminder of the old plantocratic allegations. What lay behind these, and a host of
similar complaints, was a complex set of racial attitudes which had been
shaped by slavery, distorted by the campaigns for black freedom, and then
brought into fresh focus by the results of black freedom. The idea that blacks
were lazy at heart was of course basic to the ideology of slavery. For generations past, whites involved in all aspects of the slave system had argued, in
print and less formally over their dining tables on both sides of the Atlantic,
that blacks were fundamentally and incurably indolent. Without the constraints of slavery, no black would work. Best expressed by that school of
apologists for slavery who wrote to head off the attacks of the abolitionists, this
myth of black indolence had been a persistent theme in the literature of
slavery.

Now the old plantocratic ideas about race were blossoming again, this time
in the conditions of black freedom. Adding piquancy to this renewed criticism
of blacks in the West Indies was disappointment that the ex-slaves had not
turned out as their former friends had hoped and expected. There were many
Britons who came to think that the ex-slaves in the West Indies had let them
down.

This bizarre twist to the tale infected a great deal of British thinking with a
distinct racist quality. It is easy to see how it came about. In large part it
derived from the unrealistic expectations raised in the campaigns against
slavery in the years 1787 to 1838. The abolitionists had roused themselves to
such a pitch of moral outrage, had enthused millions with a sense of indignation about slavery, that it would have proved difficult to satisfy their expectations. At heart the British had come to think that, once the slaves had been
freed, they would rise, quickly and effortlessly, to the ranks of a free peasantry,
their industry propelled forward by the urge to earn good wages in a free
market economy.[5] Much of the success of anti-slavery had hinged on the
argument that free labour was more efficient; that once the trammels and
shackles of slavery had been lost, West Indian blacks would thrive much as free
labour thrived in Europe.

It was, however, more complex than those naive abolitionists believed. In
any case, they had waxed indignant about the slaves at a remove of almost

5,000 miles and had paid little attention to the complexities of the transition from enslavement to freedom. It now seems obvious, as the planters had warned, that slaves could not easily, or immediately, be transformed into industrious peasants, working a regulated disciplined routine for their former owners.

For a start, there were few incentives to work hard. Wages were low, work irregular. As the sugar industry declined wages fell even lower and employment prospects worsened. Hard work, application, devotion to duty, discipline in all its forms – what were these to people who gained nothing from them and who, in any case, had no real experience of such discipline in a free setting? Slaves had been disciplined at the end of a whip, by cuffing and threats, by the sly doling out of material returns. Ultimately slavery was a violent, threatening labour system which secured labour by a mix of violence and seductions. How were people to learn to live and work as free labourers after a lifetime under such a system?

When the plantations declined and the West Indian sugar industry fell apart, it was easy and convincing to blame the former slaves. In their rearguard action to preserve slavery, planters had loudly and frequently declared that without the constraints of slavery, the plantation economy would collapse. And so, in the event, it did – though not for the reasons they had offered. It was in serious trouble even before the coming of black freedom. However, all that outsiders really knew about the plantations – apart from consuming their exotic produce in such volume – was the people who laboured on them. It was the labour force, the slaves, which had been the major issue in the political campaign fought in Britain and the West Indies in the fifty years before black freedom came in 1838. And it was the labour force which, again, came to prominence in British discussion about the state of the West Indies in the mid-nineteenth century.

There was a continuing strain of hostility towards the former slaves which ran like a descant through much of the literature on the fate of the West Indies. From the 1830s onwards a steady trickle of prominent British writers and visitors reported on the state of the islands. As often as not their views were impressionistic. More important, perhaps, they were often hostile towards local blacks. Blacks had, they argued, reverted to type: lazy, uncivilized, ignorant and ultimately beyond the power of improvement. This line of argument, which traced its origins to the plantocratic scribes of the late eighteenth century, was given its sharpest expression by Thomas Carlyle in his essay 'Discourse on the Nigger Question' (1849). It was an essay which dripped vituperation: 'Our beautiful black darlings are at last happy; with little labour except to the teeth, which surely, in those excellent horse-jaws of theirs, will not fail!' Carlyle's essay has, understandably, been quoted time and again. It is worth repeating if we are to catch a sense of the hatred which he directed towards the West Indian blacks – though he took pains to deny hostility.

Do I, then, hate the negro? No; except when the soul is killed out of him, I decidedly like poor Quashee; and find him a pretty kind of man. With a pennyworth of oil, you can make a handsome glossy thing of Quashee, when the soul is not killed in him! A swift, supple fellow; a merry-hearted, grinning, dancing, singing, affectionate kind of creature, with a great deal of melody and amenability in his composition.[6]

What troubled Carlyle, and those who argued a similar case in Britain, was the resolute failure of the ex-slaves to behave as they had been expected to behave. Those who campaigned for their freedom had fully expected to see ex-slaves working vigorously. Since free labour was, like free trade, better than slavery, it was only a matter of time before the combination of free black labour and free international markets saw the enhancement of material well-being on all fronts: for the ex-slaves, for their former owners, for the islands and for the mother country. Instead, the British gazed with some incomprehension as the islands went from bad to worse; the benefits of freedom did not materialize. It was as if they had been deceived into granting black freedom on false pretences. The planters had been right after all: black freedom was merely the prelude to decline and despair.

The hostility shown by Carlyle and later Trollope was not shared by everyone. There was a distinct strand of optimism in the Victorian intelligentsia's view of the ex-slaves. But that, too, was unrealistic. In truth the West Indian peasantry were on a hiding to nothing. Unless they blossomed fairly quickly into a thriving, industrious and booming work-force, they would be damned by British friend and foe alike.

Disillusionment spread from the 1860s onwards. First of all, and quite removed from the West Indies, the Indian mutiny (1857–58) had hardened British hearts against subject (and 'coloured') peoples. The savagery of the fighting, the stories of atrocities, the sharp racial antagonism generated by the Mutiny (the word 'nigger' entered the vernacular) purged ever more Britons of their benign attitude towards native peoples.[7] British material prosperity, force of arms, Christian example and culture – all these clearly did not impress millions of subject peoples who instead clung tenaciously to their own cultures, shunning what the British knew to be superior institutions. That in itself was proof, if more were needed, of the irredeemable ignorance and savagery of the people concerned. What was needed, henceforth, was the smack of firm government rather than the seductions and blandishments of cultural persuasion.

Only six years after the Mutiny, the Governor Eyre controversy in Jamaica once more raised the complex questions of race and of British dealings with subject peoples. A minor uprising in the east of Jamaica in 1865 was bloodily repressed by the Governor; some 500 died in military and quasi-legal actions (most of which were in fact illegal) in a response which was out of all proportion to the initial troubles. There followed a fierce public debate in Britain about its relationship with its native peoples.[8]

Thus did the question of race become a major political issue in mid-Victorian Britain. This debate swirled through the press with all the bitterness and prejudice which have marked similar debates in recent years. In the nineteenth century, the British argued about the politics of race at a distance from 'their' peoples overseas. A century later the argument had moved closer to home, for the descendants of those subject peoples had settled in Britain itself. In the nineteenth century a new generation of scientists added their findings to the debate about race. Anthropology and natural sciences analysed the divisions and sub-groups of mankind. The overall result was the growing conviction that the white races (and especially the British) were superior to the black and the brown; that human differences were racially determined.[9]

These arguments, often crude but sometimes subtle and too scientifically complex for popular understanding, were seized upon by journalists, speakers and politicians, by eminent schoolmasters and clergymen. The belief in the 'facts' about racial and anatomical distinctions – with the British at the top of this racial heap – rapidly took hold of British life, whatever objections were offered to the contrary. The language of race quickly gained acceptance at a popular and intellectual level. More and more effort was invested in proving British racial supremacy to be correct. Not surprisingly, it was to permeate British life well into the twentieth century; it shaped the development of educational policy (especially through the application of intelligence testing); it determined the British outlook on the world at large; and it proved to be one of the most dangerous illusions in modern British life. The British were not of course alone in this, but their imperial experience gave their racial view of the world greater potency.

The public schools were especially influential in propagating these ideas, through formal education and their almost frenzied emphasis on physical fitness and sporting activity. The Head of Marlborough claimed in 1861: 'the savage races are without a past and without a future, doomed as races infinitely nobler have been before them, to a rapid and entire and perhaps for the highest destinies of mankind, an enviable extinction'.[10] However, concepts of racial superiority were not reserved for the propertied classes, but permeated the whole of society. The printed word spread these ideas at a time when more and more British people were literate. Popular literature – newspapers, magazines, books, comics, children's literature and school texts – were suffused with the vocabulary and ideology of race. The language of race became a fundamental feature of British life.

In that crucial period between the ending of British slavery and the major British imperial incursions into Africa in the 1880s, the groundwork was laid for a racial view of the world, reinforced by disappointment with the results of black freedom. There were obvious problems with this theory. For a superior people, the British had more than their share of physical problems. How, for example, could the belief in British superiority accommodate the fact that one-third of the urban population lived on or below the poverty line? Yet it is surely symptomatic that even the poor came to be known as 'a race apart'. When social investigators stared at the poor in London, Liverpool or York, when army recruiting officers rejected droves of young men because of their physical imperfections, how did it square with current racial thought? When school doctors examined the stunted bodies of working-class children, smaller than their middle-class peers and afflicted by a bewildering range of ailments, when the data of working-class life were periodically paraded before the public, revealing levels of deprivation and physical infirmities on a horrifying scale, how could all this be accommodated with the pervading sense of racial superiority? Who, in fact, were the real Anglo-Saxons?

Such contradictions are easy to see today. They were less easily grasped in Victorian and Edwardian Britain. Doubters were pointed in the direction of British industrial strength, British military might, British imperial expansion, the longevity of its political and legal systems, and the democratic basis of British life. Where were the challenges to white dominance from black Africa, from the former slaves of the Caribbean, from the sub-continent of India? Few were prepared to accept the achievements, the institutions, the arts, the industries of other races or the religions (even of the Indian sub-continent) as remotely comparable to their British counterparts. Their religions were mere superstitions, their cultures only pale reflections of European attainments, their learning and sciences mere crudities when set against the scholarship and science of Victorian life.

Where had the old feelings gone? What had happened to that remarkable national commitment to equality which lay at the heart of the anti-slavery movement up to 1838? The abolitionists' motto had been 'Am I not a Man and a Brother?' The view that black and white were equal was, obviously, an effective political ploy, but there is no reason to doubt that many genuinely believed what they said. In the last phase of British abolitionism, between 1828 and 1838, there is an abundance of evidence which testifies to a fierce attachment to black equality. Within a generation that commitment had become the dust of disappointment. The older, more 'liberal' view of race was promoted by a dwindling band of adherents as blacks failed to live up to the expectations their white friends had of them.

Black Africans and West Indians who entered Britain in the fifty years after black freedom found precious little evidence of that brotherly identity which lay at the heart of abolitionist ideology. They were no longer objects, mere chattels owned and traded by white owners; neither were they equal, in treatment or regard, with the whites around them. They became objects of great curiosity and sometimes amusement, always distanced from their white hosts by the powerful barriers of contemporary racial thinking.

When discussing relations between black and white in the years after slavery, what importance should we attach to the fact that the British had carried more Africans into New World bondage than any other people? Is it possible to consider the rise of nineteenth-century racial thinking without considering the legacy of the slave empire, the growth of the slave colonies and their relationship to British prosperity and economic development? If anyone doubted that connection, there were reminders on all hands long after slavery had gone. Most obvious of all – but unquestioned – the British enjoyed the pleasures first created for them by their slaves. They consumed sugar in prodigious amounts, the Royal Navy endured its maritime privations thanks to the traditional tots of rum doled out to the men, and the British, like the western world at large, smoked themselves to death, courtesy of an addiction to tobacco made possible initially by slaves. And, until 1863, the British clothed themselves better than ever before, thanks to the labours of the slaves in the cotton fields of the American South. Of course all these commodities continued to be grown long after black slaves throughout the Americas had been freed.

The institution which made all this possible – the plantation – managed to survive, many of them thriving to the present day. So often, however, they are associated with their past; they invariably seem linked to problems of rural poverty and underdevelopment, the curse of those former colonies forced to live under the shadow of slavery.

Who now remembers when wandering through the splendours of the Tate Gallery that the origins of that collection lay in the nation's addiction to sugar? True, Tate and Lyle made their fortune after slavery had ended, but they merely transformed and enhanced a national taste first developed by the labours of West Indian slaves. And who, studying in the library of All Souls College, Oxford, pauses to think of the people who made it possible, slaves toiling on the Codrington estate in Barbados? Who but the historically-minded or the local antiquarian pauses to think, in Liverpool or Bristol, of the debt owed by those cities to the cargoes of Africans who pitched and rolled their diseased and filthy way across the Atlantic? Who looks at black Africa and remembers those millions of souls wrenched from their homes and dispatched to the far side of the world? People who tend to think of these issues, who make the connection between the plight of black humanity and the rise of western prosperity, are more likely to be black than white.

The black descendants of the slaves remain the most obvious reminder of slavery and its legacy. There are for instance 25 + million black Americans today, heirs to a distinctive American legacy of racism and deprivation. In the last twenty-five years successive debates about American social problems – housing, employment, the family, penal policy, military recruitment, drugs and other issues – have invariably turned to the question of slavery and its legacy. Slavery provides a setting and, for many, an explanation for that complexity of problems which have assailed black American society since 1863. All this is quite apart from the cultural impact of slavery and black life on the evolution of American society at large. No one interested in American music, sports, warfare or literature could ignore slavery. But even to express the matter in this fashion is to categorize black experience after slavery in a way which distorts the impact of black life in America.

Put at its simplest, who could envisage the growth of American society without its millions of black citizens, for so long the hewers of wood and drawers of water, in slavery and in freedom?

For a long time the British were able to feel superior about their dealings with blacks. While the USA was periodically convulsed by racial troubles, the British felt immune from such tensions. But the development of black communities in Britain before and during the First World War changed all that. The British liked to boast of their toleration, but there were plenty of signs to the contrary; of latent racism and populist violence, directed especially against Jews earlier in the century, and against Germans in 1914. In the post-war dislocations after 1918 there were new objects of animosity.

In 1919 a number of serious 'race riots', directed against local black communities, bruised a number of British ports. The seriousness of those troubles and their broader significance were ignored for almost fifty years. The number of blacks living in Britain at that time was quite small, but that did not shield them from popular animosity in areas such as employment and housing.

Now there are over 2.5 million non-whites living in Britain, the largest single group originating in the West Indies, but, inevitably, an increasing proportion born in Britain. Most live in the deprived urban heartlands, tested by those social problems which have a parallel in the USA. Those of West Indian origin are the descendants of slaves and indentured workers carried from Africa and India to undertake rural labour for the betterment of Britain and its colonies. For them at least, the history of slavery has more than a passing interest.

In the 1980s Britain had its share of urban troubles – not all of them racial. Three of the most troublesome and dangerous of the urban disturbances – in Brixton, Toxteth and St Paul's – took place in the three cities which had played so crucial a role in the development of the slave empire: London, Liverpool and Bristol formed the axis around which that lucrative and revolutionary system turned. Was it mere accident that those cities should be plagued, long after slavery had died, for the sins of their fathers?

Suggestions for Further Reading

Abrahams, Roger D. and John F. Szwed (eds), *After Africa*, New Haven, 1983.

Beckles, Hilary McD., *Natural Rebels, A Social History of Enslaved Black Women in Barbados*, London, 1989.

Berlin, Ira, *Many Thousands Gone. The First Two Centuries of Slavery in North America*, Cambridge, Mass., 1998.

Blackburn, Robin, *The Overthrow of Colonial Slavery*, London, 1988.

—— *The Making of New World Slavery. From the Baroque to the Modern, 1492–1880*, London, 1997.

Blassingame, John, *The Slave Community*, New York, 1979.

Breen, T. H., *Tobacco Culture*, Princeton, 1985.

Bush, Barbara, *Slave Women in the Caribbean*, London, 1990.

Clinton, Catherine, *The Plantation Mistress*, New York, 1982.

Craton, Michael, *Searching for the Invisible Man*, Ithaca, 1978.

—— *Testing the Chains. Resistance to Slavery in the British West Indies*, Ithaca, 1982.

—— *Empire, Enslavement and Freedom in the Caribbean*, Kingston, 1997.

Curtin, P. D., *The Atlantic Slave Trade. A Census*, Madison, Wisconsin, 1969.

—— *The Rise and Fall of the Plantation Complex*, Cambridge, 1990.

Davies, K. G., *The Royal African Company*, London, 1957.

Davis, David Brion, *The Problem of Slavery in the Age of Revolution*, London, 1975.

Drescher, Seymour, *Capitalism and Antislavery*, London, 1986.

—— *From Slavery to Freedom*, London, 1999.

—— and Engerman, Stanley L. (eds), *A Historical Guide to World Slavery*, Oxford, 1998.

Dunn, R. S., *Sugar and Slaves*, London, 1977.

Eltis, David, *Economic Growth and the Ending of the Transatlantic Slave Trade*, Oxford, 1987.

—— *The Rise of African Slavery in the Americas*, Cambridge, 2000.

Fogel, R. W., *Without Consent or Contract*, New York, 1989.

Fox-Genovese, Elizabeth, *Within the Plantation Household*, Chapel Hill, 1988.

Geggus, David, *Slavery, War and Revolution*, Oxford, 1982.

Genovese, E. D., *Roll, Jordan, Roll*, London, 1975.

—— *From Rebellion to Revolution*, New York, 1979.

Gomez, Michael, *Exchanging our Country Marks*, Chapel Hill, 1998.

Greene, Jack P., *Pursuits of Happiness*, Chapel Hill, 1988.

Gutman, Herbert, *The Black Family in Slavery and Freedom, 1750–1925*, New York, 1976.

Hall, D. (ed.), *In Miserable Slavery, Thomas Thistlewood in Jamaica, 1750–1786*, London, 1989.

Hancock, David, *Citizens of the World. London Merchants and the Integration of the British Atlantic Community*, Cambridge, 1995.

Heuman, Gad (ed.), *Out of the House of Bondage*, London, 1985.

Higman, B. W., *Slave Populations of the British Caribbean*, Baltimore, 1984.

—— *Jamaica Surveyed*, Kingston, 1988.

—— *Writing West Indian Histories*, London, 1999.

Iliffe, John, *Africans. The History of a Continent*, Cambridge, 1995.

Innes, S. (ed.), *Work and Labour in Early America*, Chapel Hill, 1988.

Isaac, Rhys, *The Transformation of Virginia*, Chapel Hill, 1985.

Jones, Jacqueline, *Labour of Love, Labour of Sorrow*, New York, 1985.

Jordan, Winthrop, *White Over Black. American Attitudes Towards the Negro, 1550–1925*, New York, 1969.

Kiple, K. F., *The Caribbean Slave. A Biological History*, Cambridge, 1984.

Kiple, K. F. and V. Himmelsteib King, *Another Dimension to the Black Diaspora*, Cambridge, 1981.

Klein, Herbert, *The Middle Passage*, Princeton, 1978.

—— *African Slavery in Latin America and the Caribbean*, Oxford, 1986.

—— *The Atlantic Slave Trade*, Cambridge, 1999.

Knight, Franklin W., *The Caribbean*, New York, 1978.

Kolchin, Peter, *American Slavery*, London, 1995.

Kulikoff, A., *Tobacco and Slaves*, Chapel Hill, 1986.

Levine, L. W., *Black Culture and Black Consciousness*, New York, 1979.

Lovejoy, Paul, *African Transformations in Slavery*, Cambridge, 1983.

—— (ed.), *Africans in Bondage*, Madison, Wisconsin, 1986.

Manning, Patrick, *Slavery and African Life*, Cambridge, 1990.

Miers, Suzanne and Igor Kopytoff (eds), *Slavery in Africa*, Madison, Wisconsin, 1977.

Miller, Joseph C., *Way of Death. Merchant Capitalism and the Angolan Slave Trade*, London, 1988.

Mintz, Sidney, *Sweetness and Power*, London, 1985.

Morgan, Philip D., *Slave Counterpoint*, Chapel Hill, 1999.

Oxford History of the British Empire. Vol. I: Origins, ed. Nicholas Canny; *Vol. II: The Eighteenth Century*, ed. P. J. Marshall, Oxford, 1998.

Price, R. (ed.), *Maroon Societies*, New York, 1973.

Rawley, James, *The Trans-Atlantic Slave Trade*, New York, 1981.

Sheridan, R. B., *Doctors and Slaves*, Cambridge, 1985.

Shyllon, F. O., *Black Slaves in Britain*, Oxford, 1974.

Sobel, Mechal, *The World They Made Together. Black and White Values in Eighteenth-Century Virginia*, Princeton, 1989.

Solow, Barbara L. and Stanley L. Engerman (eds), *British Capitalism and Caribbean Slavery*, Cambridge, 1987.

Thornton, John, *Africa and Africans in the Making of the Atlantic World, 1400–1680*, Cambridge, 1992.

Turner, Mary, *Slaves and Missionaries*, Urbana, Illinois, 1982.

Walvin, James, *England, Slaves and Freedom, 1776–1838*, London, 1986.

—— *An African's Life. The Life and Times of Olaudah Equiano, 1745–1797*, London, 1998.

—— *Making the Black Atlantic*, London, 2000.

Ward, J. R., *British West Indian Slavery, 1750–1834*, Oxford, 1988.

White, Deborah Grant, *Ar'n't I A Woman*, New York, 1985.

Wood, Peter H., *Black Majority*, New York, 1974.

Notes

Preface to the Second Edition

1 *Amistad* and *Beloved* are among the most notable movies to deal with slavery. Channel 4's TV series on slavery (1999) is the most recent televised discussion of slavery, while Liverpool's Maritime Museum exhibit on the slave trade is perhaps the best example of a permanent monument to slavery.
2 See in particular the first two volumes of the *Oxford History of the British Empire*, ed. Nicholas Canny and P. J. Marshall, Oxford, 1998 and Philip D. Morgan, *Slave Counterpoint*, Chapel Hill, 1999.
3 This is perhaps best approached in Robin Blackburn, *The Making of New World Slavery. From the Baroque to the Modern, 1492–1800*, London, 1997.
4 James Walvin, *Questioning Slavery*, London, 1996, Chapter 2.
5 Blackburn, op. cit., Chapter 4.

1 Consuming Passions

1 John Brewer, *Party Ideology and Popular Politics at the Accession of George III*, Cambridge, 1976, p. 150. On coffee houses see, B. Lillywhite, *London Coffee Houses*, London, 1963; R. Nevill, *London's Clubs. Their History and Treasures*, London, 1911; J. Timbs, *Clubs and Club Life in London*, London, 1908; A. Ellis, *The Penny University. A History of the Coffee House*, London, 1956.
2 Quoted in E. Beresford-Chancellor, *The 18th Century in London*, London, 1920, p. 136.
3 See the brilliant discussion in Sidney Mintz, *Sweetness and Power*, London, 1985, pp. 114–20. See also James Walvin, *Fruits of Empire. Exotic Produce and British Taste, 1660–1800*, London, 1997.

4   E.P. Thompson, *The Making of the English Working Class*, London, 1968 edn, p. 351.
5   Mintz, op. cit., p. 120.
6   Ibid., pp. 67; 23.
7   Elizabeth Donnan, *Documents Illustrative of the Slave Trade to America*, 4 vols, Washington, 1930–35, III, p. 8.
8   David Richardson, 'The British Empire and the Atlantic Slave Trade, 1660–1807', in *The Oxford History of the British Empire*, ed. P. J. Marshall, Oxford, 1998, Chapter 20.
9   Alan Kulikoff, *Tobacco and Slaves. The Development of Southern Cultures in the Chesapeake, 1680–1800*, Chapel Hill, 1986, p. 73.
10 Philip. D. Morgan, 'The Black Experience in the British Empire, 1680–1810', in P. J. Marshall, op. cit., p. 468.

2   Murdering Men

1   F. O. Shyllon, *Black Slaves in Britain*, Oxford, 1974, p. 169.
2   Ibid., pp. 14–15.
3   Ibid., p. 52.
4   James Walvin, *An African's Life. The Life and Times of Olaudah Equiano, 1745–1797*, London, 1998, Chapter 4.
5   Shyllon, op. cit., pp. 110–11.
6   Ibid., p. 165.
7   J. Bigelow (ed.), *The Works of Benjamin Franklin*, 1887, IV, 507, p. 11.
8   *Substance of the Debate on a Resolution for Abolishing the Slave Trade*, London, 1806, pp. 178–9.
9   John Weskett, *A Complete Digest of the Laws, Theory and Practice of Insurance*, London, 1781, p. 525.
10 *Substance of the Debate*, op. cit., p. 179.
11 Ibid., p. 180.
12 James Walvin, *Black and White. The Negro and English Society, 1555–1945*, London, 1973, p. 92; *Diary of Granville Sharp*, 1783–98, 19 March 1783.
13 The *Morning Chronicle* and *London Advertiser*, 18 March 1783.
14 Shyllon, op. cit., pp. 189–90.
15 This is addressed by D. B. Davis in his book, *The Problem of Slavery in Western Culture*, Ithaca, 1966.
16 Quoted in P. Hoare, *Memoirs of Granville Sharp*, London, 1820, p. 241.
17 O. Cugoano, *Thoughts and Sentiments on the Evil of Slavery*, London, 1787, pp. 111–12.
18 My italics; Shyllon, op. cit., p. 206.

3   Slaves, Traders and Africa

1   'The First Voyage of John Hawkins, 1562–1563', in Richard Hakluyt, *The Principal Navigations...*, 12 vols, Glasgow, 1904, X, pp. 7–8.

2   Quoted in Colin A. Palmer, *Human Cargoes. The British Slave Trade to Spanish America*, Urbana, 1981, p. 26.

3   For the story of African slavery see, Paul Lovejoy, *Transformations in Slavery*, Cambridge, 2000. But there are regular revisions, mainly in *The Journal of African History*; see, Paul Lovejoy, 'The Impact of the Atlantic Slave Trade on Africa…', *Journal of African History*, XXX, 1989, pp. 365–95; Patrick Manning, *Slavery and African Life*, Cambridge, 1990. See also, Joseph C. Miller, *Way of Death, Merchant Capitalism and the Angolan Slave Trade, 1730–1830*, London, 1988, p. 672.

4   *The Interesting Narrative of the Life of Olaudah Equiano…*, 2 vols, London, 1789.

5   Introduction, in Paul Edwards (ed.), *Equiano's Travels*, London, 1968.

6   J. F. A. Ajayi and M. Crowder, *A History of West Africa*, New York, 1972, pp. 336–7; Robin Law, 'Slave Raiders and Middlemen', in *Journal of African History*, xxx, 1989. For a recent calculation of the regional origins of African slaves see Herbert S. Klein, *The Atlantic Slave Trade*, Cambridge, 1999, pp. 208–9.

7   J. Inikori, 'The Impact of Firearms into West Africa, 1750–1807', in J. Inikori (ed.), *Forced Migrations*, London, 1982.

8   Quoted in Palmer, op. cit., pp. 32–4.

9   J. H. Boxer, *The Portuguese Seaborne Empire, 1415–1825*, London, 1969, p. 32.

10 Palmer, op. cit., p. 23.

11 K. G. Davies, *The Royal African Company*, London, 1957, pp. 240–90.

12 Ibid., p. 246.

13 Quoted in A. W. Lawrence, *Trade Castles and Forts Of West Africa*, London, 1963, p. 185.

14 Ibid, pp. 185; 278; 289.

15 Ibid, pp. 351–2.

16 Davies, op. cit., pp. 345–6.

17 A. Benezet, *Some Historical Account of Guinea*, London, 1788, p. 94.

18 Quoted in James Rawley, *The Trans-Atlantic Slave Trade*, New York, 1981, p. 269.

19 John Atkins (1735) in M. Craton, J. Walvin and D. Wright (eds), *Slavery, Abolition and Emancipation*, London, 1976, p. 33.

20 For recent estimates see Klein, op. cit., pp. 208–9.

4   Crossing the Atlantic

1   This section is based on John Newton's journal: B. Martin and M. Spurrell (eds), *Journal of a Slave Trader* (1788), London, 1962. See also, John Newton, *Letters to a Wife*, London, 1793; and *Thoughts upon the African Slave Trade*, London, 1788.

2   John Newton, 1725–1807, D.N.B., London, 1894, XL, pp. 395–8.

3   For Liverpool see James Rawley, *The Trans-Atlantic Slave Trade*, New York, 1981, Chapter IX; R. Anstey and P. E. H. Hair (eds), *Liverpool and the African Slave Trade*, Historic Society of Lancashire and Cheshire, Occasional Series, Vol. 2, 1976.

4   Elizabeth Donnan, *Documents Illustrative of the Slave Trade to America*, 4 vols, Washington, 1930–35, III, pp. 137–8.
5   James Walvin, *England, Slaves and Freedom*, London, 1986.
6   This section draws on, A. Falconbridge, *An Account of the Slave Trade on the Coast of Africa*, London, 1788.
7   Evidence of James Penny, *British Sessional Papers, Commons, Accounts and Papers*, 1789, XXVI, Pt 2.
8   For a discussion of this picture, see Marcus Wood, *Blind Memory*, Manchester, 2000.
9   Newton, *Thoughts*, op. cit., pp. 29–37.
10 H. Klein, *The Middle Passage*, Princeton, 1978, p. 229.
11 *The Interesting Narrative of the Life of Olaudah Equiano…*, 2 vols, London, 1789, I, pp. 78–80.
12 Falconbridge, op. cit., p. 25.
13 Colin A. Palmer, *Human Cargoes. The British Slave Trade to Spanish America*, Urbana, 1981, p. 51.
14 Ibid., p. 50.
15 Ibid., loc. cit.
16 Ibid., p. 45.
17 Ibid., p. 46.
18 Falconbridge, op. cit., p. 28.
19 Palmer, op. cit., p. 50.
20 Penny, 'Evidence', op. cit.
21 Falconbridge, op. cit., p. 23.
22 Penny, 'Evidence', op. cit.
23 *Interesting Narrative…Equiano*, op. cit., I, p. 71.
24 Falconbridge, op. cit., pp. 30–2.
25 Ibid.
26 Ibid., p. 30.
27 Klein, op. cit., p. 166, n. 41.
28 Falconbridge, op. cit., p. 24.
29 O. Patterson, *Slavery and Social Death*, Cambridge, Mass., 1982, p. 206; Paul Lovejoy, 'Concubinage in the Sokoto Caliphate, 1804–1903', *Slavery and Abolition*, September 1990, Vol. 11, No. 2.

5   Landfall

1   John Newton, *Thoughts Upon the African Slave Trade*, London, 1788, p. 111.
2   Newton's Journal, 3–20 June 1753: B. Martin and M. Spurrell (eds), *Journal of a Slave Trader*, 1788, pp. 80–1.
3   Elizabeth Donnan, *Documents Illustrative of the Slave Trade to America*, 4 vols, Washington, 1930–35, I, pp. 204–5.
4   Richard Ligon, *A True and Exact History of the Island of Barbados*, London, 1673; the standard account for early Barbados and much cited by historians. Reprinted London, 1970.

5   A. Falconbridge, *An Account of the Slave Trade on the Coast of Africa*, London, 1788, pp. 35–6.
6   Donnan, op. cit., I, pp. 204–5.
7   Falconbridge, op. cit., p. 33.
8   Donnan, op. cit., I, p. 205.
9   Falconbridge, op. cit., p. 34.
10   *The Interesting Narrative of the Life of Olaudah Equiano...*, 2 vols, London, 1789, I, pp. 86–7.
11   K. G. Davies, *The Royal African Company*, London, 1957, Chapter 7.
12   C. Joyner, *Down by the Riverside*, Urbana, 1984, Chapter 1.
13   Alan Kulikoff, *Tobacco and Slaves*, Chapel Hill, 1986, pp. 321–2.
14   Ibid., pp. 324–5.
15   O. Patterson, *Slavery and Social Death*, Cambridge, Mass., 1982, pp. 54–8.
16   Joyner, op. cit., pp. 217–20.
17   In P. D. Curtin (ed.), *Africa Remembered*, Madison, Wisconsin, 1967, p. 41.
18   Kulikoff, op. cit., pp. 326–8.
19   H. McNeil, *Observations on the Treatment of Negroes in the Island of Jamaica*, London, 1788, p. 44.
20   Evidence of Dr James Chisholme, in Report of the Privy Council Committee on the Slave Trade, Part III, Jamaica No. 6, *Accounts and Papers*, 1789, XXVI, 646a.
21   R. B. Le Page and André Tabouret-Keller, *Acts of Identity*, Cambridge, 1985, Chapter 2.
22   Joyner, op. cit., pp. 206–7.
23   Ibid., p. 208.
24   P. Wright (ed.), *Lady Nugent's Journal* (1801–1805), Kingston, 1966, p. 98.

6   Plantations, Slaves and Planters

1   Richard Ligon, *A True and Exact History of the Island of Barbados*, London, 1673, pp. 20–1.
2   For the story of the plantations see, Michael Craton, 'The Historical Roots of the Plantation Model', *Slavery and Abolition*, December 1984, Vol. 5, No. 3.
3   Capt. Kit S. Kapp, *The Printed Maps of Jamaica*, Kingston, 1966.
4   R. S. Dunn, *Sugar and Slaves*, London, 1977, p. 38.
5   For the growth of slavery in Barbados, see H. McD. Beckles, *White Servitude and Black Slavery in Barbados*, Knoxville, 1989. See also Hilary Beckles, *A History of Barbados*, Cambridge, 1990.
6   Dunn, op. cit., pp. 90–2.
7   Ibid., p. 169; Kapp, op. cit.
8   Dunn, op. cit., p. 188.
9   Alan Kulikoff, *Tobacco and Slaves*, Chapel Hill, 1986, p. 324.
10   Ibid., p. 325.
11   David Watts, *The West Indies*, Cambridge, 1987, pp. 207–9.
12   D. Hall (ed.), *In Miserable Slavery, Thomas Thistlewood in Jamaica, 1750–1786*, London, 1989, pp. 236–7.

13 Watts, op. cit., pp. 234–5.
14 Ibid., p. 284.
15 Ibid., pp. 340–6.
16 For the period of amelioration see J. R. Ward, *British West Indian Slavery, 1750–1834*, Oxford, 1988.
17 Hall, op. cit., p. 308.
18 B. W. Higman, *Jamaica Surveyed*, Kingston, 1988, pp. 102–4.
19 Hall, op. cit., p. 287.
20 Higman, op. cit., pp. 84–9.
21 Ibid., pp. 92–3.
22 Ibid., p. 136.
23 Ibid., p. 250.
24 Ibid., pp. 114; 117–18; 119.
25 Ibid., pp. 252–4.
26 On the growth of villages see Sidney Mintz, 'The Historical Sociology of Jamaican Villages', in his book *Caribbean Transformations*, Baltimore, 1974.
27 Higman, op. cit., p. 243.
28 Ibid., p. 247–8.
29 Ward, op. cit., pp. 23–5.
30 Hall, op. cit., p. 33.
31 Ibid., p. 218.
32 Higman, op. cit., Chapter 9.
33 Kulikoff, op. cit., p. 330. See also Philip D. Morgan, *Slave Counterpoint*, Chapel Hill, 1999, Chapter 8.
34 Ibid., pp. 330–4.
35 Ibid., pp. 336–7.
36 Ibid., pp. 337–9.
37 Ibid., pp. 340–2; Morgan, op. cit., pp. 524–30.
38 R. Isaac, *The Transformation of Virginia*, Chapel Hill, 1985 edn., pp. 30–1; Morgan, op. cit., Chapter 10.
39 B. Roberts, *Plantation Homes of the James River*, Chapel Hill, 1990.
40 Jack P. Greene, *Pursuits of Happiness*, Chapel Hill, 1988, pp. 92–4.
41 Ibid., pp. 96–7.
42 W. Alleyn and H. Fraser, *The Barbados–Carolina Connection*, London, 1988.
43 C. Joyner, *Down by the Riverside*, Urbana, 1984, pp. 13–14. For South Carolina see Peter H. Wood, *Black Majority*, New York, 1974; D. C. Littlefield, *Rice and Slaves*, Baton Rouge, 1981; Morgan, op. cit., pp. 35–58.
44 Greene, op. cit., p. 144.
45 Robert W. Fogel, *Without Consent or Contract*, London, 1989, p. 193; P. D. Morgan, 'Work and Culture. The Task System and the World of Low Country Slaves', *William and Mary Quarterly*, 1982, No. 39.
46 Greene, op. cit., pp. 147–8.
47 Ibid., p. 150.
48 Opening assertion in John Reeves, 'A Statement of the laws that at present subsist in the West Indian Islands…', 1789, *British Sessional Papers, Accounts and Papers*, 1789, XXVI.

7   In the Fields

1   P. Wright (ed.), *Lady Nugent's Journal* (1801–1805), Kingston, 1966, p. 220.
2   Ibid., p. 98.
3   Willie Lee Rose (ed.), *A Documentary History of Slavery in North America*, New York, 1976, p. 303.
4   Thomas Roughley, *The Jamaica Planter's Guide*, London, 1823.
5   B. W. Higman, *Slave Populations of the British Caribbean*, Baltimore, 1984, p. 163.
6   M. Craton, *Searching for the Invisible Man*, Ithaca, 1978, p. 214.
7   Ibid., loc. cit.
8   The description of the gang system is taken from Roughley, op. cit.
9   M. Craton and J. Walvin, *A Jamaican Plantation*, London, 1970, p. 96.
10 Higman, op. cit., pp. 182–3.
11 Ibid.
12 Roughley, op. cit.
13 *A Jamaican Plantation*, op. cit., p. 102.
14 Ibid., p. 104.
15 T. H. Breen, *Tobacco Culture*, Princeton, 1985, pp. 46–53.
16 Alan Kulikoff, *Tobacco and Slaves*, Chapel Hill, 1986, p. 325.
17 J. P. Greene (ed.), *Diary of Col. London Carter, 1752–1772*, 2 vols, Charlottesville, 1965, II, p. 606; I, p. 372.
18 Kulikoff, op. cit., pp. 396, 408.
19 Ibid., pp. 408–10.
20 Quoted in S. Innes (ed.), *Work and Labour in Early America*, Chapel Hill, 1988, p. 207
21 C. Joyner, *Down by the Riverside*, Urbana, 1984, pp. 43–5.

8   Skills

1   P. S. Foner and P. L. Lewis (eds), *The Black Worker*, 4 vols, Philadelphia, 1978, I, p. 10.
2   *Daily Advertiser*, Kingston, 7 June 1790.
3   R. S. Dunn, *Sugar and Slaves*, London, 1977, p. 198.
4   B. W. Higman, *Slave Populations of the British Caribbean*, Baltimore, 1984, pp. 170–2.
5   Thomas Roughley, *The Jamaica Planter's Guide*, London, 1823.
6   Higman, op. cit., pp. 168–70.
7   Mechal Sobel, *The World They Made Together*, Princeton, 1989, pp. 48–9.
8   Ibid., pp. 49–50.
9   Alan Kulikoff, *Tobacco and Slaves*, Chapel Hill, 1986, pp. 399–401; Philip D. Morgan, *Slave Counterpoint*, Chapel Hill, 1999, Chapter 4.
10 Ibid., p. 408.
11 Ibid., p. 413.
12 Kulikoff, op. cit., p. 405.
13 Higman, op. cit., pp. 172–4.

14 Ibid., pp. 197–8.
15 A. Blakely, *Russia and the Negro*, Washington DC, 1986, Chapter 2.
16 Higman, op. cit., pp. 92–9.
17 P. D. Morgan, 'Black Life in 18th century Charleston', *Perspectives in American History*, New Series, I, Cambridge, Mass., 1984, p. 210.
18 Higman, op. cit., p. 233.
19 Morgan, op. cit., pp. 195–6.
20 Higman, op. cit., p. 234.
21 Ibid., pp. 234–5; Morgan, op. cit., p. 200.
22 *The Interesting Narrative of the Life of Olaudah Equiano*, 2 vols, London, 1789, II, pp. 106–12.
23 Morgan, op. cit., pp. 197–9.
24 Sobel, op. cit., p. 52.
25 D. Hall (ed.), *In Miserable Slavery, Thomas Thistlewood in Jamaica, 1750–1786*, London, 1989, pp. 202–3.
26 W. Jeffrey Bolster, *Black Jacks. African American Seamen in the Age of Sail*, Cambridge, Mass., 1997.
27 Morgan, op. cit., pp. 196; 198.
28 Hall, op. cit., p. 94.
29 H. McD. Beckles, *Natural Rebels*, London, 1989, pp. 72–4.
30 Hall, op. cit., p. 156.
31 H. G. Farmer, *Military Music*, New York, 1950, p. 52.
32 See plate 5 in P. Wright (ed.), *Lady Nugent's Journal* (1801–1805), Kingston, 1966, p. 37.
33 *Felix Farley's Bristol Journal*, 12 March 1757; *Interesting Narrative … Equiano*, op. cit., II, pp. 84–8.
34 *The London Chronicle*, 17 February 1764; Henry Angello, *Reminiscences*, 2 vols, London, 1828, I, pp. 446–52.
35 I. Duffield, 'From Slave Colonies to Penal Colonies', *Slavery and Abolition*, May 1986, Vol. 7, No. 1.

9 Women

1 James Rawley, *The Trans-Atlantic Slave Trade*, New York, 1981, pp. 14; 58; Herbert S. Klein, *The Atlantic Slave Trade*, Cambridge, 1999, pp. 161–2.
2 H. McD. Beckles, *Natural Rebels*, London, 1989, p. 8.
3 Deborah Grant White, *Ar'n't I A Woman*, New York, 1985, p. 66.
4 Beckles, op. cit., p. 9.
5 Ibid., Chapter 9.
6 Ibid., p. 30.
7 Ibid., p. 35.
8 Ibid., p. 37.
9 Barbara Bush, 'Towards Emancipation. Women and Resistance to Coercive Labour Regimes in the British West Indian Colonies, 1790–1838', *Slavery and Abolition*, December 1984, Vol. 5, No. 3, pp. 225–6.

10 Ibid.
11 B. W. Higman, *Slave Populations of the British Caribbean*, Baltimore, 1984, pp. 189–91.
12 Michael Craton, *Searching for the Invisible Man*, Ithaca, 1978, p. 142.
13 Ibid., pp. 216–18.
14 Philip D. Morgan, 'British Encounters…', in B. Bailyn and P. D. Morgan (eds), *Strangers within the Realm*, Chapel Hill, 1991, p. 174.
15 White, op. cit., pp. 67–8.
16 J. R. Ward, *British West Indian Slavery*, Oxford, 1988, p. 191.
17 For studies of the plantation mistress at a later period, see, Catherine Clinton, *The Plantation Mistress*, New York, 1982; Elizabeth Fox-Genovese, *Within the Plantation Household*, Chapel Hill, 1988.
18 Mechal Sobel, *The World They Made Together*, Princeton, 1989, p. 134.
19 Ibid., p. 135.
20 Quoted in John Carey, *Reportage*, London, 1987, p. 247.
21 Sobel, op. cit., p. 136.
22 Ibid., p. 137.
23 Ibid., p. 138.
24 Ibid., p. 148.
25 Barbara Bush, 'White Ladies, Coloured Favourites and Black Wenches…', *Slavery and Abolition*, December 1981, Vol. 2, No. 3, p. 251.
26 P. Wright (ed.), *Lady Nugent's Journal*, (1801–1805), Kingston, 1966, p. 29.
27 Bush, 'White ladies…', op. cit., p. 255.
28 Wright, op. cit., p. 76.
29 D. Hall (ed.), *In Miserable Slavery, Thomas Thistlewood in Jamaica, 1750–1786*, London, 1989, p. 301.
30 Ibid., p. 46.
31 Beckles, op. cit., p. 57.
32 Matthew Gregory Lewis, *Journal of a West India Proprietor*, London, 1834, p. 60.
33 Sobel, op. cit., p. 133.
34 Beckles, op. cit., p. 58.
35 P. D. Morgan, 'Three Planters…' in W. D. Jordan and S. L. Skempt (eds), *Race and Family in the Colonial South*, London, 1987, pp. 57; 64.
36 On paternalism see E. D. Genovese, *Roll, Jordan, Roll*, New York, 1975.
37 Beckles, op. cit., pp. 59–70.
38 Ibid., p. 63.
39 Sobel, op. cit., pp. 149–50.
40 Beckles, op. cit., p. 65.
41 Hall, op. cit., pp. 44–5.
42 Higman, op. cit., p. 227.
43 Ibid., pp. 230–5.
44 P. D. Morgan, 'Black Life in 18th Century Charleston', *Perspectives in American History*, New Series, I, Cambridge, Mass., 1984, p. 202.
45 Hall, op. cit., pp. 94; 79; 80.

10   Disease and Death

1   D. Hall (ed.), *In Miserable Slavery, Thomas Thistlewood in Jamaica, 1750–1786*, London, 1989, p. 213.
2   Ibid., pp. 294–5.
3   P. D. Curtin, 'Epidemiology and the Slave Trade', *Political Science Quarterly*, 1968, Vol. 83.
4   Michael Craton, *Searching for the Invisible Man*, Ithaca, 1978, pp. 206–7.
5   R. B. Sheridan, *Doctors and Slaves*, Cambridge, 1985, p. 84; Thomas Roughley, *The Jamaica Planter's Guide*, London, 1823.
6   Sheridan, op. cit., pp. 84–6.
7   Hall, op. cit., pp. 156; 174; 188.
8   Ibid., pp. 188–9.
9   Ibid., pp. 198–200.
10   Ibid., p. 206.
11   Ibid., p. 209.
12   Ibid., p. 210.
13   Ibid., p. 38.
14   Sheridan, op. cit., p. 87.
15   Ibid.
16   Craton, op. cit., p. 132.
17   B. W. Higman, *Slave Populations of the British Caribbean*, Baltimore, 1984, p. 264.
18   Ibid., p. 265.
19   Ibid., p. 278.
20   Sheridan, op. cit., pp. 253–4.
21   Hall, op. cit., pp. 166–8.
22   Higman, op. cit., pp. 279–80.
23   Craton, op. cit., p. 123.
24   J. R. Ward, *British West Indian Slavery*, Oxford, 1988, p. 149.
25   Sheridan, op. cit., pp. 209–10.
26   Ibid., pp. 210–11.
27   Ward, op. cit., pp. 153–4.
28   Sheridan, op. cit., pp. 216–19.
29   Ibid., p. 225.
30   Hall, op. cit., pp. 125; 145; 186; 210.
31   Sheridan, op. cit., p. 201.
32   Ward, op. cit., pp. 130–1.
33   Sheridan, op. cit., pp. 200–1.
34   Ibid., p. 201.
35   Ibid., p. 204; Higman, op. cit., pp. 280–92.
36   K. F. Kiple and V. Himmelsteib King, *Another Dimension to the Black Diaspora*, Cambridge, 1981, p. 116.
37   J. S. Handler and F. W. Lange, *Plantation Slavery in Barbados*, Cambridge, Mass., 1978, p. 173.
38   Ibid., p. 174.

39 Ibid., pp. 175–82.
40 Hall, op. cit., p. 295.
41 Handler and Lange, op. cit., pp. 192–3.
42 Ibid., p. 195.
43 Higman, op. cit., p. 390.
44 Handler and Lange, op. cit., pp. 199–201.
45 Ibid., p. 209.
46 Ibid.

11 Slaves at Ease

1 Mechal Sobel, *The World They Made Together*, Princeton, 1989, p. 167.
2 D. Hall (ed.), *In Miserable Slavery, Thomas Thistlewood in Jamaica, 1750–1786*, London, 1989, p. 12.
3 Ibid., pp. 140; 131.
4 Bryan Edwards, *History…of the British Colonies in the West Indies*, 3 vols, London, 1801, III, p. 254; Matthew G. Lewis, *Journal of a West India Proprietor*, London, 1834, pp. 60–8.
5 Sobel, op. cit., p. 167.
6 *Characteristic Trails of the Creolian and African Negroes in Jamaica…*, Kingston, 1797, p. 23.
7 Richard Ligon, *A True and Exact History of the Island of Barbados*, London, 1673, p. 14.
8 Hans Sloane, *A Voyage to the Islands…*, London, 1770, I, pp. xlvii–xlix.
9 L. W. Levine, *Black Culture and Black Consciousness*, New York, 1978, pp. 15–16.
10 J. G. Stedman, *Narrative of a Five Years Expedition against the Revolted Negroes of Surinam* (1796), London, 1971, pp. 375–8.
11 John Luffman, *A Brief Account of the Island of Antigua*, London, 1789, pp. 135–7.
12 William Beckford, *A Descriptive Account of the Island of Jamaica*, London, 1790, II, p. 387.
13 J. B. Moreton, *Manners and Customs in the West India Islands*, London, 1790, pp. 152–3.
14 Stedman, op. cit., p. 362.
15 Beckford, op. cit., pp. 120–1.
16 Moreton, op. cit., pp. 152–3.
17 For music among slaves at sea, see W. Jeffrey Bolster, *Black Jacks. African American Seamen in the Age of Sail*, Cambridge, Mass., 1997.
18 J. Blassingame, *The Slave Community*, New York, 1979, p. 117.
19 Edwards, op. cit., II, pp. 79–82.
20 *Characteristic Traits…*, op. cit., p. 20.
21 George Pinckard, *Notes on the West Indies*, London, 1806, I, pp. 263–8.
22 Sloane, op. cit., p. lii.
23 John Reeves, 'A Statement of the laws that at present subsist in the West Indian Islands…', 1789, *British Sessional Papers, Accounts and Papers*, 1789, XXVI.
24 Levine, op. cit., p. 17.
25 E. Brathwaite, *The Development of Creole Society*, Oxford, 1971, p. 233.

26 *A View of the Past and Present State of the Island of Jamaica*, Edinburgh, 1823, pp. 269–73.
27 Capt. J. E. Alexander, *Transatlantic Sketches…*, London, 1833, I, pp. 95–7.
28 Levine, op. cit., p. 5.
29 Sobel, op. cit., p. 191.
30 Blassingame, op. cit., pp. 35–6.
31 B. W. Higman, *Slave Populations of the British Caribbean*, Baltimore, 1984, p. 210.
32 Ibid., p. 212.
33 For a description of Christmas in Jamaica see Beckford, op. cit., I, pp. 386–92.
34 *Characteristic Traits…*, op. cit.
35 Lewis, op. cit., pp. 50–1.
36 Brathwaite, op. cit., p. 232.
37 A. Barclay, *A Practical View of the Present State of Slavery in the West Indies*, London, 1826, p. 10.
38 Alan Kulikoff, *Tobacco and Slaves*, Chapel Hill, 1986, p. 348.
39 Ibid.
40 C. Joyner, *Down by the Riverside*, Urbana, 1984, p. 134.
41 Ibid., p. 132.
42 Barclay, op. cit., p. 10.
43 Levine, op. cit., pp. 106–7.
44 Ibid.
45 Mrs Lanigan, *Antigua and the Antiguans*, London, 1844, II, p. 115.
46 Hall, op. cit., p. 12.

12 Religion

1 D. Hall (ed.), *In Miserable Slavery, Thomas Thistlewood in Jamaica, 1750–1786*, London, 1989, p. 279.
2 Mary Turner, *Slaves and Missionaries*, Urbana, 1982, pp. 52–3; Monica Schuler, 'Afro-American Slave Culture', in M. Craton (ed.), *Roots and Branches*, Waterloo, Ontario, 1979.
3 Barbara Bush, *Slave Women in Caribbean Society, 1650–1838*, London, 1990, p. 74.
4 J. G. Stedman, *Narrative of a Five Years Expedition against the Revolted Negroes of Surinam* (1796), London, 1971, p. 364.
5 Bryan Edwards, *History… of the British Colonies in the West Indies*, 3 vols, London, 1801, II, pp. 82–9.
6 Bush, op. cit., p. 76.
7 Edwards, op. cit., II, pp. 82–92.
8 Cynric Williams, *A Tour Through the Island of Jamaica*, 1826, pp. 25–7.
9 R. R. Madden, *A Twelve Months Residence in the West Indies*, London, 1835, II, pp. 93–109.
10 Hall, op. cit., p. 217.
11 O. Patterson, *The Sociology of Slavery*, London, 1967, p. 186.
12 Turner, op. cit., pp. 56–7.

13   Schuler, op. cit., p. 133.
14   J. Boles, *Black Southerners, 1617–1869*, Lexington, 1983, p. 154.
15   Alan Kulikoff, *Tobacco and Slaves*, Chapel Hill, 1986, pp. 348–9; H. S. Klein, 'Anglicanism, Catholicism, and the Negro Slave', in L. Foner and E. D. Genovese (eds), *Slavery in the New World*, Englewood Cliffs, NJ, 1969, p. 157.
16   Peter Wood, *Black Majority, Negroes in Colonial South Carolina*, New York, 1975 edn, p. 133.
17   Ibid., p. 135.
18   Ibid., pp. 135–6.
19   Ibid., p. 139.
20   Ibid., pp. 140–2.
21   Mechal Sobel, *The World They Made Together*, Princeton, 1989, p. 180. For a recent discussion of the 'Great Awakening' see Michael A. Gomez, *Exchanging our Country Marks*, Chapel Hill, 1998, pp. 251–3.
22   Sobel, op. cit., p. 181.
23   Ibid., p. 182.
24   Kulikoff, op. cit., p. 350.
25   Sobel, op. cit., pp. 188–90; Donald G. Mathews, 'Religion and Slavery: the Case of the American South' in C. Bolt and S. Drescher (eds), *Anti-Slavery, Religion and Reform*, Folkestone, 1980.
26   Sobel, op. cit., pp. 195–6.
27   Ibid., p. 197.
28   Ibid., p. 202.
29   R. S. Dunn, *Sugar and Slaves*, London, 1977, pp. 104; 243.
30   Ibid., p. 249.
31   Ibid., p. 255.
32   H. McD. Beckles, *White Servitude and Black Slavery in Barbados*, Knoxville, 1989, p. 137.
33   Quoted in F. R. Augier and S. C. Gordon, *Sources of West Indian History*, London, 1967 edn, p. 143.
34   Turner, op. cit., p. 10.
35   Ibid.
36   Philip Sherlock, *The West Indies*, London, 1966, p. 125.
37   C. Hamshere, *The British in the Caribbean*, London, 1972, p. 137.
38   Turner, op. cit., p. 70.
39   Ibid., p. 7.
40   E. Brathwaite, *The Development of Creole Society*, Oxford, 1971, p. 255.
41   Michael Craton, *Testing the Chains*, Ithaca, 1982, p. 241.
42   Ibid., pp. 245–6.
43   Ibid., p. 246.
44   Ibid., pp. 247–8.
45   Ibid., pp. 250–1; Brathwaite, op. cit., p. 258; Turner, op. cit., p. 10.
46   Craton, op. cit., Chapter 21.
47   Ibid., pp. 281; 283.
48   Ibid., p. 288.
49   Turner, op. cit., p. 93.

13   Families and Communities

1   *The Interesting Narrative of the Life of Olaudah Equiano*, 2 vols, London, 1789, I, pp. 90–1.
2   Quoted in Barbara Bush, *Slave Women In Caribbean Society, 1650–1838*, London, 1990, p. 20.
3   Alan Kulikoff, *Tobacco and Slaves*, Chapel Hill, 1986, p. 334.
4   M. B. Norton, H. Gutman and I. Berlin, 'The Afro-American Family in the Age of the Revolution', in I. Berlin and R. Hoffman (eds), *Slavery and Freedom in the Age of the American Revolution*, Charlottesville, 1983, pp. 177–8.
5   Kulikoff, op. cit., pp. 350–60. For a recent discussion of slave families see Philip D. Morgan, *Slave Counterpoint*, Chapel Hill, 1999, Chapter 9.
6   Ibid., p. 361.
7   D. R. Wright, *African Americans in the Colonial Era*, Arlington Heights, Illinois, 1990, pp. 109–10. See also Morgan, op. cit., pp. 102–24.
8   Wright, op. cit., p. 110; Kulikoff, op. cit., pp. 368–71.
9   Kulikoff, op. cit., pp. 371–4.
10 For urban slavery see, T. J. Archdeacon, *New York City 1664–1710*, 1976; G. Nash, *Forging Freedom: The Black Urban Experience in Philadelphia*, Harvard, 1988.
11 H. McD. Beckles, *Natural Rebels*, London, 1989, p. 115.
12 Ibid., p. 117.
13 Ibid., p. 119.
14 Edmund Burke, 'Sketch of a Negro Code', *The Works of Edmund Burke*, 16 vols, London, 1826, IX
15 Beckles, op. cit., p. 129.
16 Ibid., pp. 130–1.
17 Bush, op. cit., p. 93.
18 Ibid., pp. 106–7.

14   Sex in the Slave Quarters

1   D. Hall (ed.), *In Miserable Slavery, Thomas Thistlewood in Jamaica, 1750–1786*, London, 1989, p. 18.
2   Ibid., p. 19.
3   Ibid., p. 20.
4   Ibid., pp. 31–2.
5   Ibid., pp. 32–3.
6   W. Jordan, *White Over Black*, New York, 1969, pp. 37–8.
7   Leo Africanus, in R. Brown (ed.), *The History and Description of Africa*, London, 1986, p. 187.
8   E. Jones, *Othello's Countrymen*, Oxford, 1965, p. 8.
9   John Lok's Second Voyage, in Richard Hakluyt, *The Principal Navigations...*, 12 vols, Glasgow, 1904, VI, p. 176.
10 Ibid., p. 184.

11 Jordan, op. cit., pp. 34–5.
12 A. J. Barker, *The African Link*, London, 1978, p. 126.
13 Ibid., p. 126.
14 Ibid., pp. 126–7.
15 B. Martin and M. Spurrell (eds), *Journal of a Slave Trader* (1788), London, 1962, p. 75.
16 Quoted in D. F. Littlefield, *Rice and Slaves*, Baton Rouge, 1981, p. 172.
17 R. B. Sheridan, *Doctors and Slaves*, Cambridge, 1985, p. 243.
18 Ibid., p. 243.
19 Quoted in J. Blassingame, *The Slave Community*, New York, 1979, p. 154.
20 Jordan, op. cit., Chapter IV.
21 Edward Long, *Candid Reflections*, London, 1772, p. 48.
22 *The Times*, 11–12 February 1794.
23 P. D. Morgan, 'British encounters with Africans and Afro-Americans...', in B. Bailyn and P. D. Morgan (eds), *Strangers Within the Realm*, Chapel Hill, 1991.
24 E. R. Genovese, *From Rebellion to Revolution*, New York, 1979.
25 Quoted in Jordan, op. cit., p. 156.
26 Hall, op. cit., pp. 62; 83; 86; 60.
27 Ibid., pp. 149–50.
28 Ibid., p. 78.
29 Ibid., p. 118.
30 Ibid., p. 124.
31 Ibid., p. 128.
32 Ibid., p. 218.
33 B. W. Higman, *Slave Populations of the British Caribbean*, Baltimore, 1984, pp. 292–4.
34 Gad Heuman, *Between Black and White*, London, 1981, p. 7.
35 Ibid., pp. 5–6.
36 Ibid., p. 14.
37 Jordan, op. cit., p. 80.
38 Ibid., p. 139.
39 Ibid., pp. 139–40.
40 Ibid., p. 140.
41 J. R. Ward, *British West Indian Slavery, 1750–1834*, Oxford, 1988, p. 34.
42 O. Patterson, *The Sociology of Slavery*, London, 1967, p. 163.
43 Ibid., p. 164.
44 Hall, op. cit., p. 77; Ward, op. cit., p. 26.

15 Violence

1 B. Martin and M. Spurrell (eds), *Journal of a Slave Trader* (1788), London, 1962, p. 22.
2 Ibid., p. 25.
3 Ibid., p. 80.
4 Ibid., pp. 69–70; 88.

5 Elizabeth Donnan, *Documents Illustrative of the Slave Trade to America*, 4 vols, Washington, 1930–35, II, p. 485.

6 Ibid., p. 460.

7 Ibid., pp. 486–7.

8 Herbert Klein, *The Middle Passage*, Princeton, 1978, p. 276, n. 2. See also, J. M. Postma, *The Dutch in the Atlantic Slave Trade*, Cambridge, 1990.

9 8 February 1786, in P. D. Curtin (ed.), *Africa Remembered*, Madison, Wisconsin, 1967, p. 133.

10 James Rawley, *The Trans-Atlantic Slave Trade*, New York, 1981, pp. 299–300.

11 Donnan, op. cit., II, p. 266.

12 *Interesting Narrative of the Life of Olaudah Equiano*, 2 vols, London, 1789, I, pp. 71–2.

13 Alan Kulikoff, *Tobacco and Slaves*, Chapel Hill, 1986, pp. 382–3.

14 E. P. Thompson, 'Time, Work Discipline and Industrial Capitalism', *Past and Present*, 1967, p. 38.

15 Edward Long, *Candid Reflections*, London, 1772, p. 117.

16 E. D. Genovese, *Roll, Jordan, Roll*, London, 1975, p. 299.

17 Willie Lee Rose (ed.), *A Documentary History of Slavery in North America*, New York, 1976, p. 106.

18 Genovese, op. cit., p. 65.

19 George Rawick, 'From Sundown to Sunup' in G. P. Rawick (ed.), *The American Slave. A Composite Autobiography*, Westport, 1972, I, p. 59.

20 Cited in O. Patterson, *Slavery and Social Death*, Cambridge, Mass., 1982, pp. 3–4.

21 C. Joyner, *Down by the Riverside*, Urbana, 1984, pp. 54–6.

22 Though taken from a later period of American slavery, there is no reason to believe that these examples of punishment were worse than those of earlier centuries; R. Fogel and S. L. Engerman, *Time on the Cross*, 2 vols, London, 1974, I, p. 145.

23 R. B. Sheridan, *Doctors and Slaves*, Cambridge, 1985, p. 182.

24 Ibid., pp. 180–2.

25 D. Hall (ed.), *In Miserable Slavery, Thomas Thistlewood in Jamaica, 1750–1786*, London, 1989, p. 72.

26 J. R. Ward, *British West Indian Slavery, 1750–1834*, Oxford, 1988, p. 202.

27 Thomas Roughley, *The Jamaica Planter's Guide*, London, 1823.

28 Benjamin M'Mahon, *Jamaica Plantership*, London, 1839, pp. 46–55.

29 Mary Turner, *Slaves and Missionaries*, Urbana, 1982, p. 43; Ward, op. cit., pp. 273–4.

30 Turner, op. cit., p. 134.

31 Ward, op. cit., p. 203.

32 B. W. Higman, *Slave Populations of the British Caribbean*, Baltimore, 1984, pp. 199–200.

33 Ibid., pp. 201–2.

34 James Walvin, *A Child's World*, London, 1982.

35 Fogel and Engerman, op. cit., I, pp. 146–7.

36 J. Blassingame, *The Slave Community*, New York, 1979, p. 165.

37 C. T. Davis and H. L. Gates Jnr (eds), *The Slave's Narrative*, New York, 1985, p. 106.

38 John Reeves, 'A Statement of the laws that at present subsist in the West Indian Islands...', 1789, *British Sessional Papers, Accounts and Papers*, 1789, XXVI; 'An Act for the Better Government of Negroes...', Bermuda, 1764, in Michael Craton, James Walvin and David Wright (eds), *Slavery Abolition and Emancipation*, London, 1976, pp. 175–8.

39 'An Act for the Security of the Subject...', 1730, in Craton et al. (eds), op. cit., p. 179.

40 Rose, op. cit., p. 175.

41 Ibid., pp. 179–96.

42 Fogel and Engerman, op. cit., I, p. 55.

43 Ibid., p. 129.

44 *Braco Slave Book* (formerly in possession of Mr Val Parnell, Braco Estate, Duncans, Jamaica).

45 Michael Craton, *Testing the Chains*, Ithaca, 1982, pp. 100–1.

46 Ibid., pp. 136–7.

47 Ibid., pp. 119; 264–5.

48 Genovese, op. cit., pp. 106–7.

49 Craton, op. cit., p. 317.

50 Barbara Bush, 'Towards Emancipation...' in D. Richardson (ed.), *Abolition and its Aftermath*, London, 1985, pp. 32–3.

51 Higman, op. cit., p. 22.

52 Ward, op. cit., p. 205.

53 F. O. Shyllon, *Black Slaves in Britain*, Oxford, 1974, p. 8.

54 *Royal Gazette*, Kingston, 23 December 1780; *Daily Advertiser*, Kingston, 7 June; 12 July 1790.

16 Rebellions

1 The best history of the Haitian revolt is to be found in David Geggus, *Slavery, War and Revolution*, Oxford, 1982. See also, Robin Blackburn, *The Overthrow of Colonial Slavery, 1776–1848*, London, 1988, Chapter 5. See also David Barry Gaspar and David patrick Geggus (eds), *A Turbulent Time in the Caribbean*, Bloomington, 1997.

2 James Rawley, *The Trans-Atlantic Slave Trade*, New York, 1981, pp. 130; 164–7.

3 Ibid., p. 142.

4 Blackburn, op. cit., Chapters 5–6.

5 Herbert Klein, *African Slavery in Latin America and the Caribbean*, Oxford, 1986, p. 90.

6 Roger Buckley, *Slaves in Red Coats*, New Haven, 1979.

7 Michael Craton, *Testing the Chains*, Ithaca, 1982, p. 74.

8 Ibid., p. 83.

9 D. Hall (ed.), *In Miserable Slavery, Thomas Thistlewood in Jamaica, 1750–1786*, London, 1989, pp. 14; 17.

10 R. Price (ed.), *Maroon Societies*, New York, 1973.

11 Willie Lee Rose (ed.), *A Documentary History of Slavery in North America*, New York, 1976, pp. 99–101.

12 Ibid., pp. 101–3; Peter Wood, *Black Majority*, New York, 1974, pp. 314–17. See also John Thornton, 'African Dimensions of the Stono Rebellion', *American Historical Review*, XCVI, 1991.

13 Rose, op.cit., pp. 104–5. See also Gwendolyn Midlo Hall, *African in Colonial Louisiana*, Baton Rouge, 1992, Chapter 4.

14 Ibid., pp. 105–6.

15 Ibid., pp. 107–14; Gerald Mullin, *Flight and Rebellion*, New York, 1972, Chapter 5.

16 J. O. Killen (ed.), *The Trial Record of Denmark Vesey*, Boston, 1970, pp. 136–7; William H. Freeling, *Prelude to Civil War*, New York, 1966.

17 Turner's Confession, in Rose, op. cit., p. 123–33; Stephen B. Oates, *The Fires of Jubilee: Nat Turner's Fierce Rebellion*, New York, 1975.

18 Craton, op. cit., Chapter 22.

19 Ibid., Chapter 8.

20 B. W. Higman, *Slave Populations of the British Caribbean*, Baltimore, 1984, p. 41.

21 Craton, op. cit., pp. 108; 111–14.

22 Ibid., Chapter 10.

23 Ibid., Chapter 11.

24 Ibid., p. 133.

25 Hall, op. cit., pp. 97–8.

26 Craton, op. cit., p. 138.

27 Ibid., Chapter 17.

28 Ibid., pp. 146–53.

29 Ibid., Chapter 16.

30 Ibid., pp. 155–6.

31 Ibid., Chapter 16.

32 James Walvin, *England, Slaves and Freedom*, London, 1986; *Britain's Slave Empire*, Stroud, 2000.

33 Craton, op. cit., Chapter 20.

34 Ibid., p. 266.

35 J. G. Stedman, *Narrative of a Five Years Expedition...*, 2 vols, London, 1796.

36 Craton, op. cit., Chapter 21.

37 Ibid., p. 289.

38 Ibid., p. 321.

39 Ibid., p. 321.

40 Ibid., p. 294.

17   A Leap in the Dark: Runaways

1 Rhys Isaac, *The Transformation of Virginia*, Chapel Hill, 1985, Chapter 1.

2 Ibid., pp. 329–32.

3 Michael Craton, *Searching for the Invisible Man*, Ithaca, 1978, pp. 153–6; 182–6.

4 Ibid., pp. 250–1.

5 Ibid., pp. 252–3.

6 Ibid., pp. 246–7.

7 B. W. Higman, *Slave Populations of the British Caribbean*, Baltimore, 1984, p. 393.

8   Gomer Williams, *History of the Liverpool Privateers...*, Liverpool, 1897, pp. 475–6; 478.

9   *Royal Gazette*, Kingston, 23 December 1790.

10 Quoted in R. Rathbone, 'Resistance to Enslavement in Africa', *Slavery and Abolition*, December 1985, Vol. 6, No. 3, p. 13.

11 Ibid., p. 15.

12 Ibid., p. 16.

13 Ibid., p. 20.

14 H. McD. Beckles, 'From Land to Sea...', *Slavery and Abolition*, December 1985, Vol. 6, No. 3, p. 82.

15 Ibid., p. 85.

16 Ibid., p. 87.

17 Ibid., p. 89.

18 Ibid., pp. 89–90.

19 Gad Heuman, 'Runaway Slaves in Barbados', in *Slavery and Abolition*, op. cit., pp. 101–4.

20 Ibid., p. 104.

21 Ibid., p. 108.

22 Ibid., p. 106.

23 Ibid., p. 107.

24 Ibid., p. 109.

25 Ibid., p. 110.

26 P. D. Morgan, 'Colonial South Carolina Runaways...', in *Slavery and Abolition*, op. cit., p. 75, n. 3.

27 Ibid., p. 69.

28 P. D. Morgan, 'Black Society', in *Slavery and Abolition*, op. cit., p. 139, n. 99.

29 P. D. Morgan, 'Runaways', op.cit., p. 72.

30 Ibid., loc. cit.

31 Ibid., p. 73. See also Philip D. Morgan, *Slave Counterpoint*, Chapel Hill, 1999, pp. 446–51.

32 M. L. M. Kay and L. L. Cary, 'They are Indeed the Constant Plague of Their Tyrants...', *Slavery and Abolition*, December 1985, Vol. 6, No. 3, pp. 40–1.

33 Ibid., p. 47.

34 Ibid., p. 49.

35 Alan Kulikoff, *Tobacco and Slaves*, Chapel Hill, 1986, pp. 328–9.

36 Ibid., p. 379.

37 Ibid., p. 340.

38 J. Blassingame, *The Slave Community*, New York, 1979, p. 107.

39 D. Hall (ed.), *In Miserable Slavery, Thomas Thistlewood in Jamaica, 1750–1786*, London, 1989, pp. 191–2; J. R. Ward, *British West Indian Slavery, 1750–1834*, Oxford, 1988, pp. 27–8.

40 Higman, op. cit., p. 391.

41 Ibid., p. 392.

42 Willie Lee Rose (ed.), *A Documentary History of Slavery in North America*, New York, 1976, pp. 262–6.

43   A. Kulikoff, 'Uprooted People', in I. Berlin and R. Hoffman (eds), *Slavery and Freedom in the Age of the American Revolution*, Charlottesville, 1983, pp. 144–5.
44   John Reeves, 'A Statement of the laws that at present subsist in the West Indian Islands...', 1789, XXVI.
45   Rose, op. cit., p. 180.
46   Ward, op. cit., p. 198.
47   B. W. Higman, *Slave Population and Economy in Jamaica*, Cambridge, 1976, pp. 180–1.
48   Ibid.
49   Ibid., pp. 182–3.

18   Ending it All: The Crusade against Slavery

1   William Beckford, 'A Descriptive Account...', (1790), in Michael Craton, James Walvin and David Wright (eds), *Slavery, Abolition and Emancipation*, London, 1976, p. 266.
2   'A Petition of West Indian Planters...' (1792), in Craton et al., op. cit., pp. 270–2.
3   James Rawley, *The Trans-Atlantic Slave Trade*, New York, 1981, pp. 173–4.
4   Ibid., p. 239.
5   Ibid., p. 243.
6   Barbara L. Solow and S. L. Engerman (eds), *British Capitalism and Caribbean Slavery*, Cambridge, 1987; David Eltis, *Economic Growth and the Ending of the Transatlantic Slave Trade*, Oxford, 1987.
7   Seymour Drescher, *Econocide: British Slavery in the Era of Abolition*, Pittsburgh, 1977; *From Slavery to Freedom*, London, 1999.
8   James Walvin, *England, Slaves and Freedom 1776–1838*, London, 1986, Chapter 5.
9   Stiv Jakobsson, *Am I not a Man and a Brother?*, Uppsala, 1972, p. 574.
10   Quoted in W. L. Burn, *Emancipation and Apprenticeship in the British West Indies*, London, 1937, p. 360.
11   R. W. Fogel, *Without Consent or Contract*, New York, 1989, pp. 217–18.
12   Quoted in R. Hyam, *Britain's Imperial Century*, London, 1976, p. 43.
13   Clare Taylor, *British and American Abolitionists, American Abolitionists*, Edinburgh, 1974.
14   Howard Temperley, *British Antislavery, 1838–1870*, London, 1972, p. 108.
15   For essays on this slave trade see Elizabeth Savage (ed.), *The Human Commodity. Perspectives on the Trans-Saharan Slave Trade*, London, 1992.
16   Fogel, op. cit., pp. 236–7.
17   Paul Lovejoy, 'Concubinage in the Sokoto Caliphate, 1804–1903', *Slavery and Abolition*, September 1990, Vol. 11, No. 2; S. Miers, 'Diplomacy versus Humanitarianism', *Slavery and Abolition*, December 1990, Vol. 11, No. 3.
18   See the essays in Drescher, *From Slavery to Freedom*.
19   Barbara L. Solow, 'Caribbean Slavery', *Journal of Development Economics*, 1985, XVII, pp. 99–115.

20   Barbara L. Solow, 'Capitalism and Slavery in the Exceedingly Long Run', in Barbara L. Solow and S. L. Engerman, op. cit., pp. 51–77.
21   James Walvin, *Fruits of Empire. Exotic Produce and British Taste, 1660–1800*, London, 1997.
22   David Richardson, 'The slave trade, sugar and British economic growth', in Solow and Engerman, op. cit., pp. 112–13. See also Sidney Mintz, *Sweetness and Power*, London, 1985.
23   Ibid., p. 126.
24   For the latest calculations, see Robin Blackburn, *The Making of New World Slavery*, London, 1997, Chapter XII.

19   The Plight of Africa

1   See David Henige in *Journal of African History*, 1986, XXVII, p. 2; David Eltis, Stephen D. Behrendt, David Richardson and Herbert S. Klein (eds), *The Trans-Atlantic Slave Trade: A Database on CD-ROM*, Cambridge, 2000.
2   See David Richardson, 'The British Empire and the Atlantic Slave Trade, 1660–1807', in P. J. Marshall (ed.), *The Oxford History of the British Empire. The Eighteenth Century*, Oxford, 1998, Chapter 20.
3   Paul Lovejoy, *Transformations in Slavery*, Cambridge, 2000, pp. 18–22.
4   Paul Lovejoy, 'The Impact of the Atlantic Slave Trade on Africa...', *Journal of African History*, XXX, 1989, pp. 378–9.
5   Ibid., p. 383.
6   Joseph C. Miller, *Way of Death, Merchant Capitalism and the Angolan Slave Trade, 1730–1830*, London, 1988, pp. 387–9.
7   Lovejoy, 'Impact', op. cit., pp. 385–6.
8   Walter Rodney, *How Europe Underdeveloped Africa*, London, 1972.
9   Miller, op. cit., p. 442.
10 Lovejoy, 'Impact', op. cit., pp. 389–90.
11 Lovejoy, *Transformations*, op. cit., p. 390.
12 Herbert Klein, *African Slavery in Latin America and the Caribbean*, Oxford, 1986, p. 295.
13 Lovejoy, 'Impact', op. cit., pp. 392–3.
14 Miller, op. cit., p. 155.
15 Ibid., Chapter 5.
16 Ibid., pp. 158–9.
17 Ibid., p. 681.

20   The Problems of Freedom

1   Sidney Mintz, *Sweetness and Power*, London, 1985, p. 197.
2   Hugh Tinker, *A New System of Slavery*, London, 1974. See also W. Look Lai, *Indentured Labour, Caribbean Sugar*, Baltimore, 1993.
3   Franklin Knight, *The Caribbean*, New York, 1978.

4   Anthony Trollope, *The West Indies and the Spanish Main*, London, 1859, pp. 146–52.

5   B. W. Higman, 'Slavery and the Development of Demographic Theory in the Age of the Industrial Revolution', in James Walvin (ed.), *Slavery and British Society*, London, 1982.

6   Thomas Carlyle, 'Discourse on the Nigger Question', *Critical and Miscellaneous Essays*, London, 1872, Vol. 7.

7   On the Mutiny, and reaction to it, see Christine Bolt, *Victorian Attitudes to Race*, London, 1971, Chapter 5; V. G. Kiernan, *The Lords of Human Kind*, London, 1972, Chapter 2.

8   Gad Heuman, '*The Killing Time'. The Morant Bay Rebellion in Jamaica*, London, 1994.

9   Paul B. Rich, *Race and Empire in British Politics*, Cambridge, 1986. See also Seymour Drescher, *From Slavery to Freedom*, London, 1999, Chapter 9.

10 Quoted in James Walvin, *Passage to Britain*, London, 1984, p. 42.

Index